new
babycare

new babycare

DR miriam stoppard

MD FRCP

LONDON, NEW YORK, MUNICH, MELBOURNE, DELHI

For Hazel, Oona, Tiberio and Elias

Produced for Dorling Kindersley by **Cooling Brown**
Design **Arthur Brown, Peter Cooling, Tish Jones**
Editorial **Jemima Dunne**

Dorling Kindersley
Consultant Editor **Jinny Johnson**
Managing Editor **Penny Warren, Esther Ripley**
Managing Art Editor **Marianne Markham**
Editor **Emma Maule**
Senior Designers **Nicola Rodway, Anne Fisher**
Senior Production Editor **Jenny Woodcock**
Production Controller **Alice Holloway**
Creative Technical Support **Sonia Charbonnier**
Jacket Designer **Charlotte Seymour**

First published by Dorling Kindersley in 1983
This revised edition published in Great Britain in 2009 by
Dorling Kindersley Limited,
80 Strand, London WC2R 0RL
A Penguin Company

A CIP catalogue record is available from the British Library.
ISBN: 978-1-4053-3304-7

First reproduced in Singapore by Colourscan;
this revised edition reproduced in London by Altaimage
Printed in China by L-Rex

Discover more at
www.dk.com

Preface

I've learned a lot about babycare in the last five years or so. The lessons have come from my children (four sons), my stepchildren (two daughters), my daughters-in-law and my 11 grandchildren.

The basics of child development and the principles of baby and child nurturing change little, but there's room for progress and improvement in all sorts of subtle ways. Some of these just nudge us in a different direction while others seem so fundamental we ask ourselves what took so long.

I'm grateful to all the new members of my extended family for all of them have taught me something useful – even the youngest, Maggie and Evie, my identical twin granddaughters.

It's been thrilling to listen to, observe, note, learn and inwardly digest the hundreds of small things that have refined my thinking about baby and childcare. They're all reflected in this new edition of one of my favourite books.

Contents

Introduction

There must be parents who feel nothing but joy at the news that they are expecting a baby, but they are few and far between. Once the initial excitement is over, most parents would confess to having mixed feelings about the prospect of having a baby.

Your fears are natural

Probably the most common anxiety is simply fear of parenthood. This can be fear of whether you will be a good parent or of whether you can cope with bringing up a child, or both. On top of this will be the worry about your child's happiness if you don't make a good job of it.

There will be economic anxieties. Even if both partners are working, the money that was once enough for two now has to cover the needs of three so it will be spread a little more thinly. This can mean luxuries and comforts, expensive holidays, a new car or decoration of the house may have to go by the board.

Another cause for anxiety will be the undoubted loss of freedom. No longer will you both be able to jump into the car and whizz off anywhere you like or go to a party on the spur of the moment. You can still enjoy life, but you'll have to factor in the baby's needs too.

All of these fears and anxieties are natural. There's nothing abnormal about worrying that you won't make the grade as a parent. Your feelings may be easier to cope with if you understand that both you and your child will be constantly changing. Your family unit, the way it develops and the feelings it engenders, is dynamic. There

is a natural rhythm to human relationships, especially relationships in the home. They are never at a standstill. Sometimes you may worry that your home seems less than harmonious, but this is normal family life. And as well as the lows, parenthood will give you some of the most exciting highs you've ever felt.

Mixed emotions

All the feelings of love that you have for your child will be mixed at one time or another with resentment, bitterness, anger, hostility and frustration. This is inevitable, in the same way that it's inevitable in any human relationship. The difference is that from your child you will gain rewards that no other person can give you. One of the rules that I have learned about parenting is that whatever you put in you will get back five hundred times over. So not only will your freedom increase as your child gets older, but so will the pleasures that she gives you. The sacrifices you make when your baby is young will be replaced by more and more pleasures. One of the greatest will be to see your baby turn

Your new arrival
Many of your fears will be dispelled at the first sight of your newborn baby.

from a dependent, demanding creature into a charming, thoughtful companion, an entertaining friend and a pal.

How a family evolves

The basic family unit as we know it today has been found in every race or tribe since people first inhabited the earth. The family unit is, and always has been, the cornerstone of our society and its main function is to create a secure environment in which children can be raised.

There is no one to whom the family is more important than a baby; it forms her entire universe. Within the family your child learns all the basic aspects of human

relationships. And within its security, your child learns about the good things in life: the happiness, the love and the laughter, as well as the bad things, the problems, the tensions and the anxieties. As your child grows, the family will provide the steadying, optimistic, strengthening influence that will help her cope with new and possibly difficult situations. It should always be the sanctuary to which your child can return when any conflicts seem too confusing to sort out.

The way the family is constructed and the roles played by the members of it, vary from culture to culture and family to family. In modern Western society the man has traditionally taken the role of breadwinner, provider and worker while the woman was the housekeeper and child-rearer and was mainly confined to the home. While until not long ago society accepted this as the norm, it is in fact a very recent development in the evolution of the family.

The family unit

Prior to the Industrial Revolution in the nineteenth century, the family was a working unit with mother and father and children all working towards the common good. Because of this, many aspects of family life were shared experiences; no distinction was made between worker and nurturer of children as we have it today. Women and children were very often out in the fields as well as the men, and there was never a sense at all that a woman's

Face to face
You're face to face with each other at last. Nothing bonds you more closely to your newborn baby – and him to you – than close eye contact.

duty was to rear children and do the household chores. It was a much more egalitarian arrangement.

The Industrial Revolution tore apart this happy working family unit. Instead of being together the family was split up. The wage earner, of whichever sex, but usually the man, had to go to the factory in order to do his work instead of being close to his family. At about the same time parents abdicated their role as educators of children to schools, and so the family lost much of its educational function. Thirdly, the mother was often left at home with the children and because the wage earner had to work long hours, she had to shoulder most of the responsibility for childrearing, for everyday care and for discipline. Continuing industrialization and urbanization, and the increased scope for travel, meant that families became geographically separate. As a result mothers could no longer rely on their mothers, sisters and grandmothers for help as they had done in the past. They were left alone. The family unit became small, isolated and unsupported; for the mother it became boring, repetitive, tedious and frustrating. She had no time to herself, suffered from a loss of identity and had no other outlet for her skills and capabilities. Recently, and largely because of the feminist movement, there has been a move back to the kind of egalitarian marriage that existed before.

The modern mother

Twenty-first century mothers can be divided into two main categories. The first consists of those who feel that while their children are very young they want to look after them themselves and they feel that this activity is the most worthwhile job that they can do. However, even a mother who loves her child dearly will be prepared to admit that looking after young children isn't easy. A woman who finds herself a mother shortly after leaving a job is unlikely to be well prepared for the demands, not to mention the isolation of being a mother.

Motherhood has its pleasures and fulfilment but it's very tough. It's 24 hours a day, seven days a week. It's repetitious and tedious and extremely demanding and wearing. No mother undervalues what she is doing but society does. Consequently when a young mother, particularly if she has been well trained to do a job outside the home, is asked what she is doing and all she can say is that she's a mother, she feels that the admission classifies her as inferior to women who are holding down a job. It's up to society to take a more realistic view of motherhood than the present rather idealized one.

The working mother

The other category is the working mother. For some reason the term "working mother" is still a pejorative one in our society. The general view seems to be that if women aren't prepared to devote themselves entirely to the upbringing of their children it's felt that they aren't maternal, that they're selfish and heartless.

If we go back to the pre-Industrial Revolution family we find that mothers were always working mothers. They did an equal amount of work to the father and they shared the work of the family with the father. It's a natural instinct for a mother to want to go on working even though she has had children. Also, many women today work because they have to; either because they have no partner or because there is insufficient income. Women have always made a vital contribution to the support of their families, whether it was growing food, spinning wool, making pots, weaving cotton, grinding flour, curing bacon or tanning leather. Over the centuries the economic importance of women has been equal to their domestic importance. It's only now that our priorities have become rather muddled.

Women who work nearly always have a strong drive to be independent outside the home. They want to have their own lives, their own interests and their own source of income. They cherish their own area of activity where they are respected and their efforts are prized and where they are needed for their skills and expertise. These are perfectly valid and reasonable motives for wanting to return to work after a child is born. However, the woman who opts to do this is putting herself into the category of people who work hardest and are the most stressed. In Western society today the hardest-working person is the working mother. She has two full-time jobs; that of a mother and that of a wage-earner.

The modern father

This is a father who takes responsibility for the general care of his child. Fewer fathers nowadays are prepared to be strangers to their children, missing out on all the good times in the family and, most important, missing out on their children growing up. The modern father is active rather than passive. He will arrange his day to come home early from work to see his children or work part-time so he can share the childcare with his partner. He'll spend as much time as he can playing with his children, showing them new things, helping them with their hobbies, taking them with him when he enjoys his own. He will participate from day one with the care of the baby, with nappy changing, with getting up in the middle of the night, doing the two a.m. feed, helping with bathtimes, reading stories, playing games and singing songs before bedtime. The modern father is a full-time parent, not a part-time stranger, and everyone in the family benefits from this.

A father who has a high interest in the pregnancy generally stays interested after the birth. Interest is positively related to how much he holds the baby in the first six weeks and whether he goes to the baby when she cries. Not unexpectedly, his attitude affects his partner's enjoyment of pregnancy and motherhood. The happier he is about it and the more he looks forward to fatherhood, the more she enjoys the first weeks of her baby's life too and inevitably, the better the start for the baby. The better the father is at playing his role, the more important he becomes.

A new lifestyle

As a new parent you'll notice quite a few changes in your life. A life of free and easy egocentricity will be nailed down to your new baby's inner alarm clock, to the necessity for feeds, to changing nappies and tending your baby at any time of the day and night. It will almost be a complete reversal of lifestyle, which at first may not be easy to accept. Some parents don't accept it and never let the baby dominate

their lives. They try to carry on with their free and easy way of life with a baby basket tagging along.

Other parents do exactly the opposite and give up everything to look after their baby. The baby becomes the centre of their lives and they devote all their energy towards his or her care. Neither of these extremes is a good idea; far and away the best is a happy medium in which the needs and emotions of the baby and parents more or less dovetail together.

Meeting different needs

Children need certain things from their parents. They need security and love; they need to be introduced to new experiences and they need to be recognized and loved as individuals. If a parent fulfils these needs, particularly love and affection, which are the most important things that you can give a child, then that child will develop normally and establish a pattern for forming all future relationships.

After love, the next most important thing that you can give your child is stimulation. A young child is like a sponge soaking up practically every new idea and experience she comes in contact with. Your new baby has a great potential to develop and learn and is just dying to be given the opportunity. So, to be good parents, it's important to start introducing your child to the outside world with all its wonders and excitements, first through yourselves and the immediate family, and then through your extended family.

Children also need to know that the adults they love most, their parents, approve of them. The way you should show this approval is by praise. It has often been noted that children respond much better to praise than to blame, and a positive attitude of teaching and education is far more effective than a negative one. A child who is loved has self-respect; a child who is unloved has none. A child will respond to this situation by being difficult to manage, and generally anti-social.

Although children have needs, parents have needs too. Your needs don't disappear just because you've become a parent. The elation of having a baby will be quickly dispelled if you feel that your needs go completely unheeded. All parents make sacrifices but there is no need for you to be a martyr. If your needs and those of your child are not well balanced, then resentment will build up and the chances of creating a happy, loving domestic atmosphere will be minimal.

Parents' needs

The needs of both parents must be taken into consideration. In this day and age parents can be nothing but equal, and parenting and childrearing must be equally shared. It should really be viewed as a contract: you're equally responsible for your child's conception so you should take equal responsibility for rearing your child.

The least that must happen is that you and your partner are in agreement with each other about the roles that you have to play in parenting your child. It's just not good enough for a woman to be expected to take on all the childcare without any support, while the father leaves early in the morning and doesn't return home until after the baby is asleep. In this situation everyone is missing out.

In an ideal world, the needs of parents and children would complement each other. In other words, the need of the parents to love and nurture their young baby would be matched by the infant's dependency and need for care. One of the things that triggers off conflict in a family is when the two sets of needs do not match – especially if the parents aren't mature enough to meet the demands of a young child.

Your role is important

As a parent you will be called upon to play many roles for your child. You will be your child's first friend and probably her best friend for life. At one time we thought that a child was not alert to the world around it until it reacted overtly to what was going on. Indeed Saint Thomas Aquinas saw it on an even longer scale. He said, "Give me a boy until he's seven and then take him", the idea being that a person could be formed during the first seven years.

We now know that this formative time is much shorter than that. A child starts to absorb information about its environment from the second it is born. The fact that it can't focus its eyes on a distant object until the age of about six weeks does not mean that it cannot see. It can. A newborn baby can focus perfectly well at a distance of 20–25cm (8–10in) and that's where your face and your hands should be if you want your baby to recognize you and watch you. Babies are responding to sights, sounds, smells, touches, conversations and ambiences as soon as they enter the world. If parents realize this and take this fact seriously it puts them in a highly responsible position. It means that they, and not teachers, are responsible for a child's first learning.

You will not only be teacher but playmate, counsellor, educator and disciplinarian. Your influence will be pivotal. A child learns from its parents' friendship and hostility, happiness and sadness, content and discontent, the blueprint for a loving relationship, the architecture of a conversation (indeed a baby is conversing in as short a time as two weeks so you need to know how to recognize primitive baby conversation). All the early skills – walking, talking, socializing and intellectual development – are absolutely in the parents' hands and no one else is culpable if things go wrong. This means that modern parents have to be active, interested parents who take on their roles as teachers with seriousness and dedication, the moment the baby is born.

Children need consistency

All children require one strong, constant, emotional bond early in their lives. If this is missing because the parents are inconsistent in giving their child love, sympathy and reassurance, or because the mother is replaced by several inadequate mother substitutes, your baby's early need for a secure relationship may be thwarted.

Part of your role will be to teach your child to respect other people's rights and property, and this will be enforced through discipline. For discipline to be effective it should be firm and consistent, but it should also always be sympathetic, understanding and considerate.

Very often a child's delinquent act is directed at a neglectful parent with whom she cannot communicate. Parents who don't talk to their child have very little chance of influencing her, whereas a mother or father who has observed and respected every step in their child's development and readily accepted her idiosyncrasies and failures, will nearly always be in a position to talk over problems with that child.

Setting limits for a child

Research has shown that children actually don't like a lack of boundaries nor do they thrive when they are undisciplined. In fact they do best when the limits of behaviour are clearly defined and constant; this makes them feel safe and secure. It's your role to set standards for behaviour and conduct appropriate for the age of your child, and to create a framework in which your child can get on with her life free of unnecessary control. Research has shown that both over-restrictiveness and inconsistency have adverse effects on children. Ideal parents are warm, affectionate, accepting, understanding and encouraging of independence.

One of the most important aspects of parenting is being a model for your developing child. A boy observes his father and quickly realizes what is going to be expected of him as he grows up.

He models himself on his father, he copies what his father does, he picks up habits from his father.

In the same way a daughter learns from her mother what is expected of her and what it will be like to be a woman. It's the atmosphere and behaviour inside the home from which the children first learn social behaviour and social roles. As they grow older they will determine their own moral values and their standards from those that are displayed by their parents. Children can still thrive with only one parent to learn from, but they are obviously better off with two models to check against rather than one.

It's my belief that children need the interest, the help, the support, the teaching, the counselling and the love of fathers. Certainly in matters of discipline, both parents are needed because families should make important decisions as a unit, and children should see both their parents taking an interest in and making decisions about the important times in their lives.

The importance of touch

"Spare the rod and spoil the child" was something that my mother and many of her generation quoted to her children, and most people of my age were disciplined not only with words, actions, rewards and punishments, but with some kind of physical punishment.

To my mind the word spoil is a very dangerous one because most people confuse spoiling with loving, and no baby or child can have too much loving. The first introduction to loving that a newborn baby experiences is the touch of the mother's arms. The second is the

sound of her voice. I do believe that babies "bond" to these two things. In other words they recognize the mother's touch, her smell and the sound of her voice as belonging to their carer, the person who feeds and takes an interest in them, soothes away discomfort and generally makes life happier and more pleasant. One of the most important aspects of this loving relationship is touch and the first touches a baby experiences should be soft, gentle, welcoming and cushioning.

We are not the only animal to whom touch is important; it is important throughout the whole animal kingdom, as some controversial and rather moving animal experiments show. Some of the first of these were done with baby Rhesus Monkeys. They were divided into two groups, having been taken away from their mothers at a young age, but old enough to survive on their own. The groups were given two substitute "mothers". One was a "wire mother", which was simply the shape and body of a mother monkey made out of wire. The other was a "soft mother": the wire body was covered in material such as lamb's wool. For the first group, the wire mother provided food via a nipple attachment; for the second group, the soft mother did. The experimenters thought that the monkeys would prefer whichever mother had the food. However, it was found that the young monkeys clung to the soft mother whether it provided them with food or not, and only

Your baby's first conversations
At this magic distance – 25cm (10in) between you – your baby can see you clearly and "speaks" to you with mouth and tongue movements.

Father's role

There are so many things you can share with your child. For example, it's never too early to start showing him how to brush his teeth.

went to the wire surrogate occasionally to eat. Sometimes they were prepared to go without food in order to snuggle up to the soft mother, so great was their need for softness, comfort, and touching. In some intensive care units where premature babies are nurtured, the babies are put on soft, fluffy sheets because this makes the babies feel as though they are being touched. The astonishing fact is these babies thrive better and put on weight more quickly than a child who lies on a linen or cotton sheet. The upshot of all this is very important for a parent. If you want your baby to be happy, to thrive and to put on weight, one of the most important things you can do for her is to cuddle, and cuddle, and give more cuddles. Take every opportunity to stroke, pat, touch and love your child through gestures. If you can accompany these touching movements with a soft, loving voice, a big smile and your face held 20–25cm (8–10in) away from your newborn baby, you will be giving her a flying start in life.

Love is not exclusive

Until quite recently the commonly held view of the mother–child bond was that it was exclusive. It was thought that a strong, healthy bond between mother and child was essential for a child's mental health, but more importantly that a child's care should be monopolized by one mother figure. It was also felt that a child was unable to form attachments to more than one person who was, of course, the mother. This placed a huge psychological burden on the mother and made her the subject of great pressure by everyone who cared to exert it, be it partner or family.

Research has shown that this is almost certainly not the case. Babies are not confined to a single bond. Once your baby has reached the stage of forming an attachment to anyone then she is probably capable of maintaining a number of attachments at the same time. As they grow up, most babies form specific attachments simultaneously – as many as five or more. By the time children are 18 months old, almost a third have formed attachments with neighbours and grandparents but, above all, with their fathers. Another aspect of the research has shown that being attached to several people at the same time does not mean that the baby has a shallower feeling towards each one. An infant's capacity for attachment is not like a cake that has to be cut. Love in babies has no limits.

Given this basis of a baby's ability to form attachments with several people, there is no reason why "mothering" can't be shared by several people. Furthermore, the mother need not be the biological mother. There's no evidence at all to suggest that firm attachments won't grow between children and unrelated adults who take on the parenting role by fostering or adoption, for instance. The belief that the mother, simply by virtue of being the biological mother, is uniquely capable of caring for her child is without foundation. There are no medical, physiological or biological reasons for confining childcare to women. In fact the argument in favour of equal sharing of parenting between both parents is irresistible.

Consistency of care

An infant can form multiple attachments and research has shown that such attachments depend more on the quality of the interaction than on its duration. Controversy about whether the mother has to be the infant's constant companion throughout each day is over. A minimum period of togetherness is desirable, but there is nothing that can be said about how much. It is the personal qualities that the adult brings to the interaction that are the most important. Provided that these can be given full play there is no reason why mother and baby should not spend a portion of the day apart (the mother at work for instance and the child in some kind of day-care arrangement that the family is comfortable with).

There is, however, one important proviso: that is the stability and quality of substitute care. If the people responsible for the child's care are constantly changing the child could well become disturbed. A child may not need uniformity of care, but she does need consistency of care. It's your job to make sure this is given if neither of you is going to stay at home.

1 The newborn

Soon after delivery your baby will be examined and his weight, head circumference and length will be measured in order to form a baseline against which his future development will be assessed. Incidentally, don't try to compare your baby with others; doctors and midwives don't. The only comparisons that should be made are with himself at different stages. The average birth weight is 2.5–4.5kg (5lb 8oz–9lb 12oz), but if your baby is smaller, don't worry. The normal range varies according to such factors as genetics, race and nutrition. The average length of a baby at term is 48–51cm (19–20in), but again big variations are common.

Physical impressions

The head

Size The average newborn baby's head circumference is about 35cm (14in). It may seem large in comparison with the rest of his body as it comprises a quarter of his length compared to one eighth in an adult.

Shape Your baby's head is unlikely to be perfectly rounded after birth, but, no matter how bumpy or swollen it looks, your baby's brain will not have been damaged. This is because the bones in the head are specially designed to move over each other during birth so that the head, which is the largest part of the baby's body, can pass down the birth canal easily. The head will soon regain its rounded shape.

Sometimes a baby has a large, firm swelling on one or both sides of the head that doesn't go down immediately. Called a cephalhaematoma, this is again caused by the natural pressure exerted by the uterine muscle during labour. It's really a large bruise of the scalp and it's outside the skull. The swelling puts no pressure on the baby's brain and subsides, without treatment, within a few weeks.

Bruising is quite common after a forceps delivery, as are shallow indentations on either side of the head. They are both rectified naturally within a couple of days.

The fontanelle The fontanelle is the soft spot in the top of your baby's head and it is the space where the skull bones have not yet joined. They don't fuse until your baby is about two years old. The baby's

Holding your newborn
Next to your skin, breathing in all those lovely reassuring body smells, will be your newborn baby's favourite position.

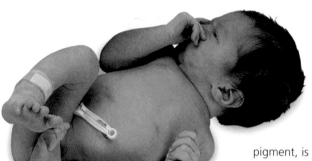

Your baby's body
A newborn baby's abdomen may seem very rounded and his limbs small and thin, but these proportions are normal and will soon change.

scalp covers this space and is really quite tough, but make sure that the fontanelle is never pressed very hard. The purpose of the fontanelle is to allow the soft skull bones to "mould" (this means to ride over one another) without damage to the baby's brain as it passes through the birth canal. You need take no special care of the skin and hair that cover the fontanelle. However, if you ever notice that the skin over the area is taut, if there's a bulge or if the area's abnormally shrunken, contact your doctor immediately.

The eyes

Condition Most babies are born with rather puffy eyes as a result of the natural pressure during birth. The swelling usually goes down within a couple of days.

Never accept a discharge from your baby's eyes as normal. In all probability it's a common, mild infection called "sticky eye", but it should always be treated by a doctor, not by yourself. Never use proprietary drops or ointments.

Colour All babies are born with blue eyes. This is because melanin, the body's natural

pigment, is not present in the skin or eyes at birth. If a baby is going to have brown eyes or a dark brown skin, the colour will gradually develop over a period of weeks or months. The eyes and skin may not reach their permanent colour until the baby is six months old.

Eye function You may find it difficult to get your baby to open his eyes at first, but never try to force them open. One of the easiest ways I have found to get a baby to open his eyes is to hold him above my head. The tendency then is to open them.

You might notice when your baby does open his eyes that he appears to squint. Don't worry about this. Your baby hasn't yet learnt to use his eyes synchronously, as a pair, to focus on things. The squinting will gradually disappear as he learns to focus when he's one or two months old. Check with your doctor if your baby is still squinting after three months.

Tears Tiny babies don't shed tears, as you'll find when your baby cries. It usually takes about four or five months for a baby to produce "real" tears when he cries.

The mouth

Lip blisters Such blisters, usually in the centre of the mouth, are caused by the baby's sucking. They cause no harm and will go away of their own accord.

Tongue-tie Your baby's tongue may appear

to be almost fully attached to the bottom of his mouth. This should not be a cause of worry. The baby's tongue grows mainly from the tip throughout the first year.

The skin

The vernix The skin of your newborn will probably be covered with this white, greasy substance. Some babies have vernix all over their face and body, while others only have it on isolated parts such as their face and hands. Hospital practices in relation to vernix have changed. Whereas it used to be meticulously cleaned off after birth it is now left on because it provides a natural barrier against minor skin infections. It is generally considered unnecessary to clean it off not only because of the vernix's protective qualities, but also because it is naturally absorbed into the skin within two or three days. However, if there are large accumulations of vernix in skin folds it may be wiped away in case it causes irritation.

Texture Your baby may be born with dry peeling skin (most noticeable on the palms of the hands and soles of the feet). This is not eczema nor does it mean that your baby will be permanently dry-skinned. In most cases the dryness soon disappears.

Colour The top half of your baby's body may be pale while the lower half is red. This is due to the baby's immature circulation, which causes the blood to pool in the lower limbs. The difference is rectified by moving your baby about.

You may notice that your baby's hands or feet have turned rather blue, especially if he's been lying down. Once again, this is due to your baby's relatively inefficient circulation. The colour will change if you pick up or move him. Try to keep your baby's room at an equable temperature, around 16–20°C (65–68°F). Blue marks (also called Mongolian blue spots), which look like bruises, often occur on the lower backs of babies with dark skin tones (nearly all African and Asian babies have them). They are completely harmless and fade away naturally.

Jaundice Many healthy newborn infants develop slight jaundice – a yellowish discolouration of the skin and the whites of the eyes – on about the third day of life. This is known as physiological jaundice, because it is not a disease. It is due to the baby's blood having a high content of primitive red cells, which are broken down after birth. When red cells are broken down, one of their constituent parts, the yellow pigment called bilirubin, increases in the blood and causes the skin and eyes to colour. Physiological jaundice should clear by the end of the first week as long as the baby is feeding well.

The umbilicus

Immediately after birth the umbilical cord is cut about 8–10cm (3–4in) from the baby's abdomen. Pressure is exerted on it by a clamp and the stump shrivels and drops off within ten days or so. Some babies develop umbilical hernias (small swellings near the navel), but these nearly always clear up within a year of their own accord. If your baby has one and it enlarges or persists check with your midwife or health visitor.

The breasts

Both male and female babies can have swollen breasts at birth; they may even have a slight discharge of milk. This is caused by the presence of maternal hormones in the baby's body and it resolves itself naturally. Never try to squeeze any of the milk out. The swelling will subside within a couple of days.

The genitals

The genitals of both boys and girls are naturally larger at birth than the rest of their bodies. The scrotum or vulva may even look rather red and inflamed. This is a natural occurrence and is caused by the mother's hormones crossing the placenta into the baby's bloodstream. Such hormones may also cause a clear or white discharge in female babies, and even a small amount of vaginal bleeding. Once again, this is perfectly normal and will clear up naturally after a couple of days. However, if you're at all worried by this, contact your doctor.

Stools

A baby's first stools are usually dark green and sticky and have very little smell. This is because they are mainly meconium, which is digested mucus from the mucus glands in the bowel. It is the only kind of motion your baby will pass for the first two or three days. Gradually over the next three or four days you will notice that the stools change colour. The appearance and consistency of the stools will then depend on whether your baby is having breast or formula milk (*see p.134*).

COMMON BLEMISHES

Birthmarks

Quite commonly there are small red marks on a baby's skin, particularly on the eyelids, on the forehead and, if you lift up the hair, at the back of the neck just under the hairline. They are due to the enlargement of tiny blood vessels near the surface of the skin and are traditionally called stork marks. Both of my sons had them and they disappeared, as they do in most children, by the time they were six months old. In some babies, however, these marks may not disappear until they are about 18 months.

Another common birthmark is the so-called strawberry mark. This appears after a couple of days but usually fades before three years old. If you're at all worried by your baby's birthmark ask your health visitor for advice and reassurance.

Spots

It is not unusual for a baby to have small white spots over the bridge of the nose, called milia. These spots are not abnormal so never, ever squeeze them. They are caused by the temporary blockage of the sweat glands and sebaceous glands that secrete sebum to lubricate the skin. They nearly always disappear after a few days.

Weals and rashes

Many babies develop a skin condition that looks rather like nettle rash, called urticaria neonatorum. The baby's skin becomes red and blotchy, with small white spots that appear and disappear quite rapidly. The whole rash only lasts for a couple of days and will disappear without treatment. If you're in doubt get medical advice.

Body hair

Babies are born with varying amounts of hair, called lanugo, on their bodies. Some babies have only a soft down on their heads, others are covered in quite coarse hair over their shoulders and down their spines. Both are quite normal, and the hair usually rubs off quite soon after birth.

Newborn behaviour

If you concentrate on your baby and observe him carefully over the first two or three days of life you will become familiar with normal infant behaviour and will become accustomed to your baby's idiosyncrasies. It is essential that you learn to understand his signals; stay with him as much as possible, to watch him, nurse him, and play with him.

If you watch him closely you may notice that he does several unexpected things: he may shiver quite suddenly for no reason; he may make such snuffling noises that you wonder if his nose and air passages are blocked; he may even stop breathing all together for several seconds. None of these is abnormal. In the first weeks of life your baby will be given a hearing screening test by the hospital.

Sounds

Breathing A newborn baby's lungs are small and breathing will seem shallow when compared to ours. When you first go to your baby you may be unable to detect that he is breathing. Don't be frightened by this because the breathing will get stronger each day.

All newborn babies make strange sounds when they breathe. Sometimes the breathing is fast and noisy and at other times it may be irregular. Your baby may snuffle with each breath in and out and you may think he has got a cold. This is not necessarily so. In most babies it is because the bridge of the nose is low, and the snuffling noise is caused by the air trying to get through the very small nasal passages. As your baby grows older the bridge of the nose will get higher and the snuffling sound will gradually stop.

On the other hand, if you find that the snuffling interferes with your baby's freedom to suck then you should talk to your midwife, health visitor or doctor, as he may need treatment with nose drops before feeding. Nose drops should only be used under medical supervision.

You should, however, be concerned about your baby's breathing if it ever becomes laboured, especially if you notice that the chest is being sharply drawn in with each breath and the breathing rate has risen to 60 or more breaths per minute. Any of these signs warrants immediate medical attention (*see p.310*).

Sneezing Babies are very sensitive to bright lights and sometimes sneeze whenever they open their eyes for the first few days. This is because the light stimulates the nerves to the nose as well as to the eyes. (You can try this out for yourself the next time you feel a sneeze coming on: if you look into a bright light you will find that you are able to precipitate the sneeze.)

Even if your baby is sneezing quite a lot it doesn't necessarily mean that he has a cold. The lining of a baby's nose is very sensitive, and sneezing is essential as it clears out the nasal passages and prevents dust from getting down into the lungs.

Hiccups Newborn babies hiccup quite a lot. This is normal, too, and it shouldn't bother you. Hiccups are caused by sudden, irregular contractions of the diaphragm and are a sign that the muscles involved in respiration, those between the ribs, the diaphragm, and the abdomen, are getting stronger and trying to work in harmony.

Reflexes and movements

All newborn babies have reflexes that are instinctive movements designed to protect them. These reflexes last until voluntary movements on your baby's part take their place, generally around three months old. Two of the most easy reflexes to elicit are those to protect the eyes and to maintain breathing: your baby will close his eyes if you touch his eyelids and will make struggling movements with his hands if you gently hold his nose between your thumb and forefinger.

The rooting reflex If you gently stroke your baby's cheek you will find that he turns his head in the direction of your finger and opens his mouth. He makes this rooting movement when he is searching for your breast to start feeding (see p.91).

The sucking reflex Every baby is born with the reflex to suck and yours will begin to do so if something is put in his mouth or if you press on the upper palate just behind the gums. Sucking movements are extremely strong and they last for quite a long time after the stimulation to suck, like a finger or a nipple, has been removed. If you want to breastfeed it is important that you put the baby to the breast as soon after delivery as possible. Your baby has to get used to the actual technique of breast-feeding, just as you do, so it helps if he has the powerful desire to suck as a stimulus.

The swallowing reflex All babies can swallow when they are born so they can swallow colostrum or milk straightaway.

The walking reflex A newborn baby will move his legs in a walking action if you hold him upright underneath the arms and let his feet touch a firm surface. This is not the reflex that encourages a baby to stand

NEWBORN REFLEXES

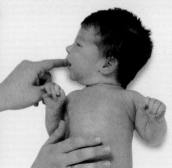

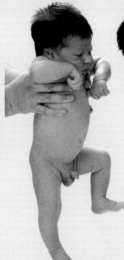

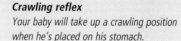

Crawling reflex
Your baby will take up a crawling position when he's placed on his stomach.

Rooting/sucking reflex
Your baby will instinctively turn his head in the direction of your finger when you gently stroke his cheek.

Walking/stepping reflex
When you hold your baby under the shoulders in an upright position with his feet touching a firm surface, he'll move his legs in a walking action.

upright and walk (*see p.188*). If you hold your baby upright and let the front of his legs gently touch the edge of a solid object he'll automatically bring his foot up in a kind of stepping movement.

The crawling reflex When placed on his stomach your newborn baby will assume what appears to be a crawling position. This is because his legs are still curled up towards his body as they were in your womb. When your baby kicks his legs he may even be able to shuffle in a vague crawling manner and may actually move up his cot slightly. This "reflex" will disappear as soon as his legs uncurl and he is able to lie flat.

The startle or Moro reflex If your baby hears a loud noise close to him, or if he's been roughly handled, he will throw up his arms and legs with fingers outstretched in an attempt to catch on to something. He'll let his limbs fall back slowly towards his

body and will then bend his knees and clench his fists. This is a large or "gross" response to a stimulus and many newborn responses are like this. For instance, when your young baby sees you he uses the whole of his body to greet you. It's only when he gets to about eight or nine months old that he simply smiles and reaches out his arms to you as a more mature greeting.

The grasp reflex A newborn baby will automatically tighten his fingers around anything that is pressed into the palm of his hand. He can grasp very tightly, and immediately after birth this reflex is so strong that his whole weight can be supported if he grasps onto your fingers. This reflex is generally lost by the time he is around three months old. If you touch the soles of your baby's feet you will also notice that his toes curl downwards as if to grip something.

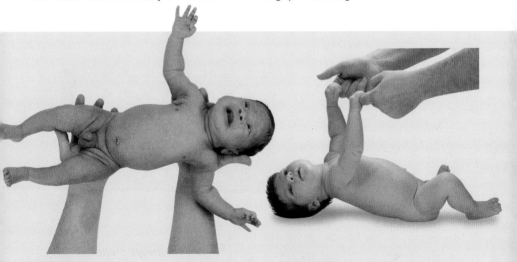

Moro reflex
Should your baby's head drop back, he will throw his limbs up with fingers outstretched, then let them fall back slowly towards his body.

Grasp reflex
If you put something such as a finger in the palm of your baby's hand, he will clench it surprisingly tightly.

Bonding

A newborn baby sleeps for most of his first days, so you should spend all of his waking time with him. Research has shown that physical contact with you, the sound of your voice and the smell of your body are very important during the first few days of life. During this time your baby forms a bond with you which, if encouraged, is unique and unbreakable.

This bonding process is nature's way of ensuring that children are nurtured and that the human race, as a whole, survives. However, in the normal course of events, whether you are breast- or bottle-feeding your baby, he will automatically get the close contact he needs while you are feeding, changing and holding him. He will get to know you, your smell, and the sound of your voice.

If, for any reason, your baby is taken away to the nursery for observation, or to the neonatal (special care) unit, make every effort to visit him as often as possible. Even if he has to be cared for in an incubator, you can touch and caress him through the portholes, talk to him and, if possible, feed him. It is important to take all the steps you can to reduce the time you are separated from your baby.

Eye contact is essential

All research points to the fact that physical contact between mother and baby should start as soon after birth as possible. Furthermore, eye contact should follow immediately after birth wherever possible. Most child development experts used to say that babies could not see properly until their eyes could focus, but babies can interpret shapes and outlines. The shape and outline of your face will be recognized by your baby within 36 hours. Research has shown that it is your eyes that your baby searches for and concentrates on once he has found them. Furthermore, babies can do this within a few hours of birth. Certainly when my second son was born and I lifted him on to my stomach and called his name he opened his eyes instantly on hearing my voice and flicked them around the room until they came to rest on my face.

It has been shown that mothers who make early eye contact with their babies and continue to do so, particularly during feeding times when they face their babies and look deeply into their eyes, are much more likely to be mothers who are sympathetic and understanding. These mothers tend to solve problems calmly and by logical discussion. They rarely resort to physical punishment of their children.

Early physical contact

Following on from the first few days you should try to keep your baby in contact with you as much as possible. By contact I mean on your body, for instance in a sling. It has been known for decades that the children who are carried on their mother's backs, such as those in Indian, Inuit and some African tribes, rarely cry. The newborn infant finds the close physical presence of the mother very reassuring. She is soft and warm, her smell is familiar. When the baby lays his head against the

mother's body he hears the familiar heartbeat that he has been hearing for nine months in the womb. The baby feels secure and at home in his surroundings. It is more natural for your baby to be jogged about on his mother's body especially as it could bring back memories of his cushioned ride in the womb, than to lie completely still on a mattress in a cot.

The importance of smell

We know that your smell is one of the first associations that your baby makes with you. You give off a smell to which your baby is very sensitive and to which he responds biologically. Whenever you go into your sleeping baby's room he wakes. When other people, even your partner, go in he stays asleep. This is because the baby's very sensitive sense of smell picks up your chemicals called pheromones, and he wakes because he recognizes you as his main source of comfort, pleasure and food.

First impressions
Your newborn baby will be still covered in cheesy vernix. It's no longer washed off after birth – it's the best moisturizer known.

Sounds and their effects

Newborns do not like loud noises. While your baby is becoming used to your voice, speak or sing in a gentle, soothing, cooing voice. Research at Oxford University has shown that babies respond better to the high-pitched female voice rather than to the lower-pitched male voice. To a baby the mother's voice is almost like therapy. You should chat, sing or croon to your baby whenever you are with him. Even young babies enjoy nursery rhymes and simple songs, particularly if they have a pronounced rhythm and rhyming sound. Research suggests that children who were sung to early in their lives rapidly develop a feeling for and a facility with words and tend to speak and read slightly earlier.

Mother love

Most mothers are exhilarated, although exhausted, after the delivery of a baby and feel great love for the child. Some mothers, however, find they feel nothing at first.

We now know that mother love, put very simply, is a response to hormones. There are certain hormones produced in the brain almost immediately after delivery, namely oxytocin or prolactin, which trigger lactation and are also responsible for maternal feelings. Different women have different emotional responses to these hormones and may find that their love for their babies takes longer to develop.

A mother's feelings for her baby can also be affected by other factors, like the actual delivery and her own expectations of the birth and the baby. It's not uncommon for the baby's arrival to be something of an anti-climax. Even if it is short and perfectly normal, labour is a very dramatic event and it is a hard act to follow.

Conversely, if the labour has been very hard and long, and if drugs have been used, the mother may be too exhausted and numbed to feel great love for her child. Also, she may have unrealistic expectations of her response to her newborn baby. She may, for instance, expect to recognize him instantly as her

Instant recognition
In some babies you can immediately recognize their inherited features; in others they are less obvious. Parents will always know their own baby.

own flesh and blood, and to look physically similar to herself and her partner. In fact, this is rarely the case and so it's important to be aware of it.

Most women, however, find that their love grows gradually over the 48 or 72 hours after their babies' births until on the third day they feel a palpable love for their new babies. But don't be surprised if it takes two weeks or more.

Spend time with your baby

A mother's response to her baby can be affected by the amount of time she spends with him during the first few days of life. In one study on this, a group of mothers were permitted only routine contact with their babies on a hospital ward. Another group of mothers in the same ward was allowed to have contact with their babies for an extra 15 hours during their three days in hospital. The two groups were interviewed one month after delivery and a year later and revealed a number of quite surprising differences. The mothers who had been given extended contact were found to be more reluctant to leave their babies, to be more responsive to their crying, to engage in more eye-to-eye contact during feeding and to be generally more attentive. The remarkable thing is that these differences are accounted for by just 15 hours of additional contact during the first three days of life.

While it's undoubtedly true that early physical contact helps bonding, it's not the only factor involved in the development of maternal or paternal feelings. In a study of premature babies, where the most extreme form of early separation arises because the baby has to stay in an incubator for an extended period, mothers were allocated to two groups. In the first, the standard hospital procedure was used and each mother was permitted only to look at her baby during the several weeks he stayed in the incubator. In the second group the mothers were permitted to handle their babies in the incubator from the second day onwards.

Both groups of mothers were questioned after one week and one month and then after discharge from hospital. It was impossible to find any consistent differences between the two groups. This important piece of research suggests that a mother's attachment to her baby may not be seriously affected by a temporary separation immediately after her baby's birth. That's just as well, otherwise there would be little hope for adoptive parents and their children.

Mothering instincts

Mothering is much more complex than a simple dependency on the hormonal changes that occur at childbirth. The most likely explanation for the way a woman develops mothering instincts is that they stem from the mother's own childhood. Love develops early on in life on a reciprocal basis. It stems from the experience of being loved by parents who give a child the capacity for loving others. It enables the child to return love when it is given and to transfer it to others later on in life. In other words, when a child is loved it makes him fit for love; if a child is deprived of this experience the ability to love is stunted. This is why it's so important for your child to have your loving attention, care and concern.

2 Equipment

Go shopping for equipment in the last couple of months before your baby is due, while you can still shop on your own and you feel reasonably energetic. You'll be faced with a seemingly endless choice of "essential" items, but don't be swayed by clever advertising. Ask friends or relatives which items of equipment they found useful and, more important, which ones they bought and never used.

Choosing equipment

Shop around and find out what's available before you make your final choices, and always think of the equipment in relation to your lifestyle. For example, if you feel perfectly relaxed about bathing your baby in the sink, don't bother buying a baby bath just because most people do.

Similarly, if you really like the idea of a large carriage pram and you have a big enough hall, an easy route to shops and parks, and you can afford one, then go ahead and buy a pram. Some people think it unlucky to buy too many things before the birth. Check to see if you can choose what you need but not pick it up until you're ready.

Second-hand can be fine
It isn't essential to buy everything new. Babies grow so quickly that some items that are essential for a brief time are useless within a couple of months. Many families are quite happy to lend or sell such items, so keep an eye open in newsagents,

local papers and clinics as well as at house and garage sales and on Internet sites. The only stipulation I'd make when buying second-hand, apart from checking for general wear and tear, is to check that surfaces are smooth and rust-free and that, where applicable, they still comply with the latest safety regulations.

However, never buy a second-hand car seat. It may have been damaged in an accident and will probably not have the original instructions so may be difficult to fit correctly.

Don't buy too many baby clothes before the birth. You will need to have the basics (see pp.40–42) ready, but you'll find that relatives and friends love buying for a new baby and you'll probably find that many items are duplicated.

Buy a car seat
This is a basic purchase, you can't bring your baby home from hospital in a car without a baby seat. Check that it is comfortable to carry; some also clip into a special pushchair frame.

CHANGING AND BATHING EQUIPMENT

New baby

- Changing unit with storage drawers
- Padded changing mat
- Changing bag for going out, with a folding changing mat
- Baby bath
- Cotton wool
- Baby wipes
- Baby oil
- Barrier cream
- Large soft towels
- Flannel or sponge
- Baby's hair brush
- Blunt-ended scissors
- 4 packs disposable nappies
  or
- 24 towelling nappies
  Nappy liners
  Pins/fasteners
  Plastic pants
  2 nappy buckets

Older baby

- Toothbrush
- Bath seat and/or non-slip mat for big bath
- Potty
- Standing block for reaching the sink

Choice of potties
Get a potty towards the end of the first year, before your child needs one.

Changing and bathing

If you like the idea of having a special changing area, but don't want to build one or convert a piece of furniture like a chest of drawers, then a changing unit is probably right for you. Make sure that it's stable and has plenty of storage space. Alternatively, many parents find a padded changing mat on a chest of drawers or on the floor is sufficient.

If you don't want to bath your baby in the sink or a household basin, you'll need a baby bath. Some are designed to use on the floor while others fit on a stand or across a bath. Choose one that won't be too heavy when full and is easy to empty.

Baby bath and changing mat
For a young baby you can use a flat-based baby bath with a stand or it can be rested on a flat surface. A changing mat is an essential item for most parents.

Feeding

If you're breast-feeding you'll need the minimum of equipment – feeding bras and breast pads for you, and a couple of bottles and a breast pump if you want to express some milk. Bottle-feeding mothers will have to buy a complete feeding kit (*see right*). There are many kinds of bottles and teats. Some teats are moulded to the shape of the baby's mouth; others are designed to move in and out like a human nipple when sucked.

When your baby starts on solids you'll need equipment for mashing food into a smooth enough purée. You'll also need unbreakable dishes to serve it in. Special dishes that keep the food hot are available, although they're not essential. Bibs, however, are. Probably the most efficient style is the plastic bib with a trough that catches all drips or pieces of food and can be washed easily.

For an older baby you'll also need some form of highchair and there's a wide variety to choose from. Make sure that the chair is stable, that it has washable surfaces, a tray with a rim to catch spilt liquids, and a safety harness. Make sure you can release the harness quickly if your baby chokes on food. Some highchairs have adaptable footrests and seats so can be used at the family table for an older child for many years.

FEEDING EQUIPMENT

New baby/breast-feeding
- Feeding bra
- Breast pads
- Breast pump if you need to express milk
- Bottles or breast milk storage containers for expressed milk

New baby/bottle-feeding
- Bottles
- Teats
- Formula
- Sterilizing equipment – cold-water unit, steam sterilizer or microwave steam sterilizer
- Bottle brush

Older baby
- Plastic bowls
- Weaning spoons and forks
- Trainer cups
- Blender or liquidizer
- Bibs
- Highchair and/or booster seat
- Safety harness

Double breast pump
Expressing milk with a double pump is excellent for stimulating milk production. Each breast produces more milk and it's richer, creamier and more nutritious.

Sleeping

The best choice for your newborn is a Moses basket or a carrycot/pram, both of which are easy to move from room to room. You'll need a cot when your baby outgrows whichever you've chosen.

Choose a cot with two mattress heights, so you don't have to bend too far in the early days, and with sides that drop down – it's much easier to get to the baby. Do make sure that the cot's side rails are set closely together, so your baby's head can't get stuck. The cot mattress should fit snugly, allowing no more than one finger to slide between the mattress and the cot side. Foam mattresses are best and some have air holes that allow your child to breathe if she turns on to her front while asleep. Fold-up, fabric-sided travel cots are useful for holidays and going out with the baby in the evening. Baby sleeping bags are useful for older babies. All equipment must comply with safety standards.

Avoid cot bumpers and fleeces as they increase the risk of overheating – babies who get too hot are at a greater risk of cot

Moses basket and baby chair
A Moses basket makes a simple lightweight bed for a newborn. A bouncing chair is useful for babies before they can sit up. Always place it on the floor.

death. Don't put cot bumpers in cots, or use a duvet for babies under one year.

As soon as your baby shows signs of being able to clamber out of her cot you'll need to buy a bed – some cots are designed to convert into beds.

Outings and travel

Slings are a popular way of transporting a newborn baby; they're light and comfortable, and allow you to carry your baby close while keeping both hands free. The sling should be used with a neck attachment until your baby can support her own head. Back-packs, which have supportive frames that make it easier to bear a larger baby's weight, are suitable once your baby can sit up by herself.

You'll also need some form of pushchair. The one you choose will depend on both your budget and your lifestyle. A large pram is impractical if you live in a small flat, three flights up; a foldable

---

SLEEP EQUIPMENT AND ACCESSORIES

New baby
- Moses basket or carrycot
- Waterproof sheet to protect mattress (tie-on sheets are good)
- Cotton sheets
- Cotton cellular blankets
- Fleecy blanket
- Baby monitor

Older baby
- Full-size cot with foam mattress
- Cot duvet (not for babies under 12 months)

lightweight pushchair or a pram with a removable carrycot would be much more suitable. However, a pram or a pram/buggy is much more comfortable for a young baby than a lightweight pushchair, which does not usually offer enough support. For the first three months your baby must be able to lie flat in whatever you choose.

Any kind of pushchair or pram needs to be easy to push, have good brakes, integral harness, or rings for a safety harness and mechanism to prevent the frame from collapsing. You will also need a waterproof cover and a sunshade for it.

Car seats

Whenever you take your child in a car you must comply with safety regulations. A car seat is one item you cannot do without if you intend taking your baby in your own or anyone else's car. Never buy a second-hand seat unless you can be certain that it has not been damaged in an accident.

All babies under 13kg (28lb) should travel in a rear-facing seat, which provides better protection for a young baby's head, neck and spine. These seats are portable so can be used for carrying your baby to and from the car. Never put a rear-facing seat in the front of the car if your car has airbags, unless they have been fully deactivated.

An older baby can have a forward-facing seat, which must be fixed in the back seat of the car. These are larger and heavier than rear-facing baby seats and designed to be left in the car. Some need to be fitted into the car, others use existing seat belts. Newer cars have special fixings for children's car seats. The latest guidelines state that children should use car seats up to the age of 12.

Additional equipment

Even young babies like to see what's going on around them and a bouncing baby chair is useful for a baby before she can sit. Always place the chair on the floor and make sure she is safely strapped in.

Although many people find playpens reminiscent of a baby prison, some find them invaluable. If you decide to buy one your choice will be between a collapsible nylon-meshed pen and rail, or a square wooden pen; both have a padded base.

CARRYING EQUIPMENT

- Front-carrying fabric sling with neck support for newborns; make sure it's washable.
- Back-pack for an older baby.
- Carriage pram with solid body and collapsible fabric hood,
  or
- Pram with removable carrycot,
  or
- Fold-flat pushchair with lie-back facility for young baby (there are many types available, ask other people which they prefer),
  or
- Pram/buggy combination – can be used as a carrycot on wheels for young baby and converts into a buggy that can face towards you or forwards. There are also combinations called travel systems available that include a car seat.
  or
- All-terrain, three-wheeler pushchair.
- Parasol for summer.
- Waterproof cover for pushchair.
- Rear-facing car seat for baby up to 13kg (28lb).
- Front-facing car seat for older child – this is compulsory up to age 12 depending on height.
- Changing bag to carry spare clothes/nappies when you are out.

Your baby's room

A baby's room doesn't have to be smart or filled with lots of expensive furnishings, but it does need to be warm, clean, safe and attractive. Make sure furniture is easy to wipe clean and has smooth rounded edges. Any paint used should be non-toxic and lead-free. Always use flameproof fabric for bedding, upholstery and curtains. And most important, your baby's room should be fun, with plenty of bright colours, pictures and mobiles in it to stimulate her senses. The colours of nature – blue, yellow and green – are said to be soothing for your baby. Paint the walls in cheerful colours, use splashes of primary colours for curtains and accessories and put plenty of things to look at on the walls.

BASIC FURNISHINGS

- Moses basket or carrycot and stand.
- Cot (you can put a Moses basket in the cot to begin with).
- Changing area with storage for nappies and other items.
- Storage for clothes and toys.
- Baby monitor so you can hear her if she wakes or cries.
- Low chair where you can sit when feeding.
- Good thick curtains or blinds to keep the room warm and dark.
- Dimmer switch to provide low levels of light for night changes or feeds.
- Shelves for books and toys.
- Mobiles hung over the cot and changing area.
- Pictures on the walls and on a pinboard in her room – even on the side of the cot. Change the pictures regularly to keep her interested.

What your baby will need

You'll need plenty of storage space, especially above or to the side of the changing area. If you plan to build your own changing area you'll want a wide, flat surface on which to place the changing mat. Wide-topped chests of drawers make ideal changing tables because they have a large surface area and plenty of storage space for nappies and clothes. All you have to do is build shelves above wherever you place it. Make sure that the surface is smooth, then cover it with a washable covering and put a padded changing mat on top. The floor covering should be hard-wearing and easy to keep clean; consider cork tiles or vinyl with a couple of non-slip rugs. Carpet is warm and absorbs noise but is harder to keep clean.

Room temperature

A baby's room doesn't need to be very warm, but should be kept at a constant temperature. Around 18°C (65°F) is suitable if your baby is covered with two blankets and a sheet. If the room is warmer, she should have fewer blankets. If you don't want to heat the entire house at this level, put a thermostatically controlled heater in her room.

Adapting the room for a toddler

Your baby's room is going to have to evolve to suit her needs as she gets older and more mobile. She'll need plenty of floor space for crawling and taking her first steps so keep furniture to a minimum. What there is should be steady and stable

Planning a baby's room
A new baby's room doesn't need a lot of special furniture. The essentials are a cot, a nappy changing area and a comfortable chair for you when feeding.

so she can use it to pull herself up without accidents. Be extra aware of the safety risks linked with a small, inquisitive toddler and follow the recommendations on p.296.

At some stage she will need to move from her cot to a bed, but don't rush her. Most parents make the switch between the ages of two and four. You must do it when a child becomes able to climb out of a cot. Once she has a bed she can get out of it by herself and explore her room so you need to be certain that everything is safe.

Storage space
Make sure there are plenty of places to keep toys so it is easy for your child to keep her things in good order. It's much more fun to play with toys if you can find them easily and don't have to search in

several different places for all the bits. This needn't be expensive shelves and drawers or ready-made toy boxes; wicker baskets, plastic stacking boxes or laundry baskets all provide good storage for children's things. Don't worry too much about tidiness though – it's having a good time together that counts.

A blackboard or a special wall area where your toddler knows that she can scribble and chalk on may also be welcome as soon as she's ready to do so.

ADAPTING A ROOM FOR A TODDLER

- Non-slip rugs on wooden floors to make them cosier for sitting on.
- Bedside table for night-light and drinks; make sure she can't pull wires.
- Low table and chair where your toddler can sit and draw and play.
- Low hook where she can hang up her coat.
- Pinboard where she can put special pictures.
- Toy boxes on wheels.

3 Clothing

All parents take great pride in their new baby's appearance and it's very tempting for you and your family and friends to rush out and buy lots of clothes for him. It's up to you what you choose, but there's absolutely no need to spend a lot of money. Remember that your child is going to grow rapidly during these first years, and he'll grow out of clothes very quickly. As far as your baby is concerned he doesn't mind what he wears as long as it is soft and comfortable and can be put on and taken off without too much trouble.

Choosing clothes birth to 1 year

Your newborn baby won't be very active, but that does not mean that he's going to stay scrupulously clean. There will inevitably be accidents and leaks from nappies, and he's bound to posset and dribble sometimes – all of which will mean fairly frequent changes of clothing. Before your baby is born, make sure that you have enough clothes to keep up with his needs. Make sure too that everything is machine washable and colourfast.

Initially, there is no need to make a distinction between day- and nightwear, and by far the most suitable nightclothes are stretch suits. As your baby gets older, sleep suits make a cosy alternative. If you buy vests or body suits, buy wide-necked ones so that they go on over his head easily – babies hate having their faces covered. Body suits are useful as they can be fastened under the baby's nappy. Buy brightly patterned suits that can be used as T-shirts if it's warm.

BASICS FOR A NEW BABY

- 6–8 T-shirt/vests or body suits
- 6–8 stretch suits
- 2 cardigans/sweaters (4 for winter babies)
- 2–3 pairs of socks and padders
- 2 pairs of scratch mittens
- 2 nightgowns (choose those with drawstring bottoms to keep feet warm)
- 1 blanket or shawl
- Protective clothing and sunhat for sun protection
- All-in-one outdoor suit (for winter)

All-in-one stretch suits
These are ideal for babies of any age. Stretch suits are easy to put on, they keep your baby warm and allow freedom of movement.

BUYING CLOTHES FOR A NEWBORN

- Whatever sizing system the manufacturer uses, make sure that you buy a size that will last until your baby's at least two months old. He won't be bothered if it's slightly too big and it's more practical than the newborn size, which he'll quickly grow out of.
- Buy only machine-washable, colourfast clothing for your baby.
- Make sure that any clothing you buy allows easy access to the nappy, so there's the minimum of undressing involved. Stretch suits with poppers in the crotch or right down the front and legs are the easiest to put on.
- In the early weeks you may find it simplest to use nightdresses that can just be lifted up to get at the nappy.
- Clothes that open down the front or have wide, envelope necks are the best because babies hate having their faces covered.
- Clothes that fasten up the front also mean that you don't have to turn your baby over when you're dressing him.
- Material should be soft and comfortable with no hard seams or rough stitching; check the neck and waistband before buying. Buy towelling, cotton or pure wool clothes; if you buy clothes made of man-made fibres do check that they feel soft and comfortable.
- Buy non-flammable clothing.
- Avoid lacy shawls or cardigans – your baby's tiny fingers can easily get caught in the holes.
- Avoid white – it gets dirty quickly and needs more care when washing. Babies suit bright colours just as much as the pastels traditionally specified for them.
- If you do buy a hat either buy one with a chinstrap, or sew some ribbons on. Many babies hate wearing hats and pull them off unless they're tied on under their chins.

Additional clothing for a baby

The kind of clothes you buy on top of the basics will be determined by finance and personal taste. There is no one essential piece of clothing, but there are some items that are more practical than others.

In summer, for example, cotton T-shirts and shorts or cotton dresses are the most suitable because they're cool and leave the baby's limbs free; in winter, mini tracksuits and dungarees are practical alternatives to all-in-one stretch suits. Once your baby is mobile he'll need clothing that gives adequate knee protection. As when your baby is very young, stick to clothes that give you easy access to his nappy, because by the time he's crawling he's not going to want to lie still for very long.

Check fit regularly

Keep an eye on how tight the legs, neck and wrists are on all clothes and buy the next size up accordingly. Bear in mind that clothes with poppers at the neck quite often last longer. Babies often outgrow clothes because their heads can no longer go through the neck opening; with poppers you can just leave them undone to accommodate your baby's head.

You'll probably learn how to gauge your baby's size quite accurately, but if you're at all worried always go by the height and weight charts given in shops, not by age. Unfortunately, different countries and manufacturers use varying size notations so if you're confused about sizes, ask the sales assistant's advice. If in doubt, buy the larger size: looser-fitting clothes are much more comfortable than tight-fitting clothes and your baby will soon grow into them.

Dressing a baby birth to 1 year

Babies need changing frequently in the first months and, initially, you may not be fully confident about supporting your rather floppy baby and dealing with the clothes at the same time. Don't worry: it's perfectly normal to be a bit awkward at first, and any fears that you have are easily overcome with practice and patience on your part.

With a new baby, always dress and undress him on a flat surface: a changing mat, on the bed or the floor, is ideal because it allows you both hands free. Secondly, keep the amount of time that he's undressed to a minimum and don't get flustered when your baby cries as you take off his clothes. Young babies hate being undressed; they're scared of the air on their naked bodies and the removal of the comforting fabric that they were wearing makes them feel very insecure. When your baby feels like this he's going to cry, very loudly. It's not because of you, so don't think that you're a bad parent. Keep calm and get on with the task in hand, but always have something to attract your baby's attention, like a mobile.

Using your lap

When your baby has more muscle control and you feel more confident you can sit him on your lap to take off his clothes. If you sit with your legs crossed your baby can sit neatly in the hollow of your legs; your arm should cradle your baby. Or, you

PUTTING ON A VEST

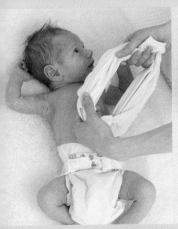
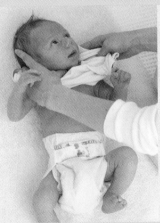
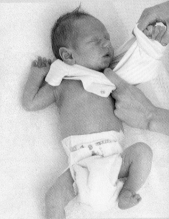

1 Lay your baby on his back on a flat, firm surface. Stretch the neck opening of the vest or body suit as wide open as you can with both hands.

2 Slide the vest over your baby's head. Take it over his face first, then gently lift his head up to bring the vest over the back of his head down to his neck.

3 Widen each sleeve or armhole with your fingers and bring your baby's arms through, fist first, one at a time. Draw the vest down over his body.

PUTTING ON A STRETCH SUIT

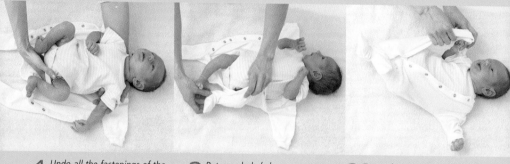

1 Undo all the fastenings of the stretch suit and lay it on a flat surface. Then, lay your baby on top of the suit so that his neck lines up with the neck of the suit.

2 Put your baby's legs one at a time into the legs of the suit, feet first. Fasten the suit under the nappy area so he can't kick his way out again.

3 To put his arms in, roll back one arm of the stretch suit and guide your baby's arm in, fist first. Roll the sleeve up into place. Repeat with the other arm.

could combine sitting your baby on your lap with using a flat surface. For example, it may be easier to put on the top layer in your lap, but to deal with the bottom half on a flat surface. You'll probably need to distract your baby in some way, so have some toys for him to hold.

Dressing an older baby

Once your baby can crawl he won't want to stay still for long and dressing may proceed "on the move". However, towards the end of the first year this will be coupled with the ability to help as you put on the clothes. For example, if you ask your 11-month-old baby to make a fist, or stretch out an arm, he'll probably do so and you'll be able to slide the jumper or jacket on without having to draw his hand through yourself.

Name the clothes as you put them on or take them off, and make a game out of the whole procedure. For example, make it

into a kind of hide and seek, peek-a-boo game: "Where's your arm gone, then?" "Oh, look, here it comes now." Always try to undress your baby when he's occupied with something else. For example, if your baby has a favourite song that he likes joining in with, always sing it while dressing or undressing him.

Washing your baby's clothes

Once your baby starts eating solids he's bound to get messy, even when he's wearing a bib, and once he starts walking his clothing will get dirtier as well. Make sure everything can go in the washing machine. If possible, have enough changes of clothes so you don't have to do the laundry every day.

If you need to use an enzyme-containing washing powder to remove stubborn stains, wash the garment in your usual powder afterwards to remove any traces of potentially irritating enzymes.

UNDRESSING A NEWBORN

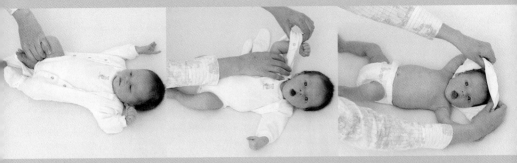

1 First, unfasten your baby's suit. If his nappy needs changing, gently pull both legs out of the suit so that his top half remains covered while you change him.

2 Grasp each sleeve by the cuff and slide his hand out. Roll his vest up towards the neck and gently pull his arms from the sleeves, while holding him by the elbow.

3 Pull the neck wide open and lift the vest over your baby's head, keeping the fabric off his face. Support his head while you carefully remove his vest.

DEALING WITH STAINS

Vomit/faeces	Use an enzyme-containing washing powder after you've removed the vomit and rinsed the garment with cold water.
Milk	Remove milk stains by rinsing the clothing thoroughly in cold water and then using an enzyme-containing washing powder.
Egg	If there is an egg stain on clothing, soak in cold water for an hour before laundering in the usual way.
Fruit and chocolate	Douse tough stains such as chocolate or grape juice with soda water, rub until the discoloration has gone and then wash as usual.
Blood	Soak bloodstains in cold water for thirty minutes, if they don't come out use an enzyme-containing washing powder. If this fails, try a few drops of ammonia on the stain.
Lipstick	Dab stain with soft white cloth that's been dipped in denatured alcohol; or use a proprietary stain stick, then wash as normal.
Grass	Remove grass stains with alcohol if they are resistant to laundering.
Chewing gum	Soften the gum with methylated spirits before gently pulling the gum away from the fabric, or freeze the garment and scrape it off.

Choosing clothes 1 to 3 years

As your baby grows your main concern when buying clothes will be that they're comfortable and, when he's more active, that they allow easy movement. Your baby will no longer spend most of the time asleep and as he starts to move about more he's going to need more clothes. They'll have to be suitable for various weather conditions (rain, cold, sun), and they'll also have to be tough enough to withstand the wear and tear that your toddler will give them. Once he can crawl he'll need sturdy protection for his knees and once he can walk he'll need shoes to protect his feet.

As before, buy clothing in a material that moves with your child so that however active he is there's no risk of him being uncomfortable, or of the material tearing. Towelling, cottons and corduroys are ideal. When he's being "toilet trained", clothing must be easily pulled down or up, and when he's learning how to dress or undress, avoid buying clothes with zips or fiddly fastenings, and use elasticated waists for as long as possible.

It'll take a while for your child to develop the co-ordination needed to dress himself, but by the time he's 18 months he'll be trying, even if it's just pulling off socks. Any attempts at dressing or undressing should be encouraged. They're a sign of growing independence and maturity, not to mention co-ordination.

Try laying out his clothes in such a way that your child can go up to them and manoeuvre them on easily. Even if he seems to be fumbling, don't step in until it's really necessary. You will, however, have to deal with most of the fastenings until your child has adequate dexterity to cope with them.

Room for growth
Pinafores or dungarees with buckles are ideal as they can be adjusted to fit your child as she grows so can be worn for longer. And she'll enjoy learning how to manage the buckles for herself.

Buying clothes

Keep your child's measurements jotted down in your diary and, as your child is growing very quickly, make sure that you take new measurements frequently.

- Buy unisex clothes when you can. There is no reason why a girl shouldn't wear boys' clothes, and they are usually sturdier anyway.
- Get outdoor clothes on the large side so that extra layers can be worn underneath. As such clothes are often more expensive, the larger size should allow your child to "grow into" it. With items that are worn every day, buy the best quality you can afford; they will last longer and may even be passed on to siblings or friends.
- Brightly coloured clothes are useful if your toddler wanders off – he'll be easier to spot in the playground for example.
- T-shirts can double up as pyjama tops.
- Buy patterned vests so that they can double up as T-shirts.
- Put extra buttons on dungaree straps so that they can be gradually lengthened as your child gets taller.
- Young children find short zips difficult to manipulate so buy trousers with elasticated waists for as long as possible.
- Buy tube socks without shaped heels so that they "grow" with the child. Buy all socks in the same brand and the same colour so that you don't have trouble matching them.
- Buy clothes with elasticated waistbands and trousers or skirts with shoulder straps so that they can be let down.
- Avoid "fitted" clothes – your toddler will grow out of them more quickly.

- Avoid man-made fabrics – they don't "breathe" like natural fibres and could make your child uncomfortably hot, especially in summer. Look for natural fibres such as pure cotton or a fabric with a high cotton content.
- A loose coat, like a duffle coat, will last your child for two winters: one as a coat with the sleeves rolled back, and the second as a jacket with the sleeves at their usual length.
- Some sleepsuits have plastic soles on the feet. So that your child's feet don't sweat, cut a small hole in the middle to let the air circulate.

Dressing toddlers

- Stop your toddler's overall straps slipping down by crossing them over at the back (and front if necessary).
- When you're teaching your child to handle buttons show him how to button from the bottom upwards.

MAKING CLOTHES LAST

- When sleepsuits get too short for comfort cut off the feet for an extra few months' wear.
- Reinforce the knees on the inside of new jeans with the extra fabric you trim from the bottoms of the legs, or use iron-on patches.
- Make summer shorts from long winter trousers that are too short or have become worn at the knees.
- When your child outgrows an expensive jacket, cut out the sleeves and let your child wear it as a waistcoat.
- Run a dark blue crayon, indelible pencil or a fountain pen filled with blue/black ink over the white line when jeans have been let down.

Getting dressed
By about the age of two your child will be trying to dress herself. Choose trousers with elastic waists to make the task easier.

- Wherever possible use Velcro fastenings, but don't use this near the neck as it may rub and cause sore patches.
- Tiny hands find zip fasteners difficult to manage so put a key ring through the zip fastener for easy handling.
- When your child is learning to use a zip fastener, teach him to pull the zip away from both skin and clothes to prevent the zip fastener catching on his skin.
- Put a badge or clear marking on the front of a garment so that your child can tell front from back.
- Mark the hole in a belt that your child should use with a stick-on gold star or a piece of tape.

- Until your child learns to hold a sweater when he is putting on a coat, sew elastic loops inside the cuffs so that the child can hang onto those and stop the sleeves being dragged up as the coat is being put on.
- If the zipper is sticking, run a soft lead pencil or a bar of soap over the zipper "teeth" to make it run smoothly.
- If your child is unwilling to make a fist when you're putting on a jumper, put a small treat such as a raisin into your child's hand. He will grasp it and make a fist allowing you to push the sleeve on.
- Attach gloves or mittens to a long piece of tape that you can thread through the arms of the coat.
- Wet shoe laces before tying – the bows won't slip and they will stay tied.
- When you first put on your baby's new shoes, cover the slippery soles with a piece of adhesive tape so that he won't slide on a slippery floor; or score the soles with scissors so that they grip.
- If the ends of your child's shoelaces become frayed, coat them with clear nail polish or wrap some sticky tape around them until you can replace them.
- Always buy boots large enough to accommodate an extra pair of socks. Wellingtons aren't very warm so put a pair of thick socks over your child's usual socks to keep his feet warm.
- When your child first starts to use buttons, sew large buttons onto the clothes so that he can handle them more easily and, if you can, sew them on with elastic thread.
- Once practical concerns are taken care of, let your child have a say in what you buy and choose his favourite colours.

CHOOSING SHOES FOR TODDLERS

There's no need to put your baby into shoes until he's walking. The bones in your baby's feet are soft and pliable – so pliable that even the pressure of tightly fitting socks can misshape the toes if your baby wears them regularly. When it's very cold, or when he starts to crawl, you can put on socks or cotton baby "boots", but do make sure that there's plenty of room for his feet to move about.

When buying shoes go to a reputable shoe shop and make sure the assistant has been trained to measure and fit children's shoes. She should always measure the foot for width and length before bringing any shoes for your child to try on. Once the shoes are on she should press the joints of the foot to check that the foot's not restricted in any way and check that the buckle or laces hold it firmly in place and don't let it slip about. Ask your child to move about in the shoes to check that the toe doesn't crease up and hurt when he's walking and to double-check that there's no slipping.

The type of shoe that you buy will be determined by when and where it is to be worn. Your child will need a sturdy, well-made pair of leather shoes once he is running about and playing outdoors, and some

New independence
Children love having new shoes, and spend hours taking them on and off.

Wellington boots for wet weather. In summer, leather sandals, canvas shoes or trainers are fine as long as they fit properly. What you should never do is buy second-hand shoes. Good shoes are an essential means of ensuring that your child has good feet in adult life.

Uppers should have no hard seams or stitching that might hurt the foot and cause chafing

Arch should be well-formed to give support

Healthy feet
Good shoes are essential for the healthy development of your child's feet. At first, most young children find it easier to cope with buckles or Velcro than laces.

Toe should be wide enough for the child's toes to fan out without restriction. The box over the toe should be high enough so that no pressure is exerted on the toenails

Sole should be light, flexible and non-slip

Fastenings should be adjustable and the foot held firmly in the shoe

The heel should grip snugly and shouldn't be higher than 4cm (1½in)

4 Holding and handling

In the first few weeks of life your baby will seem very vulnerable, and many parents are rather nervous of picking up their newborns, fearful that they may somehow accidentally damage their child. It's important to get used to holding your baby properly, not just for your baby's comfort but for your own sake; you'll never manage to feed or bath her successfully if you are unsure about how to hold her.

Handling your baby birth to 1 year

Most babies like to be handled in a firm way, especially in the early weeks when the sensation of being tightly enclosed (whether by your arms, by clothing or by a swaddling shawl), gives a great sense of security. When it comes to actually moving your baby, do it as slowly, as gently and as quietly as you can.

It's an instinctive reaction to hold your baby close to you, to talk soothingly and lovingly as you look into her face and eyes, and many experiments have shown that children do need and benefit from this physical contact. For example, premature babies gain more weight when they are laid on soft, downy sheets simply because the fluffy sheets give them the impression of being touched. Your newborn baby will be comforted by any kind of holding, cuddling or caressing, and skin-to-skin contact, with both of you lying naked in bed, is probably the best of all. In this way she can smell your skin, feel its touch and warmth and hear your heart beating.

Picking up your newborn baby
Don't worry about picking your baby up; she's much tougher than you think. The only thing that you really have to take care of is her lolling head. Until she is about four weeks old she'll have little control over it so whenever you pick her up do it in a way that supports the head.

Putting down your newborn baby
When you lay your baby down you must make sure that her head is supported. Unless you do, her head will flop back and may give your baby the sensation that she is going to fall; her body will jerk and she'll stretch out both arms and legs in the Moro or "startle" reflex (*see p.27*). Either put your baby down in the way I suggested for picking up, so that your whole arm supports spine, neck and head, or wrap your baby fairly tightly in a shawl so that her head is supported and her arms held close against her body. Once she is lying down in the cot, gently unwrap her.

Playing with an older baby
Babies need to be picked up and cuddled. She will enjoy conversations and contact with you.

HOW TO PICK UP A NEWBORN BABY

1 *Slide one hand under your baby's neck to support her head. Slide the other under her back and bottom.*

2 *Pick her up gently and smoothly, so you don't startle her, making sure her whole body is well supported.*

3 *Gently swing her round so she is against your chest. Holding her close makes her feel safe, especially if she can see your face.*

Swaddling your baby tightly makes her feel secure, so it's a useful way of comforting and calming a distressed baby.

Newborn and very young babies should be placed on their backs to sleep, with feet against the foot of the cot. The latest medical opinion and research suggests that this is the best and safest position in which to minimize the risk of SIDS (Sudden Infant Death Syndrome) and it is no longer believed that in this position there is an increased risk of the baby bringing up her feed and possibly choking. By four or five months, your baby will instinctively choose the position she finds suits her best.

Carrying your young baby
When you are carrying your baby, gently support her head in the crook of your arm. Hold her so you can see her face and she yours.

Support your baby's head
Whenever you are putting your baby down to sleep, remember always to support her head and body to prevent her head from flopping back.

Carrying your newborn baby

In your arms There are two main positions for carrying your baby in your arms. The first is with the baby's head in the crook of either arm, slightly higher than the rest of the body, which rests on the lower part of your arm encircled by the wrist and the hand that support her back and bottom. Your other arm provides additional support, to the baby's bottom and legs. This position allows you to talk to and smile at your baby.

The second way is to hold your baby against the upper part of your chest, with your forearm across her back and her head resting on your shoulder supported by your hand. This position leaves the other hand free, which is useful if you need to pick something up. Otherwise it can provide support to the baby's bottom.

In a sling There is no reason at all why your newborn shouldn't be carried in a sling, as long as it provides adequate support for the baby's neck and head, and it envelops the baby's body so that she can't slip out of either side. The best kinds of sling are the very soft, pouch-like ones that allow the baby to take up her curled form. Most parents feel happiest with the sling worn on their chest because there they can see and cuddle the baby easily and generally protect her more efficiently.

Picking up your older baby

Once your baby has control of her head there is no need to take the kind of care you did when she was newborn because the head and body will now stay aligned when she's picked up. When she reaches this stage the best way to pick up your baby is to put your hands under her armpits and to lift her towards you. Once she's been picked up carry her in the crook of your arm or against your shoulder. Or, as her back, neck and head muscles become stronger, she can be carried astride your hip with your arm going across her back and holding her thigh.

Carrying your older baby

By the age of four or five months, most parents carry their baby on one of their hips; which one is determined by whether the parent is right-or left-handed. You'll inevitably develop your own methods of carrying your baby and these may well vary

HOW TO CARRY AN OLDER BABY

On one hip
Your baby is now able to support herself well enough to sit astride your hip. This allows her to look all around, while still feeling secure and close to you.

Facing forwards
Hold your baby securely around the waist, face outwards so that she can look around her. You can use your other hand to support her or keep it free.

Rocking
You can hold your baby under her tummy and make this into a boisterous game by swinging her quite high, or just rock her gently from side to side to soothe her.

according to her mood. For longer journeys you can still carry your baby in a front sling (though she may be getting heavy now) or in a back-pack.

Putting down your older baby

You don't have to be as careful putting down an older baby as a newborn one. She is now stronger and can control her head so can be put down in exactly the same way as she is picked up. Alternatively, you can support the upper part of your baby's body with one hand curved diagonally across her back with the other hand supporting her bottom.

If you are lifting your child to put her into a highchair, support her under the armpits and let both legs dangle so that she can place them easily between tray and seat. Don't forget to strap her in.

Handling your child 1 to 3 years

A toddler needs much less holding and carrying than a young baby but there will still be times when she'll signal that she wants to be carried, just like she used to be. If you ignore these signals she'll probably cry.

Cuddling and security

You may find that she wants to be carried when she's tired; when you've been out for a long walk; when your toddler's cutting a tooth; if she isn't feeling well; if she's fearful or if you have been away. Don't hesitate to give this kind of physical support and affection. She will give you a clear signal when she is reassured and will wriggle down and run off.

We never outgrow the need for physical affection. Always recognize this in your children; never scoff at it and always give it. When my children were growing up, they

Keep cuddling her
All babies love a cuddle and as they grow up, they need the reassuring and loving embrace of caring parents more, not less.

liked a cuddle every now and then, especially when they were tired or had had a difficult day at school, if they were fearful about my departure or absence or if the world simply didn't feel right. Even when children are quite old they may still want to sit on your knee occasionally. In unfamiliar circumstances they may even like to sit on your knee while eating, particularly if strangers are present and they feel that they are under observation. Don't ridicule your child for wanting this. If it is convenient, let

AVOIDING BACK STRAIN

Babies and toddlers inevitably require lots of lifting and carrying, not to mention the prams, pushchairs and other equipment that go along with them, so it is important for the protection of your back that you learn a lifting technique that avoids injury and strain. Don't lift with straight legs and curved back, as this puts strain on the back. Instead, keep your back straight, bend your knees and lift, using the powerful thigh muscles to take the weight.

her sit on your knee; there is absolutely nothing wrong with it and a few moments of your touch will give your child the confidence to handle the situation in her own way. To my mind, a child should never have to go to bed without some cuddling to provide a sense of security and the reassuring feeling that you really do care.

Reassurance and sympathy

When your young child is hurt, worried, puzzled or frightened, always be there with an encircling, comforting arm and a sympathetic word. But do give such reassurances as these in the form that your child wants and don't overpower her with your physical affection when she makes obvious signs that she doesn't require it. Of course there are some children who don't like to be handled or cuddled very much. They usually show this from a very early age by stiffening their bodies and crying when you hold them. This can be quite difficult for a parent to cope with because it seems like rejection (see p.239). These babies usually grow up to be children who avoid physical contact and usually turn their heads away if you lean to kiss them. They make no physical overtures themselves and can be really quite difficult children to show affection to and to love in an overt way. They may never learn how to accept physical affection nor to be comfortable with it. If your child is like this, the only way for you to treat her is to not make the discomfort worse by thrusting physical affection on her. Respect your child's diffidence. Wait for her to come to you and only give your physical affection when she shows you by her actions that she wants it.

Holding and handling older children

As children get older they become more independent and we may think of them as needing less touching, stroking, holding and cuddling. This is true, up to a point, but don't make the mistake of thinking that they don't need physical affection at all – especially boys, who may be expected to keep a stiff upper lip much younger than they are capable of doing so.

I personally made it a rule to tell my children every day that I loved them, whenever the whim took me. I think that parents should make similar resolutions about holding and touching their children even if it's just letting them sit on your knee at the breakfast table, or putting an arm around your child when you read a book or look at the paper. Always give your children a cuddle as you talk over the day when you put them to bed.

Children need you

As your children get older, they often become somewhat shy about public demonstrations of affection, and even more so about the need for it. Choose private moments for this and they won't feel they're being soppy when they luxuriate in your care, attention, and love.

If you have several young children it can be very difficult to spread yourself out evenly between them. I remember a friend

of mine who had twins; from necessity, she adopted a pragmatic approach to the problem. Instead of trying to ensure that each twin had an equal share of her time and attention at all times, she concentrated instead on attending to whichever twin needed her at any one moment, and assumed that over the months and years it would all even out.

This is the attitude I tried to pursue when my own children were growing up,

Kiss it better
When a young child is upset about something, nothing is as comforting as a hug from you and a kiss to make everything better again.

and it is an invaluable approach for a mother of twins. Of course, for much of the time you will be giving your children equal attention, but if one demands more than the other, give it; she is asking for it because she needs it.

5 All about nappies

Until your child starts to use the potty, probably some time during the third year, he'll have to wear nappies both day and night. During the first few months life may seem like an endless round of nappy changing. But don't despair. As your child grows and gains more control over his bowel and bladder muscles he'll go for longer without excreting and urinating and the number of nappies you need to change will decrease. By about two and a half he'll probably become aware of wanting to go to the lavatory. It's at this point, and not before, that you should start toilet teaching.

Nappies and changing birth to 1 year

Your first choice in nappies will be between reusable and disposable types. Many parents prefer disposables, although an increasing debate on environmental issues has led other parents to consider reusables.

Yet the issue is not clear cut: the detergents required to clean reusable nappies can be viewed as pollutants to the water supply, and the energy required to wash them might also be regarded as wasteful. While fabric nappies are cheaper than disposables in the long run, you need to consider the increased electricity bills for frequent washing-machine runs, and the cost in your time.

What is clear is that providing that the nappy is changed as often as necessary, and that the basic rules of hygiene are observed, your baby will be happy. The techniques for cleaning and caring for your baby's bottom will be the same.

When to change a nappy
Change your baby's nappy whenever you notice that it is soiled or wet. The number of times the nappy needs to be changed will vary from baby to baby and from day to day. However, you'll probably always change the nappy when your baby wakes in the morning, when he's put to bed at night, and when he's been given a bath. In addition, you'll find that your baby will need to be changed after a feed because of the gastrocolic reflex that stimulates the elimination of faeces when food is taken in.

Always change your baby on a soft, warm, waterproof surface; padded changing mats are ideal for this. Usually

Nappy changing can be fun
Make nappy changing time a chance to chat to your baby and enjoy her company instead of a chore. She's less likely to get upset if you're chatting and laughing.

made of a foam-filled, waterproof material, they have a slightly raised edge to prevent the baby rolling off. They can be placed on whatever surface suits you best – floor, table or bed. As your baby gets older and starts to wriggle when you change his nappy, you may find it safer and easier to change him on the floor or on a low bed, whether or not you use a mat. Never leave your baby alone on any surface that is above floor level.

Changing a nappy

This is always easier if you are well prepared. Make sure that everything you need is within easy reach. The last thing you want to discover halfway through changing your baby is that you've left the clean nappies downstairs and the cotton wool or baby wipes in the bathroom.

There's no need to wash your baby's bottom with soap at each change: just gently wipe the faeces with a nappy corner then clean your baby's bottom with water or a baby wipe. If your baby has only wet the nappy, use a water-soaked flannel or cotton wool. When you change your baby, watch out for any redness and take the appropriate action (see p.68).

If your baby is very wriggly and restless during nappy changing, have a toy handy to act as a distraction. With an older baby, involve him in the process by letting him hold something, or give him a book to look at. Talk to your baby all the time – nappy changing is a great opportunity to interact with your baby.

Boys often urinate when changed, so cover the penis with a clean nappy as you take the old one off.

CLEANING A GIRL

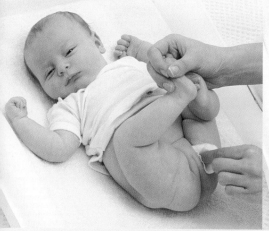

1 Lift your baby's legs by holding her feet or ankles. Use cotton wool dipped in warm water or baby wipes to clean the labia on the outside only.

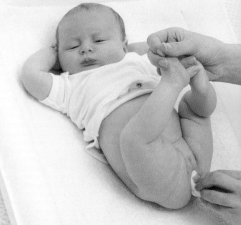

2 Use a clean piece of cotton wool or a baby wipe to clean the vulva, always wiping from front to back. Clean around the leg creases.

Disposable nappies birth to 1 year

This type of nappy makes nappy changing as simple as it can be. They are easy to put on – no folding, no pins, and no plastic pants – and can be discarded when they are wet or dirty. They are convenient when you're travelling because they are more absorbent so you need fewer nappies. You also need less space to change them in, and you don't have to carry wet, smelly nappies home with you to be washed. You will, however, need a constant supply so, to avoid having to bring home loads with your shopping, buy them in large batches and have them delivered to your home.

Even if you've chosen to use the fabric variety, it's always useful to keep a stock of disposables in the house. They're a good back-up if you've run out of your usual nappy, or if your baby develops a rash because of your washing methods.

Disposable nappies are available in a variety of sizes, suitable for newborns to toddlers, and in a range of styles. They have elasticated legs for added protection against leaks, a plastic outer covering and an absorbent inner layer, sometimes topped with a one-way nappy liner. They are secured with adjustable adhesive tabs. There are special disposables for your baby to wear when swimming and a pull-on type for toddlers that can be pulled up and down like a pair of pants. Try different brands and styles until you find what's best for you and your baby.

CLEANING A BOY

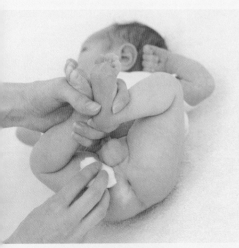

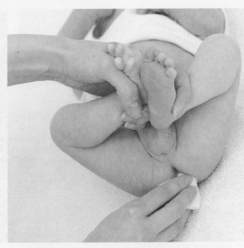

1 Lift his legs by holding both ankles. Clean around the genital area. Use a new piece of cotton wool each time you wipe.

2 Still holding your baby's legs, make sure that all soiling is removed. Work from the leg creases in towards the penis.

HOW TO PUT ON A DISPOSABLE NAPPY

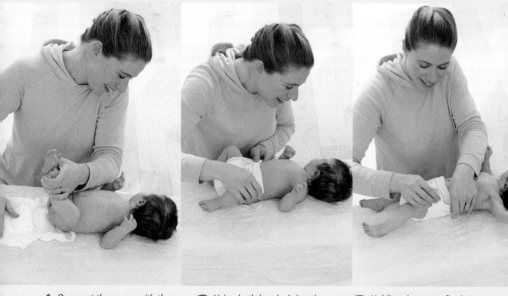

1 Open out the nappy with the adhesive tabs at the top. Lift your baby's legs and slide the clean nappy under her, gently lifting her buttocks into position.

2 Using both hands, bring the front of the nappy up between your baby's legs, as high as it will go. Tuck in the corners securely around her waist.

3 Holding the nappy firmly in place with one hand, fix the adhesive tabs firmly on to the front flap of the nappy. Make sure the nappy is not too tight.

Disposing of a disposable

All disposable nappies are designed to be thrown away: the whole of an all-in-one nappy, plastic backing included, can be discarded, but not put down the lavatory. You can throw used nappies straight into the bin, or wrap them in old plastic bags if you prefer. You can also buy special tie-up biodegradable nappy sacks that reduce the smell – very useful when travelling or away from home.

Special nappy bins are also available. These are designed to wrap and seal individual soiled nappies in odour-proof plastic film, ready to put in the dustbin.

CHOOSING DISPOSABLE NAPPIES

There are many different types of disposable nappy to choose from and they come in a variety of sizes to suit the age and weight of your baby. When trying them consider the following:

- How absorbent is the nappy and does it keep your baby's bottom dry?
- Is it comfortable round the legs and does it fit round the body well? Check for any hard edges that might irritate your baby.
- You'll need to balance price against efficiency. Buying cheaper nappies might be a false economy if they are not as absorbent or effective as a more expensive brand.

Best for you both
Your baby will need to
wear nappies for at least
two years until he has
full bowel and bladder
control, so it's worth taking
the time to find out what
kind of nappy is best for
you both.

Reusable nappies birth to 1 year

Although initially more expensive than all-in-one disposables, these nappies can work out cheaper over the years. Made of terry towelling or muslin, in a variety of styles, they have to be rinsed, sterilized, washed and dried after use and therefore involve much more labour than disposables. Because they have to be washed regularly you'll need a minimum of 24 nappies. Obviously, the more nappies you have the less often you'll have to do the washing (and the more economical your washes will be). Buy the best you can afford. They'll last longer and be more absorbent.

NAPPIES AND ACCESSORIES

Here is a selection of reusable nappies and equipment. Provided your baby is changed regularly he will be happy in any style.

PLASTIC PANTS

FABRIC NAPPY WITH
VELCRO FASTENER

FABRIC NAPPY
LINER

LINERS AND
SAFETY PINS

Towelling squares These traditional nappies are thick and absorbent and can be folded into a variety of shapes according to your baby's size and needs. They can be bulky on very small babies and newborns. Buy them ready-hemmed to avoid fraying when they are washed. Towelling nappies are more absorbent than the majority of disposables and are therefore very useful at night. You can also use a disposable pad inside a towelling nappy for extra absorbency at night.

Muslin squares These are about the same size as towelling squares, but they are softer. They are ideal for newborn babies because they are soft and comfortable, but they are not very absorbent so need changing frequently.

Shaped terry towelling These T-shaped nappies are made of a softer, finer towelling than ordinary squares and have a triple-layered central panel for added absorbency. They are shaped to fit neatly around the baby's legs and are more straightforward to put on.

Plastic pants These pants, which come in several designs, are used over towelling nappies to prevent wet or dirty nappies soiling clothes or bedding. Buy six initially. You'll need to replace them as they get old, torn and unusable.

All-in-one reusables These offer all the features and convenience of a disposable nappy, but are produced using fewer chemicals, are made of cotton, and don't contain dye, latex or perfume. They're machine washable, can be brightly coloured, have Velcro closing tabs and elasticated legs.

Made of several layers of absorbent fabric, they have an anti-leak outer layer, so you don't need to put plastic pants on top of them. Your baby's faeces are collected in liners and the used nappy can be stored in a nappy bucket until you have sufficient to make up a load for your washing machine.

Nappy pins/nappy grippers Nappy pins are especially designed for use with fabric nappies and have locking heads. You'll need at least 12. Grippers are easier to use than pins and safer. These little plastic devices hook into the nappy and fasten it securely without the worry of pins.

Nappy liners You'll need these with reusable nappies. They are placed inside the nappy and go next to the baby's skin. Choose the "one-way" variety that's made of a special material that lets urine pass through but remains dry next to the baby's skin. This minimizes the risk of a sore bottom due to friction or moisture, so reduces nappy rash. They also catch most of the faeces and prevent the nappy from getting badly soiled. Liners can be lifted out with any faeces and flushed away if biodegradable, or if made of fabric, washed with the nappies.

HOW TO PUT ON AN ALL-IN-ONE REUSABLE NAPPY

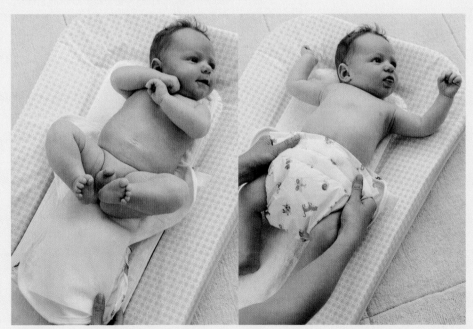

1 *Shaped reusable nappies are as easy to put on as disposables. Begin by sliding the clean nappy under your baby. Position it so your baby's waist aligns with the top edge of the nappy.*

2 *Bring the nappy up between his legs and hold it in place while you fold the sides into the centre. Check that the nappy is fitting your baby snugly and fasten with the Velcro tabs at the sides.*

Baby on the move
Once your baby is crawling it's even more important
that his nappy is comfortable and not too bulky so that
it doesn't restrict his movements .

powder; the wet nappies are simply rinsed out thoroughly, then dried. Whenever you wash nappies use pure soap flakes or powders. Avoid strong detergents and biological enzyme powders as these will irritate your baby's tender skin.

If you have to use a fabric conditioner because the towelling has become stiff, make sure that you rinse it all out; despite manufacturers' instructions to the contrary, this too can cause irritation. Unless the nappies are very stained, or have become rather grey, there is no need to boil them. Hot water is sufficient for both rinsing and washing after using sterilizing tablets. Never add coloured clothing to the sterilizing solution – the colour will run. Even if the clothing has been soiled, just remove the worst of the mess, rinse the item and then wash as normal.

Nappy washing routine

To balance the chores of feeding, changing and nappy washing, try to develop a routine whereby you wash the nappies in sufficiently large loads. The pre-requisite of this routine is a large supply of nappies – I suggest no fewer than 24. In order to sterilize the nappies you will need two plastic bins: one for soiled nappies, one for wet ones. They should be large enough to hold at least six nappies, plus solution, and they must have lids and strong, reliable handles. Don't, however, buy such a large bin that you can't carry it fully loaded to the washing machine or bath. Special nappy bins are sold but any

Nappy washing and sterilization

Your baby's reusable nappies must be thoroughly washed to remove all traces of ammonia and faecal bacteria that would otherwise cause irritation for your baby and possible infection (*see p.68*). Special nappy sterilants are available that make this process much easier and less time-consuming. With this method the nappies are soaked in a sterilizing solution for a specified length of time and then only the soiled nappies have to be washed with bin of a decent size with a lid is suitable. Bins designed for beer-making are ideal and they are also reasonably priced.

Each morning fill the bins with the required amounts of water and solution. Rinse a urine-soaked nappy in cold water, squeeze out the excess moisture and put it into the bin. Remove as much faeces as possible down the lavatory, then hold the soiled nappy under the water as you flush it to remove the excess. Wring out the nappy and submerge it in the solution. After the required time, wring out both sets of nappies. Rinse the urine-soaked ones thoroughly in hot water before drying them. Wash the soiled ones in a washing machine and dry them.

To reduce the environmental impact of laundering reusable nappies, it's best to wash them in as large a load as possible at lower temperatures.

You might like to consider using a nappy-laundering service, available nationwide, except in very isolated areas. You store dirty nappies in a deodorized bin that has a biodegradable liner. For a weekly fee, the nappy-laundering service takes away your dirty nappies and replaces them with fresh ones. You may need to have a bigger supply of nappies though.

Washing plastic pants

If plastic pants become soiled or wet they should be washed in warm water with a little washing-up liquid. If the water is either too hot or too cold the plastic hardens and becomes unusable. Pat the pants dry after washing and leave them to air before using. One way of softening plastic pants is to tumble dry them with a load of towels.

TIPS FOR USING FABRIC NAPPIES

- Use a disposable inside a towelling nappy for extra absorbency at night. You can also use this method when you're travelling and want to avoid an awkward change.
- Use stretch towelling pants over plastic pants – they look neater than plastic pants on their own. Frilly and patterned plastic pants are also available if you want something prettier.
- Always keep your fingers between the nappy and the skin if fixing with a pin.
- When you've put on the nappy run your fingers round the legs to check they are not too tight.
- To save time, fold all the nappies ready for use and put the nappy liners in position.
- Make sure that the nappy fits snugly around your baby's body. It gradually gives, so if it's too loose it will slide down.

Tips for washing fabric nappies

- Keep plastic gloves near the bucket for lifting nappies out; alternatively use plastic tongs.
- If you use powder sterilant, always put the water in before the powder. Otherwise the powder spreads through the air when you add the water and you may inhale the powder.
- Both drying in the open air and in a tumble drier keep the fabric softer. If you use radiators to dry nappies they tend to harden the fabric. It's better to invest in a rack that can be placed over the bath or to use a pull-out line if you can't dry outdoors or with a tumble drier.
- Always keep any nappies changed at night in a separate bucket, or in a large plastic bag, and add them to the new day's solution the following morning.
- Some buckets have special holders for air-fresheners. If yours doesn't, hook a piece of wire through a freshener and attach it above the water line.

Nappy rash

If left for any length of time in a nappy or on the skin, urine is broken down to ammonia by bacteria from the baby's stools. Ammonia is an irritant: it burns the skin and results in nappy rash.

Nappy rash can range from a mild redness to an inflamed area of broken skin and puss-filled spots. The bacteria that produce nappy rash thrive in an alkaline medium. The stools of bottle-fed babies are alkaline, unlike those of breast-fed babies that are acid. For this reason, bottle-fed babies are more prone to nappy rash. To minimize the possibility of your baby suffering from nappy rash:

- Change your baby's nappy as often as necessary; never leave him lying in a wet or soiled nappy.
- Put a one-way disposable nappy liner next to your baby's skin. This allows urine to pass straight through to the nappy below, so keeps the skin dry.
- Leave your baby's bottom open to the air whenever you can. Just slide a nappy under his bottom to catch any mess.
- Pay particular attention to washing fabric nappies. Make sure they are well rinsed to remove all the ammonia.
- At the first hint of nappy rash stop using plastic pants. These help to keep the

NAPPY RASH CHART

Appearance	Cause	Treatment
Redness and broken skin in the leg folds.	Inadequate drying after bathing.	Meticulous and thorough drying. Do not use powder.
Rash that starts around the genitals rather than the anus. Strong smell of ammonia.	Ammonia dermatitis.	General nappy rash treatment, above. If this doesn't work, seek medical advice.
Spotty rash all over the genitals, bottom, groin and thighs, which eventually leads to thick and wrinkled skin.	Extreme form of ammonia dermatitis.	Seek medical advice if rash persists after trying general treatment, above, first.
Rash that starts around the anus and moves on to the buttocks.	Thrush.	Get medical advice. You will probably be given nystatin cream and medicine.
Brownish-red scaly rash on the genitals and buttocks and anywhere the skin is greasy.	Seborrhoeic dermatitis.	Ointment for rash, prescribed by your doctor. You might also get a special lotion if the scalp is very scaly and sore.
Small blisters all over the nappy area.	Heat rash.	Don't use plastic pants, and leave off the nappy as much as possible.

urine close to the skin and promote the formation of ammonia.

- At the first sign of broken skin start using a special cream for the prevention of nappy rash.
- Don't wash your baby's bottom with soap and water. They dehydrate the skin and can cause it to become cracked.
- Don't use talcum powder on a baby. Powder can become caked and irritating in the skin creases, which increases the risk of nappy rash.

Treating nappy rash

You may find, despite your precautions, that your baby develops a sore bottom. If you are satisfied that he doesn't require specific treatment (see chart opposite), then the most successful remedy will be a combination of the tips here, plus a few more, below.

- Change the nappy more frequently.
- At night, put a disposable pad inside a resusable nappy for extra absorbency. This is especially useful for older babies who are sleeping through the night and who will therefore not be changed from evening until morning.
- Do not apply barrier creams when changing your baby's nappy as this prevents air getting to the skin. Although it also keeps the skin dry, it is more important that the skin be well aired when your baby has nappy rash.

Using nappies 1 to 3 years

A one year old still urinates automatically, but because the bladder can hold an increasing amount of urine he'll be dry for longer periods. You'll use fewer nappies – on average 50 per week as opposed to the 80 used on a newborn. If you hesitated to use disposables before because of the price, you may consider them now as they're neater and less bulky than reusable nappies. This is important because your increasingly mobile child will find it difficult to walk with a cumbersome wad of nappy between his legs. If you use fabric nappies, now's the time that shaped all-in-one reusables are more suitable than folded terry nappies.

When it comes to changing a nappy you'll find your toddler far less willing to lie still. Make sure that you've got some books or toys as distractions or you'll find that each change becomes a battleground. Clothes that give easy access to the nappy save your time and energy.

Early bladder and bowel control

At some time during the third year your child will probably gain conscious control over his bowel and bladder muscles and your days of frequent nappy changes should be over. When your child stays dry during naps you can start leaving off that nappy (see p.138). You may also want to use trainer pants that can be pulled down quickly when your child tells you that he wants to go to the lavatory. You can either buy special plastic knickers lined with towelling – you'll need at least six pairs – or get the special pull-up disposable nappy pants, to give protection against accidents.

6 Bathing and hygiene

Part of your daily routine will be to keep your baby clean. This will be reasonably easy when she's very small, but as your baby becomes more active you'll find that you will not only have to clean her more often, but also that it will require a bit more effort to manage the daily bath. By the time she's two she may want to try washing herself.

Washing your baby birth to 1 year

Most young babies don't need bathing very often because, apart from their bottoms, faces, necks and skin creases, they don't get very dirty. There is no reason why you shouldn't go for two or three days without bathing your baby as long as you clean her face, hands and bottom every day. You can do this without even putting the baby in the bath by topping and tailing (*see p.72*). It's also advisable to wash her hair regularly to help prevent cradle cap forming (*see p.75*) on her scalp.

Some parents feel apprehensive the first few times they bath their baby. However, if you set aside half an hour, have everything you need around you and try to relax you will probably enjoy it. After the first two or three times it will become fairly routine and you'll wonder what your first bathtime nerves were all about.

Where to bath your baby
Until she's big enough to go into an adult bath you don't have to wash your baby in a bathroom. You can use your baby's room, the kitchen or any other room that is warm and has enough space to lay out all that you need to bath her in comfort. The baby's bath can be filled in the bathroom and then carried to the chosen room (make sure you don't fill it too full or the water will splash out as you walk from room to room).

A small baby can be washed in a specially designed, sculpted plastic bath with a non-slip surface (*see p.34*). As it is most comfortable for you if you don't have to bend too much, the bath should be placed on a table or worktop of a convenient height. Alternatively, you could place it on an adjustable stand (although they tend to be rather flimsy) or on a rack that straddles the bath.

If, however, you don't have a baby bath there are some inexpensive, practical

Keep her warm
After bathing your baby, wrap her up in a towel immediately so she doesn't get cold. Pat her dry all over, being extra careful with folds and creases.

TOPPING AND TAILING A YOUNG BABY

This means cleaning your baby by washing her face, hands and nappy area, without undressing her completely. Remove her clothes, leaving her vest on.

Place your baby on a changing mat or towel. Use cooled, boiled water for her eyes and warm water for her face and body.

1 *Using moistened cotton wool, gently wipe each eye from the inner corners outwards. Use a clean piece for each stroke and eye.*

2 *Wipe her face, ears and neck, then her hands and feet, using clean cotton wool each time. Pat her dry thoroughly.*

3 *Clean her nappy area, then wipe with cotton wool moistened with warm water. Wipe from front to back, then pat dry.*

alternatives that you can use until your baby is old enough to go into the big bath. For example, a plastic household basin functions in exactly the same way as a baby bath and is useful because, like a baby bath, it can be carried anywhere you choose. Kitchen or bathroom sinks are also practical because they are generally at a comfortable height so you don't have to bend over too much, and they often have additional counter space to the side.

However, if you do use the kitchen sink, it's important to make sure that the taps are well out of reach of your baby's kicking legs. If they aren't, wrap them up with cloths or towels so that they can cause no harm. If the "bath" surface is too slippery, either use a plastic suction mat or line the sink with a small towel or nappy to provide a non-slip surface for your baby's bottom.

Bathing a young baby

Get everything that you need for washing, drying and dressing ready before you start.

• Ideally wear a waterproof apron, and lay a large, soft towel across your lap and up your front so that when you cuddle up your baby after the bath she will feel warm and comfortable.

• Very young babies can't regulate their own temperatures very efficiently, so keep the time she's undressed to a minimum.

• Try using a towel with a hood: she'll feel even more secure and snuggly, especially if you put the towel over a radiator for a while first so that it's warm.

• Only fill the bath with a few centimetres of water until you are used to bathing.

• Never use baby powders. They are very drying to a baby's skin and may cake in the creases, causing irritation and rashes.

GIVING YOUR BABY A BATH

It's important that your baby doesn't get cold when being bathed, so make sure the room is warm with no draughts, and that you have everything you need to hand: bath, two large towels, facecloth, cotton wool, nappy-changing equipment, clean nappy, nappy liner and clean clothes.

1 *Fill the bath 5–8cm (2–3in) deep, putting cold water in first. Test the temperature with your elbow or wrist; it should only feel warm, not hot.*

2 *Undress your baby, clean her nappy area (see opposite) and wrap her in a towel. Clean her face and ears gently with moistened cotton wool.*

3 *Holding your baby in a football carry, under one arm, lean over the bath and wash her head. Rinse well and pat dry. A gentle brushing is good for cradle cap.*

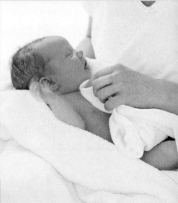

4 *Support your baby's shoulders with one hand, holding on to her upper arm, and support her legs or bottom with the other. Place her in the bath.*

5 *Keep one hand under your baby's shoulders so that her head and shoulders stay out of the water, and use your free hand to wash her. Talk to her throughout.*

6 *When she is clean and rinsed, lift her gently onto a towel, supporting her as before, and dry her thoroughly. Don't use talcum powder, it could irritate her skin.*

GIVING YOUR BABY A SPONGE BATH

If you're nervous about giving your baby a bath, or if she hates being undressed, give her a sponge bath. Get everything you need ready. Sit your baby on your lap and take off only the minimum amount of clothing at a time. Alternatively, sit your baby on a changing mat, using the same techniques.

1 *Have a bowl of warm water near you. Undress her top half and wash her front with a cloth or sponge. Dry her, then lean her forwards and wash her back.*

2 *Put clean clothes on her top half and remove her lower clothing and her nappy. Clean her nappy area with a new cloth (see p.72) and dry thoroughly.*

3 *Using a sponge or cloth, wash your baby's legs and feet. Gently pat them dry, especially between her toes. Put on a clean nappy and dress her again.*

Using a bathtub

Between three and six months old your baby will outgrow most small baths and you will have to start using an adult one. If you think that your baby may be frightened by the size of this new bath, you can continue to use the small bath but place it inside the large, empty one until she gets used to it.

It is much more awkward to wash a baby in a big bath, but you must still hold on to your baby's arm until she can support herself. Don't bend over the bath or you'll strain your back. Instead, kneel by the bath and have everything that you need next to you on the floor. Use a plastic suction mat on the bottom of the bath to prevent the baby sliding about and keep the water shallow (no deeper than 10–13cm/4–5in). It doesn't take much for a wriggly, kicking baby to slip under the water so you must be vigilant at all times. Never, ever, leave your baby alone in the bath, even for a moment; don't even turn away to attend to something else in the same room. If the phone rings, either ignore it or take your wet baby with you. Leaving your baby, even for a second, is just not worth the risk.

As your baby gets older she'll spend more and more time crawling about on the floor and, as a result, will need to be washed more often; baths will become a regular feature of the day. By this time she will no longer be scared of being undressed and will feel quite secure in the water. In fact, she will almost certainly have begun to enjoy bathtimes so it's your job to make them fun and as trouble-free as possible.

As soon as your baby can sit up, always have a period at the end of the bath when she can enjoy splashing and playing with toys. Have some boats, ducks, sponges or plastic cups on hand so that she can experiment with them and see what they do. If you have two children, try occasionally bathing them together so that your older child can share games and can teach your baby about the things that water does. It's exciting for your baby to see how containers can be filled and emptied or water poured from one to the other, and she'll love watching how some toys float and others sink slowly to the bottom of the bath.

Many household items can be adapted for bathtime. Babies love seeing water pour out of objects and this makes plastic fruit boxes with their airholes ideal. Other good toys include measuring spoons, small watering cans, ice cube trays and colanders.

Care of the hair

To prevent cradle cap from forming you should wash your newborn's head every day with a soft bristle brush and a little baby shampoo. To prevent any scales forming you should comb through the hair, even if she has very little. If cradle cap does appear, smear a little olive oil on her scalp and wash it off the following morning. This will dissolve the scales, making them soft, loose and easy to wash away. Don't be tempted to pick them off with your fingers.

After about 12–16 weeks wash your baby's head with water every day and once or twice a week with baby shampoo. You can either use a football carry (if your baby is quite light) or you can sit on the edge of

Hair washing
Pick up your baby in a football carry by tucking her legs under your armpit and supporting her back along your arm. Cradle her head in your hand. Wash the hair using mild shampoo and rinse gently with warm water.

the bath with your baby across your legs, facing you. (This method is especially useful if she's scared of the water.) Make sure that you use a non-sting variety of baby shampoo, but nevertheless take care to avoid getting it near her eyes. Don't worry about your newborn's fontanelles. They are covered with a very sturdy membrane and you can do no harm if you are gentle. You need not scrub the hair. Modern shampoos remove dirt and oil within seconds, so you just have to bring the shampoo to a lather,

BATHTUB BATHING TIPS

- Always run the cold tap first, if you start with the hot tap, the bottom of the bath may be too hot and could burn the baby.
- Cover up hot taps with a flannel or towel so there's no risk of scalding.
- Don't pour more hot water into the bath when your baby is in it – she may get scalded.
- Make sure that you put your baby in the bath (and lift her out of the bath) with your back straight, taking the strain with your thighs.
- Don't let your baby stand up in the bath without your support – she could slip and fall.
- If your child starts to jump up and down in the bath – no doubt rejoicing in a newly found skill – be very firm about making her sit down again; she could easily topple over.
- Don't be tempted to see if your baby can sit unsupported. She could easily tumble under the water and get a bad fright – bad enough to put her off baths for a while.
- Never, ever, leave your baby alone in the bath. Watch your baby all the time; even if you turn around for a moment she could slip under the water and drown.
- Don't pull the plug out when your baby's in the bath. She may be frightened by both the disappearing water and the noise.
- Don't dust your baby with talcum powder after a bath – it's very drying to the skin and can cause irritation.
- If you're at work during the day, make the most of bathtime – it can be a great time to play and relax with your baby.
- Keep some toys exclusively for use in the bath to make bathtime a special treat.

count to 20 and then rinse it off again. One wash is quite enough, and your baby's hair will be absolutely clean at the end of this operation. Rinse your baby's hair by simply dipping the flannel into the basin of warm water and wiping it over her head. Try to get as much lather off as possible, but if your child is complaining it really doesn't matter if you leave slight traces on the hair. Dry her head with the end of the towel, taking care not to cover your baby's face or she may become very distressed and panicky.

Care of the skin

A newborn has no need of soap. It is dehydrating and your baby's skin is delicate. She needs to preserve all the natural oils so use only water until about six weeks. After then, any gentle soap can be used – you may want to try a special liquid soap that is simply added to the bath water and needs no rinsing off. Make sure that you wash any folds and creases properly by running a soapy finger along

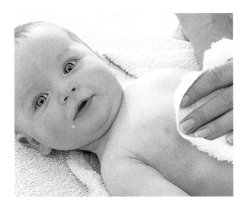

Caring for the skin
Dry your baby's skin thoroughly after a sponge bath or bath. It is especially important to dry in any folds of skin and creases around her arms, legs and neck.

them then rinsing well. Dry the skin thoroughly – any moist creases will lead to irritations; never use talcum powder.

Care of the eyes

For a young baby, when you wash her eyes, squeeze a couple of cotton wool balls in cooled boiled water. Use a different piece of cotton wool to wash each eye, starting from the inner part of the eye and working to the outer part.

Care of the nose and ears

The nose and ears are self-cleaning organs so you should never try to put anything inside them or in them or interfere with them in any way. Pushing something the size of a cotton bud up a baby's nose or into a baby's ears, will only push whatever is there further in. It is much better to let whatever is in the nose come down naturally. Never put drops into the ears or nose unless your doctor advises it.

Never try to scrape wax out of a baby's ears even if you can see it. Wax is the natural secretion of the skin lining the canal of the outer ear. It is antiseptic and it prevents dust and grit getting to the ear drum. Some babies make more wax than others, but removing it will only result in the production of even more. Removing wax irritates the skin, so leave it alone and check with your health visitor or practice nurse if you are concerned. Wash your baby's ears and nose using moist cotton wool (*see p.73*).

Care of the nails

There is no need to cut a newborn baby's nails for about three or four weeks, unless your baby is scratching her skin. Nails are

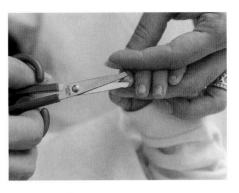

Trimming nails
If you're going to use scissors lay your baby on a flat surface, talk soothingly to her, and then gently cut the nails following the shape of the fingertips.

easiest to cut after a bath when they are soft so have a pair of small, blunt-ended scissors nearby when you take your baby out of the bath. If you do them right away you'll be able to cut the nails of both hands and toes in less than half a minute. But if you're worried about cutting your baby's nails try doing it when she is asleep.

Care of the navel

The umbilical cord will have been clamped and cut immediately after delivery, leaving a 5–8cm (2–3in) stump protruding from your baby's abdomen. This may be clamped by a plastic clip. Over the next few days the cord dries and shrivels, and will then drop off. Let the area stay open to the air as much as possible to help speed up the shrinking and healing process. If you notice any redness, discharge or other signs of infection, ask your health visitor or doctor for advice. You don't have to wait for the navel to heal before you give your baby a bath, as long as you dry it carefully and thoroughly afterwards.

Some babies develop umbilical hernias (*see p.23*). They generally clear up within a year or two. If your baby has one and it enlarges or persists, seek medical advice.

Care of the genitals

You should never try to open the lips of your baby girl's vulva to clean inside; there is no need. Just wash the exterior nappy area (*see p.60*) and dry it well. However, you should take care to wipe from front to back – that is, towards the anus – whenever you are cleaning her nappy area. This minimizes the risk of bacteria spreading from the bowels to the bladder or vagina, causing infection.

An uncircumcised baby boy should not have his foreskin pulled back for cleaning.

It's quite tight and could get stuck. Just wash the exterior of the nappy area as normal and dry carefully, particularly the skin creases; the foreskin will retract naturally at three or four years of age.

If your baby has been circumcised, it is important to keep a careful watch to make sure that his penis is not bleeding. A dressing may or may not be applied, but in either case you will be given advice about bathing your baby and special care of the penis. Following circumcision, the penis is nearly always swollen and slightly inflamed for a few days, and occasionally there may be a few drops of blood: this is normal and will gradually settle down. However, if bleeding persists or there is any sign of infection, seek medical advice.

Possible bathtime problems birth to 1 year

Fear of undressing

Many young babies become extremely distressed when they are undressed. They hate the feeling of air on their bodies, preferring instead the security of being fully clothed or wrapped tightly. When your baby's very small you can get around this by topping and tailing *or* giving sponge baths (*see pp.72–74*).

Fear of bathing

If your baby is absolutely terrified of having a bath, skip it for a couple of days and then try again, very gently, using only a little water in the bath. Until your baby is ready to go back into the bath give sponge baths or top and tail.

If, after some time, she still doesn't like being bathed and remains frightened of

water, try to overcome it by introducing bathtime in a play context. In a warm room (but not the bathroom), lay out a towel with a large plastic bowl full of water next to it. Put some floatable toys and plastic beakers into the bowl, undress your baby and encourage her to play with the toys. She'll gradually get used to the idea of being near the water.

When she seems happy and confident help your baby to paddle in the water: if your kitchen is warm put a towel on the draining board, fill the sink with warm water and let your baby dangle her feet while sitting on the towel. Make sure that you keep a firm grip on your baby with one hand while you play with toys and beakers with the other, and that all the taps are bound up with a cloth.

Bathtime games
The evening bath is a wonderful time for creative play. You'll find your baby is endlessly fascinated by filling things, pouring and splashing water.

Do this a couple of times then swap the bowl or kitchen sink for a baby bath and let your baby play in the same way as before. You'll know she's overcome any fear when she struggles to get into the water with the toys. Let your baby do this a couple of times before you turn it into an occasion for washing as well.

Fear of the big bath

Once your baby is splashing about and making a mess in the small baby bath, she is ready to go into a big bath. However, if your child is frightened of getting into a big bath, you'll have to build up to it gradually. Place the baby bath inside the big bath and put a towel or a rubber mat next to it so that she can't slip. Sit her in the big bath along with some toys and fill up the baby bath with warm water as usual. Then let her climb into the baby bath. Once she is happy doing this, you can introduce a few centimetres/inches of water into the big bath, with the towel or rubber mat in the bottom and all the toys, as before, and the baby bath full of warm water. She will then probably climb in and out of the baby bath and quickly get used to sitting in the big bath in just a few centimetres of water. You can then increase the amount of water in the big bath, leaving the baby bath there until she is no longer interested in it. This makes the transition fairly painless, and at the same time does quite a lot to increase your child's confidence.

Dislike of hair washing

Even a baby who thoroughly enjoys having a bath may hate hair washing and she'll probably develop this dislike when she's around eight or nine months old. Even though you may be very gentle and take every precaution to make sure that your child isn't frightened or upset by hair washing, you may find that it remains a problem until your child is of school age, so it is worth getting the technique right from the start.

Young children hate to get water in their eyes, let alone soap or shampoo. So do everything you can to keep your baby's face and eyes dry throughout the whole operation of hair washing. Never pour water over your child's head just to prove that it won't hurt. Few children under the age of six can stand this, and if it is done to them suddenly they find it extremely unpleasant. Don't continue the washing operation if she screams or struggles and never forcibly hold your child so that you can get her hair washed. You may have an accident, like getting some shampoo into her eyes, or her slipping over in the bath and getting ducked under the water, which will make the whole incident much worse. It will also make all future attempts to wash your child's hair very difficult and fraught experiences for both of you.

Once your child strenuously objects to hair washing, give up and don't try again for a few weeks to give your child a chance to recover. Bathtimes are generally happy

Safety in the bathtub
When washing your baby in the bathtub, use a non-slip mat to prevent her from slipping or sliding about. Keep the water shallow – no more than 10–13cm (4–5in).

for most children, so it is better to dissociate hair washing from bathtimes so your child doesn't start to dislike taking baths as well. Keep her hair reasonably clean by sponging it to remove any dirt or bits of food, or brushing it out with a soft, damp brush. It really doesn't matter if your child's hair is greasy for a week or two; it will come to no harm.

Another way of keeping the water from your baby's face is to use a specially designed shield. This fits like a halo around the hairline and allows you to rinse off any shampoo without getting soapy water all over your baby's face. You may find that

Bathtime routine

Bathing is a perfect opportunity for the cuddling and playing that babies come to relish. Make it part of the bedtime routine, a signal to her it's time to wind down.

your baby is less distressed if you wash her hair while she sits on your lap. Have a basin of warm water near you, and use a flannel to wet her head before you use a non-sting shampoo. So that no water gets onto her face, rinse the water off with a damp facecloth, not by pouring water over her head. She won't be disturbed by this because she won't feel any water trickling over her head or her body.

Washing your toddler 1 to 3 years

As your child gets older she will probably regard bathtime primarily as playtime. Most children love playing with water and the bath is one of the most convenient places for them to do it, so provide plastic cups, beakers, boats and ducks, allow plenty of time, relax and let bathtime be fun. Encourage your child to wash herself by having a special sponge that she can use. Until her co-ordination is more developed she won't make a perfect job of it so be prepared to go over the same areas with another facecloth. Soap both your child's hands by holding a bar of soap between them, and show her how to spread the soap over her body and arms.

Baths should be carefully supervised as a child of this age is still at risk of slipping and falling under the water. Toddlers are generally keen to do things for themselves so there is the added risk that your child may turn on the hot tap or grab the soap

ENCOURAGING DAILY HYGIENE

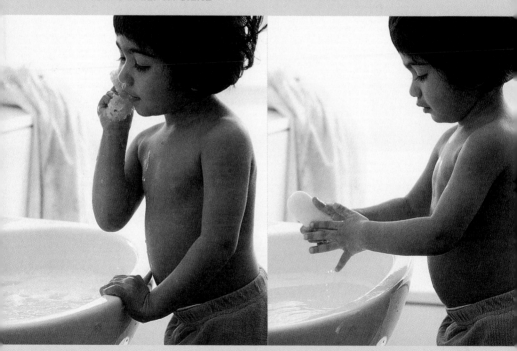

Face washing
If your child objects to washing her face, suggest that she use a sponge instead of a flannel. This is more fun, and much softer on the skin.

Hand washing
Encourage your toddler to wash her hands from an early age. Give her a step so she can reach the basin and make that she knows which is the hot tap.

or shampoo and get some in her eyes. Covering the taps with a towel is a good way to soften any falls or bangs.

Daily routine

Most children need a wash in the morning but it's probably best to leave it until after breakfast. Children are often ravenously hungry when they wake up, and you'll only have time to change the soggy nappy before food becomes imperative. After your child has eaten she'll probably be more willing to stand still to have her face and hands washed, teeth brushed (*see p.203*) and hair combed.

By the time your child's about one and a half she'll be able to rinse both hands under water and, with improving co-ordination, will learn to soap them. Do bear in mind, though, that she won't always remember the routine of hand washing: sleeves may not be rolled up, jumpers may get wet and soap may slip out of tiny fingers. So always be close by to lend a hand should she need it.

Hygiene

Start hygiene routines young and, where possible, teach by example. For instance, from the time that your child starts to crawl and get her hands dirty, washing before eating should become automatic. If you start by washing your hands with your child (and I mean with), by getting your hands soapy together and washing each other's hands, it can become fun. While you're teaching your child how to wash you can make a game of it by trying to blow bubbles with the soap film that forms between your forefinger and thumb when you make a circle. Dry your hands together

as well. Afterwards, let your child inspect your hands and then you look at hers.

If you start like this it makes it much easier to apply hygiene rules at other times. For example, hand washing should always follow visits to the lavatory. But you should start at the potty stage and do it with your child every single time. You can help her become more independent by providing a stable, non-slip standing block in the bathroom, so she can reach the basin and toilet easily and safely by herself.

Give your child a soft toothbrush to start with and encourage her to use it after meals, especially once her molars are through (*see p.202*).

Pets and hygiene

There are important advantages for your toddler in having a pet, but you may be concerned about the possible health risks involved. However, if you follow a few simple rules about handling pets, you should have no cause for concern. Encourage your child to wash her hands after playing with her pet – especially before touching or eating food. Also, you should stop your child from kissing her pet, especially near its nose and mouth.

The most common problems caused by pets are infestations of fleas and worms. Both of these are easily avoided by regular use of the appropriate preventive treatments. If infestations do occur, treat promptly and stop your child from playing with the pet until treatment has worked. Ringworm is a contagious skin condition that can be caught from pets, and is commonly seen in children. If you suspect ringworm, ask your pharmacist for advice on treatment.

Possible problems 1 to 3 years

Fear of hair washing

If your child really hates having her hair washed, keep the hair very short so that it needs only sponging to keep it clean (*see p.80*). One of the major reasons why children hate having their hair washed is that they don't like water going over their faces. To overcome this you'll have to encourage your child to believe that hair washing won't hurt and that it won't feel nasty when water is rinsed over her head. Use non-sting shampoo, and you can still use a hairwashing shield on an older child.

Another problem that can make hair washing unpleasant is when your child has the kind of fine, curly hair that gets very tangled; combing through tangles after hair washing can become a nightmare. If you don't want to cut her hair short, try using conditioner: after rinsing off the shampoo, work conditioner through the hair, gently comb through with a wide-toothed comb, then rinse it off with a spray attachment. Then just pat her hair dry with the towel to absorb the excess water. You can buy anti-tangle spray to put on dry hair before you brush it.

Family bathtime
Older children in the family will love helping to bath a baby and like to join in. Bathtime can become a riotous affair with lots of shouts and splashing!

Make a game out of hair washing. It will become much more fun from your child's point of view if you get into the bath as well and wash your own hair. Rinse it with a plastic jug of water and make out that it's great fun pouring water over your head.

If you have an older child you could prove that it doesn't hurt by letting the younger child help you wash the elder's hair. Once you've lathered up the shampoo, hold the frightened child and allow her to rub both her hands through the bubbles. If possible, get the child to help pour the rinsing water over, too. Or, you could wash a doll's hair in the bath with your toddler's assistance. Let your child help with the rinsing and then suggest that you do it to her own hair. With any luck she'll just take this as part of the game. Alternatively, encourage your child to wet her own hair with a facecloth then put a tiny bit of shampoo into her hands so that she can put it on her hair.

An older child is also useful in proving that a wet face isn't unpleasant. For example, the elder child may well be proud of holding her breath under water and once your child is about three she might want to join in with this game, even if it means only putting nose and mouth under the surface for a count of five.

Fear of water

A few children hate water and bathtimes for these children and their parents will be very distressing. Probably the easiest way of overcoming this fear is to make bathtimes as happy and relaxing as possible, with plenty of playtime included. Try to find out what is frightening your child: is it the size of the bath; is it the amount of water in it;

is it related to an incident, for example slipping and suddenly being ducked under the water? If it is the size of the bath that causes the worry, introduce alternatives, like the kitchen sink or a large washing-up bowl. Your child will probably sit quite happily on a towel on the draining board, playing and dipping her feet into the water. This should also help if she's scared of the volume of water, as will playing with a shower attachment or a garden hose (as long as the flow is gentle). Ironically, swimming can be used to overcome your child's fear of water although you'll have to introduce the subject gently, see below.

GETTING HER USED TO WATER

Another way of getting your child used to water on the face is to take her swimming. Once she's got used to splashing and getting wet hair you'll be able to start hair washing. This is especially easy if you have a shower after swimming. You can then gently and deftly introduce the idea of having a shampoo in the shower using a non-sting baby shampoo: a quick shampoo should only take a couple of minutes.

You can also use the shower attachment at home, encouraging your child to play with the spray, playing it up to her shoulders and eventually on to her hair and face. Once again, when she's used to wet hair, you can quickly shampoo and rinse it.

If she likes swimming in the pool, take advantage of any swimming classes that you can attend with your child and where you do most of the teaching (with help from an instructor if you need it). Being able to swim may save your child's life and, if possible, it's always a good idea to make sure that she has learned to swim before she starts school.

7 Feeding

The main aim of infant feeding is to provide adequate nutrition. It helps to bear in mind also that while breast-feeding is undoubtedly best if, for whatever reason, you don't breast-feed your baby, he'll still thrive on bottle feeding. Don't feel guilty if you make this decision; concentrate on the needs of your baby. As important as any milk is the love and affection that you give your baby while you're feeding. And once he's on solids, the important rule to remember is to take your lead from your child; as long as you offer a wide variety of foods he doesn't have to have "essential" foods every day. Remember, above all, that food is a pleasure.

Nutritional needs birth to 1 year

A baby grows more quickly during the first six months than at any other time in his life. Most double their birth weight in around four months and triple it by the time they are about a year old. In order to grow, your baby needs protein, vitamins, minerals and carbohydrates. Until he's at least six months old your baby will receive these in the form of milk. When he's started on solids he will get all he needs from a well-balanced diet. During the first six months, a baby needs slightly more than 100 calories per kilogram (2lb), and from six months to one year slightly less than 100 calories per kilogram (2lb).

Protein

Most of the protein that a baby takes in is used for growth, and the protein requirements during the first year are correspondingly higher than at any other time of life; they are three times greater than those for adults. Milk, as long as it is given in adequate amounts, provides all the protein that a newborn infant needs.

Vitamins and minerals

Breast-milk is short of nothing except vitamin D. The main source of this is the sun, which stimulates the skin to manufacture it. If you live in a cold climate, or if your child has a very dark skin, you may need to give vitamin D supplements; ask your doctor for advice. If you bottle feed your baby all vitamin needs will be satisfied by the formula.

The rapid growth of bone and muscle during the first year means that babies have a greater need for minerals like calcium, phosphorous and magnesium

than adults. All babies are born with a supply of iron that will last for up to four months; after this, iron has to be added to the diet, usually in the form of solids, but possibly as iron supplements. Breast-milk and cow's milk are both pretty low on iron; formula milk usually has iron added.

Fats

The body needs minute traces of fatty acids for growth and repair. The fat content of both breast and formula milk is about the same, but in human milk the droplets of fat are smaller and so more digestible.

Carbohydrates

These are major energy providers. Both breast and formula milk contain the same carbohydrates, although the carbohydrate level is slightly higher in breast-milk.

Feeding comfortably
Make sure you're comfortable when feeding. Sit with both feet firmly on the ground. Support your back and arms with pillows and place a pillow on your lap to raise and support your baby if necessary.

Trace elements

Your baby needs traces of certain minerals like zinc, copper and fluoride. The first two are present in both breast and formula milk. Fluoride, however, is not and infants need fluoride to protect them against dental decay. If fluoride is added to the drinking water in your area a low-fluoride toothpaste will provide enough additional fluoride. If it's not, you may need to use a high-fluoride toothpaste for your child or even give supplements, but only with your dentist's guidance. If you're in doubt, contact your water authority.

Breast-feeding birth to 1 year

Human breast-milk is tailor-made for a baby: it contains just the right amount of protein, carbohydrates, minerals and vitamins to sustain your growing baby. Apart from its nutritional worth, breast-feeding makes sound sense for the following reasons:

- Breast-fed babies are less prone to illness than bottle-fed babies. There are fewer cases of gastroenteritis, chest infection, and measles and this is directly attributable to the antibodies that the baby receives. All babies receive some antibodies from their mother's placental blood, via the umbilical cord, but in the case of breast-fed babies these are supplemented by antibodies in both the colostrum (see p.90) and in the mother's

milk. In your baby's first few days of life they exert a protective influence on the intestine (reducing the likelihood of intestinal disturbance), and because they are also absorbed into the bloodstream they form part of the body's protection against infections. Some antibodies, such as those against poliomyelitis, are in the breast-milk, so the mother can actively protect her newborn while he is breast-feeding. (The baby will still have to be immunized, however.)

- Breast-milk is more easily, and quickly, digested than cow's milk. Breast-fed babies don't get constipated: they may pass stools infrequently but this is because the food is so efficiently and completely used up. The stools of breast-fed babies are soft and comparatively odourless, and they don't contain the bacteria that generally causes ammonia dermatitis, so these babies are less prone to nappy rash.

- Breast-fed babies rarely become overweight. Each baby has his own appetite and metabolic rate – it won't be the same as the baby next door, so don't worry if your baby is fatter or thinner than your neighbour's. He'll be the right weight for his own body.

- Breast-feeding is convenient. The milk is always at the right temperature, you don't have to waste your time sterilizing

Ensuring a good supply of breast-milk
When you are breast-feeding, make sure you are eating well and drinking lots of fluids, especially in hot weather when your baby will be more thirsty too.

and making up bottles, and you save money by not having to buy all the equipment. Breast-fed babies have less wind, sleep longer, posset less and the posset smells less unpleasant.

- Breast-feeding is good for your figure. Research has shown that most of the fat that is gained in pregnancy is shed if a woman breast-feeds. During breast-feeding a hormone called oxytocin is released and this encourages the uterus to return to its normal size, as well as stimulating the production of milk (see p.90). Your pelvis returns to normal more quickly and so does your waistline. Contrary to popular belief, breast-feeding does not affect the shape or size of your breasts. They may get bigger, smaller, or sag after pregnancy, but changes are not contingent upon breast-feeding; they are due to being pregnant.

- Breast cancer is rarer in parts of the world where breast-feeding is traditional. Breast-feeding may provide some protection against the disease.

Breast-feeding and contraception

Because the hormone that activates milk production also suppresses ovulation, it is unlikely that you will conceive while breast-feeding. However, you should never rely on this as a means of contraception. See your doctor for advice.

Preparing to breast-feed

Ideally, try to decide whether or not you want to breast-feed your baby well before delivery so that you can plan for it. If you are having your baby in hospital, tell the nursing staff as soon as you are admitted that you intend to breast-feed. Be assertive

MILK SUPPLY AND DEMAND FEEDING

All mothers are anatomically equipped to feed their babies and there is no such thing as mother's milk that does not suit a baby: the milk the breasts produce is the baby's natural food and he will not reject it.

- There is no such a thing as a mother physically incapable of feeding her baby: the size of your breasts bears no relation to the amount of milk that you can produce, although breast enlargement or reduction surgery can affect the ability to breast-feed.

- Milk is produced in deeply buried glands, not the fatty tissue of the breasts, so don't worry if your breasts are rather small: they *are* adequate. The amount of milk that you produce is dependent on how much your baby takes, hence the expression supply and demand. For example, if your baby's appetite is not very great then your breasts will not produce very much milk because they're not being stimulated by your baby to do so. If your baby is an eager feeder, your breasts will respond and produce more milk. The amount of milk available for your baby will fluctuate throughout the whole time that you breast-feed, according to how much your baby takes.

- If your baby is hungry half an hour after being fed, don't worry. Your breasts will have produced some milk for your baby to feed on, and they'll soon build up a supply for his new needs. When the need for more feeds slows down the breasts will produce less.

- A newborn needs 60–100ml (2–3½floz) of milk per 500g (1lb) of body weight, so a 3.5kg (7lb 11oz) baby will need 400–650ml (14–24floz) daily. Your breasts each produce 40–60ml (1½–2floz) of milk in three hours so your daily output of 700–1000ml (24–35floz) is ample.

about asking for help from them. Ask to see the staff nurse or sister if necessary. Ask her to sit with you for an entire feed, and to give a running commentary of what you should and shouldn't be doing. The best way to learn is to have someone who knows a lot about breast-feeding watching and encouraging you.

Few women breast-feed without encountering any problems. So while you shouldn't expect to find it difficult, neither should you be surprised if you have a run of problems. The thing to bear in mind is that most breast-feeding difficulties can be put right (see pp.98–101).

COLOSTRUM

During the 72 hours after delivery the breasts don't produce milk. Instead they manufacture a thin, yellow fluid called colostrum. This fluid is made up of water, protein and minerals and it takes care of all your baby's nutritional needs during the first days of his life before your breast-milk comes in.

Benefits of colostrum

Colostrum contains invaluable antibodies that protect your baby against diseases like polio and influenza, as well as intestinal and respiratory infections. It has an additional laxative effect that stimulates the excretion of meconium (see p.24). It's important to put your baby to the breast regularly in the first days, both to feed on the colostrum and to get used to latching on to the breast (see opposite).

Every time your baby cries in the early days you can put him to the breast but for only a couple of minutes each side at first so that the nipples don't get sore. Putting your baby to the breast also helps the uterus to contract.

The first contact

It is good for both you and your baby to try suckling as soon as the baby is born. There are two important reasons for doing so: suckling naturally stimulates the production of oxytocin, a hormone which, among other things (see p.89), makes the uterus contract and expel the placenta soon after birth. Suckling also helps to form a very strong bond between mother and baby immediately after birth.

Incidentally, you needn't worry about your baby choking. The natural reflex to suck is very strong, and he is able to swallow at birth.

The let-down reflex

When your baby suckles at the breast the pituitary gland in the brain is stimulated to release two hormones: prolactin and oxytocin. Prolactin activates the actual manufacture of milk in the milk glands; oxytocin is responsible for the milk being passed from the milk glands to the milk reservoirs behind the areola. This process happens within seconds and is known as the let-down or draught reflex. You may feel this reflex very powerfully: in fact, the very sight or sound of your baby may trigger it off, and milk may actually leak out of your nipples in anticipation of feeding.

How to hold your baby

Support your baby along the length of his back and use your hand and fingers to support the back of his neck to bring him up to your breast. He should be able to reach your nipple without effort. Support your back and arms with pillows and place a pillow on your lap to raise and support your baby if necessary.

The rooting reflex

The first few times you put your baby to the breast to feed he may need some encouragement and help to actually find the nipple. Cradle your baby in your arms and gently stroke the cheek nearest the breast. This will elicit the rooting reflex. Your baby will immediately turn towards your breast, mouth open and ready. If you put your nipple in now he will happily clamp both lips around the areola and settle down to suckle. Many babies lick the nipple before they take it into their mouths and it sometimes helps to express some colostrum as an added incentive.

After a few days your baby will need no artificial stimulation and will happily turn and latch on to the breast as soon as he is picked up and held close to your body.

Never try to guide your baby's head to the nipple by holding both his cheeks between your fingers, or by squeezing the mouth

The sucking effect
The baby stimulates milk to flow by pressing the tip of his tongue against the areola. Then he presses the back of his tongue up towards his palate to squeeze milk from your nipple into his throat.

open. The baby will become very confused by the conflicting stimuli of both cheeks being touched and will turn from side-to-side in a desperate bid to find the nipple.

Putting your baby to the breast

The key to happy, trouble-free breast-feeding is knowing how to get your baby's mouth correctly fixed or latched on to your breast. Try to get your nipple well inside your baby's mouth. This is important for two reasons. Firstly, unless he takes a good proportion of the areola into his mouth the

GIVING A BREAST-FEED

1 Gently stroke the cheek nearest to you, so that your baby turns to your breast. He will turn to your touch, open-mouthed, searching for your nipple.

2 Cradle your baby's head in your hand and make sure he latches on correctly. The baby should take the nipple and a good proportion of the areola into his mouth.

3 To break the suction when he's finished or it's time to move to the other breast, slip your little finger into the corner of his mouth. Your breast will slip out easily.

milk will not be successfully sucked from your breast. Your baby extracts milk from the breast in a kind of chomping, sucking motion: the baby's mouth forms a seal around the areola, and as he sucks, the tongue pushes the nipple up against the roof of the mouth. The milk is then drawn out in a rhythmic combination of sucking and squeezing. It can only be successful if the baby can exert pressure on the milk ducts behind the areola. Second, if you position the nipple well into the baby's mouth, you minimize the chances of developing sore or cracked nipples (see p.101). Your baby has a very strong sucking action and if only the nipple is in his mouth he will effectively shut off the openings of the milk ducts and little milk will get out. Your nipples will become extremely sore and your milk supply will eventually be reduced because the milk is not being drawn off (see p.89). Your baby will quite naturally become frustrated and bad-tempered with hunger.

BREAST-FEEDING TIPS

- You may find that because your let-down reflex is too efficient your milk pours out too quickly and chokes the baby as soon as he sucks. You can slow the flow down by expressing a little milk first (see p.96).
- If your nipple is soft and small and your baby has trouble finding it, put a cold, wet cloth on it for a moment – your nipple will firm up and protrude, making it easier for your baby.
- Milk flows in both breasts at every nursing and it's best to use both breasts at each feed. Start with the heavier breast.

Bonding

Once your baby is happily sucking at your breast, settle down and look at him. If your baby's eyes are open, make eye contact with him. Smile, talk and chat softly while he is feeding so that he associates the pleasure of feeding with the sight of your face, the sound of your voice and the smell of your skin.

How long on each breast

Your baby's sucking will be strongest in the first five minutes when he will take 80 per cent of the feed. As a general rule, keep your baby on the breast for as long as he shows interest in sucking. If your baby continues to suck after your breasts have emptied, it may be that he is just enjoying the sensation; this is fine if it's not making your breasts sore. You'll find that your baby will lose interest in his own individual way: it may be that he starts to play with your breast, slipping his mouth on and off the nipple; he may turn away; he may fall asleep. When he appears to have had enough of one breast gently take the baby off your nipple (see below) and put him on to the other breast. If your baby does fall asleep after feeding from both breasts he's probably had enough: you'll soon learn whether this is the case or whether he's going to wake, hungry again, after ten minutes, or so. Similarly, if your baby appears to have taken all he wants from just one breast, don't worry. You can start the next feed off on the other breast.

Removing baby from breast

Never pull your baby off the breast – you'll only hurt your nipple. To get the baby off, slip your finger down between the areola and your baby's cheek and put your little finger into the corner of the baby's mouth. This will make his mouth open, breaking the suction, and your breast will slip out of his mouth easily instead of being dragged off. In the first few days this is particularly important because your nipples are rather soft and they need a chance to become less sensitive.

What to wear to breast-feed

It is most important that you wear a bra when you are breast-feeding. One that supports your breasts underneath, has front fastenings and wide straps to avoid hurting your shoulders is best. On top you should wear whatever you feel most comfortable in but, obviously, the top should allow easy access to your breasts. Large T-shirts are both comfortable and practical; front opening shirts are quick to open but some women feel more exposed wearing them.

Breast-feeding positions

You can feed your baby in whatever position you choose, as long as your baby can latch on to the nipple and you are comfortable and relaxed. Experiment and do whatever feels most natural. Do try to change positions throughout the day – this will ensure that your baby doesn't only exert pressure on one part of the areola, and minimizes the risk of a blocked milk duct. If you sit down to feed your baby, make sure that you're comfortable, with your arms and back supported with cushions or pillows if necessary.

It's also nice to lie in bed to feed your baby, especially in the first few weeks and at night, and there's no reason why you shouldn't do this. Lie on your side, propped with pillows if that's more comfortable, and gently cradle the baby's head and body alongside you. You may need to lay a small baby on a pillow so that he's at the right

BREAST-FEEDING POSITIONS

Sitting position
Make sure your arms and back are supported with cushions or pillows and you are relaxed. Use a pillow to raise your baby to a comfortable level.

Lying position
This is good when you're tired or to keep your baby off a Caesarean incision. Lie on your side and lay your baby alongside you so he can reach your lower breast.

Feeding twins
While it can be easier to feed them singly in the early days, once breast-feeding is established you can try feeding your babies together.

height for your nipple, but a larger baby should be able to lie on the bed next to you. Make sure that the muscles under your arm aren't strained as this will slow down the flow of milk. Alternatively, lay your baby on a pillow under your arm, with his feet tucked behind you. Your hand can support your baby's head as he faces your breast. Always put your baby back in his own bed after feeding; don't fall asleep with him in your bed.

The position you choose initially may be affected by the delivery you've had. For example, if you've had an episiotomy you'll probably find sitting down extremely uncomfortable, so feeding on your side will be more suitable. Similarly, if you've had a Caesarean section your stomach may be too tender for your baby to lie on so try the football-hold position with your baby's feet tucked under your arm. Alternatively, try feeding your baby while he's lying on the bed alongside you.

Frequency of feeds

Babies need frequent feeding because of their body size. Breast-fed babies may need more feeds than bottle-fed babies because they digest their milk more quickly. Babies should be fed on demand (*see p.89*), and parents will quickly learn to recognize the cries that mean their baby is hungry (*see p.158*). Newborn babies may need to be fed every two hours, having as many as eight to ten feeds a day. By about one month, babies are usually taking food every three hours, and at two to three months approximately every four hours. However, every baby is different.

Most babies sleep through the night after their late evening feed by the time they are three months old, but you shouldn't even consider trying to drop the night feed unless your baby indicates his willingness by sleeping through.

Supplementary bottles

We have all heard tales about women not having enough milk to feed their babies and, even though the fear may be only subconscious, when problems arise during the early days of feeding a woman may use this as an excuse to justify giving up on breast-feeding. Please don't succumb to this pressure; resist it even if your midwife suggests it to you, and certainly when friends and relatives do.

Every woman comes equipped with the means and capacity to feed her baby. Breasts respond to the demand for milk by producing it, so if your baby is not taking off all your milk in the initial stages you should try to express the rest so that the demand for milk from your breasts is kept up. Most breasts respond to this approach with a good flow of milk.

As your child gets older and perhaps has bouts of crying, someone will nudge you and say the baby is hungry. You may have just fed your baby, in which case he may be simply thirsty. This occurs, of course, as soon as you start mixed feeding because food needs liquid to dilute it and to be digested. So initially you can try your baby with 15ml (½floz) of plain, cooled boiled water to quench his thirst.

Every new mother is worried about how well she can feed her baby and may feel a pressure to go onto supplementary bottles. The attraction of the bottle to an anxious mother is that she can see instantly how much milk the baby has taken – an assurance not available when breast-feeding. But try to be logical and rational about it, and above all have confidence in your ability to feed your baby. Remember that a baby takes 80 per cent of the feed in the first two to three minutes on each breast. So although the baby may become rather bored with being on the breast, if he has been sucking for at least five minutes, he has almost certainly had enough milk to satisfy his hunger.

ENSURING A GOOD MILK SUPPLY

- Rest as much as you can, particularly during the first weeks after the birth of your baby. This is a time when you should sit rather than stand, and lie rather than sit.
- Your milk flow will be affected if you are tense so go through your antenatal relaxation routines and make sure that you have a period to yourself every day when you can lie down.
- Go to bed as early as you can. You will be quite tired anyway and your sleep patterns will probably be broken by your baby.
- As far as the house is concerned, let the housework go. Don't do anything but the most urgent things.
- Make sure that your diet is well balanced and fairly rich in protein. Don't eat a lot of highly refined and processed carbohydrates (cakes, biscuits, sweets, chocolates, etc).
- You may need some iron supplements and possibly some vitamin supplements, so ask your doctor about this.
- Drink about 3 litres (5 pints) of fluid every day while you're breast-feeding; some women find they need a drink by them while breast-feeding.
- Most of your milk is produced in the morning when you are rested so if you consistently rush about or become tense during the day you'll find by evening that your supply is poor.
- If your baby doesn't take all the milk available in the early feeds of the day, express the remainder. This will ensure that the supply is topped up throughout the day.
- Get help and support from everyone around you who is positive and optimistic. Use your midwife and health visitor; speak to friends who've had babies and get advice from them.
- If you are unable to give your baby a feed because you're away or because you're ill, express milk to keep the supply going.

There may be times, such as when you have a blocked duct or a very sore nipple when it is painful to breast-feed. Hard as it is, it's best to avoid offering your baby formula if you possibly can if this happens. There are so many benefits to your baby being exclusively breast-fed for the first six months if possible.

When feeding is painful, many mothers prefer to express milk from the affected breast and use this in a bottle. Giving supplementary formula feeds can undermine the production of breast-milk.

A baby who has become used to the nipple may dislike plastic teats. Unfortunately, it can be difficult to tell whether your baby just dislikes the teat, or is not hungry. If you persist, he'll eventually get used to the bottle, but you may then find that he doesn't want to go back to the breast. If your breasts are very sore, try giving your baby the expressed milk from a sterilized spoon or cup.

Expressing milk

Bottles of your own expressed milk can be given to your baby when you are ill, extremely tired, or are leaving the baby with someone else. Expressed milk can be kept in sterile containers in the refrigerator for up to 48 hours, or frozen and kept in the freezer for up to six months. This will enable your partner or child-minder to feed your baby with your milk. Also, because breasts produce milk in response to demand, you may need to express milk in order to keep your supply going – if your baby is premature and can't yet breast-feed, for example.

Milk can be expressed by hand or with a breast pump. Electric pumps are more expensive but easier to use than the manual versions. They imitate a baby's natural sucking cycle more closely and are best if you need to express often. Even if you use a pump, it is worth learning the technique of hand expressing in case you

EXPRESSING BY HAND

1 Wash your hands. Massage your breasts with flat hands, beginning at your ribs and working towards your areola, gradually going over the whole breast.

2 Roll your fingers and thumb together below and above your areola so that you press on the wider milk ducts behind the nipple. Work gently and rhythmically.

3 If the milk doesn't begin to flow, keep on trying. Once it starts, continue for about five minutes, then move onto the second breast.

need it. Before you start, get a bowl, a funnel and a container that can be sealed, and sterilize all of them, either in a sterilizing solution or with boiling water. Make sure your hands are clean.

Hand expressing is nearly always a bit difficult in the first six weeks as the breasts have not reached full production, but do persevere. The best time to express milk is in the morning, when you'll have the most milk, although when your baby drops the night feed you may find the evening the best time. You'll be able to express 30–60ml (1–2floz) without too much trouble.

The more relaxed you are, the easier it will be to express your milk. If the milk won't start to flow, place a warm flannel over your breasts to open the ducts, or try expressing in the bath. If you have to lean over a low surface, expressing may give you backache, so make sure you are comfortable and that the container is at a convenient height.

EXPRESSING TIPS

- Expressing milk should never hurt. If it does you're not doing it correctly; stop immediately.
- Every piece of equipment and all containers should be sterile; your hands must be clean.
- If you're worried about your baby not going back to breast-feeding having got used to the bottle, try giving the expressed milk from a cup, with a spoon. They should both be sterilized.
- Milk must be stored correctly otherwise it will go off and make your baby ill. As soon as you've collected your milk put it into the refrigerator until it is needed; it will keep for 48 hours. You can also freeze the milk for up to six months; the expressed milk should be put into sterile plastic containers that can be sealed. Don't use glass – it might crack.

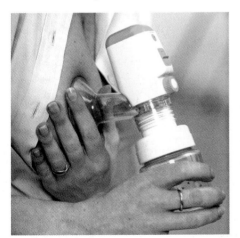

Using an electric pump
An electric pump is best if you need to express milk often. The operation varies from brand to brand so follow the manufacturer's instructions.

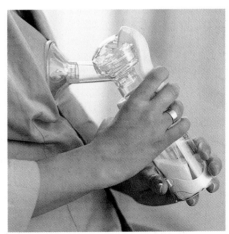

Using a manual pump
Start by fitting the funnel of the pump over your areola to form an airtight seal. You then operate the lever or plunger of the pump to express the milk.

Possible breast-feeding problems birth to 1 year

Some women find that breast-feeding goes without a hitch from the beginning, but be prepared to be a bit clumsy the first few times, for your baby not to suck vigorously or for very long during the first 24 to 36 hours, and for your breasts to be a bit sore.

Refusing the breast

One of the most common reasons for a baby having problems taking the breast is that he has difficulty breathing. Your baby can't breathe through his nose and swallow at the same time, so always check to make sure that your breast is not covering his nostrils.

Your baby may be reluctant to take the breast if there has been a delay in starting to breast-feed after birth. For both you and your baby, the sooner you start the better. Babies learn to take the breast quickly in the first 48 hours but find it increasingly difficult the longer it is left. This does not mean, however, that your baby will never take to the breast. It just means that you will have to be patient and persevere. If, for example, your baby is premature, you could ask that he be given your expressed milk (so that your supplies of milk continue), and when you get home you can introduce the breast.

Another reason for your baby refusing to take the breast may be that he's fretful. If he's woken up, keen to feed, only to find that he's either ignored, fussed over, or changed, you may well find that he's too distressed to take your breast. If this happens you'll have to hold your baby firmly and talk soothingly and not even try to feed him until he's calmed down.

"Sucky" babies

For many babies, sucking on their mother's breast is the most pleasant experience of the day. You'll soon learn to distinguish between sucking for food and sucking for comfort. During a feed you may see and feel your baby making strong, rhythmic sucking movements but if you look closely, you'll see that he isn't swallowing. There's no reason, however, why your baby shouldn't suck as long as he wants, as long as you're happy about it and your nipples aren't sore.

Sleeping through feeds

During the first few days your baby may not be all that interested in feeding. Don't be put off. Still try suckling your baby for about five minutes on each breast, at each feed. If your baby goes to sleep at the breast don't worry; it is a very good sign that your baby is contented and doing well. (This is not the case, however, with premature babies who sleep a lot and need to be awakened and fed frequently.)

Don't stick to a rigid routine. If your baby sleeps through a feed, leave it for half an hour and then wake him up gently and try the breast. If he wants to go on sleeping, let him do so: just give the feed when he wakes. If he is hungry he'll perk up when food is offered.

Startled babies

Most babies are easily startled by any sudden, loud noise or violent movements in their first few weeks. When you pick your baby up for a feed, hold him firmly and talk soothingly all the time. Lower your head towards your baby so that your face and eyes are all that he sees. Make sure that there are no disturbing noises around you and, if possible, pick your baby up before he starts to cry.

Biting

This is a natural impulse and your baby may well bite you even before his teeth have come in. When it happens you will automatically jerk back and may even let out a cry. Your baby will be startled by this and if you say "NO", quite firmly but without shouting, he will soon learn not to do it – even at a very early age.

Anxiousness on your part

If you meet a minor obstacle such as your baby refusing to have a feed, try not to get worked up about it. Nervousness may lead to more difficulties, which will make you more discouraged and may even put you permanently off breast-feeding.

Nervousness may also affect your milk. As far as your baby's health is concerned, even a few days of colostrum and breast-milk give a good start to life and are better than none at all. You should never get worried about your baby going without food because you can always fall back on bottle-feeding. Don't let small problems lead you to hasty decisions. You may be tearful and easily upset during the first week or so after delivery anyway, and it would be a shame to give up breast-feeding when you are in this rather unsettled state. Try to persevere and ask your midwife or health visitor for advice.

If you are worried about breast-feeding, make it as easy on yourself as you can. If you are embarrassed about it, make sure that you are not in a public place when feeding time comes around. Don't invite visitors to the house when you know you will be feeding, unless you are prepared to feed your baby in front of them if he wants food in a hurry.

Overfeeding/underfeeding

You cannot overfeed a breast-fed baby. He regulates how much he wants (*see p.89*), so unless you give something other than breast-milk (like badly made-up supplementary bottles), he'll take what he needs and his weight will be correct.

It is highly unlikely for a breast-fed baby to be underfed, but if you are worried that your baby isn't getting enough milk, talk to your midwife or health visitor.

IF YOU'RE ILL

As long as you feel like breast-feeding, continue to do so – even if you have to go to hospital. You may have to make special arrangements with the nursing staff, but if this is what you want, argue firmly for it, and don't be dissuaded.

- If you have to have an anaesthetic you will not be able to breast-feed – not only will you be too groggy afterwards, but the drugs you have been given will have passed into your milk.
- If you have an advance warning of an operation, try to express and freeze your milk. This way the baby will not miss your milk, even if he misses the pleasure of feeding from you.
- If you are confined to bed with a bad cold or flu, you can express your milk so your partner can feed the baby if you feel too weak.
- If you're too ill even to express milk your baby will have to be given formula milk by bottle or by spoon. He'll probably protest at first but will acquiesce as he becomes hungrier.

Care of your breasts

Take good care of your breasts: they are going to be working quite hard for the next few months. The first step is to buy yourself a couple of the best maternity bras that you can afford. Ask the assistant to measure you and make sure that the bra gives you good support both below your breasts and on your shoulders. The drop-front kind (see below) is very good because it makes feeding quick, convenient and hygienic and your breasts are never left to sag. Towards the end of the first week when lactation becomes well established, your breasts may become full, sore, tender to the touch and quite hard because there is so much milk. A good bra will minimize discomfort; so will expressing (*see p.96*).

Pay attention to the daily hygiene of your breasts and nipples. Wash them every day with water – don't use soap because it is drying to the skin and can aggravate a sore or cracked nipple. Always handle your breasts carefully: pat them dry gently after both feeding and washing. Leave your nipples open to the air whenever you can: still wear your bra for support, but leave the front flaps down.

Once the milk really starts to flow it may leak out quite a lot during the day. Put breast pads or clean handkerchiefs inside your bra to soak up the leaking milk. Change the pad frequently for cleanliness.

While there are no muscles in the breasts themselves, exercise can help keep them in good shape. By shortening the connecting fibres that attach your breasts to your chest muscles, you draw them up and maintain their firmness. The following "top-lift" exercise is most beneficial once you've weaned your baby, but you can also use it once breast-feeding is well established. You can do the exercise either sitting or standing. Raise your arms to shoulder level; grasp the left forearm with your right hand and vice versa, and simultaneously, press and push with each hand towards the elbow with a jerky movement. Repeat for as long as feels comfortable. Do the exercise for a minimum of six weeks for the best results.

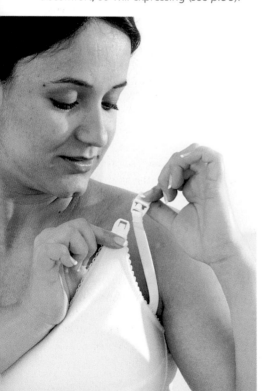

Nursing bras
A good supportive bra will minimize discomfort if your breasts become sore. Drop-front styles are convenient and easy to undo.

BREAST PROBLEMS

Problem	Prevention	Cure
Cracked nipples Shooting pain when the baby suckles.	Feed little and often in the first few days. Keep the nipples dry by using disposable breast pads or clean hankies.	Keep feeding if at all possible. If necessary, express the milk by hand (not by pump), and feed the baby by bottle or spoon.
Engorgement Extremely full and painful breasts with a swollen areola.	Feed your baby frequently and try to encourage him to empty your breasts regularly.	Have a hot bath and gently express some milk, or encourage it to flow by massaging towards the nipple.
Blocked duct A hard red patch on the outside of the breast where the duct lies. This can often occur as a result of engorgement or when your bra or clothes are too tight.	As for engorgement. Wear a properly fitting bra and keep feeding the baby in different positions throughout the day.	Frequent feeding, offering the breast with the blocked duct first so that it is properly emptied. Express the breast if necessary.
Mastitis Acute infection of the milk duct resulting in a pus-filled lump.	As for a blocked duct.	Antibiotics prescribed by your doctor. If this fails it will have to be drained surgically. You can, however, continue to feed, even if you need an operation.
Breast abcesses This infection, which results from an untreated blocked duct, can make you feel feverish; you may have a shiny red patch on your breast.	As for a blocked duct.	As for a blocked duct, although you will probably be prescribed antibiotics by your doctor. Unless instructed otherwise, you can continue to feed your baby from the affected breast.

If you can, avoid all drugs when breast-feeding; many medications pass into the breast-milk and can affect your baby. If you are already taking medication, or if you see your doctor for any new problem, make sure he knows that you are breast-feeding.

Sore nipples

Painful nipples are the most common reason for women giving up breast-feeding. However, there are ways to avoid them. Make sure your baby is correctly positioned and properly latched on, and never pull your baby off the nipple (see p.91). Ask your health visitor for advice if you have problems. Keep your nipples as dry as possible between feeds and make sure they are dry before putting your bra back on. If they do become cracked, ointment, such as Vaseline, may be helpful. You can also try using a nipple shield. This is made of soft silicone and fits over your nipple. The baby sucks through a small teat on the front; sterilize it before use.

Bottle-feeding birth to 1 year

Once you make the decision to bottle-feed, stick to it and don't feel guilty about it. Many babies are bottle-fed at some point, including those who started out on the breast. All of them thrive. Your baby will do well on infant formula (powdered cow's milk). Just make sure that he has the same attention and closeness at feeding times as he would have if you were breast-feeding.

Mother's milk is important to your baby, but it is not as important as your love. Fill the hours you spend with your baby, particularly feeding times, with your love, affection and care. These are just as important to your baby's physical and emotional well-being as your milk.

Most women feel pressure to breast-feed their babies, and worry quite a lot if they decide not to, but there are some good reasons for deciding that breast-feeding is not for you. Despite your very best efforts you may simply not be successful at it. In that case, the best thing is to forget about it and concentrate on giving your baby a good bottle-fed diet:

he will do just as well. Other women find it emotionally or psychologically difficult, some feel that they may be too tied down by a breast-feeding routine and that it will curtail many of their activities, including return to work. Some couples are opposed to it because it excludes the father.

One of the good things about bottle-feeding is that the new father can be just as involved as a new mother at feeding times. Make sure that your partner feeds the baby very soon after you get home from the hospital, so that he gets used to the technique and isn't afraid to handle the baby. The sooner he learns to do all the things that your baby needs the better. If possible your partner should share the feeding equally with you. If not, he should give at least two out of the six feeds a day.

Choosing the bottles

Buy unbreakable bottles that have a wide neck so that they're easy to fill and to clean; the 250ml (10floz) size is the most suitable. The teat should ideally be one shaped to fit the baby's mouth. Disposable bottles are useful for travelling, and for when you run out of sterilized bottles.

Sterilizing the bottles

Buy your feeding equipment well in advance of having your baby so that you can practise with it before your baby is

Bottles and teats
There is a wide range of feeding bottles and teats now available. You may need to try a few to find out what suits your baby best.

born. Major department stores and chemists sell bottle-feeding packs that contain all the essential equipment.

All feeding equipment needs to be sterilized to reduce the risk of your baby getting ill. There are a number of ways of sterilizing bottles, but the most popular are cold-water sterilizing units and steam units. Whatever method you choose, always read the manufacturer's instructions carefully and follow them exactly. With cold-water sterilizing units bottles can be left in the solution. Before using a bottle shake off any excess solution from both the bottle and the teat or rinse with cooled boiled water from the kettle. If using a steam sterilizer, equipment should be re-sterilized before use if not used straight away. Dummies and teething rings should also be thoroughly cleaned before use.

HYGIENE AND PREPARATION TIPS

- Always wash your hands before sterilizing, preparing and giving feeds.
- Make sure that everything that comes into contact with your baby's food is thoroughly cleaned or sterilized before use and always clean the work surface before starting to make up the feed.
- Follow all sterilizing instructions to the letter.
- Sterilize every piece of equipment that you use for making up your baby's feeds.
- Make up the feed according to the instructions. Never add any extra feed.
- Give the feed to your baby as soon as it is ready. Do not make up feeds in advance.
- Never give your baby leftover milk. Throw away any milk that's left after a feed.

CLEANING EQUIPMENT

Washing bottles and teats
Wash all equipment in hot soapy water. Scrub the insides of bottles with a bottle brush and rub teats thoroughly to remove milk. Rinse well in warm running water.

Boiling
To sterilize bottles by boiling, you should boil them for at least ten minutes. Then remove them from the water and allow to cool down before using.

Cleaning in a dishwasher
Once your baby is over 12 months old you can wash feeding equipment in a dishwasher. Clean teats before they go in. Run the machine on the normal cycle.

The flow of milk

Milk simply runs out of the breast at the beginning of a feed so there is hardly any need for exertion when your baby is sucking. I feel that bottle-fed babies should find feeding just as easy. To make this possible for them the hole in the teat should be large enough to let drops fall in a steady stream when the bottle is inverted. If it takes a few seconds for a drop to form, then the hole is too small; if the stream is continuous, it is too big.

- You can buy teats with different-sized holes; alternatively to make a hole bigger you need a fine, red-hot needle. Simply insert it gently through the hole in the teat and the rubber, or plastic will melt. Have a few spare teats as it is not as easy as it sounds, and you may end up with holes that are much too large. I certainly did the first time I tried it.

- It is worth spending time getting the size of the hole just right, because if it is too large your baby will get too much too fast and cough and splutter. If the hole is too small, your baby will get tired from sucking before he has taken a full meal, and he may swallow too much air.

- Buy sculpted teats if possible. These are shaped to fit the baby's palate and allow the baby more control over the flow.

The first feed

There is no artificial equivalent to colostrum. Even if you're not going to continue to breast-feed you will be giving

MAKING UP A POWDER FORMULA

Bottles must be made up strictly in accordance with the proportions of powder to water recommended by the manufacturer or by your health visitor or doctor. Make bottles when you need them. Bacteria can multiply fast in bottles of warm formula, so don't make up bottles in advance and store them.

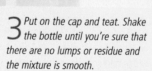

1 *Fill the bottle to the correct level with fresh tap water that has been boiled and left to cool for half an hour. Fill the scoop with milk powder and level it off.*

2 *Add the milk powder to the water. Make sure you add exactly the right number of scoops – no more and no less than the manufacturer recommends.*

3 *Put on the cap and teat. Shake the bottle until you're sure that there are no lumps or residue and the mixture is smooth.*

your baby a great head-start if you put him to the breast in the first days (*see p.90*).

Don't worry if your baby doesn't gulp down all that's in the bottle. It's perfectly normal for all babies, breast- or bottle-fed, not to take very much in their first 48 hours and they take a while to get into the swing of feeding. Like a breast-fed baby, yours will let you know with a cry when he wants to be fed. Follow your baby's lead and develop the supply and demand system explained on p.107, just as for a breast-fed baby.

Milk formulas

A variety of milk formulas is available, all carefully formulated to make them as close as possible to breast-milk. In fact, formula milk has added vitamin D and iron, levels of which are quite low in breast milk.

Most formulas are based on cow's milk. Some formulas are available both in powder and ready-mixed forms. There are soya-based formulas available, but never give these to your baby without the advice of your doctor, midwife or health visitor. Ready-mixed milk comes in cartons or ready-to-feed bottles and is ultra-heat treated (UHT), which means it is sterile and will keep in a cool place until the "best before" date. Once the carton has been opened, the milk will keep for 24 hours in a refrigerator. Ready-mixed milk is more expensive than powdered formula, but it is very convenient when you are travelling.

Giving a bottle-feed

Make sure that you have a quiet, comfortable place to sit and that your arms are well supported with cushions or pillows if necessary (*see p.93*). Lay your baby in

BOTTLE TEMPERATURE

Make sure that the milk is cooled to the right temperature before you feed your baby. Never keep warm milk in a vacuum flask or leave a bottle standing overnight in a bottle warmer. Never warm a bottle in a microwave as it can cause "hot spots" that can scald your baby.

Testing temperature
Test the temperature of the milk on your wrist before feeding the baby: it should be neither hot nor cold to the touch.

Cooling a bottle
If the bottle is too hot, put the bottle in a jug of cold water, or hold it under cold running water for a short while, then test again. Always leave the cap on the bottle covering the teat.

your lap with his head in the crook of your elbow and his back supported along your forearm. Make sure that your baby is not lying horizontally. He should be half-sitting so that breathing and swallowing are safe and easy and there's no risk of choking.

Just before you start feeding, test the heat of the milk by letting a couple of drops fall on to the inside of your wrist. The milk should feel neither too hot nor too cold. You should already have tested the flow of milk (see p.104). Loosen the cap of the bottle very slightly so that air can enter to take the place of the milk that your baby sucks out. If you don't do this quite a lot of negative pressure can build up inside the bottle that will flatten the teat and make sucking very hard work. Your baby will become bad-tempered and angry and refuse the rest of the feed. If this happens, gently pull the bottle out of your baby's mouth so that the air can get in and then continue feeding, as before.

To elicit your baby's sucking reflex, so that he takes the bottle, gently stroke the cheek nearest to you. As your baby turns to your touch you can gently insert the teat into his mouth. He should latch on to a fair amount of teat so that the tip is far back into his mouth, like a nipple would be. You should, however, be careful not to push it so far back that he gags on it.

Let your baby set the pace of feeding. He might want to pause mid-feed to look

GIVING A BOTTLE-FEED

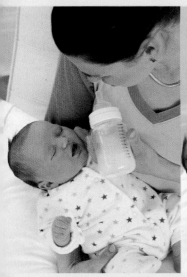  

1 *Gently stroke your baby's nearest cheek to elicit his sucking reflex. Insert the teat carefully into his mouth. If you push the teat too far back he may gag.*

2 *Chat to your baby as you feed. Let him pause mid-feed if he likes. Change him on to the other arm at this stage to give him a new view, and your arm a rest.*

3 *If you want your baby to release the bottle from his mouth, gently slide your little finger into the corner of his mouth and lift it out.*

around or play with the bottle and he should be allowed this pleasure. From the very beginning make feeding times as pleasant as possible. Face your baby and make eye contact. Don't sit in silence: talk, sing to him, make any kind of sound you like. Just make sure that your voice sounds pleasant, happy and responsive. This is the first conversation that your baby will enjoy, so he will react to your movements, gestures and smiles.

Half-way through the feed, change your baby on to the other arm. This will give your baby a new view to look at and your arm a rest; you may also want to wind him at this point (see p.108).

Bottle-feeding patterns

Bottle-fed babies tend to feed less frequently than breast-fed ones. This is because formula milk takes longer to digest; it also contains slightly more protein that therefore provides more calories and delays hunger for longer.

After the first two or three days bottle-fed babies usually settle on a four-hourly regime. They will therefore be having six feeds, probably one less than if they were being breast-fed. When your baby is first born he will probably not take more than 60ml (2floz) milk at each feed but as he gets older the feeds will get bigger and the number of feeds, per day, will be fewer.

Let your baby determine when he's to be fed; never, ever, feed your baby according to the clock. Feed him when he tells you with cries that he is hungry, not when you think he should be.

Don't feel that your baby has to finish the bottle at each feed. Like everybody else, your baby's appetite will vary, so if he seems satisfied, but there's a little left in the bottle, don't try to make him take it. He will only get too full and may posset it back (see p.109). What's more, he may become overfed and fat. On the other hand, if your baby always seems ravenous, give some extra from another bottle. If he regularly wants more milk, start to add the extra amount at every feed.

BOTTLE-FEEDING TIPS

- Don't feed your baby lying flat; it is very difficult to swallow in this position and your baby may gag or even be sick.
- Never leave your baby with the bottle propped up on a pillow or cushion. Not only is it very dangerous because your baby could choke, but he could become very uncomfortable if he has to swallow a lot of air along with the feed because of the angle at which the bottle's been propped. Moreover, your baby misses out on the cuddling and affection that he should enjoy while he feeds.
- Don't try to force your baby to finish the bottle after he has stopped sucking: he knows when he's had enough.
- Even if you think the milk formula doesn't suit your baby don't change it without first consulting your midwife or health visitor. It is very rare for a brand of milk to be responsible for a baby not feeding well; very rarely a baby is allergic to cow's milk, and you may then have to use a hydrolized (broken down so more easily digested) formula, but always seek medical advice first.

Possible bottle-feeding problems birth to 1 year

Overfeeding

Fat cells are produced by an infant in response to the amount of fat that is taken in with the food. Once produced these cells can't be removed, so if your baby develops an excessively large number they will still be present when he's an adult and can lead to health problems.

If you overfeed your baby he will become fat; unfortunately, it is easier to overfeed a bottle-fed baby. There are two major reasons for this: first, it is tempting to put extra formula into the bottle. You should always follow the instructions to the letter (*see p.104*), otherwise you'll be giving the baby unseen (and unnecessary) calories. Second, because you can see the amount of formula he's taking it may be hard to resist encouraging him to finish the last drop. You should always let your baby decide whether he's had enough or not. Other causes of over-feeding include giving sweet, syrupy drinks and introducing solids to your baby too early.

Underfeeding

This is rare in bottle-fed babies, but it can happen. Your baby should be fed on demand and not according to the clock. Although most babies will be ready for a feed every four hours by the time that they are two to three months old, their individual appetites may vary from day to day. Say, for example, your baby's at the age when he can take five 180ml (6floz) bottles a day, but at one feed he only takes 115ml (4floz) out of the bottle. If you insist on feeding to a schedule, don't give any extra milk in these scheduled bottles and

don't allow any of the interim feeds that your baby will be crying for, he won't be able to catch up with the total volume of milk that he needs, and won't gain weight.

You should also be flexible about how much feed you make up. The figures on the packages are given as a general estimate but, for example, if your child consistently drains each bottle you give and also seems fretful and upset, he may well be hungry. Make up an extra 60ml (2floz) of formula and see if he wants it. If he takes it then he needs it and he won't put on extra weight.

If you find that your baby is demanding frequent feeds but doesn't take much and remains fretful, check that the teat hole isn't too small. It may well be that he's having a hard time actually sucking the milk out of the bottles and is therefore not getting enough nourishment.

Winding

The point of winding is to bring up any wind that has been swallowed during feeding or crying prior to feeding. The reason for bringing up wind is to prevent it from causing your baby discomfort. Babies vary a great deal in their reaction to wind, and in my experience the majority of them aren't noticeably happier or more contented for having been burped.

Babies also vary a great deal in the amount of air that they swallow during feeding. Some, including all breast-fed babies, swallow very little. Swallowing air is much more common in bottle-fed babies but even then it doesn't seem to be a problem. If very small quantities of air are swallowed

Winding your baby
Hold your baby on your shoulder with a bib or a nappy over your shoulder to catch any dribble. Gently rub or pat her back between the shoulder blades.

during feeding they form small bubbles in the stomach that cannot be burped up until they have coalesced into a large bubble, and this can take a great deal of time. Small bubbles in the stomach are very unlikely to give rise to discomfort. The one point in favour of winding is that it makes you pause, relax, take things slowly, hold your baby gently and stroke or pat him in a reassuring way. This is very good for your baby and very good for you, too.

My attitude towards winding, therefore, is that by all means do it, even if it is just for your peace of mind, but don't become fanatical about it. And don't pat or rub your baby too hard while you're winding as you may jerk your baby as this may make him bring up some of the feed. A gentle upward stroking movement is usually preferable to firm pats.

Some experts advise that you stop the feeding halfway through to wind your baby. I don't think there is any need to do that. Wait until your baby pauses naturally in the feed and take advantage of this little rest to try winding. As your baby gets older you will probably find that he finishes his whole bottle quite comfortably without needing to burp.

Possetting

Some babies never posset at all. Others do so with surprising ease, and this can be a cause of concern to parents. My youngest son had a tendency to posset, and I worried in case he wasn't getting enough to eat. I simply followed my own instinct, which was to offer him more food. If he didn't take it, I assumed that he had possetted an excess that he didn't need. In very young babies, the commonest cause of possetting is overfeeding. This is another reason why you should never insist that your bottle-fed baby finishes his feed.

If your bottle-fed baby shows a tendency to posset, check the hole in the teat. If it is too large he may be taking too much, too quickly. If it is too small he may be sucking in a lot of air because he has to suck very hard.

Forcible (projectile) vomiting, especially if it happens after consecutive feeds or goes on for more than a day, should be reported immediately to your doctor. Vomiting in a very small baby can quickly lead to dehydration, and you need to get medical advice as soon as possible.

Night feeds birth to 1 year

Because you will be responding to all of your baby's demands for food you may find that feeding him takes up quite a lot of your time – feeding can take at least 30 minutes each time. This will mean you are feeding for more than three hours out of every 24. With night feeding on top of all the other things that you have to do to take care of your baby you may find yourself becoming extremely tired and tense. It won't be so much the number of hours sleep that you lose, but more the way in which your sleep patterns are broken up over long periods of time.

It is very important that you get adequate rest both day and night, so you need your partner to share the work with you. There should be equality of child-nurturing between you, and as you are doing most of the feeding it is only fair that he takes over some of the other jobs for the baby. In fact, even if you've decided to breast-feed, the night feeds shouldn't be your entire responsibility. If your baby sleeps in another room, ask your partner to bring him to you as soon as he cries, and get him to take your baby back and change the nappy after he's been fed. He could take a turn at feeding with expressed milk.

Reducing night feeds

Until your baby weighs about 5kg (11lb) he won't be able to sleep for more than five hours at a time without waking with hunger. However, once this weight is reached you can try stretching the time between feeds with the aim of giving yourself about six hours of undisturbed sleep, and of painlessly getting your baby to drop the early morning feed. Your baby will have his own routine, but as a general rule, it's sensible to try to juggle your baby's last feed so that it's given at around the time that you go to bed.

But do be flexible; it may be that your baby doesn't want to drop the early morning feed, and no matter how much you try to alter the routine he will still wake up and want feeding. If so you'll just have to try to make the night feeds as straightforward as possible and look forward to the time when he drops them.

TIPS FOR NIGHT FEEDS

- Feed your baby in bed so that you are warm and comfortable, but always put him back in his cot afterwards.
- If you're very tired, and you are breast-feeding, express enough milk for the night feed and put it into a sterile bottle, and arrange for your partner to give the baby the bottle.
- Keep some nappy-changing equipment in your bedroom so you can feed and change your baby with the minimum of disturbance.
- It's easy to get cold sitting up in bed so have a sweater or dressing gown nearby.
- Have a drink by your bedside in case you get thirsty while feeding.
- If your baby's in another room and you're concerned about not hearing his cries, invest in a baby alarm.

Introducing solids 6 months

At some stage during the first year you will have to start to wean your baby off milk and on to solid food. Official advice is that milk is sufficient for your baby for the first six months, but you may find friends and relatives pressure you to start weaning your baby earlier.

You should, however, resist all such pressure for the following reasons: first, breast milk (or its formula equivalent) is the only food that your baby needs in the early months. Second, the introduction of solids to too young a baby can lessen the desire to suck. In the case of breast-fed babies this decreases the amount taken from the breasts, which respond by producing less milk. Either way, your baby will end up having an unsatisfactory diet for his needs. Third, until your baby is at least six months old his digestive tract is incapable of digesting and absorbing complex foods. If you introduce solids before this time not only will they pass through largely undigested, but you will be putting an increased strain on his immature kidneys.

When to introduce solids

In the early months milk provides all the calories required to make your baby grow. The more he grows, the more milk he'll need to drink. But your baby's stomach can only hold a certain amount of milk at each feed, and he will eventually reach a point when he's drinking to full capacity at each feed, but still won't have enough calories to keep going. This is the point at which you'll have to introduce solids, and you'll recognize the sign when your baby starts to demand more milk and appears very unsatisfied after each feed. He may suddenly start wanting a sixth feed, having been quite content on five for the previous couple of months, or he may wake at night after previously sleeping through.

In many babies this happens at around six months and it's also an ideal time to start solids because it generally coincides with a tapering off of your baby's intense desire to suck.

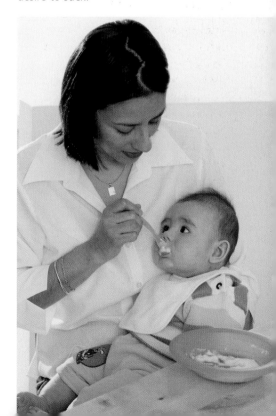

First tastes
Choose a time when he is not too hungry or tired, such as halfway through his midday feed. Scoop some food on to a spoon and insert it gently between his lips.

What foods to give

Up until the sixth month your baby will have had a diet of milk. It is therefore only sensible to start with bland, semi-liquid, foods with a smooth, creamy consistency: unsweetened purées of fruit (bananas, dessert apples, ripe pears and peaches) and vegetables (potatoes, carrots and cauliflower), and gluten-free rice cereal are ideal. Although specially manufactured "first foods" are available, it's better to make up your own. Apart from being cheaper, you'll know exactly what is in the food and that it has no additional sugar, salt, or preservatives.

Food safety

By the time your baby is ready for weaning you don't have to sterilize all cooking utensils meticulously – but you must follow the general principles of good hygiene. Wash your hands before preparing the baby's food and before feeding, make sure that all the utensils are clean and that any made-up food is kept in the refrigerator. Purées of fruit and vegetables can be kept for two days in the refrigerator or frozen in individual portions in ice-cube trays.

Giving the first solids

Start off by giving your baby one or two teaspoons of food along with a normal milk feed; the one around midday is ideal because your baby will be quite alert and not ravenously hungry. Your baby, although ready for the calories that solids provide, will be hungry for what he knows is satisfying – milk – so feed from one breast first, or give half the usual bottle. As he gets more used to solids he may want to be given them before he takes the milk.

Having decided which feed to start the solids on, prepare the small amount that you'll need and then settle in your normal position to feed the baby. When you've given him half of the milk feed, sit your baby on your lap then, using a small spoon, scoop up some food and place it gently between his lips so that he can suck the food off. Be very careful not to push the spoon in too far or he may gag on the unexpected food on the back of his tongue. He's bound to be messy at first, maybe pushing more food out than he manages to take in. If so, gently scrape the excess off the baby's face and place the spoon on to his lips as before. Your baby will signal that he's had enough by turning away from the spoon with lips shut, maybe even crying. Never force your baby to take any more food than he wants. When he's taken the solid food you can give the rest of the milk feed.

TIPS FOR FEEDING

- Give your baby only one new food at a time and then wait for several days to see if it suits.
- Use dry infant cereals that you have to make up rather than ready-mixed cereals; they contain more iron and are more nutritious for your baby.
- Only give cereal once a day.
- If he doesn't like taking food from a spoon, try dipping a clean fingertip into the food and let him suck it off.
- If you find it awkward to feed the baby on your lap, put him in a baby seat on the floor.
- Keep plenty of kitchen paper nearby to mop up any mess.
- Even early solids can stain clothes, especially banana, so put a small cloth bib on your baby.

Establishing solids 6 months to 1 year

Once your baby happily accepts one or two different solids it's important to introduce a variety of textures and tastes. As the year goes on he'll be able to deal with foods that have only been mashed or chopped and will learn to enjoy chewing and sucking on chunks of food. He'll soon move from the stage of milk feeds with "tastes" of solids to three established solid meals a day with accompanying drinks of water, diluted fruit juice or milk.

The amount of food you give your baby can be gradually increased over the weeks until he takes most of the calories that he requires for growth from solid food and not from milk. As the number of solid meals that he takes increases, the amount of milk needed correspondingly decreases. When your baby is thirsty, give him plain water or diluted fruit juice to drink, rather than milk. It is best to avoid encouraging a taste for sweet drinks, so never give your baby a commercial drink containing sugar and colourings. It's difficult to specify the amount a baby should be eating because every baby has different requirements and appetites. You'll be the best judge of how much your baby wants. If you are not sure, make slightly more of each food than you think he needs and feed as much of each individual portion as your baby wants. Freeze the leftovers.

Finger foods
It won't be long before your baby starts wanting to feed herself. Start with rusks or other easily held pieces of fruit or vegetables; be prepared for a mess. Never leave her alone while she is eating.

What foods to give

When your baby has got used to taking cereal and fruit or vegetable purées, you can start to introduce other foods – including meat, fish and dairy products –

into his diet, until he is eating virtually all the foods that you normally eat. As these gradually replace milk as the main source of his nutritional requirements, you will have to ensure that he has a balanced diet that includes foods from all the main food groups (*see p.122*).

When first starting on solids, your baby will cope best with foods of a smooth, creamy consistency. After cooking, mash, sieve or purée the food, then thin down with milk, stock or the water that the vegetables were cooked in.

By about nine months of age you can gradually introduce your baby to food with a more lumpy texture. This can be mashed with a fork or finely chopped with a sharp knife. You don't have to wait for your baby's teeth to appear before introducing lumpy food, as he can chew with his gums.

Food safety
In the first few months of your baby's life, it is essential that all feeding equipment is sterilized by one of the various methods available (*see p.103*). By the time he starts eating solids, however, it is no longer necessary to sterilize everything used at

FOOD INTOLERANCE AND ALLERGY

Don't worry too much, but do take some sensible precautions with the foods you give your baby – especially if you or your relatives have allergies.
- Don't give your baby foods containing wheat flour or gluten before he is seven months old as he may find them difficult to digest.
- Avoid giving your baby soft-boiled eggs until he is about one year old.
- Don't give a baby under one year of age honey as it can cause infant botulism, a rare but serious disease.
- Don't give your baby very high-fibre breakfast cereals as they are too difficult to digest.
- Avoid unpasteurized cheese until your baby is at least two years old.
- If your baby has a relative who suffers from an allergic condition, avoid giving peanuts, or foods containing peanuts, and shellfish until he is at least three years old.

feedtimes – although bottles and teats used for milk should still be sterilized as before. For cups, bowls and cutlery, thorough washing in hot, soapy water followed by rinsing with hot water, is adequate. However, as your baby is weaned onto solids and his diet expands to include a wider range of foods, more general questions of food safety become important, especially in the light of much publicized outbreaks of salmonella and listeria poisoning, as well as other concerns about food safety. As babies – along with the elderly, pregnant women and people suffering from illness – are among those most vulnerable to the harmful effects of bacteria in food, it is vital to have clear guidelines about the safe preparation, storage and cooking of food for infants, although the advice is equally applicable to the whole family.

Kitchen hygiene
Wash your hands with soap and hot water before handling food. Ensure that you and your family wash your hands thoroughly (not at the kitchen sink) after using the toilet and nappy changing, and after playing with pets.

Keep the kitchen scrupulously clean, especially work surfaces, chopping boards and utensils used in food preparation. Dry dishes with clean tea-towels, or leave them to dry in a rack after rinsing with hot water. Wash your dish-cloths regularly. Keep waste bins clean and covered and empty them often.

Don't leave any food out without covering it first; likewise cover food before putting it in the fridge. If you are feeding your baby from jars of baby food, it's all right to give it to him straight from the jar if you know he is going to finish the contents at one meal. Otherwise transfer some to a bowl and leave the remainder in the jar with the lid replaced, and refrigerate until the next meal.

Buying food

The rule is to shop often, choosing fresh ingredients wherever possible, and to use it quickly. Avoid bruised or damaged fruit and vegetables, and wash fruit if it is not to be peeled before eating. If buying canned goods, check that there are no dents or signs of leakage on the can, and that seals on jars are unbroken. Check sell-by dates, and avoid cut-price items that have reached their expiry dates.

Storing food

Store food in clean, covered containers in the refrigerator, and use as soon as possible. Don't store cooked and raw foods alongside each other, and put raw meat or fish on a plate at the bottom of the refrigerator so that juices cannot drip down onto food on to foods below. Don't keep food in the freezer longer than the time

TIPS FOR FOOD PREPARATION

- Before steaming and puréeing fruit, peel, remove the seeds and any bits that may choke the baby and cut up into fairly small pieces. Do the same for vegetables.
- Give your baby meat, cooked any way you like and then puréed. Don't forget fish, chicken and chicken livers, which are cheap, quick and easy to prepare. Thin down the meat with vegetable water or soup.
- Always choose the freshest looking vegetables (not wrinkled or dull-looking ones), and cook them as soon as possible.
- Handle fruit and vegetables gently. Don't cut them until you have to and don't crush and bruise them as this destroys any vitamin C present.
- Cook vegetables and fruit in as little water as possible, with a tightly fitting lid, so that they are cooked by steaming rather than by boiling; this helps to retain the vitamins.
- Cook soft-skinned fruit and vegetables in their skins because this helps to retain the vitamins and it will also give your child fibre. You may have to remove the skin if it's tough and therefore likely to choke the baby.

- Use cast-iron cooking pots. A little iron is absorbed into the food and so helps to keep your child's iron supplies topped up.
- Always make the food a suitable consistency for your baby's age. For example, a thick milk for your six-month-old baby; a thicker cream for your seven-month-old baby and a slightly chunky mash for a nine month old.
- Don't use copper pans for green leafy vegetables as copper breaks down vitamin C.
- Don't cook tinned foods for too long – you will destroy the vitamins.
- Don't add salt or sugar to your child's food; the immature kidneys can't handle a heavy salt load and you will be doing your child a favour if you don't encourage a sweet tooth.
- Avoid using too many saturated fats in your cooking – use safflower or corn oil instead.
- Don't prepare vegetables or soak them in water a long time before you cook them or you will destroy the vitamins.
- If making food in advance, cover it and leave to cool slightly. Put it into the refrigerator as this will discourage bacteria from growing.

recommended by the manufacturer, according to the star rating of your model. Foods that have been frozen must be thoroughly defrosted before cooking, and defrosted foods must never be refrozen.

Cooking and reheating food

The only safe rule as far as babies' food is concerned is to always cook thoroughly; this is especially true of meat, chicken and eggs. Never give raw eggs to babies. Try to avoid giving reheated leftovers to your baby, but if you do, make sure they are thoroughly heated through first. Chilled or frozen food should be heated up once only and any leftovers thrown away. If you're preparing food in advance, cool it as quickly as possible before storing in the refrigerator or freezer. If you put hot food straight into the fridge it may raise the temperature and warm other foods.

Ready-prepared foods

Whether you make up your baby's foods yourself or buy ready-made foods in jars is up to you. Bought foods are certainly convenient if you're travelling or you are in a hurry, but they are more expensive than home-made meals, and may not be as nutritious. However, there are now some excellent ranges of freshly prepared food. If you are going to use ready-prepared foods on a regular basis, follow the guidelines listed below.

Preparing food for babies

You'll probably already have a liquidizer or food mill; if you haven't, buy a cheap easy-to-use, hand-operated blender. You'll only have to purée food for the initial months of your baby's new diet; thereafter it can be mashed or chopped finely. At the beginning you may find it easier just to sieve the food, especially when you're not making up big batches. If you've frozen portions of food, a small pan is ideal for heating them up quickly.

For thinning down your home-prepared foods simply add water; the water in which you've steamed fruit or vegetables (with no additional salt or sugar), is ideal, but you can also add expressed milk, cow's milk,

READY-PREPARED FOODS

- Check the list of ingredients on the tin or jar. They are listed in order of concentration, so never buy anything in which water is listed first.
- Make sure that the jar is vacuum sealed when you open it, otherwise it may be contaminated.
- Don't buy "mixed dinners"; they usually contain a lot of thickener.
- If possible, buy meat and vegetable dishes separately and then combine them if you want a "mixed dinner".
- Don't keep opened jars in the refrigerator for longer than two days. Throw them away after that.

- Don't buy anything that has added salt, sugar, modified starch or monosodium glutamate (MSG).
- Never store food in opened tins; put it into a dish or bowl and keep it covered in the refrigerator.
- Don't heat the food up in the jar – it may crack.
- It is very unhygienic to feed the baby from the jar then keep the rest for a second meal, as it will have become contaminated with saliva. It's all right to feed your baby from a jar if he's going to eat the lot or if, for example, you're on the move and you don't mind throwing away what's left when he's had enough.

soup, tomato, orange or apple juice. For thickening, use ground, wholegrain cereals such as wheatgerm or rice, cottage cheese, yogurt or mashed potato. If you feel that you need to sweeten foods use naturally sweet fruit juice or dextrose. Never use refined sugar – brown or white. Our bodies don't need to have it, it's bad for our teeth and it only encourages a sweet tooth.

Giving drinks

While you're introducing solids, milk will remain an important part of your baby's diet, and will make up a large part of the daily caloric intake. By the time he's nine months old it will be safe for him to have cow's milk, either from a cup or in food. Although the milk doesn't have to be boiled, any containers that it is given in have to be thoroughly cleaned every time the baby's had a drink out of them.

As soon as your baby is having any quantity of solid food he'll need water as well as milk to drink. Start him off with 15ml (½floz) water or diluted fruit juice between and after feeds (it's a good idea to try giving it from a cup, *see right*). Thereafter he can be given it whenever he's thirsty during the day. Do bear this in mind, especially in summer or in a warm atmosphere. Avoid syrups, cordials and cola drinks and any drinks with added sugar or saccharin – these are very high in calories and also bad for your baby's teeth. Stick to water or natural, unsweetened, diluted fruit juice.

Where to feed your child

At first you will probably feed your baby on your lap or in an infant seat, but once your baby's back muscles are strong enough to

WEANING YOUR BABY ON TO A CUP

At around six months introduce your baby to drinking from a cup as part of the process of weaning from breast or bottle. The best feeds to use the cup are the lunchtime and late afternoon feeds when he'll probably be keenest to eat solids. Give the solids first and then try the cup.

There is a variety of special cups on the market. Beakers with spouts are best at the beginning as they let the liquid drip out and the baby has to half suck and half drink to get anything. Hold the beaker yourself and offer only a few sips of milk at first, but release it as soon as he wants to take it from you. As he gets more dexterous he can use a two-handled cup; the ones with specially slanted lips are ideal because they don't have to be tipped very far before the liquid comes out. Some babies, however, prefer an open cup.

Your baby will gradually wean himself off the morning feed. He'll still want a breast-feed or a bottle before bedtime until he's at least a year old – more for comfort than for food.

Using a trainer cup
Give your child water or juice in a cup. You will need to hold for him at first, but as he becomes more dexterous he will be able to hold it himself.

support him you'll probably want to get a highchair. Make sure the model you buy complies with safety standards. Chairs with a wide base are safest as they make it less likely that the chair could topple over if your child wriggles or jumps around. Check the chair regularly for any sharp edges or loose fittings. Always give the chair a good clean after meals so food doesn't gather in the nooks and crannies.

When your baby first starts using a highchair you may have to prop him up with cushions. Most highchairs have harnesses to stop the child slipping or falling out. While these are important safety features and should be used, always make sure you know how to release them quickly in case your child should choke or gag while he's eating.

If he does gag on some food, and he's almost bound to at some stage, pat your child firmly on the back until whatever food is caught dislodges itself. When you give your child a new texture, he may gag out of surprise. Talk soothingly and gently rub your child's back and he'll be able to swallow whatever was worrying him. It is essential that you know how to react quickly in any situation like this. Should the child's choking be severe, and especially if he loses consciousness, you must know what to do and the appropriate first aid procedures (see p.299). Never, ever leave your child alone while he is eating.

Feeding your child

Your baby will soon look forward to solids – not only to eat, but to play with. Feeding times will become messier so it's advisable to put newspaper or a plastic sheet below the highchair or table to catch the worst of the mess. Keep your baby well away from expensively covered walls – remember, he can throw food now.

After a month on solids your baby will have grasped the technique of getting food successfully off the spoon, and by the time he's taking two solid meals a day he will be prepared to open his mouth ready to take the food.

Self-feeding

Your baby will leave you in no doubt when he wants to feed himself: he will simply take the spoon from you. Let your baby experiment and be prepared to put up with the mess. Encourage all attempts at self-feeding because it is such a huge step forward in your baby's development, both physically and intellectually, and also because it will give your baby a feeling of accomplishment and confidence. It will help your baby to become manually dexterous and to co-ordinate muscles and

SELF-FEEDING TIPS

- Tuck a few tissues under the neckline of your baby's bib to stop his neck getting wet as he practises drinking.
- If a baby won't wear a bib, put a coloured scarf round his neck to protect his clothes.
- If your baby is going to sneeze get out of the way or you will be covered in food.
- Fit a kitchen towel holder on the back of the highchair or near it.
- Keep the highchair well away from your walls – your baby will be quite capable of throwing food by now.
- Get a non-slip bowl if you can as it will stay in place while your baby is trying to put the food on to his spoon.

movements. There is nothing that will speed up the co-ordination of eye and hand faster than getting a spoonful of food to the mouth.

Your baby will take several months to become proficient at self-feeding. His food will be a plaything and you may also worry because most of the food seems to be on the floor and not in your baby's stomach. Nature has taken care of this. At a time when a baby starts to self-feed, the initial growth spurt is beginning to slacken off and so he needs less.

Until he can manage to get the food successfully into his mouth, have a spoon each. When he can't scoop the food up, swap your full spoon for the empty one.

Be flexible about feeding

Try not to get tense at mealtimes. This will be easier to do if you don't spend too much time preparing the food and then feel resentful if it isn't eaten, and if you

Preparing foods
Make sure cooked vegetables are easy to hold but soft enough for her to chew. Congratulate her when she manages to get the food into her mouth.

FINGER FOODS

If self-feeding with a spoon seems to frustrate your baby, but his appetite is good, try finger foods. Your baby will be able to handle them easily, and even if the food is hard your baby will suck it.

Fruit and vegetables
- Any fresh fruit that is easy to hold, cut into slices minus the skin or pips, e.g. bananas
- Any vegetable that you can make into a stick or shape that is easy to grasp, e.g. carrots, broccoli
- Mashed potato

Grains and cereals
- Small pieces of sugarless dried cereal
- Little balls of cooked rice
- Wholemeal bread (without the complete grains)
- Wholemeal rusks (without the complete grains)

Protein
- Cubes of low-fat cheese
- Macaroni and cheese
- Fingers of cheese on toast
- Hamburgers and patties cut into small, easily held pieces
- Scrambled eggs
- Cottage cheese
- Any kind of meat, preferably white meat, in pieces that are easy to pick up
- Chunks of firm fish, taken off the bone
- Hard-boiled eggs in slices

SAFETY TIPS

- You should take care not to give your child food of a size that might stick in his throat or be inhaled, so you should avoid nuts, fruit with pips and seeds, unpeeled fruit with tough skins and raw vegetables.
- Don't ever leave your child eating or drinking alone in a room. If he gags, chokes or vomits, he needs immediate help (see p.299).
- Don't be obsessive, but be careful with mealtime hygiene. Use clean utensils, a clean highchair and a clean bib.
- When you are storing food in the refrigerator, cover containers with film, and never put cooked with uncooked meat.

take a few precautions so you don't have a lot of clearing up to do. The most important rule of all is not to pit your will against your baby's. In the end there is no way that you can force a baby to eat and you should never reach that point. Even if you are worried that your baby isn't taking enough food – he is. If he doesn't want to eat, his needs have temporarily shrunk. A child will always eat if he is hungry, and will eat to satisfy his needs. A period of eating very little will probably be followed by a period of eating a lot.

Balanced nutritional intake

Think in the long-term. Don't think of your baby's nutritional intake as what has been eaten that day but rather what has been eaten that week, and try to balance it out in this time scale. You may find that for a couple of days your baby will refuse everything but cereal and then on the third

day go on a fruit-eating binge, or want only cheese. A baby, like most animals, is self-regulating. He knows what he wants and when he wants it.

As with many aspects of child-rearing, take your lead from your baby on feeding. As a note of reassurance, a baby's chosen diet will be a balanced one as long as he has the correct foods to choose from.

Daily eating patterns

Regardless of the guidelines already given, or what some baby books say about nutrition, your baby doesn't have to have every kind of food at each meal. He can take a whole day's ration of protein at one meal, and the ration of carbohydrate at the next. Try to let go of the urge to control your baby's diet, and not to think that being a good mother means that he has to eat "good" food at every meal. Think of a balanced diet over a week rather than worrying about every meal he eats.

Your baby won't need more than one or two big meals a day. In between times he'll simply need a snack. Don't confine eating to meal times; with a stubborn baby they can become pitched battlegrounds. Of course, encourage your baby to have regular feeding times, but if he is going through a difficult phase, bend a little and supplement a small meal with a snack later.

If he stands up or tries to get out of the highchair take your baby out and forget about the feeding. He will come back to the food or ask for it when he is hungry. If you argue you will get upset, your baby will get upset and mealtimes will become unpleasant. Your baby will come to associate mealtimes with unhappiness and this will lead to feeding difficulties.

Food and eating 1 to 2 years

For your toddler to be strong and healthy he must have a diet with sufficient amounts of protein, carbohydrate, fats, vitamins and minerals. He will get this if you provide a wide variety of foods from which to choose (*see p.122*). The amount your child eats will largely be determined by how active he is and whether the body is going through a growth spurt. For example, the body slows down around the first birthday, but speeds up again when the child learns to walk. Thus, by the time he's 18 months old he'll need about three times the number of calories per day for his body weight that an adult does because of the speed of growth. To provide enough energy for this your child should have roughly 45 calories for 500g (1lb) weight. He'll also need 25g (1oz) protein a day, which although less than for infants, is still twice that of adults.

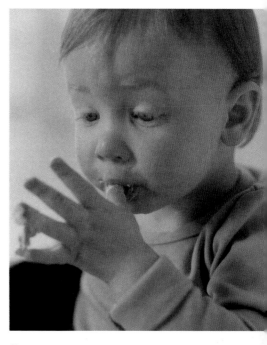

New tastes
Now that your child is eating family meals, encourage him to try different tastes and feed himself. Eating is still likely to be a very messy process.

What foods to give

By the second year your child will be able to eat more or less the same diet as you. There is no one essential food that your child has to eat in order to be healthy – he just has to have plenty of sensibly cooked, fresh foods from which to build up a balanced diet. Milk will remain an important part of the diet as it is a useful source of protein, but drinks of water should also be given when he's thirsty.

Give your child at least one nutritious protein dish at each meal, and at least five servings of fruit and vegetables a day. He'll be able to eat an increasingly large amount of food at each meal; exactly how much

DON'T GIVE YOUR CHILD:

- Whole nuts
- Popcorn
- Very rough wholemeal bread, with pieces of whole grain
- Small pieces of raw fruit or vegetable
- Fruits with stones or pips, such as plums
- Unpeeled fruit with thick skins
- Highly spiced dishes, unless he enjoys these and specifically requests them
- Salty foods
- Sugary drinks

FOOD GROUPS

Food group	Food	Content
High protein	Chicken, fish, lamb, beef, pork, offal, eggs, cheese, legumes	Protein, fat, iron, vitamins A, D, B
Milk and dairy products	Milk, cream, yogurt, ice cream, cheese	Protein, fat, calcium, vitamins A, D, B_2
Green and yellow vegetables	Cabbage, sprouts, spinach, kale, green beans, squash, lettuce, celery, courgettes	Minerals, including calcium, chlorine, chromium, cobalt, copper, manganese, potassium and sodium
Citrus fruits	Oranges, grapefruit, lemons	Vitamin C
Other vegetables and fruits	Potatoes, beetroot, corn, carrots, cauliflower, pineapples, apricots	Carbohydrates, vitamins A, B, C
Breads and cereals	Wholemeal bread, noodles, rice	Protein, carbohydrates, B vitamins, iron and calcium
Fats	Butter, margarine, vegetable oils	Vitamins A, D

will depend on his appetite, but he'll probably be able to take a third to half a standard adult portion each time.

Help your child to develop good eating habits by not sugaring or salting the food and by not giving "empty" calories in the form of cakes, biscuits and sweets. Don't give your child sweet puddings – fruits, yogurts or fruit purées are much better.

Eating patterns

By the time your child is toddling he will eat three smallish meals a day with a snack in the morning and the afternoon. Be prepared for your child's appetite to be a bit erratic during this year: he may be starving one day and eat everything that you serve, but the next day eat hardly anything. And don't worry if your child goes on food binges, eating only one food

and refusing all others; it is a perfectly normal occurrence at this age (see p.125). Similarly, don't be alarmed when he goes through periods of little appetite – your child knows exactly what he needs and will eat to keep pace with himself.

Giving sweets

I believe that it is wrong to deprive children of sweets. Deprivation very often leads to furtiveness and dishonesty. I do believe, however, in sweet rationing. But I am not beyond giving sweets as a reward as this kind of reward is immediately understood by your child. I rationed my own children to one sweet after lunch and supper. This scheme worked with all four of them and encouraged self-control and good eating habits. They should always brush their teeth afterwards.

SAMPLE DIET FOR A 14-MONTH-OLD CHILD

Day 1	Day 2	Day 3
Breakfast 1 scrambled egg, ½ slice buttered brown toast	**Breakfast** 1 cup diluted fresh orange juice, 125g (5oz) yogurt, 1 tablespoon baby muesli, ½ tablespoon wheatgerm, 50ml (1½floz) milk, ½ mashed banana	**Breakfast** 50g (2oz) cereal plus milk, 1 cup diluted fresh orange juice, ½ banana
Mid-morning 1 cup diluted orange juice, 1 apple	**Mid-morning** 1 cup diluted fruit juice, 1 biscuit	**Mid-morning** 1 cup water, 1 apple
Lunch 50g (2oz) white fish, ½ brown bread roll, 1 tablespoon green beans, 1 cup diluted fruit juice	**Lunch** 1 cup milk, 1 cup water, 2 fish fingers, 1 tablespoon peas	**Lunch** Egg florentine, (2 tablespoons spinach, 1 poached egg, 25–50g/1–2oz cheese), 1 sugar-free fruit yogurt, 1 cup milk
Mid-afternoon 1 cup water	**Mid-afternoon** 1 cup water	**Mid-afternoon** 2 cups diluted apple juice, 1 oat cookie
Dinner 150g (6oz) baked beans, 50–75g (2–3oz) potatoes, 50g (2oz) grated cheese, ½ banana, 1 cup milk	**Dinner** 1 egg omelette with 25g (1oz) cheese, 1 tablespoon fresh green beans, 1 cup milk, ¼ slice brown bread	**Dinner** Ham sandwich with wholemeal bread, cubes of cheese, raw carrot, cubes of melon

Eating at the table

Introduce your toddler to family mealtimes by pulling the highchair up to the table when you have a meal. He'll be able to see everything that is going on and will gradually become more accustomed to family meals and to mealtime behaviour and good manners. To make sure that he feels included give your toddler the same food that you are eating, but prepare it in a way that he can manage to spoon or pick up without your help. This process will be much easier if your child is quite neat and able to eat without much mess.

However, if your child is very messy you may find it more successful to feed him before the rest of the family and to then bring the child to the table with a few favourite finger foods when you eat.

Don't expect your child to automatically adopt adult behaviour, especially at the beginning. Around the age of 12 months he'll be used to crawling and "cruising" and will probably not be far off walking, so don't be surprised if your child is unwilling to sit still for long. If he insists on getting down, let him do so; he'll probably come back for more food in a few minutes and

will soon learn that food means sitting still and eating. If, however, he shows no signs of wanting to come back don't insist that all his food is eaten. If he is hungry he'll make up for it at the next meal.

Messy eaters

Some children take so much pleasure in eating that they find it hard to concentrate on the job of getting food from plate to mouth. Try to be philosophical about the mess your toddler makes at mealtimes. It is a transient phase during which he will be learning how to co-ordinate. You may think that he's learning this at your expense, but do try to stay cool and calm. And remember, being tidy is nowhere near as important as your child being happy and eating the way he wants to. Make mealtimes pleasant and minimize the tidying up by following these tips.

- Stand the highchair on a plastic table cloth so that you can mop up spillages easily; otherwise just surround the

Eating as a family
Even if your child has finished her own food, she will enjoy sitting at the table with you while you eat. Take the opportunity to try her on new tastes.

highchair with newspaper that can be gathered up after each meal.
- Draw a circle on the highchair tray to show your baby where he should put his cup down. Make the positioning of the mug into a game.
- Most toddlers don't like having their faces wiped with a cloth. Use your own hand dipped into water; for some reason, this is much more acceptable and will do the job just as well.
- If your child is very messy, take him over to the sink to be washed. Make a game out of washing hands; let your child play some water games while you're there.
- Let your child dip both his hands into a bowl of water when he's still sitting in the highchair and then just wipe them dry with a towel.

Possible feeding problems 1 to 2 years

Food fads

Between the age of one and two your child will begin to show pronounced preferences for certain foods. It is common for children to have these food fads, eating one food and refusing everything else. He may, for example, go right off meat and want to eat only yogurt. A week of this may be followed by a dislike of yogurt and desire to eat cheese and fruit.

Being a good parent means not making a fuss about any of this. There is nothing magical about any one food and there is always a nutritious alternative to the one that your child rejects. Don't spend time cooking food that you know your toddler will refuse and then feel resentful when he does. Take the easy way out and cook food that you know he really wants, even if it's something of which you disapprove.

Research has shown that as long as you offer your child a wide variety of foods, the diet that he chooses will be a balanced one. There is, after all, no reason on earth why your toddler should eat the food that you choose. His tastes are not necessarily yours and, if it is your child's happiness and well-being that you are concerned about, you will soon realize that it is more important that he eats something that he likes than that he doesn't eat at all. Be flexible about what you give your toddler.

Disliked foods

I really don't believe in camouflaging a disliked food, mixing it with a food that is well-liked, or bribing a child to have a spoonful of a disliked food with a spoonful of one that is liked.

If your child dislikes something, give him an alternative food that provides the same nutrients and that you know he likes. If your baby shows a profound dislike for one food, trying to trick or bribe him into eating it may well result in the child refusing other foods as well. When you introduce a new food do it when you know your baby is hungry and he's more likely to take it.

The only thing that you must be on your guard against is your child excluding all of one food group. If this happens then his diet will become unbalanced. Other than that there is absolutely nothing wrong with odd fads, and don't forget, the more worked up you get about them the more your toddler will display them because he'll very quickly learn that it is a way of manipulating you. So play them down.

Weight problems

If your baby is offered the right kind of food he can be neither underweight nor overweight. Your baby will always regulate his food and will take in just enough to supply his needs at any particular time. An underweight or overweight baby is, therefore, the fault of the parent in offering the wrong kind of food.

Overweight Excess weight in a baby is nearly always due to too much fatty meat, too many sweetened drinks and refined carbohydrates (cakes, biscuits, jams and sweet foods) in the diet. It may also be because you curb your toddler's activity by keeping him in a pram or playpen and not allowing him to use up energy by crawling and walking. Always encourage your child to be active by playing games with him yourself – the livelier the better.

Underweight Unless purposely deprived of food, very few toddlers are actually underweight, even if they weigh less than another baby of the same age and sex. Many parents worry unnecessarily about having a small, thin toddler; some children, like some adults, are naturally (and healthily) small and thin.

If you are giving your baby a balanced diet and he is happy, contented and developing normally (see p.189) then you probably have nothing to worry about. However, if you are concerned, check with your doctor or health visitor.

Food and eating 2 to 3 years

Your child's daily calorie requirements will continue to increase as he grows, and during the third year he'll need roughly 50 calories a day for every 500g (1lb) that he weighs. His nutritional requirements will remain the same and he'll need a variety of well prepared foods with sufficient vitamins and minerals. Because he is growing, he still needs more protein and calories for his body weight than an adult.

TIPS FOR FEEDING TWO YEAR OLDS

- Always make sure that a meal contains at least one food you know your child likes.
- Always serve small amounts and allow second helpings. A large piled-up plate is intimidating for a child.
- Keep foods simple. Children like to see what they are eating: they don't like messy foods.
- Always offer a variety of foods to guarantee a balanced diet.
- Try livening up your toddler's meal by using more colourful food.
- Until your child is going to school, include a finger food in a meal where possible.
- Include foods that are fun to eat like jelly, potato wedges, or ice cream from a cone.

What foods to give

Between the ages of two and three years, children tend to like dairy products like milk, yogurt, ice cream and cottage cheese as well as breads and cereals. They dislike, and may even reject, meat, fruit and vegetables. Don't get worked up about this; try, instead, to find a couple of meats and some fruits and vegetables that he does like and stick to them until your child seems to want a change.

Give your child two or three servings of protein, and five or more servings of fruit and vegetables a day. Provide four or more servings of wholemeal bread and cereal – a serving of bread being ½ a slice, and one to two tablespoons of cereal. Avoid high-calorie, starchy foods.

Eating patterns

Your child may continue to have food fads (see p.125) throughout this year, and may also demand rituals at mealtimes. A ritual is something that your child has to have repeated. For instance, it may become a ritual to have a sandwich cut on the diagonal: your child will refuse a sandwich that is cut in any other way. Some children

Decorative food
One way to encourage your child to try different foods is to decorate it or make interesting shapes. Then ask your child to try the whiskers, or eat the ears and nose.

want their plate set in a certain way and will throw a tantrum if it is not. The best way to approach both of these rituals is with patience. After all, adults have food rituals too: we sit in certain positions at the table, and may prefer our tables set in a certain way. As long as it is reasonable, you should indulge your child's ritual. On the other hand, if a ritual interferes seriously with the intake of food or disrupts the family, try to reason with your child and explain that such behaviour is not fair on others. Be firm, but be prepared for it to take several attempts to break an undesirable ritual.

Organizing mealtimes

Your child should be getting quite familiar with the social aspects of eating but don't expect too much from him. It is very difficult for a child to concentrate on eating with a spoon, not spilling the drink, not making a mess and being quiet while eating at the table. He is trying to listen to what you are all saying, to participate in the conversation, and to concentrate on the food. He is trying to learn a great many new skills all at once, and viewed like this it is not surprising he can get a bit excitable, just to break the tension, and there are bound to be accidents. Again, be understanding and flexible.

MAKING MEALTIMES FUN

As with all feeding, the key word is flexibility. You and your child should enjoy yourselves, so give a little thought to making mealtimes entertaining for all of you.

- Ice cream cones don't have to be used just for ice cream. Fill one with cheese and tomato chopped together or a tuna fish salad. This means that you can give your three-year-old a snack on the move.
- Encourage your child to sometimes "build" his meal from sandwiches, cubes of cheese, vegetables and dried fruit. He could build a house or a car or a boat, and when it is finished eat it.

- If he wants to use a knife, give your child a plastic or blunt-ended one.
- Let your child use a straw for drinking sometimes. So that he won't tip the drink over cut the straw off so that there is no more than 5cm (2in) above the cup, or use a bendy straw.
- Be open to innovation and occasionally serve your child's meal on a doll's plate or on a flat toy.
- Fill a cake tin with lots of different finger foods such as cubes of cheese, bits of cold meat, raw vegetables, fruit and tiny sandwiches and let your child pick out what he wants.

Possible feeding problems 2 to 3 years

The overweight toddler

Obesity in a young child is nearly always caused by lack of exercise combined with a poor diet that is high in "empty" calories, for example, highly refined starches and carbohydrates such as those found in cakes, biscuits, sweets, chocolate, ice cream and sweet drinks. If your toddler is overweight, consider doing some of the following things:

- Look at the amount of sugar your child is consuming (especially "hidden" sugars added to foods). There is absolutely no need for your child to take in any added sugar with his foods
- If you have been adding sugar to food, stop now so your child gets used to the natural sweetness of food such as fruit.
- Look at the amount of food your child is eating as snacks. Try cutting them down and changing them to low-calorie, healthy snacks (see p.130).
- Reduce the amount of fat you use in food preparation. Your child probably won't even notice. Don't fry in fat but grill; buy the leanest meat that you can and trim off any fat; cut down on cheese; give him semi-skimmed not full-fat milk once he's over two.
- Make sure your child is getting every opportunity to be active and to play. Encourage active sports. Invite friends to the house for a game of football or go outside with your child and play an active game with him.
- Look at the amount of milk your child is consuming. If he is taking a lot of protein, plus a lot of milk, he is probably getting too much. Cut down.

- Try giving your child more homemade and uncooked food. Pre-packaged foods, especially salty, fatty snacks, are often high in calories.

Refusing to eat

This is one of the first signs that your child is ill, so observe him carefully. Is he more clumsy than normal, rather pale and fretful? If so check his temperature and get medical advice if you're worried. At other times your child may simply not be hungry. He may have had a lot of snacks before a meal – for example, if he's had a snack or a drink of milk in the hour before the meal it's not fair to expect your child to eat with his normal enthusiasm.

Sometimes your child may appear to refuse food for no reason at all. What you must never do in this situation is try to force your child to eat, so don't be taken in by your child's capricious behaviour. Try to be casual about it and get on with something else. If you insist, mealtimes can quickly become a battleground and in the end you'll always lose. If you ignore your child he'll eat when he's hungry; if he doesn't, don't worry. He'll make it up for it at the next meal.

Food allergy

This should not be confused with food intolerance. Food intolerance simply means that some food doesn't suit you as well as others. Food allergy, however, is quite specific and quite rare. Most cases of suspected food allergy turn out to be simple intolerance, or the combination of a fussy child and a fussy parent.

Picky eaters
Make a game out of eating. Give her little pots
containing different foods, and some chopped
vegetables so she can "make" her own meal.

Allergy is the body's reaction to a foreign protein or chemical. It is a protective mechanism and produces symptoms ranging from a headache, a slight rash and a feeling of indigestion, to profuse vomiting, swelling of the mouth, tongue, face and eyes, widespread red blotches in the skin, diarrhoea and an extremely ill child. When first exposed to the allergen the reaction may be very slight but, if exposure is repeated, the allergic response may get worse and worse.

One of the reasons why food allergies have attracted so much attention is that they have been blamed for behavioural disturbances in children, but the number of cases where this can be proven is infinitesimal. The only proof of a true allergy as the cause of behavioural problems is when the food is withdrawn and the child's behaviour changes markedly, then when the offending substance is reintroduced the child reverts to the previous bad behaviour. Nothing else counts as proof; improvement on its own is not proof, there has to be confirmation by the reappearance of the child's symptoms after the reintroduction of the substance.

In a very small number of cases there is proof, although even then it is very difficult to decide whether the child is responding to the removal of the food or the added attention he has received from parents, doctors, nurses and relatives. It may be, and in many cases it undoubtedly is the case, that bad behaviour is a cry for attention, love and affection and if this were given the behaviour improves anyway. Parents should not sidestep this issue, and should try changing their ways before any food is withdrawn from a child's diet.

Talk to your doctor
The reason I am so concerned about allergy and intolerance is that many a child has needlessly had his diet seriously curtailed and robbed of nutritious foodstuffs in the name of this unproven association. Parents should never attempt to isolate a food allergy on their own or change the child's diet, without a doctor's advice: a clear diagnosis from a paediatric allergist should always be the first step.

Snacks 1 to 3 years

Studies performed on the eating habits of children show that under the age of four or five children prefer to eat, indeed their bodies require them to eat, frequently throughout the day. This is largely because their tiny stomachs can't cope with three adult-sized meals a day, and we shouldn't try to impose an adult eating pattern on them. The actual range of how often a child eats is quite wide – from three to 14 times a day, with the average being around five to seven times. The size of the meal he'll want will vary throughout the day, but as a general rule the more often a child eats, the smaller the meals will be. On average, children take in the same amount of nutrients, regardless of the number of times they eat in the day. However, what is important is not the number of times that your child eats but what he eats.

Sensible snacks are those that provide adequate calories in a healthy and nutritious form but contribute little to tooth decay. They include fresh fruit and vegetables, cubes of cheese, cheese sandwiches with wholemeal bread, and fresh fruit juice.

Most commercial snack foods, especially those bought from vending machines and fast-food stores are highly refined and processed, contain a lot of calories and very few nutrients. Avoid foods like biscuits, sweets, cakes, ice cream, raisins and other dried foods.

Planning out snacks

Snack food should contribute to the whole day's nutrition, so don't leave them to chance; plan them out carefully. It is important to introduce variety as snacks can become boring to children just as meals can. Some of the ways in which you can do this are as follows:

Fruit smoothies

Purée some soft fruit and add milk and/or yogurt to make your child a drink packed with vitamins and minerals; he might like to help you make it as well.

- Try to co-ordinate meals and snacks so that you serve different foods in the snacks and in the meals.
- Try to make the snacks amusing. Place a tomato on top of an open wholemeal sandwich so that it looks like a smiling face, for instance, or cut up pieces of fruit in unusual shapes.
- Try to involve your child in planning and, more important, helping to prepare part of the snack.
- Take advantage of the activity to make the snack exciting and even educational. For example, have your child help you shell peas or make bread and then use whatever you've prepared together as part of the snack.
- You could think about serving an ordinary food in a different form: yogurt, which your child might not like straight out of the tub, becomes more like ice cream if you freeze it.
- Drinks are one of the best kinds of snacks, particularly if they are milk-based – though you should use semi-skimmed or skimmed milk once a child is over two years. Milk-based snacks are nutritious because they contain protein, calcium, iron and many of the B vitamins.

Snacks and tooth decay

Food encourages the development of tooth decay. Every time we eat, small amounts of food are left on and between the teeth, and these particles, particularly if they are starches, are broken down to acid by bacteria in your mouth. It is these acids that dissolve the outer enamel layer of the tooth and cause tooth decay.

Carbohydrates and starches form the major food source for bacteria in the mouth. Refined sugar (sucrose) found in sweetened drinks, cakes and sweets is more easily converted to acid by bacteria than any other form of food. It has been shown that the higher the sugar content of the food the more acid can be made by the bacteria and the greater the likelihood of tooth decay. Fruit juices can also be acidic and should be given with food, or confined to mealtimes.

Not surprisingly, sticky foods such as raisins stay on the teeth for longer, so the bacteria are given more time to convert the starches into acid. Sticky foods, therefore, give rise to more tooth decay than sweet foods that don't remain in the mouth for long, getting trapped between, or coating, the teeth. A sticky toffee, for example, will lead to tooth decay more easily than the same amount of sugar taken in a drink. The same applies to other chewy foods.

In considering the snacks that you give your child you must consider the effect they will have on tooth decay. You can start early in your baby's life by never adding sugar to the food. Nobody needs refined sugar; the body can manage perfectly well without it, so do your children a favour and don't encourage a sweet tooth.

Another precaution you can take is to encourage your child to brush his teeth after eating any food. Ask your dentist for advice on which type of toothpaste you should use. In addition, you can avoid ending a meal with a sweet dessert. It is much better to finish off with fruit or, better still, a piece of cheese. Cheese is alkaline and neutralizes the acid in the mouth, therefore helping to prevent tooth decay in the long term.

8 Bowel and bladder function

The most important event in relation to the passing of urine and stools will be when your child manages to stay dry and clean both day and night. However, this won't happen until she's physiologically and mentally mature enough to co-operate. You can't speed up this process – you can only help your child as she gradually gains control over her own body.

Passing urine birth to 1 year

In young babies, the bladder empties itself automatically, and a baby will pass urine frequently during the day and night. This is because the bladder is unable to hold urine for any length of time and as soon as it contains a little the bladder wall is stretched and stimulates emptying. This is perfectly normal, and you cannot expect your baby to behave any differently until the bladder has developed enough to hold urine. This rarely happens before the age of 15 months.

Bowel movements birth to 1 year

For the 24 hours after delivery your baby will excrete a sticky black substance called meconium. This filled the intestines when your baby was in the womb and has to be eliminated before normal digestion can take place.

Your baby will soon settle into a regular routine, and the stools will become firmer. As long as your baby is healthy, happy and gaining weight, you should pay very little attention to her bowel movements. Don't become obsessive about them and don't worry about them.

Though babies vary a great deal in the number of stools that they pass, there is a tendency for them to become fewer as the baby grows older. At the beginning your baby may pass three or four a day, but at the end of a couple of weeks she may only have a bowel movement every other day.

This is perfectly normal. In fact, all the following are normal: loose, unformed stools; a totally green stool; a bowel movement after every meal or up to six stools in the first few days.

Using the potty
A baby who isn't ready can't be potty trained. A baby who is doesn't need any training. Don't try to force your child. Take your lead from him.

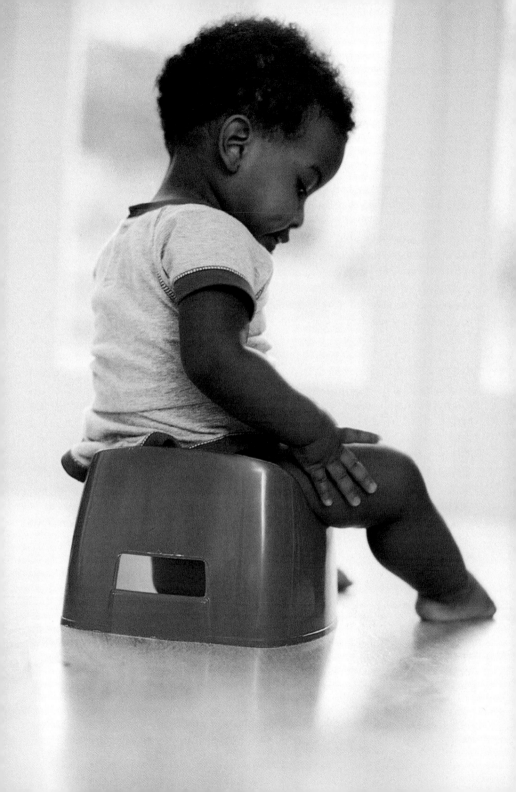

Stools of the breast-fed baby

During the first day or so, the stools will be greenish-black, smooth, sticky, meconium ones; afterwards, the light-yellow stools typical of the breast-fed baby will appear. The number of stools per day is quite unimportant. Some babies have several, some have few, and some may have a bowel movement every time they feed. The stools may be pasty or they may be no thicker than cream soup but they are rarely hard or smelly. Breast-fed babies hardly ever suffer from constipation; they absorb practically all of the milk so there is very little waste. It is therefore quite logical that they might not move their bowels more than once every third day.

Stools of the bottle-fed baby

Once the digestion has settled down, a baby fed on formula tends to have more frequent stools and the stools tend to be firmer, browner and smellier than those of a breast-fed baby.

You may find that your baby's stools are soft, like scrambled eggs, but the commonest tendency is for the stools to be rather hard. The easiest way to put this right is to give your baby cooled, boiled water to drink in between feeds, tipping it gently into the mouth with a spoon. Once your baby is on solid food you can soften the stools by adding a little prune juice to your baby's drink, or by giving her a few teaspoonfuls of sieved fruit thinned down with water.

Never add sugar to your baby's bottles, but if the formula has a high sugar content, your baby's stools may be loose, green and curdy. If this goes on ask your doctor for advice.

Changes in bowel movements

As long as your baby is doing well, it really doesn't matter if the stools change in appearance from one day to the next. A slightly lighter or a slightly darker colour doesn't mean anything serious. A slightly less well formed or a harder stool doesn't mean to say that there is anything wrong. If you are ever worried, however, do consult your midwife, community nurse or doctor who will be glad to give you advice. Looseness of the stools per se doesn't indicate an abnormality or an infection. On the other hand, watery stools that are accompanied by a sudden change in colour, a sudden change in the frequency of passing stools, plus a change in the smell of the stools, should be mentioned to your doctor or health visitor, especially if you feel that your baby is "off colour". As a general rule, changes in the number and colour of the movements are much less important than changes in the smell and the amount of water in the stools.

As your baby gets older be prepared for the stools to change whenever you add a new food, particularly fruits and vegetables. If the stools become very loose after introducing a new food don't give it again for several days and then try it again in a very small quantity. Don't forget that beetroot can turn the stools red and that it is quite normal for a stool to turn brown or green if left exposed to the air.

Streaks of blood in the stools are never normal. Even though the cause may be quite minor, like a tiny crack in the skin around the anus, you should consult your doctor. Large amounts of blood, pus or mucus may herald an intestinal infection, so seek medical advice immediately.

Possible bowel problems birth to 1 year

Constipation

This is hard, infrequent stools. Infrequent means less often than every three or four days, and hard means hard enough to cause discomfort or pain. Constipation itself cannot make a child ill, and old theories that constipation poisoned the system were discarded long ago.

Constipation without any other signs of illness is nothing to worry about. However, if your baby is straining a great deal to pass a hard stool and it causes discomfort, you should consult your doctor to see if it is necessary to get any medicine to soften the stool. Doctors are loathe to use laxatives or purgatives for a young child, and it is hardly ever necessary to resort to such treatments. In a very small baby constipation is rare and it is nearly always due to not giving the baby enough water. It can, therefore, nearly always be cured by giving your baby more drinks or by adding a little extra water to each bottle. Don't try the old-fashioned remedy of adding sugar to your baby's feeds – it doesn't work, your baby doesn't need sugar, and it will only encourage a sweet tooth.

By far the best way to soften the stools is to alter the diet and to add a little more fibre and roughage. A couple of teaspoons of prune juice added to your baby's water drink will help, and when she's on solids, two teaspoons of sieved stewed prunes with the evening feed should bring results.

Once your child is on a varied diet, he should never be constipated unless his meals don't include enough fresh fruit, vegetables, whole-wheat breads and whole grains. It is very easy to prevent him becoming constipated once he is eating solids: you simply add more of these foods to his diet. In a young child, the bowel always responds to the addition of complex carbohydrates (which are contained in root and green vegetables), because the cellulose within them holds water in the stools and makes them more bulky and soft.

There are really only two reasons why a child should become chronically constipated. The first is due to an over-fussy parent who has become obsessive about the regularity of the child's bowel motions. The second is if a child has previously felt great discomfort and pain when trying to pass a motion, and retains the stools to prevent that pain recurring.

It is fairly common for your child to have a few days of constipation after having an illness with a high temperature. This is partly because she has taken in very little food so there are no waste products to pass, and partly because of the loss of water due to sweating with the fever. The body conserves all the moisture it can by absorbing it from the stools and this makes the motions hard. This kind of constipation needs no treatment at all and it will correct itself when your child goes back on to a proper diet. Don't use patent medicines, laxatives, suppositories or enemas without seeking medical advice.

Diarrhoea

True diarrhoea – very loose, frequent, watery stools – is a sign that the intestines are irritated and that the food is "hurrying" along. Once your child is on solids, a change of diet, such as the introduction of a new fruit or vegetable, may be enough to cause it.

Diarrhoea in young babies is always serious because the intestines are not given sufficient time to absorb the water essential for life, and severe dehydration can develop quite rapidly. There is no need to be concerned about the odd loose stool if your baby remains well, eats normally and is perfectly happy. However, if your baby has very watery stools, if they are green and smelly, if she refuses food, has a fever of 38°C (100°F) or more, has blood or pus in the stools and is listless with dark rings under her eyes, then you should contact your doctor immediately.

If your baby is very young (under four months) seek medical advice or go to the hospital emergency department as soon as possible. With an older baby, stop all food and just give drinks of water until you can see your doctor. If your baby has mild diarrhoea and no other symptoms, you can start treatment immediately yourself. If you are breast-feeding your baby continue to nurse. Diarrhoea usually clears up well on breast-milk. If you are bottle-feeding, make up the next bottle at half-strength, with half the regular formula to the usual amount of water. Let your baby take as much of this mixture as often as she likes. She may be off food, taking only small amounts, and will become hungry more quickly. If mild diarrhoea doesn't improve within two days, seek medical advice even if your child seems well.

Once the diarrhoea has cleared up you can start re-introducing normal food. The best foods to start off with are mild, milky ones. Start off with a third to a half the usual serving on the first day and on the second day a half to two thirds of the usual amount. On the third day, if all is going well, and she has a good appetite, you can go back to regular servings.

Gaining control 1 to 2 years

I believe that there's only one way to approach the whole subject of bowel and bladder control and that's to take signals from your child and to help, not train, your child. Control over the bowel or bladder is rare before the age of 15 or 18 months; sometimes it is very much later.

Gaining bowel control
It is not uncommon for babies to empty their bowels during a meal or very soon after as early as three months. Some parents take this to be an early sign of readiness for toilet training. It is not at all. It is simply the working of the gastro-colic reflex that stimulates the passage of food down the intestines to the bowels when food is eaten.

Your child will be ready for your help when she can make the connection between inner sensations and the physical reality of passing urine and faeces. You'll notice this awareness when, for example, she suddenly stops what she's doing and points to the nappy, or otherwise attracts your attention with a cry or a shout then fills her nappy. Your child's awareness of having a full rectum and a full bladder will probably occur at about the same time. However, her ability to deal with the two sensations will be different.

Introducing a potty

It's much easier to "hold on" to a full rectum than it is to a full bladder, and your child will probably achieve bowel control first. Because of this it's sensible to help your child use the potty for bowel movements first. It's also sensible from your point of view because bowel movements are more predictable, so you can prepare for them on your child's behalf. When your child makes her special movements or sounds, suggest that she use the potty. Make things easier by deliberately leaving

off any clothes or nappies so that nothing hinders her getting on to the potty in time.

After she's been on the potty, wipe her bottom (front to back in girls) with some toilet paper. Put the wipes in the potty and flush the whole lot down the lavatory. Remove any trace of faeces and rinse out the potty, then wash it with disinfectant.

Never force your child to sit on the potty. It will have the reverse effect, so that when you next suggest that she use it you'll be faced with a point-blank refusal or even a tantrum. Instead, just forget about the potty for a few days and then re-introduce it in a casual way.

Using a potty
Keeping a potty for your child's favourite doll or teddy bear can encourage her to sit on the potty too.

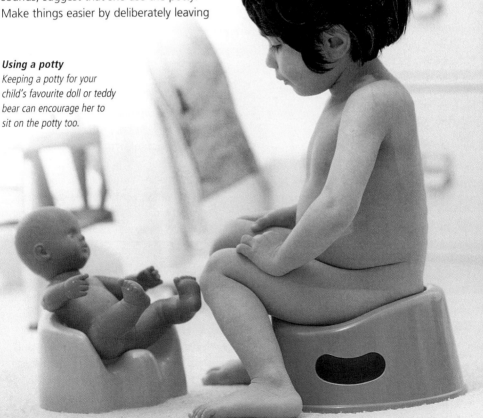

Gaining bladder control

This process will have to be gradual and for it to be successful your child's bladder will have to be capable of holding more than a little urine without spontaneously emptying. One of the first signs of this maturity is your child's nappy being dry after a reasonable length of time (for example, after an afternoon nap). Once your child stays dry regularly throughout this nap you can start to leave off that nappy. Before you put your child down for her nap, encourage her to empty her bladder. If she does, congratulate your child; if she doesn't, don't make a fuss, just try it again another day.

When she can do this successfully and can indicate to you that she wants to go on to the potty, you can start leaving off nappies completely during the day. Never start this until she can wait quite comfortably for a few minutes while you take down her clothes.

TIPS

- Do let your child develop at her own pace. There is no way that you can speed up the process, you can only be there to help your child along.
- Let your child decide whether or not to sit on the potty. You can suggest that she does but you should never force the issue.
- Do treat your child's faeces in a sensible manner, and never show any disgust or dislike for them. They're a natural part of your child and initially she'll be very proud of them.
- Do not delay once your child has signalled as control is only possible for a short time.
- Praise your child and treat her control as an accomplishment.

There will be accidents so be prepared for them and always be sympathetic. Never scold your toddler if she has an accident: it's not her fault. Just mop up and change any clothing without making a fuss.

Toilet "training"

I'm whole-heartedly against toilet training. For me there are no arguments in favour of it, only arguments against it. I believe that toilet training proceedings and the attitudes that advocate "training" a child's bowel movements and bladder function should be eradicated from child care and child development.

The reasons I feel this so strongly are as follows. It is impossible to train a child to do anything unless the body has developed to a point where it is anatomically and physiologically able to perform the tasks that you demand of it.

When applied to bowel and bladder function this means that it is impossible for your child to control either of these unless the bowel and the bladder muscles are strong enough to hold urine and faeces, and that, at a given order from the brain, the nerves to the bowel and bladder are mature enough to obey the order and evacuate. If this level of development has not been reached there is nothing that your child can do to adhere to your "training" programme.

You can see immediately what a dreadful position this puts your child in. She is aware of what you want, but her body is unable to perform the task. Your toddler's desire to please you overrides almost all other desires, and in this she is frustrated. She becomes unhappy at not being able to please you and may then feel inadequate, ashamed, guilty and finally resentful. If you insist on a toilet programme when your child's not ready for it, the result can only be sadness. The relationship with your child will deteriorate. You will become a source of unhappiness, and bowel movements and potty training will become a battleground of your baby's will against your nerves, and you'll always be the loser. You cannot make your baby pass a stool, or keep a nappy dry, and if you try to do either of these things you'll make your child suffer every time the inevitable accident occurs.

Gaining control 2 to 3 years

While it is likely that your child has already shown signs of both muscle control and has an awareness of urination and bowel movements, it is also possible that she hasn't. If this is the case, don't worry. The procedure for helping your child to understand her bodily requirements is the same, no matter what age she starts.

If, however, your child has gained some control, you'll find that she'll continue to improve during this year. It has been shown that by two-and-a-half years old approximately 90 per cent of girls and 75 per cent of boys have complete bowel control and even go to the lavatory alone. However, the same study showed that more than half the children of that age were still wet at night, although they could go without a nappy during the day.

Staying dry at night

Bladder control at night comes last of all. It is often not possible for a two-and-a-half year old child to hold urine for much longer than four to five hours, and it is often much less than that. The signal to start leaving off the night-time nappy is when she wakes up with a dry nappy regularly. When this happens, leave off the nappy, but take the child to the potty and encourage her to empty her bladder before she goes to sleep. Leave a potty beside the bed and suggest that she use that if necessary during the night. Do leave a night light on so that she can see what she's doing and be prepared to give any assistance if necessary.

It's a big step for your child to stop relying on you and to take responsibility for using the potty herself. Encourage your child as soon as she shows any signs of taking this responsibility because it is important that you help and that she feels a sense of confidence.

Be prepared for accidents, but never get upset by them. You can minimize the amount of work by:
- Protecting the mattress with a rubber sheet, putting your usual sheet on top.
- Putting a small rubber sheet on top of the child's ordinary sheet, with a half sheet over that. If there's an accident you can quickly remove the half sheet and spare the rest of the undersheet.
- Making sure that night wear is free of zips so that your child can take down her clothes without any trouble.
- Avoiding any confrontation by not forcing your child in any way. Gentleness and understanding invariably pay off.

Getting used to the lavatory

Once your child is using the potty regularly introduce her to the idea of using the lavatory. To help your child feel safe and secure, get a special seat that fits inside the lavatory rim for her to sit on. If she's worried, suggest that she holds on to the sides of the seat, and always stay near at hand. You'll probably need to put a small step or box in front of the lavatory so that she can get up easily. Show your little boy how to stand in front of the lavatory and aim at the bowl. Put a piece of toilet paper in the bowl for him to aim at.

If your child wants to do everything alone, respect her wishes. However, do teach your child how to wipe her or himself after using the lavatory, especially your little girl. It is very important that she learns to wipe from the front to the back to avoid spreading any bacteria from the rectum to the vagina.

Possible bowel and bladder problems 2 to 3 years

Late developers

Some children acquire bowel and bladder control much later than others, and this may present a problem to the parents. In nearly all cases it is wrong to blame the child. Often there is a family history of lateness in acquiring bladder control. If your child is wet during the day and night, most doctors feel that there is no need to investigate this difficulty before your child is three years old, and if she is only wet at night your doctor may feel that these investigations may be put off until she is five years old. Whenever you go along to your doctor about a urinary problem with your child, take along a specimen of urine.

Bed-wetting

Many children, more especially boys, will not be able to be dry at night until well after the age of four and this is perfectly normal. If they are dry, then a change of surroundings or routine, such as the arrival of another baby, an illness or a spell of unhappiness, such as starting school may cause them to start wetting the bed. If your child has a bed-wetting problem, lightly suggest that she thinks about going for the whole night staying dry – positive

Encourage good hygiene
Girls are generally more receptive to being taught good hygiene than boys. Let her flush the lavatory if she wants to, but remind her to wash her hands afterwards.

TIPS

- Whenever you travel, make sure that you have a potty with you so that your child can go under any circumstances without having to wait. Put the potty on the floor in the back of your car so that you can stop anywhere along the road instead of having to worry about finding a public lavatory in a hurry.
- If she sits down and can't do anything, turn on the taps; this works for babies as well as adults.
- If you keep star charts for different accomplishments, keep one for each success.
- If you have a potty in the bathroom, you and your child could go to the lavatory at the same time.
- Let your child accompany you to the lavatory at an early age so that she can learn from watching you. This works particularly well with boys.
- Tell your child quite firmly and sympathetically that accidents will always be ignored and forgiven, and that she's not to worry about them.
- Get a potty well before you think your child will need it. You can explain why it is there and that when she is old enough she'll be able to use it. This may give your child an incentive to have a go.
- Be wary of flushing the lavatory when your child's with you – many are frightened by the noise, and by the fact that "part of them" is being taken away.

thinking may help. Don't make a big thing of it – she'll worry and you'll have defeated your purpose. No matter how long it goes on, assure your child that it will eventually stop, because it does. She will just outgrow it, so be calm and sympathetic at all times.

Regression

If your child suddenly seems to lose her bladder and bowel control, and regresses to an earlier stage, the cause could well be a physical illness or some emotional disturbance. Sometimes the cause is obvious – a new baby, for example, may make your child feel dethroned and rejected. It would be quite normal for her to try attention-seeking behaviour to detract from the new baby, which may include wetting and soiling her clothes. Starting at nursery school or moving to a new house or your absence could all stimulate the same pattern of behaviour. If none of these has happened, consult a doctor about

investigating your child. She may have developed an infection or a have a minor anatomical abnormality in the urinary tract.

Toddler diarrhoea

Some toddlers, who are healthy and eat well, often have diarrhoea that contains undigested food. The exact cause of this toddler diarrhoea is not known, but may be linked to drinking too much fluid, particularly fruit juice, not eating enough fat, or eating too quickly. If your child is otherwise well and there's no underlying illness, changes in her diet usually help.

- Give your child water or milk to drink instead of fruit juice. Clear apple juice seems to be a particular culprit.
- Slightly increase your child's fat intake. Give her whole milk, add butter to her meals and don't give her low-fat foods.
- Encourage her to eat plenty of fruit and vegetables but don't give her excessive amounts of fibre.

9 Sleeping

A newborn baby spends most of the time asleep but as he gets older quite regular sleeping patterns will emerge. By the time he's three months old he'll have one main wakeful period a day, usually at the same time and quite often in the late afternoon or early evening. By the time your child's 12 months old he'll probably be having two naps a day, one in the morning and one in the afternoon, and will be sleeping through the night. Although the sleeping patterns will gradually come to resemble those of an adult during the second and third year, your child will still need a brief nap during the day because of the energy he's using in growing and in play.

All about sleeping birth to 1 year

Unless your newborn baby is hungry, cold or otherwise uncomfortable, he'll spend most of the time between feeds asleep. The amount of time he sleeps will depend on individual physiology, but the average is about 60 per cent of the day. Don't, however, expect your baby to sleep all the time and don't get worried when he doesn't. Some babies are naturally more wakeful than others right from the start.

Even though your baby will follow his own sleep pattern it is important that he learns to differentiate between day and night and there are several ways of helping your baby to do this. For example, when you put your baby down in the evening make sure that the room is darkened and make an extra effort to see that he's comfortable and contented. When he wakes to be fed in the night simply give the feed but don't play or otherwise distract your baby. As he gets older and more aware of what's going on, develop an evening routine so that he has the evening feed, a bath, a story, games and songs before going to bed happy.

Occasionally a baby is sociable rather than sleepy after a meal and this is something to enjoy, although it needn't stop you from trying to set up the routine of bed after the evening meal.

If your baby is habitually wakeful after the meal, don't cause unhappiness for all of you by insisting that he stays in the cot. He'll only get upset and you'll end up with a baby who is very hard to pacify and your nerves will be worn to shreds. If, like me, you are a working mother and spend a good deal of your time away from home, your child will naturally see the night time

as your mothering time and will want to spend that time with you. The probability is that you'll want to spend time with him, too, in which case there is nothing wrong with being flexible about the time he goes to bed. In our house, when we discovered that we had two sleepless young children, we had to abandon the idea of routine bedtimes and the whole household was far happier for having done that. However, we didn't abandon bedtime routines.

Where your baby should sleep

As long as your baby is warm and comfortable he'll be able to sleep almost anywhere. Most parents start their baby off in a basket or carrycot (*see p.36*), because that way the baby is portable, and they can therefore keep him close both day and night. However, when your baby outgrows whichever of these you've used, he'll have to be put in a cot – preferably

Keep him close by
Your young baby will be happiest going to sleep hearing your voices in the background so keep his Moses basket near you.

one with drop sides and an adjustable mattress height (*see p.36*), so that he can be picked up and put down easily.

Whichever room you put your baby to sleep in, it must be warm. Your young baby doesn't have full control over his body temperature: he'll lose body heat easily but won't be able to generate it again by moving about or by shivering. For this reason you must keep the room at a constant temperature of about 16–20°C (60–68°F). If you don't want to keep your whole house that warm you could buy a thermostatically controlled room heater (approved by a recognized safety board), which will maintain your baby's room at a constant temperature.

Whenever you leave your baby to sleep outside, make sure that he's not in direct sunlight. Either put the pram under a shady tree or use a sun shade, and if there's a breeze, put the hood up and point the front of the pram into the wind so that there's an effective wind-break. Make sure that you put a cat net over the front of the pram, even if you don't have cats yourself.

What your baby should wear

Young babies don't like being changed so in the early weeks, when he's going to need changing quite frequently, you'll want something that gives easy access to his nappy but causes the minimum of disturbance. Nightdresses are useful initially, but once your baby has settled down, probably within a month, all-in-one stretch suits are equally practical.

When your baby's about four months old you may want to use a sleeping bag, especially in the winter (*see p.36*). Your baby will stay snugly warm inside and there

WHAT BEDDING TO USE

Temperature	What to use
14°C (57°F)	Sheet and four blankets or more
16°C (60°F)	Sheet and three blankets
18°C (65°F)	Sheet and two blankets
20°C (68°F)	Sheet and one blanket
24°C (75°F)	Sheet only

will be no risk of the blankets being kicked off on a cold night. Choose a lightweight sleeping bag and make sure it is the right size, so your baby can't slide down into it. If the weather's very cold, put your baby in a stretch suit as well. Otherwise just leave on his vest and nappies. In summer your baby may not need any covering at all, although you'll probably want to put him in a vest or body suit.

Many parents worry about whether their baby's too hot or too cold once he's been put down. You can tell by touching the back of his neck, but make sure that your hand isn't too hot or too cold when you do this. If the back of his neck feels about the same temperature as your skin then he's at the right temperature; if it feels damp and sweaty he's probably too hot. If you've got blankets on his cot, take one off. If his neck feels cool, add an extra blanket (but check the room temperature – see chart above). Never judge your baby's temperature by feeling his hands. Babies' extremities are often cooler than the rest of their bodies, and are quite often bluish in colour. This is nothing to worry about.

BED-MAKING TIPS

- Your baby will be most comfortable wrapped in sheets and blankets made of natural fibre – cotton is ideal.
- Avoid blankets with fringes – he may suck them.
- Avoid lacy, open-work shawls as your baby's fingers might get stuck in the holes.
- Use your own old sheets, cut up to the correct size, in addition to bought ones. The more sheets you have, the less frequently you'll have to do the washing.
- Use a pillowcase as a sheet – just slide the mattress into it. When one side gets dirty just turn the mattress over.

Putting your baby down to sleep

The safest position in which to lay your baby down to sleep is on his back. He will not be more liable to choke in this position. As a result of research, doctors now believe that the risk of Sudden Infant Death Syndrome (cot death) is reduced when the baby lies on his back. When he is about four or five months, he will be able to roll over to find the most comfortable position, regardless of how you put him down. Put your baby down with his feet touching, or close to, the bottom of the basket or cot.

It's best not to use a cot bumper as it impedes air circulation and later on your baby may use it to try and climb out of the cot. Once your baby has fallen asleep don't change his position or he's bound to wake up. Similarly, don't keep on going in to the room to check that he's all right. However, there's nothing wrong with carrying your baby in a sling while he's asleep; he'll be soothed by your constant closeness.

There's no need to keep the house quiet when you put your baby to bed. In fact, it's good to encourage him to get used to going to sleep while all the household noises are going on.

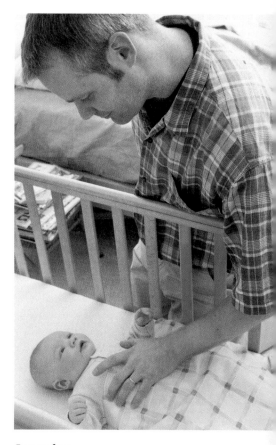

Feet to foot
Lay your baby on his back with his feet touching the foot of the cot, even if his head is halfway down the mattress. That way he can't wriggle under the covers.

Getting your young baby to sleep

Your newborn baby will undoubtedly fall asleep whenever he's tired, and in almost any situation, but there are a few precautions that you should take to guarantee this:

- Wrap your baby before he's put down, at least during the first month. He'll feel much more secure and contented with something firmly wrapped around him. Swaddle him in something that is not too heavy, however, and make sure his head is uncovered. Note that swaddling is instead of, not as well as, other bedding and don't let him get too hot.
- Darken your baby's room at night.
- In the winter leave a hot-water bottle in the bed for half an hour before he's put down. Don't forget to remove it before putting your baby to bed.
- Make sure that the room is warm enough (*see p.143*).

- Place your hand on your baby's back or on one of the limbs to soothe him; rock your baby slightly.
- Use a musical mobile.

Getting your older baby to sleep

By the time that your baby's about nine months old he'll be able to keep himself awake, even when he's actually quite sleepy. As a result he can become over-tired and so tense that sleep is impossible. The main reason why he does this is attachment to you; you provide love, security and excitement and he doesn't want to lose these, even for a moment.

Another reason, which is also linked to the desire for security, is that he doesn't like routines being changed. For example, if you've been on holiday or if your baby has been moved to another room, he may become disturbed by the change. Whatever the cause, this period of clinginess and insecurity will be brief, so treat it as calmly and sensibly as possible and remember, yours isn't the only child in the world who refuses to go to sleep.

Security objects

By about nine weeks your baby may be showing signs of becoming attached to a comfort object such as a blanket, a muslin square, a handkerchief, a doll or his own thumb. There is nothing wrong with any of these. There's no particular age at which comforters should or shouldn't be used and, like bed-wetting, children grow out of them. So, if your baby takes up a security object, don't try to prevent it. If you really feel dubious about letting him use one, look at it in this way: in using one your child is showing self-reliance; he has found a way of coping without you. However, I think the time to question your baby's use of a comforter would be if he used it the whole time, even when you were there. If he clings to it occasionally when he's going down with an illness, or when he's very tired, that's understandable. But if he persistently uses it there's a good chance that you're not providing the kind of comfort and love that he needs, so your baby's having to resort to an artificial source of comfort in place of you.

SLEEPING TIPS

- Keep the hour before bedtime as happy and pleasant as possible.
- Try giving a comfort suck whether from the breast or the bottle just before he's put to bed.
- Develop a routine and stick to it. Don't just put your baby straight to bed: work out a routine of play, then bath, teeth, bed, story, song and then say goodnight. But don't leave the room; quietly tidy up so that your baby learns that he can drift off to sleep without actually "losing" you.
- Let your baby develop comfort habits (see above).
- Rock your baby's cot if he finds that soothing.

- Play a musical mobile. Many babies are fascinated by the movements they make and are soothed by the sound.
- Don't take your older baby out with you in the evenings, even if you used to do this earlier with no problems. He'll be used to his own routine and own room and will be frightened by being moved somewhere else.
- When he does cry, always go back but don't pick the baby up immediately – see what's wrong first – he may just need you to change his position or adjust the temperature.

Day-time naps

Once your baby sleeps through the night he'll need one or two naps during the day to revive his energy. What time he takes the naps depends on the individual baby – it may be after breakfast, it may be mid-morning, after lunch or at four o'clock. At the beginning, what's more, the time may change from day to day and from week to week. By the end of the first year, a set pattern will probably emerge. Apart from special occasions (when, for example, you want your baby to be awake at a special time), the length of the nap should be left to your baby – some sleep only 20 minutes a day, others need four hours. However, if he wants to sleep through the afternoon but then stays up for most of the evening you may want to encourage him to wake up earlier so that he'll go to sleep at a

more sociable time for you. This won't harm your baby and it will make life easier for the whole family if the routines of adult and child can dovetail.

Going out at night

Until your baby is about six months old, and really requires a regular routine at bedtime, you can take him with you whenever you go out at night. In fact, it's a very good thing for the parents, and the mother especially, to have some relaxation in the early period, and because your baby will sleep anywhere it's easy to get around.

However, once he starts sleeping through the night, it's advisable to try to stick to a regular bedtime routine. You can't expect your baby to be as adaptable as an adult, and if you want trouble-free bedtimes it's best to follow a routine.

Possible problems birth to 1 year

Early wakers

From the very beginning, try to encourage your baby to be happy alone in bed when he wakes. Put an interesting mobile just above the cot that will swing in the currents of the air and make moving patterns for your baby whenever he's awake. Put a round-edged mirror on one side of the cot so that he can look at his own reflection and not feel lonely and, once your baby can reach up, put a string of objects within arm's reach so that he can move and play with them. These need not be expensive and can be simple household articles, such as a small wooden spoon, an empty bobbin of cotton or clothes pegs strung on to a length of string

and attached to the cot. It will also help if you put a few favourite toys in the cot so that there is always something interesting to play with and to distract his attention without screaming for yours. Make sure that the room isn't too dark in the mornings so that he can at least see what he's playing with. If the room's very dark leave a night light near the cot or consider hanging lighter curtains.

You can help to train your baby to stay happily in bed by training yourself first. Don't lie there waiting for the first wakening murmur and then leap out of bed to see if he is all right. Leave your baby to snuffle and chatter to himself as long as you possibly can, and only get up if he

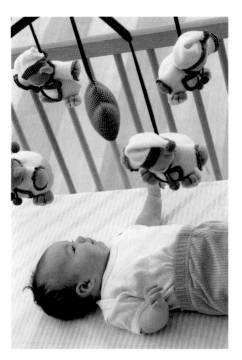

Keeping your baby amused
Unless your baby is hungry or uncomfortably wet he'll lie happily if he has something to hold his attention. A bright mobile above the cot stimulates young eyes.

Until your baby drops the night feed and sleeps through the night, you're always going to have to get up at some stage during the night. To cope with this you should try the following:

• Work out a routine with your partner so that you can go to bed early at least once or twice a week.

• If you are bottle-feeding, get your partner to give some night feeds.

• If you are breast-feeding, and your milk is well established, you could make the night feed a bottle of expressed milk that your partner can give. There is absolutely no reason why you shouldn't do this, although your baby may not readily accept the teat (*see p.96*).

appears to be getting restless and upset. Always wait to see if he quietens down; you will be teaching your baby self-reliance and independence if you do so, even at this early age. If, however, he becomes fretful, don't delay; go at once and give all the comfort and affection you can.

Night wakers

Young babies It is absolutely essential that you get enough rest. If you have a baby who wakes at night, you and your partner should bear the burden equally from the very beginning and take alternate nights on and off duty. Whatever the cause of the crying, you should always go to your baby immediately. If you don't, he'll become increasingly distressed and the end result will be a baby difficult to pacify and a fraught parent.

• If you breast-feed your baby, make sure that your partner helps you by collecting the baby if he's in another room, by changing the nappy after the feed and by putting the baby back to sleep.

• Many mothers find it difficult to get back to sleep if they have been woken up. Don't lie there fuming with resentment: try some relaxation exercises, read a book that you've been wanting to catch up on, tackle some work, or get up and do something that you've been putting off.

• If you've lost sleep during the night, you must make it up the following day. Completely relax your routine and do as little in the house as possible so that you can have a nap when the baby's sleeping.

Older babies In the second half of the year your baby should sleep through the night. However, there may be occasions when, for whatever reason, he wakes up. Try the following:

- Make sure that he's not too hot; if he is, remove either some clothing or some of the bedclothes.
- Check that he's not too cold, having kicked off the bedclothes. Either use a sleeping bag (see p.36), more bedclothes, or leave a safety heater in the baby's room to provide a constant temperature.
- Check that he doesn't have nappy rash. If he does, the discomfort of it could wake him up. Deal with the rash immediately (see p.68).
- Don't constantly go into the baby's room to check that he's sleeping well – your anxiety will be more of a disturbance.
- If he's had a nightmare, provide comfort and stay until he's asleep again. If it happens on more than one night in succession look for some external reason – are you getting upset with him rather a lot; is he being looked after by a new baby minder; is he just disturbed by your not being there during the day?

Wakeful babies

Some babies just don't need as much sleep as others and as a result are much more demanding of their parents' time and energy. Such babies should never be left lying alone in their cots with no amusement. They should either have mobiles or activity centres in their cot, or should be carried by the parent if they're moving around a lot. For example, you could put your baby in a sling and still move quite easily around the house. Whatever you do, don't fret because your baby sleeps less than anticipated. When he's awake he's learning all the time, and you'll inevitably be rewarded with an eager, bright child.

All about sleeping 1 to 2 years

Most toddlers will sleep an average of about 11 hours through the night, and will make up any extra sleep that they need in naps. If your baby needed a lot of sleep in the first year he'll probably continue to do so in the second; if he needed little sleep, then this trend will continue, too. Although he sleeps through the night he'll still need two naps a day. How long these naps last will depend, as before, on your baby. What may change this year will be the times at which he wants to take the nap. For example, you may find that the nap that he used to take at around 9–9.30am gets later and later. This means he'll want to sleep immediately after lunch, at around 1.30 or 2pm. On other days, however, he may take a nap late in the morning but then not want another one until the middle of the afternoon. As far as these changes are concerned, you have to take the lead from your child; there's no point in trying to make him sleep to order and you'll have to accept that the napping pattern varies from day to day. Fit into the baby's routine so that if he establishes a pattern whereby he gets sleepy towards 11.30am and wants to have a nap around noon, you start having lunch around 11.30. He'll then be able to have a satisfying nap after lunch, and you'll have a much less grumpy baby. Alternatively, you could wait until he wakes up before having lunch – it depends on your baby.

Around the age of 15 months your toddler will reach a period where two naps a day are too many and one nap a day is not quite enough. He'll happily play through the first nap, but because he can't last without sleep until the second one he has to have a later nap than usual. This inevitably means that he's alert enough to go through the usual afternoon one, but then because he's too tired to last out until bedtime he has to go to bed early. As with everything else in childcare, you have to be flexible. The period where he has to drop one nap won't last long and he'll soon sort out his own napping routine. By the end of the second year he'll probably take a single nap at the end of the morning, or in the early afternoon.

Until he settles into a napping routine do make sure that he is having adequate rest during the day. Even if he doesn't seem to be all that tired and is rushing around, eager to learn new games or play with exciting toys, it's quite easy for him to become over-tired. Keep an eye on your child and if he becomes bad-tempered or fretful, or shows a sudden lack of co-ordination then make sure he rests or plays a quiet game.

Whenever your toddler takes a nap, give him a chance to wake up gently from it. It may be a restorative sleep, but he's unlikely to wake up perfectly refreshed and active. He'll need a quarter of an hour or so of being cuddled and talked to gently and quietly before he's ready to be active again. If you have to go out immediately after your toddler's nap, make sure that you leave enough time for the recovery of his good humour.

HELPING YOUR TODDLER TO SLEEP

During the day

- Make up a nap time box for your child with favourite toys and books that he can look at as he gets sleepy before a nap. Don't leave good or expensive books – they may get ripped up. Leave board books or old books. A good alternative is to make up your own books by pasting interesting pictures from magazines on to board and then covering them with clear plastic film.
- Give your child an occasional treat by letting him take a nap in your bed, or somewhere near you.
- If your child won't take a nap, make sure that he has a rest time where he is calm and quiet.
- If your toddler won't go to sleep, put on a long-playing tape or CD. Teach your child that the rest time is not over until the music stops.

In the evening

- Don't put your child to bed immediately after an exciting game or rough-and-tumble – he will have great difficulty settling down, which will be frustrating for you. Give him 10–15 minutes to quieten down, sitting with you watching TV or looking at a book.
- Even a small child likes looking at a book in bed so, if your baby is quite happy, leave him with a favourite, non-scary book.
- Put a dab of your perfume or aftershave on to your child's pillow and suggest that he breathes it in deeply. Deep breathing is relaxing and calming and will help your child go off to sleep.
- Give your toddler a bath before bedtime and follow this with a warm drink and a story in bed.

Bedtime routines

Your baby's bedtime routine will change this year. He'll need more diverting games and more of your attention; give him both. The essential thing to remember is that bedtimes should be play times and happy times, and even although you're worn out, you should try to be calm and relaxed. If you are not, your baby will pick up your anxiety and be fretful, and you may have to spend twice as long trying to put him to sleep than if you had spent an extra five minutes of your undivided attention in a quiet, direct way.

Where your toddler should sleep

At some time during this year your baby may try to get out of his cot to come to you. Obviously a fall from the top of a cot could be dangerous so either lower the mattress and effectively make the top of the rails out of reach, or put your child into a single bed. If your toddler is quite young when he's first put into a "big" bed get a safety guard or put cushions on the floor beside the bed.

Time to read together
Children like routines, and bedtime is a great time to sit down quietly together and read a favourite book; he may even want the same book every day.

Possible problems 1 to 2 years

Waking in the night

It's been estimated that 15 per cent of two year olds wake regularly in the night and this can be a source of great worry to parents who also need sleep. No matter how often this happens, or how irritating it may be, don't leave your toddler to cry; go to him immediately, provide comfort and try to find out what the problem is. It may be something easily remedied – he may be cold because the blanket or quilt has fallen off; he may be too hot; he may be thirsty; he may be teething.

On the other hand, it may be something less tangible: he may have woken up for none of these reasons and may just be afraid after a bad dream. The difficulty is that he can't explain what's upsetting him and you can't tell your toddler that he's got nothing to fear. What you should always do is provide love and affection, without any fear of spoiling.

Dealing with a sleepless child

I'm very sympathetic to parents with sleepless children having had two myself, one of whom was sick if he wasn't reached within a minute or so of starting to cry. I would like to give the parents of such children a hopeful message. Neither my husband nor I enjoyed an unbroken night's sleep for six years and on many days we were almost too tired to drag ourselves around; but we got through it and we've forgotten the dawn vigils. When I look at our two loving, outgoing, affectionate sons I sometimes think that I wouldn't have had it any other way. We gave them love in the night, they gave us five hundred times as much back every day.

At the time we were so desperate for sleep that it became our over-riding priority; once it did our worries were half over. We decided to do anything to ensure a full night's sleep, at least now and then. I had never believed that taking the baby in to our bed could do him or us any harm. I could not believe staying with my baby when he wanted me could do him any harm, so I followed my instincts and threw any so-called rules to the wind. If you want to try something like this I suggest that you try it sooner rather than later. I'm convinced you're not buying problems,

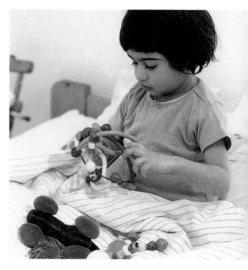

Early risers
Leave some special toys or board books beside your child's bed to keep her occupied when she first wakes in the morning, or after her nap.

you're only being a good parent to your child. Never take your baby into bed, however, if you have been drinking alcohol, taking drugs or using medications that make you drowsy. Keep his head uncovered and use lightweight bedclothes.
• My husband and I did alternate nights "on duty". One stayed with the child; the other remained undisturbed unless there was an emergency.

TIPS FOR EARLY WAKERS

• Put a pile of cloth or board books at the bottom of the cot or bed for early morning "reading". Make sure that there is enough light to see by; if there isn't, leave on a low-wattage night light when you put your toddler to bed.
• Put a soft box or plastic bucket at the side of the bed or cot with small toys, crayons, paper, bits of

cloth or interesting household articles in it, so he can sort through and play with them.
• Leave a paper bag with some fresh fruit or bread at the bottom of the bed; never put the food in a plastic bag for safety reasons.
• Leave a drink in a beaker or cup within reach of your child.

- We put up a camp bed next to the cot, and later the bed, so that we could put out a reassuring hand to pat him as he started to cry. This way neither of us really woke up at all.
- We gave the child 15 minutes to settle to any of our strategies, then we tried taking him in to our own bed – a sure-fire success.
- We only ever gave water or fruit juice at night, never milk, so as not to accustom the child to food.

Refusing to go to bed

According to the correspondence I get, there are more "difficult" babies around than most people realize, and they pose great problems for their parents. The baby who doesn't go to sleep at night is classically intelligent, physically very active, interested in everything that is going on around and openly affectionate. During the day these children are delightful and very rewarding, but you pay the penalty at night.

Two of my four sons were sleepless, demanding babies so I devised a few guiding principles for coping. You have to get your priorities right: no one can function properly for long without adequate sleep and you, as a parent, are no exception. Sleep is too important to miss and you are justified in doing whatever is necessary to get it, so adopt a few pragmatic rules as opposed to old-fashioned dogmatic ones:

- There is nothing magical about bedrooms. Let your child go to sleep where he is most comfortable: at your feet on the floor, on a couch, in your lap.
- Be flexible about bedtimes. Left to

themselves, most children go to sleep at around seven or eight o'clock in the evening, whether you put them to bed or not. Why should they be unhappy in a room on their own, instead of being happy in your company?
- Give your child an early evening bath. This often relaxes children and makes them sleepy.
- If your child is proving difficult to get to go to bed, still put on his nightclothes before he's brought into the living room. If he falls asleep you won't have to wake him up again, you can just put him straight in to bed.
- If problems persist, talk to your health visitor. They are trained to support parents coping with common behaviour problems and should be able to suggest helpful strategies and techniques.

Rapid-return technique

If, for some reason, your baby starts to get out of bed every night or calls for you constantly, cries when put down and won't settle in his bed at night, try this technique. It can take a few nights, but it does work.
- Go in, remain silent and put your baby down again.
- Repeat this immediate action of settling your baby back down in his cot as many times as it takes.
- Be patient and don't give in. You may have to repeat these actions up to 50 times on the first night.
- Follow through on the second night. You still may have to go to your baby as many as 20 times.
- The third night will be much better and your baby should be back to normal in about four nights.

All about sleeping 2 to 3 years

By the time your child is two years old he usually needs 12 hours of sleep at night and about one or two hours of napping during the day; once again, the actual amount will depend on the child. In general, the nap or rest time will shorten during the year, but bedtime will usually stay the same. The amount of time that your child sleeps at night won't decrease until he's around six years old when he'll reduce it half an hour at a time, per year.

Around the age of three many children stop having naps, although the majority still need a rest period indoors after lunch until they are about five or six.

Sleep routine

Children around the age of two and three sometimes start delaying tactics at bedtime. There may be the desire to go to the lavatory or to have a drink and, of course, there's the possibility that he may just appear at your side with no excuses, wakeful and charming. In these circumstances I think you have to decide how to act according to what your previous routine has been. If you have been pretty flexible about bedtimes and never insisted that your child went to bed in his room, cot or bed, then you can't suddenly change tactics when your child is two or three: your child will simply not accept the inconsistency, and will quite rightly baulk at the new regime. In these circumstances, I think it is better to be practical and to let your child play in the room with you until he is tired; to let your child fall asleep beside you and to then carry him up to bed.

On the other hand, if the bedtime routine has been carefully set and this new behaviour is a departure, then I think your child will only benefit from your being firm about the re-establishment of routine.

TIPS FOR MAKING BEDTIMES EASY

- Mark the bedtime with an alarm or a timer, so that you can give your children five minutes warning of bedtime.
- For a young child, have a toy clock next to the real clock and set the hands of the toy clock to bedtime. When the hands of the real clock match up with the toy clock, that is the time for bed.
- Keep a child's bedtime as near the same time as you can every night to help establish regular sleeping patterns.
- Children are quite often not sleepy at their bedtimes. They like the time to slow down just lying in bed looking at a new toy, reading a new book, or just chatting to one another. It is quite often a good idea to have children who are near each other's own age sharing the same bedroom until they require their privacy.
- Once your children get into a proper bed, have a little snuggle down with them before you leave them to go to sleep. It is very nice for them; it warms up the bed, and their last memories are of your closeness. It is also very relaxing for you: I did it with my children and I nearly always found that I dropped off before they did. It was a tradition we started when they were young, but continued after they went to school.

Night-time comfort
It is about this age that a child may like a particular doll or toy to take to bed with her. If this happens it is worth keeping an identical spare in case the first is lost.

No doubt you will get a few whimpers and a few doleful pleas, but you have already established with your child that you are loving and will come if he is in real need, so you can afford to be firm. You have a lot of credit to draw on and your child will learn this lesson quite quickly, and soon stop repeating it. However, if you give in, then your child will certainly pick it up as a new habit.

The way you handle these situations depends quite a lot on how much energy you have left and how much you are prepared to have your evenings interrupted. If you have been with your children all day, you probably feel with some justification that the night times are your own, and if you've brought your children up to recognize this you can be quite firm in insisting on it.

Keeping bedtimes happy

It is important to keep bedtimes happy. Personally, I was prepared to make quite a lot of concessions to make sure that my children didn't go to sleep unhappy. I forgave certain misdemeanours, which would normally have been punished earlier in the day, so that they didn't go to bed with the memory of my angry voice ringing in their ears. I tried to avoid them feeling upset or crying with distress. It is worth making pre-bedtime activities especially joyful and friendly: as your child gets older spend the time between supper and bed (about 30 minutes) in their company –

even if you are only sitting in the same room reading a newspaper, or getting on with some work. Having your presence in the room is very comforting and consoling and will calm your child so that he'll be in a happy mood when he makes the transition from the living room to the bedroom. If you can, watch a suitable television programme together, or read a book or play a game before you take your child to the bedroom.

Bedroom rituals

Most children like a bedtime ritual. Mine always had half a dozen favourite songs they liked me to sing, and a storybook they liked their father to read. When we were home together we would share the bedtime routine: ten minutes with me on songs and ten minutes with him on a story. We would both stay in the bedroom and, as there were three children going to bed, bedtimes were communal with the children sitting or lying on each other's beds. It was a family time. My husband lay on the bed while I sang the songs. I stayed and lay on a bed while he read a story.

When the story and songs were over, it was lights out, except for a low night light, although we often stayed and talked over what had happened during the day. Sometimes we lay under the bedclothes for a short while to give our children the extra loving feeling of companionship.

In our household this sometimes rather protracted but worthwhile bedtime routine worked. The last thing we did was to switch on the hall light so that the children could see their way to the bathroom during the night or to our room if they needed us. It's quite useful if the light has a dimmer switch so that it gives a suitably low enough light so that no doors have to be shut.

Possible sleep problems 2 to 3 years

Delaying tactics

Your child may try to stop you leaving by saying that he simply doesn't want you to go. Here again, you have a choice of action. You can stay with your child until any possible fears have gone and he is feeling calm enough to go to sleep, either with you or without you. Or you can call your child's bluff and leave. I think the latter action is dangerous as it can cause your child to get so frightened that he becomes hysterical. This is bad both in the short term – he will have great difficulties in going to sleep that night – and in the long term – you may make your child fearful of going to bed for several years to come. I would never advocate it.

Another way is to say "If you lie still for five minutes I will come back" and then come back in exactly five minutes. Make sure that he's comfortable and say that you will come back in another five minutes and do so again. In your absence, leave some music playing or let your child continue to read the book he has been reading or to enjoy the game he has been playing, so that he is not left alone with fearful thoughts, waiting for you to return. On the third or fourth occasion you'll probably find he's asleep.

As a last resort, take your child downstairs with you. Rest assured that there is absolutely no harm in it, although you will have to be prepared for this to become a long-term habit. It makes for some very rewarding family evenings, as long as you don't get too tired and you aren't too jealous of your privacy. Use the method most suitable for you all.

Fear of the dark

If your child delays going to bed because he is fearful of being left alone or of being in the dark, then you yourself can allay both of these fears. If your child is scared of being alone in the dark sit and distract him by reading a story, playing a game or singing nursery rhymes. Make sure that he is calm and sleepy, and actually sit and pat his back until he has quietly dropped off. Fear of the dark is perfectly normal and reasonable in a small child, so don't insist on the bedroom being dark. Provide a low-voltage night light which will be a comfort to him and will help you to see your way in the child's bedroom late at night.

Bad dreams and sleep walking

Your child probably won't have a nightmare before the age of three, though children sometimes wake up with a scream and a frightened look, suggesting that they have had a bad dream. Many children have the odd nightmare and this is normal, although it can be quite frightening for the parent if the child doesn't become conscious straight away. Nightmares are not abnormal unless they happen often or are accompanied by regular sleep-walking. This behaviour suggests that the child is having to exercise a great deal of self-control to overcome anxieties when he is awake and only loses this control when he is asleep. If you can, the treatment is to find out the cause of the tension and to remove it. If the cause isn't obvious, like a new baby in the house, or starting at nursery school, talking things over with your doctor may be of help. If nightmares are a real problem, your doctor may recommend a child psychologist.

A night terror is different. Your child's eyes may be open although he won't actually see you. He may shout abuse at you in a strange, garbled language and be rude and angry. Ignore all this; he is not in control of himself and, don't forget, during the night terror he'll be very frightened.

Very often there is little you can do to relieve your child's fear, even though that is your greatest wish. There's no point in trying to speak to him rationally about what's going on. He can't even understand the words you say in many cases. During the nightmare don't ask your child to do anything. This puts further pressure on him and only increases his anxiety. The only way for you to behave, even though the nightmare may last as long as half an hour, is to remain by his side, and be entirely sympathetic, calm, softly spoken and caring. Never, ever, leave your child with a night terror. Stay the whole time until it is over. Your nearness and comfort are all that is required. Speak soothingly and quietly about anything you like; don't suggest that he tries to pull himself together; never raise your voice and never scold your child as this may make him hysterical.

Locked doors

Never lock your child's door to keep him separate from you. This is just admitting to a failure in your ability to handle your child and is cruel. Locked doors and barriers shouldn't be used as childcare devices. They are no substitute for you teaching your child, even as early as two years old, about respecting other people's privacy, including your own. A three-year-old child is open to reason and you can explain to him that he cannot just get out of bed when he pleases, and that you will put him back no matter how often he does it. If you are firm, but reasonable, your child should respond.

If your child habitually gets out of bed put a guard across his bedroom doorway or top of the stairs for his own safety.

10 Crying

Many newborn babies cry quite a lot, so be prepared for it. If you expect your baby to cry, and treat it as normal when she does, you'll find it easier to cope with. If your baby is one of the few who doesn't cry much, think of it as a bonus. In order to understand why your baby is crying, and how you can provide comfort, bear in mind what upsets a baby, and what comforts her, changes as she develops. A new baby may cry when she's undressed for a bath; a one year old may cry when you leave the room. The new baby will be comforted by being snugly wrapped up in a towel; the one year old will be comforted by the sight of you returning.

All about crying birth to 1 year

Your newborn baby has a limited repertoire of communication, and crying is almost her only way of telling you that something is wrong. Remember that for several months she's been floating gently in the dark, in a constant temperature with a constant food supply. As a result, bright lights, hard surfaces are unexpected, so it's not surprising if she cries when she's cold and hungry. But crying doesn't necessarily mean that your baby is in danger.

Recognizing different cries

Cries can be identified quite accurately by mothers and fathers who become increasingly able to distinguish different kinds of cries from their baby during the early weeks following birth. This is not a one-sided distinction; babies become increasingly able to anticipate their mother's responses to their cries. Most parents worry quite a lot about why their baby is crying, and the interpretations seem endless. Is it hunger, boredom, anger, loneliness, overtiredness, stomach pains or colic? Does she want a cuddle or is she just plain miserable? But after the first four weeks mothers pay much less attention to the type of cry than to lots of other information, such as how long is it since the baby last had a feed? Did she feed well last time? Is she too cold/too hot?

Responding to crying

The way you respond to your baby's distress can affect how your baby behaves and how she grows up. Your response to the crying and the way you comfort her can influence the bond that grows between you over the years. This goes

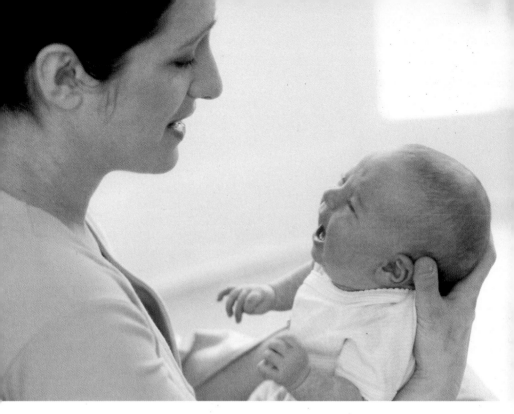

beyond the issue of "spoiling" your baby to the central question of how your child's early experiences with you will affect her later development.

Some research with mothers and newborn babies has shown that over the first few days of life a slow response to crying may well lead to more, rather than less, crying. In another study, it was found that babies whose crying was ignored early on tended to cry more frequently and more persistently later in the first year and that after the first six months this persistent crying discouraged the mothers from responding. The same research showed that mothers who had responded quickly to their babies had children who were much more likely to be advanced in "communication skills", as measured by comparing the range of facial expressions

The newborn baby
Crying is her only way of communicating with you in the early days. Always respond to her, and she will come to learn and recognize the sound of your voice.

in each baby. Further studies give a picture in which the sensitive and prompt response of the mother promoted a harmonious relationship with the child who was content, obedient, secure and competent as a result. This research supports the belief that mothers are programmed to respond immediately to their babies. Some psychologists have attributed the difficulty some mothers have with demanding children largely to the erosion of a natural mother and baby relationship, produced by anxiety about spoiling their children. Mothers who do not respond promptly are "insensitive" and "going against nature".

Comfort through movement
When your baby cries, rock her in your arms to comfort her. Most babies are soothed by gentle rocking movements; it is what they were used to in the womb.

Never leave your baby to cry

The factors that prevent a child from forming deep, loving relationships with their parents, are parental apathy and lack of response and they are more important as inhibitors of the child's attachment than even a parent causing distress, say by physical violence.

I have heard mothers say "If she is clean and dry, winded and well fed – let her cry". Or "He needs to cry for an hour, it is the only exercise his lungs get, so leave him alone". I am very strongly against these attitudes. In my opinion a baby should never be left to cry. In the first place, a crying baby may swallow air, which will cause discomfort and make feeding difficult. Prolonged crying may make your baby feel very tired, even exhausted, and she will become irritable and difficult to soothe. More important than either of these reasons is that she will quickly learn that pleas for attention go unheeded, and that there is no loving human response when she needs it.

All the research that I have read supports not letting your baby cry. It also suggests that if you let her cry she'll very soon stop asking for attention, which may seriously damage her ability to form relationships with others while growing up. A baby's pattern of behaviour, first with the mother, then with the father, and later on with family and friends, is worked out during the first year of life and probably starts as early as the first six weeks. If friendship is denied to a child in these early weeks, she may grow up introverted, withdrawn, shy of displays of affection, and repulsed by physical contact. Don't give your child such an unfair start in life.

Spoiling your baby?

In my opinion a baby cannot be loved too much. I don't share the belief that too much picking up or nursing will spoil a child. A child under one year of age cannot be "spoiled" enough, if picking up, nursing, loving and cuddling mean spoiling. To me, none of this behaviour constitutes spoiling. A child who is picked up and nursed is learning about loving, human behaviour. The model for this behaviour, which she'll retain for life, is the early relationship with her parents.

What we tend to call spoiling is both a natural response of a mother to a distressed child, and the natural need of the baby. A mother's behaviour is "built-in" just as much as the behaviour of the baby. She is genetically programmed to respond to her baby's crying, although she may suppress her instinctive response with a learned response that interferes with her natural drives, which are to pick up, soothe and nurse her crying baby. Society has suggested that she will spoil her baby if she does this, and so she is torn; she should not be. She should follow her natural instincts. The protective instinct in a mother (which is what she is displaying when she picks up and tries to soothe her crying child) is the basis of her maternal instinct, and essential to her biological function as a mother. Babies require this physical contact with a soft, warm, loving human being. The need for this is so strong that it almost overrides the need for food.

The mother's response

Undoubtedly crying, and your prompt response to it, play an important part in the way your baby becomes attached to you. Every child in a family will become attached to both parents, but the quality of the attachment depends on the sensitivity of the mother. It is the promptness and appropriateness of the mother's response to the child's distress, in other words how much she is attuned to her child, which is the most important part of this sensitivity, and it is critical for the development of a

stable and happy relationship between baby and mother and then between baby and other people as she grows up.

So my unequivocal answer to the question, "Is it possible to spoil a baby?", would be "No".

Crying spells

Spells of crying are likely to go on for three, four or even six weeks, while your baby becomes acclimatized to the outside world. When she has developed a routine that takes account of any likes and dislikes, the frequency of crying usually decreases.

Everyone finds it harder to cope with crying during the night. When your sleep is interrupted you'll feel, along with every other parent, some degree of impatience. Your feelings aren't abnormal; everyone has them. Don't panic when your baby starts to cry. It's inevitable that she will, and your tenseness will only make matters worse.

If you feel that your baby seems to be crying rather a lot, you can take comfort from some research that has shown that babies may cry quite independently of any discomfort they may be feeling or of the effectiveness of the comfort you give. For instance, babies who were born after a long labour, or whose mothers were given drugs during labour, were more likely to cry frequently and sleep in short bouts.

Mothers who were highly anxious during pregnancy tend to have more irritable and difficult babies. It's also well known that male babies are more vulnerable to stress at the time of birth than female babies, and at least one American study has shown that boys are more irritable at the age of three weeks than girls.

Causes of crying birth to 6 months

Hunger

This is the most common cause for crying in young babies, and parents soon learn to recognize it. Studies have confirmed what parents know – babies cry more before feeding than after. Experiments have shown that it is the actual feeling of a full stomach that brings most comfort, and not being held, sucking or swallowing.

GENERAL CRYING CURES

If your baby still seems fretful try some, or all, of the following remedies as part of your crying cure. Most babies are soothed by both sound and movement, and many parents find it relaxing too.

Movement
- Rock your baby – rocking chairs and swings are ideal for this.
- Walk or dance with your baby.
- Bounce your baby gently in your arms or on a bed or in the cot.
- Put your baby in a bouncing seat that will move gently.
- Take your baby for a ride in the car or in a pram or a sling, even at night.
- If you are on your own, put your baby in a sling and just let her cry and get on with whatever you want to do and try to ignore the crying.

Sound
- Talk, sing or croon to your baby.
- Put on the radio or television.
- Put on the vacuum cleaner, or let a tap run forcibly into the sink for a few minutes.
- Give your baby a noisy toy. Shake and rattle it.
- Play tapes or CDs of calm music.

- Feed on demand. Don't be inflexible about feeding times, and never feed by the clock. Remember, she's very young; she may want feeding every two or three hours and a feed given 15–30 minutes earlier than expected will do your baby no harm at all.
- If your baby seems only to want to suck give her cooled boiled water as a drink between feeds (from a sterilized spoon).
- Give your baby a dummy to suck; hold it in the baby's mouth if necessary. You could also use a clean finger.

Lack of contact

Some babies cry whenever you put them down in their cots, but stop as soon as you pick them up again. This is perfectly natural, and means that your baby feels happiest when she is physically close to you. In many cultures babies are swaddled or held in close contact with their mothers' bodies, and these babies rarely cry.
- Pick your baby up as soon as she cries.
- Carry your baby around with you in a sling or a shawl so that she can hear and feel your heart beat.
- Rock your baby until you get tired then hand her over to your partner until the baby's calm again.
- Wrap your baby tightly. The texture of the cloth should be warm and fluffy – cool fabrics are far less effective.
- Lay your baby across your lap, tummy downwards, and massage her back and her arms and legs.
- Lay your baby across a warm hot-water bottle on your lap or on a bed.

Temperature

Heat and cold (and humidity) have important effects on the amount of time that a baby sleeps, cries and is active. Young babies sleep more and cry less if they are in relatively warm environments (16–20°C/65–68°F), but equally they do not like to be too hot.

Wet or dirty nappies don't in themselves cause a baby to cry unless the wet nappy gets cold, too, in which case it is the drop in temperature that is a potent cause of distress.

- Make sure your baby's room is at the desired temperature.
- Feel the back of your baby's neck to test whether she's too hot or too cold (if it feels sweaty, for example, she's too hot). Either add another layer of clothing if she's too cold or take a layer off if she feels too hot.
- Check your baby's nappy to see if it's wet or dirty; change it if necessary.

Undressing

Most babies hate being undressed, even when the room is warm and they are awake and contented immediately before their clothes are removed. The effect of undressing is consistent and it gets worse over the second and third weeks: as soon as the baby senses that the clothes are being removed she tenses up and finally breaks down when the piece of clothing nearest the skin comes off. The cause is not the cold, but the fact that the skin is no longer in contact with the familiar and reassuring texture of the clothing.

- Keep undressing to a minimum in the early weeks. Try topping and tailing your baby (*see p.72*), so that you only have to undress her a little at a time.
- Whenever you have to undress your baby fully, lay a towel across her body – the contact with the fabric will help her.
- Talk soothingly and reassuringly and try to get the undressing over quickly.

IF CRYING IS DIFFICULT TO COPE WITH

One of the things you should be aware of is that every parent at some time or other contemplates doing something physically violent to her/his children. Most mothers with newborn babies who are exhausted and trying to pacify a screaming baby will confess that they have thought of doing anything to stop the baby crying. It is not abnormal to think such things. It's only abnormal to do them.

It can be particularly difficult to cope before your period. Mothers who are ideal parents – very loving and caring, sympathetic and patient for the rest of the month – can become far less tolerant for the few days prior to menstruation.

Most mothers are aware when they begin to lose hold on themselves and are able to control violent behaviour against their children. But if you feel yourself sliding down the slippery slope you should seek help, first from your partner or from a friend, but also from your health visitor or doctor.

Get help if necessary
If you ever find yourself hitting or shaking your baby, don't feel that it is an admission of failure to seek help. You must do so, both for your child's sake and your own. Equally don't stand by and let your partner injure your child: try to make her/him see that what she or he is doing is wrong, and if she or he is impervious to your pleas, seek help on behalf of both of you. Contact your doctor, health visitor, the police or your local health authority immediately.

COLIC

This term describes recurrent bouts of unexplained crying usually in the late afternoon or evening, but can be at any time. The crying may be intense and brief or last for hours and is not generally pacified by the usual remedies. The baby's face is red and she draws her legs up.

All sorts of causes have been put forward, such as overfeeding, underfeeding, wind in the bowel, being picked up too much or too little, indigestion and tension. It has always struck me that tension is the most likely cause. You're busy in the evening and it's likely that your baby picks up on the tension and responds by crying.

As your baby is likely to cry every night for 12 weeks I'm against using any medicine to forestall it. Of course try to soothe your baby, but don't expect her to respond readily. Try to take comfort from the fact that these colicky spells come only at night and usually only last for three months. Colic generally stops without you doing anything and is rarely serious.

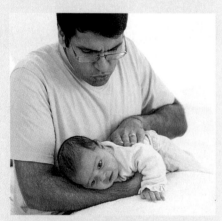

Colicky babies
It's not known why colic happens, but it usually starts in the first three weeks of a baby's life. Try laying her across your lap supporting her abdomen, and gently massage her back.

Pain

This is a very definite cause of crying, but the actual cause of the pain may be hard to determine. It may be the discomfort of colic (*see left*); it may be something quite obvious like sore bottom or a very tightly fitting garment. If, for example, the pain is caused by an earache you'll probably notice your baby putting her fist against the affected ear.

- Go to your baby immediately. Hold your baby close to you, cuddle and talk soothingly to her.
- Always remove the source of pain if it's easily discernible.
- Stay with your baby until she's completely calmed down.
- If no amount of comforting on your part works, and your baby seems ill, seek medical advice.

Violent or sudden stimulation

Sudden changes in the level of stimulation of your baby, be it light, noise, jerking movements, being played with too roughly or the sensation of falling, will cause great distress. In the latter case your startled baby will throw out both arms and legs in the Moro reflex (*see p.27*), and will invariably begin to cry.

- Hold your baby close to you and use the general pacifying methods of contact, movement and sound.
- Avoid moving your baby in such a sudden way next time.
- Avoid sudden stimulation with bright lights, loud noises or sudden jerky movements. A baby can stand quite loud noises or quite bright lights over a long period of time but a sudden change will cause immediate distress.

Tiredness

Many babies cry when they are tired. It took me almost two weeks to understand my tired newborn son's message. "Clever baby," I thought, "Dumb mother." Some babies (like adults) twitch or jerk just as they are dropping off to sleep. This may cause a baby to wake up again and, if it continues, will result in a fretful sleep.

• Lay your baby in a quiet, warm, dimly lit room.
• If she's particularly twitchy, wrap her up firmly before you put her down to bed.

Misreading your baby's signals

Not reading your baby's signals to you, whether they be "I'm hungry", "I'm tired", "I want to be cuddled not played with",

can all result in tears. For example, if your baby is ready for a feed, but you ignore this and give her a bath first, then your baby is bound to cry. If, while you're breast-feeding, you fail to notice that your baby can't suck properly because she's being smothered by your breast and she is finding it difficult to breathe, then she's bound to cry.

• Be alert. Look at your baby, listen to her gurgles and grumbles and interpret what she's saying to you. She will be saying something to you if you are attentive enough to understand.
• Resolve whatever is causing the alarm immediately to reduce her stress.
• Use the general crying cures (*see p.162*) to soothe your baby.

Causes of crying 6 months to 1 year

Your baby will still cry if she's hungry, if she's in pain and if she's too hot or too cold and the cures for these will remain the same as for newborns (*see pp.162–163*). However, as she gets older she will also be distressed by new things.

Boredom

Your baby will spend longer periods awake during the latter half of this year and she may cry out of sheer boredom if she's just left to lie in a cot, unattended, with nothing to look at or play with. Similarly, she'll be keen to stay with you and see what you're doing all the time because at the moment you're a constant source of amusement and affection. When you leave your baby, especially if she can hear you

elsewhere, she's bound to cry.
• Hang a mobile or similar toy above your baby's cot so that she can swipe at them and watch how they move about. Leaves on trees, curtains blowing by an open window, lampshades moving – they all provide amusement for your baby.
• You'll have a more contented baby if you keep her near you whenever she's awake; she will always sense your presence.

Anxiety

Your baby may well become increasingly wary and scared, especially of strangers and of you going away. During the second half of this year she will be extremely clingy and, in parallel with this increasing dependence on you, she will begin to form

attachments to comforters like her own thumb; a blanket or a dummy. The source of comfort varies with individual children but the need for it is common to all of them. The intensity and persistence of these attachments can last for two to three years. The objects are usually suckable or strokable, and children use them in moments of anxiety and tiredness to simulate the effects of continuous stroking and contact.

- Understand that this is just a period in your child's development that she has to go through.
- Never force her to go to a stranger if she really can't stand it.
- Let your baby have a comforter, even if it's a dummy. She'll grow out of using it in time.
- Give your baby lots of cuddles.

Frustration

Your baby's increasing physical capabilities may well lead to tears of frustration. Once she's started crawling she'll be able to

Boredom and frustration
Your baby may cry because she wants to be with you all the time, but it may also be because she's bored. Try leaving a few toys in her cot for when she wakes.

move away from you more quickly and will want to explore her surroundings. What this in fact means is that she'll frequently have to be checked and stopped from doing what she wants to do, for her own safety, as well as to protect whatever it is that she's trying to explore.

- Make your home as "child-proof" as possible by removing breakable objects from low tables and shelves and by using the correct safety fittings throughout your home (*see pp.292–298*).
- Remove the baby from the source of frustration. If, for example, she keeps going up to a dog and pulling its tail, either remove it or the baby from the room. Your baby's memory is very short at this time so she'll soon forget the object of her curiosity.
- Distract your baby with other games.

All about crying 1 to 2 years

In the one to two year old most crying is due to emotional disturbance: to fear, anxiety, separation, deprivation of her parents and parental love.

Insecurity

Between the ages of one and three, children spend less and less of their time physically close to, and touching, their mothers. But in contrast to this apparent independence there will be moments when your toddler becomes rather frightened and anxious.

There is usually a period, around the age of one, when this happens. You may notice that she's quieter and less mischievous than usual; that she's become very shy of strangers and strange situations and clings desperately to your legs; she may even be off her food. These are all signs of anxiousness to which you should respond immediately.

- The best way of coping with these anxieties is to give your toddler extra affection and, while doing this, to encourage your toddler to be curious and adventurous, and to have a growing sense of self-confidence. Praise and reward each feat, each new achievement. Your toddler requires your approbation and will do almost anything to get it, including showing off her new independence, so it really is quite easy to encourage her.
- A child who is securely attached to at least one of her parents (mother or father) uses that parent as a base from which to explore, and will go on to explore confidently. Much research has shown the importance of the presence of the person with whom the child has a secure attachment enables her to cope with new, possibly fearful, experiences and with the accompanying anxiety.

Fear of separation

Simply because a toddler is so attached to the parent, separation becomes one of the greatest causes of distress, and fear of separation is one of the most potent causes of anxiety. When fear, insecurity, anxiety or separation cause great distress, crying ensues. The degree of distress varies according to your child's age (you may find that it is much less by the time she is 15 months than when she was ten months); the way you actually leave the toddler; and the familiarity of the situation. Of course, it also depends upon your toddler's previous experiences of being separated. If it was unpleasant the first time, your toddler is likely to find it more unpleasant when it happens a second time.

Children, undoubtedly, don't like being left. In a way, the better parent you are, the more your toddler is likely to cry when separated from you.

- Never be scornful of fears and always try to be sympathetic and supportive. Reassure your child, more by actions than by words, that you are to be trusted and relied upon. If you say you will come back in half an hour, do so. If you say you are just going into the next room, go no further. If you say you will pop back in five minutes to check on a game, do so.

One of your baby's greatest sources of confidence is that she can trust you.

- In your attempts at sympathy and reliability do your best not to be over-protective. This will only curb your child's adventurous spirit, and stop her from building up self-confidence.

Frustration

Towards the end of the second year, your toddler's sense of adventure will almost certainly outstrip her co-ordination and degree of mobility. She will attempt tasks that are beyond her dexterity, sense of balance and physical strength, and this will cause great frustration. It's also inevitable that you will be the source of frustration because you have to stop her doing certain things she wants to do for her own safety.

- Try to be patient. The best form of support you can give is your help. Help with the painting; help with building a tower of blocks; help with climbing; help to make sand castles; help to prop up soldiers or farmyard animals. If the frustration at her inability causes crying, you can easily distract your child into another favourite game.

- If she gets frustrated when she tries to copy older children's games, or tries to do something that an older child can do easily, suggest that you play a game together that you know she can physically cope with. While it's important for your toddler to try new things, and to continue trying when she doesn't immediately succeed, too many defeats could have a retrogressive effect.

- Don't be drawn into battles with your toddler – whether they're over using the potty or eating a certain food. She'll want to assert her independence and, where possible, respect this and don't force the issue. Let her decide whether she wants to use the potty, and don't worry if she wants only to eat green beans and ice cream. A calm acceptance of facts is better than arguing.

Possible crying problems 1 to 2 years

Temper tantrums

A temper tantrum is an attention-seeking device. The tantrum will go on as long as you are giving your child your attention; it will be shortened abruptly if you withdraw it. The best thing to do is to leave the room; your child will come to no harm. A breath-holding attack is self-limiting, and your child will take a breath as soon as she becomes at all short of oxygen. If she is kicking and screaming, simply move articles out of reach so that she cannot be hurt and leave her to kick and scream. Don't be tempted to cajole your child, to lose your temper, to smack or to threaten punishments. None will do the slightest good to bring the tantrum to an end, or to avert the next one. The only course of action is to leave your child alone.

Night-time crying

Quite a few babies cry as they are going to bed at night. You can do a lot to avoid this if you establish a bedtime routine. This doesn't mean that you are inflexible, rather that you give the evening a rhythm that you and your baby get used to. Bedtime and bathtime should ideally be happy. From the time your baby is six months old she should be enjoying her bath and if you treat it as playtime you are off to a good start. By the time bathing is over, your baby should be relaxed and getting a little sleepy. If supper is also casual, informal and happy, with a drink, a story, a game or a song – whichever your child prefers – followed by bed and a firm but loving goodnight, then just leaving your baby should work. As children get older they tend to express preferences for particular songs that they even like sung in a certain sequence, or favourite stories that they will follow with you in their storybook. Some of them will drop off to sleep by listening to music or while you sit by them quietly reading or singing. Find the bedtime routine that suits your child best and follow it every night without fail (*see p.151*). Familiarity brings security and that brings a happy child at bedtime, and she is more likely to go to sleep without a fuss.

Prolonged separation

The effect of prolonged separation varies a great deal with age. Before the age of six or seven months, there are usually no signs of distress when, for example, babies are admitted to hospital or are separated from their parents for extended periods. From the age of six months to four or five years, however, children are acutely distressed, and it is possible that boys are more

Comfort while you're away
Leaving one of your garments that smells of you, such as a scarf or a sweater, may go a long way to easing the pangs of separation.

disturbed by separation than girls. If young children have had an unhappy first experience of separation, they are more likely to be upset by a second. The longer the separation, the more disturbance the child shows, especially if it is separation from mother, father and/or siblings.

The effects can be mitigated by receiving mothering from another individual, say a foster parent or a loving nurse, especially if the following are noted:

- Care is given to follow the baby's known daily routine and the pattern of child-rearing to which she is used.
- A brief period of familiarization is arranged so that the child can meet the person who is going to take care of her before the separation occurs.
- Memories of the past are kept fresh in the child's mind by the caregiver talking about them.

All about crying 2 to 3 years

As your baby gets older the reasons for crying become much more complicated. Her thinking becomes increasingly sophisticated and she has a much wider appreciation of the world and what is going on in it; she has insight into your motivations and understands your more subtle expressions of approbation and disapproval; she is becoming acutely aware of her own position in the family, among friends and in the world in general; she has new insecurities and anxieties. Fears are no longer confined to simple ones like the fear of separation and there are all sorts of new and unusual things happening every day that may cause fear. Because your child's appreciation of the world is growing, there is increasing potential for her to become upset by events. While she is gaining in self-confidence she is also becoming sensitive and more likely to feel shame, resentment, frustration, anger, jealousy and dislike, all of which may be upsetting and cause her to cry. Also, because she knows more of the world she is becoming aware of the threats that are around and how they may affect her. She has to face quite a lot of them alone. It is not easy for anyone, let alone a small child, and it is not surprising that she resorts to tears fairly often.

TIPS FOR MAKING SEPARATION EASIER

Separation anxieties

Children well over the age of three still dislike being separated from their parents, even if you are only going to spend the evening out of the house. Up to the age of five or six it is quite usual for a child to shed a few tears until she is reassured about some of the details of the evening.

One of the most difficult separations for a child of this age is when her mother goes into hospital for the birth of a new baby. Apart from the jealousy that most children feel at this time (see p.253), there is the additional upheaval of the separation from the mother. Prepare your toddler well in advance of the birth by talking about the new baby, about you going into hospital, and who will look after her while you are away. Ideally it should be someone she knows well who understands her routine and who can ensure that it continues while you are away. Try to let her visit you as often as possible while you are in hospital.

Making separation easier

- Always spend a few minutes with your child quietly doing something nice before you leave. Never rush off without proper leave-taking.
- If you make a promise that you will be back by a certain time keep it and, as you are going, remind your child that you will always come back. If you are delayed, telephone to explain why.
- Have a goodbye ritual – to tell a story or play a game, to give a hug, to blow a kiss as you get into the car, to wave to your child as she stands on the step, or to honk your horn as you leave.
- Think up a few games – kiss a child's palm and fold her fingers around it. Tell her if she needs a kiss while you're away there is one for her.
- Never keep the fact that you're going out a secret from your child. Talk about it well ahead of time.
- If you are going to have a babysitter ask her to come a good half hour before you leave so she can start a game with your child before you go.

Fears real and imagined

Children suffer from classical fears between the ages of two and three. The fact that your child suffers from them is not a sign of abnormality. Two of the most common are described below.

Fear of the dark This is very common and not at all abnormal. Help your child by leaving a night light on in the bedroom. You don't have to go to any expense; just replace the standard bulb in her bedroom lamp with a low-wattage coloured one. You can also help your child by showing that darkness is nothing to fear. So go for a walk at night and point out all sorts of interesting things that you don't normally see during the day, like the stars or the moon, or some nocturnal animals (the nocturnal house in a zoo, which you often have to walk around in darkness may also be a good idea). In the summer take your child out in the garden and lie on the grass, covered by a blanket.

Fear of thunder Most children are fearful of thunder and lightning. The best you can do is to distract your child while it's overhead. You can tell a favourite story;

Walk away
A child won't persist with a tantrum if there's no audience. Try to walk away slowly so your child can catch you up for reconciliation and lots of hugs.

turn the television set up loud, play music or get out that game you bought "especially for a rainy day".

Dealing with fears

Encourage your child to talk about fears as soon as she is able to. Listen intently and show your child that you are interested and sympathetic. Hear her out even if she finds it difficult to put the fears into words. Try to help by giving examples, and show that you identify with such fears.

Never tease or shame your child about what she is feeling – that will only encourage her to hide her fears, and could drive your child away from you. You should always be the sympathetic friend who will give help and comfort in a frightening situation. You are going to have to show your child how to face up to fears and there are several different ways that you can actually do it.

- One of the best ways of reassuring your child is to show her that you are exactly the same as she is. All children love hearing stories about when you were little, like them. Tell your child some of the fears that you had, and explain how you managed to overcome them with your parents' help.
- If your child develops fear of a piece of household equipment, for instance the washing machine, help her to overcome it by explaining what it's for and how it works. Tell your child that machinery is nothing to be afraid of and to prove it, hold her in your arms while you fill it, and give a running commentary of exactly what you are doing. Go through the routine of putting in the washing powder and switching the machine on.

DEALING WITH INJURIES

You don't want your child to grow up being babyish about minor injuries, but you should never underestimate one, especially if you can see the damage. There is no point in saying that a small scratch doesn't hurt, because the sight of blood will scare your child and she will use pain as an excuse for your attention. Whenever your child comes to you with an injury give sympathy and support and use placebos whenever you can. The best possible placebo is a kiss and a cuddle and a gentle word. Next, try a favourite drink or snack, then suggest a small treat – perhaps your child's favourite food for the next meal, or having tea as a picnic in the garden. Always keep your "magic" ointment handy. In our house it is 0.5 per cent cetrimide cream, a simple antiseptic that can be used for all cuts and abrasions. It is very soothing and if your child believes that an ointment will work and take away the pain you are halfway there.

Put your hand on it to feel the vibration and then slowly and gently put your child's hand on it with yours on top so that she knows that you are not frightened, and that with your support she needn't be frightened either.
- If your child is scared of getting lost or of being in an accident, talk her through it. For instance, you can say things like, "If you got lost what is the first thing you could do? Well, I think probably the best thing would be to go to the first shop that you come to, go to the counter and say, 'I am Jane Brown. My address is ... my telephone number is ... Please will you ring my mummy and daddy?'"
- Never ever brush off a fear as though it isn't serious. It is serious to your child and you should treat it as such. So, for example, if your child is worried by the lamp in her bedroom, which casts an unpleasant shadow on the wall, try moving the light, or the bed, to a position where there are no shadows.

Dealing with irrational fears

One of the best ways to deal with irrational fears is to dispel them with some kind of physical activity. If your child is afraid of monsters or ghosts, say that you are a parent who can do magical things to them. Say that you are able to blow them away and give a big blow; promise that you will be able to get rid of them with the vacuum cleaner and switch it on; guarantee that you can flush them down the toilet and do so. There are some people who say indicating to your child that you believe in monsters and ghosts in this way encourages your child to believe in them too, and that a better alternative is to say that there are no such things as ghosts. The one trouble with this ploy is that your child won't believe you. She can't; she can only believe you if her fears are rational, which they aren't.

Crying from overtiredness

This is one of the most common reasons for crying, especially in the evening. The child may have been allowed to stay up later than usual, perhaps because of a visit from friends or relatives, or on a special occasion such as Christmas Day, when children tend to be thrown out of their usual routines, with more excitement than they can cope with. The result is an exhausted child whose overexcitement will spill over into tears at the slightest problem. The more you try to jolly her out of it (and this is especially true when visitors are involved), the more hysterical and inconsolable her crying will become. It is clearly better to prevent these situations developing in the first place, by trying not to let your child become overexcited and by ensuring that she has a rest in the middle of the day if you expect to let her stay up later than usual in the evening.

If you haven't been able to avoid it, and your child does become overtired and tearful, try to deal with her as calmly as possible. Take her off quietly to her room and cuddle her until she has calmed down; if she has a favourite book or song, and she has quietened down enough to be receptive, read or sing to her. Or let her have a quiet, relaxing bath, get her ready for bed, and stay with her until you are sure that she has completely relaxed and is ready for sleep.

Pre-school nerves

There are very few children who skip off happily to playgroup or nursery school with a cheery goodbye and hardly a backwards look. Prepare your child well in advance, no matter how self-confident she seems.

The first thing you have to do is to look at the various schools in your area. Visit each one, talk to the teachers at some length, and sit in on at least a couple of classes so that you can get a good feel for the atmosphere and for how interested the teachers are in the children and how much individual attention they are prepared to give during different activities. One of the most important things you have to establish is that there is a rapport between you and the teachers. If there isn't, there is no point in sending your child there, no matter how good the school appears to be.

Take your child to the nursery

Most nursery schools suggest that you take your child along for a brief visit several weeks ahead of when she is going to start. Don't make a big thing of it. Fit it in between errands and don't stay for any longer than about 15 minutes. Don't push her into it. Make the point of your visit a chat to one of the teachers and just let your child look, listen, observe and absorb. Let her wander around, touch, pick up and play with things, but don't force your child to do so. Some nursery schools will let your child visit more than once.

On the first morning be prepared for a shaky start, and for the necessity of staying with your child for the whole morning. Many nurseries welcome this and they will suggest that you help your child by participating in the lessons and staying

quite near her. This may not be necessary. As soon as your child feels that you are not going to leave, she will be quite happy if you sit at the back of the room. Take some work or a book along with you so that it is not a complete waste of time as far as you are concerned. If your child seems quite happy, say that you are just going to pop out to get something from the car and will be back in five minutes. Come back in exactly five minutes. If your child is distressed when you leave, don't go. If, on the other hand, she is quite happy, you might let another half hour pass and say that you are just going to do an errand and that you will be back in 20 minutes. Be sure that you are back in time.

Take the lead from your child

Over the next few days, using your child's reaction as a guide, see if you can leave her for longer. Some children adapt very quickly to a nursery and you won't need to stay after a few days. Others may still want you to stay for about half an hour at the end of two weeks. Just fit in with them. The most important thing is that your child should feel that school is a happy place and that it is not associated with the unhappiness of being separated from you and of feeling entirely alone. A good teacher, who feels confident about your child and confident about herself, will very firmly suggest that you leave when she thinks the time is right. Being overprotective about your child at a nursery school only makes it harder rather than easier for your child, especially if she's capable of coping without you. If you have a good rapport with the teacher you should feel happy taking her advice in this.

All of my children liked a ritual when they first arrived at nursery school. No matter what it was, we always did something that took about five to seven minutes before I said goodbye, and then they always came to the window and waved. This seemed to keep a child of not yet three quite happy when I departed and you may like to try a similar routine.

Possible crying problems 2 to 3 years

Temper tantrums

A good method of handling temper tantrums when you are on your own with your child, and in the privacy of your own home, is to ignore them completely (*see* p.168). Alternatively, you could try to distract your child by saying something

Fear and anxiety
When a young child is upset about something, there's nothing like a cuddle from his mum or dad to make everything feel better.

unusual, amusing or silly, or try a tactic like switching the light on and off, or opening and closing the door several times.

However, as your child gets older, and there is a greater chance of her throwing a tantrum in a public place, there are a few different ways that you can handle them. The majority of temper tantrums are caused through anger and frustration – anger that she can't have her own way or that her body is not physically strong enough or well enough co-ordinated to do what she wants it to do, and every now and then your child needs, like everybody else, to give such anger full vent. You can help her by doing some of the following:

- If your child is having a temper tantrum in a public place, don't get flustered; just take her out of the room into another as calmly as you can. If you're in a shop, take her out into the street, or even to your car. If you're in a restaurant, take her to the toilet. It's easier to deal with the tantrum more calmly where there are fewer people about.
- Don't ever forget to congratulate your child and praise her when the tantrum is over and she has got control again. After all, it's only a stage she's going through.
- A lot of anger and aggression can be got rid of by physically active games outdoors. That is why toys such as tricycles, scooters and footballs are so good, because strenuous physical activity re-directs antisocial behaviour.
- If your child is expressing anger by shouting, join in for a few sentences and then gradually quieten your voice down, encouraging her to do the same, until you are both whispering. Then have a good giggle about it together.

BREATH HOLDING

As your child gets older she may try breath-holding attacks and her face might become quite blue during them. In this instance try any of the following tips:

- Blow gently on to your child's face.
- Sprinkle a few drops of cold water on to your child's face or apply a cold cloth.
- Gently pinch your child's nostrils together for a second or two.

- Give your child some paper and crayons or fingerpaints and ask her to paint or draw exactly what she is feeling.
- Let your child know that there's a set of "angry" toys like a drum to beat loudly, or a musical instrument to play such as a xylophone, or a particular marching song that can be shouted.
- It can help your child quite a lot to talk about anger and to let her know that you consider it to be a reasonable and valuable emotion to feel. It lets off steam but it also draws boundaries. Your anger tells her when she has overstepped the mark in all sorts of directions. Her own anger can be just as useful.
- Try to discuss with your child the causes of anger. Try to get to the root of the problem. It is one of the ways you can teach your child about sharing, tolerance, love, kindness, thoughtfulness for others, etc. If ever you think that such anger is justified, say so, and tell her why you think it is reasonable to be angry about something that has happened and then discuss the different ways that you might have reacted that wouldn't have been so hurtful and destructive.
- Show your child that anger is just as well expressed in words as in physical violence or destructiveness and let her know that angry words are much more acceptable to you than blows or breaking things.

Phobias

A phobia is different from ordinary fear. If your child is afraid of snakes, she is only afraid when she meets one at fairly close quarters. The rest of the time she doesn't give snakes a second thought. However, if your child has an actual phobia about snakes, she will become hysterical when she actually sees one, when she sees a picture of one, when she thinks of one, or when something reminds her of one.

One of the things you have to understand is that, even as your child gets older, the explanation of a phobia really doesn't make any difference: she is not open to rational explanations. The only way you can help your child overcome a phobia is to convince her in some way that the object of her fear is harmless. There are a variety of ways in which you can help her understand this:

- You can help your child to realize that such fears are unfounded by letting her know that you don't have the same fear but don't do it in a way that makes your child feel inferior.
- Another way is to show that peers aren't afraid of the phobic objects. If, for example, your child is afraid of dogs, it is quite a good idea to ask one of your friends who has a dog to bring it to the nursery school at pick-up time when your toddler can see that the other children are quite unafraid of it.
- Never, ever ridicule your child's fears. No matter how unrealistic they seem to you, they are very real to her. Give rational explanations wherever you can and always behave in a sympathetic, helpful and rational way.
- If the phobia starts suddenly, look for something in your child's life that is causing stress. If it is associated with something such as a parent going away, the death of a pet or starting nursery school, then there is a good chance that the phobia will be transient.
- But your child may be emotionally upset about something that is difficult to fathom. You can try some real therapy by very gently introducing the object of her phobia at the same time as she is doing something very pleasant, for example, while she's eating one of her favourite foods such as ice cream.

FAMILY CONFLICT

Of course your children have to grow up knowing the facts of life, one of which is that adults disagree occasionally, get angry and have rows, but for heaven's sake don't let them be frequent.

Don't row in front of the children

If your partnership is going through a sticky patch, don't row in front of the children. Children, of course, want their parents to inhabit an ideal world where there is no rowing, no anger and no acrimony, and they get very insecure when the people they love most don't seem to love each other. The greatest deterrent to having a row with my husband came when my second-youngest son,

at four-and-a-half years old, snuggled up next to me a few minutes after we'd had a row, looking very doleful. When asked what was wrong he said, "I don't know, but the world doesn't feel right".

Most children have an instinct to be peace-makers; mine certainly did. As soon as they heard a raised voice or an opinion vehemently expressed they'd start diversion tactics like "Do you want a cup of coffee, mum" and then actually interject with, "Please don't get in a woos", their term for getting in a state. It's very hard to lose your temper when a young child is pleading with you to stay calm. If you remember the damaging effect witnessing a row can have on children, it can act as a great deterrent.

11 Physical development

Watching your baby grow and develop is one of the most exciting aspects of being a parent, and during the first year you'll be astounded by how quickly your child changes. With each passing week he'll gain control over the various muscles in his body so co-ordination will improve, and with this improved co-ordination he'll be able to sit, crawl, stand and, eventually, walk and run. His manipulation abilities will improve and gradually, over the months, he'll develop fine control over his movements.

General development birth to 1 year

Every child develops at his own rate, and the ages at which various skills or aspects of co-ordination are achieved, are only approximations. Never try to force your child to go more quickly than he wants to – it will serve no purpose. Let him go at his own pace, while at the same time providing all the encouragement and help that you can.

The main changes that occur in your baby's general appearance in this first year of life, besides those of size and weight, are his proportion, posture and body control. Your baby's head gradually gets smaller in proportion to the rest of his body and his limbs lengthen and strengthen, ready for walking. During the first year your baby gains general control of his body so that it's no longer floppy and he can move it purposefully.

Your baby goes through the fastest growing phase of life in the womb. Growth and weight will continue to be rapid during the first six months, but the rate will slow down towards the end of the first year. In general, a baby of average weight will increase his length by a quarter during the first six months, and double his weight. His head will increase in circumference by about twice as much in the first 12 months as it will in the next 11 years.

Long-term changes

Most size/weight charts plot the baby's weight in kilograms or pounds against the baby's age in weeks and his length in centimetres or inches. Except for the first few weeks of life when weight gain is watched rather closely, it's best not to watch your baby's weight obsessively. If your baby looks healthy and acts in a healthy way, then it's highly unlikely that there's anything wrong. It is the long-term trends that are important.

When you look at your baby's growth you should pay attention to the regularity of weight gain rather than the amount. As long as your baby's weight is increasing over the weeks, even if it is a bit erratic, and he shows signs of being happy and thriving, then you should not worry about weighing him too often. Furthermore, all size/weight charts are constructed for an "average" child. The average child is a theoretical statistic. Your baby is unique and his pattern of growth and weight gain will probably be quite different from any other babies that you know. That doesn't mean that he's abnormal.

Milestones

These are stages or "punctuations" in a baby's growth and development.

Grasp reflex
Your baby is born with a "grasp reflex", which means that he will keep his fingers tightly closed over anything that is put into them; he loses this after a few weeks.

They always follow the same order, as each one depends on the previous stage. They come along with such regularity that it is possible to forecast with some accuracy when they will occur for most babies.

This does not mean, however, that all babies will develop at the same speed. Just as there is a wide spread in the growth of size and weight, so there is for the development of physical capabilities. While no two babies will develop at the same rate or in the same way there are some general principles that apply to physical development in all babies.

MILESTONES: BIRTH TO 6 MONTHS

Month	Milestone
Birth	• **Head control when on his back** If you grasp your baby around the upper chest and lift his body from the mattress, his head will be so heavy and floppy that it will just hang back. This is why it is so important to support his neck and head carefully. • **Sitting** Your baby won't be able to sit up at all without support. If you hold him in a sitting position his back will be round and his head will loll forward. He'll be very wobbly, and will collapse immediately unless supported. • **Crawling** Your baby will be born with a crawling reflex (*see p.26*), but will lose this as soon as his body uncurls from the fetal position.
1	• **Mobility** Your baby will have lost his very newborn appearance, but his legs will still be bent. He may lift his head. • **Manipulation** Your baby's hand will be held in a tight fist; he'll reflexively grasp anything put in his palm. • **Head control when on his stomach** Your baby will lie with his head to one side, with his bottom pushed up in the air and his knees slightly bent underneath his body. • **Sitting** Your baby's back will still be rounded and he'll only be a little steadier. However, he'll try and hold his head up for a second or two when held by you.
2	• **Mobility** Your baby continues to stretch himself. When lying on the floor, he can lift his head to a 45-degree angle and hold it for a few moments. • **Manipulation** He'll hold his hand open more often and his grasp will become voluntary. • **Head control when on his back** If you lift your baby from the mattress by holding on to his hands he'll be able to hold his head in line with the rest of his body for a second or so. • **Head control when on his stomach** Your baby's body will be more fully stretched out and he'll be able to lift his head from the mattress for a moment or two.
3	• **Mobility** Your baby's body will be completely uncurled and his legs will be extended. He'll hold up his head. • **Manipulation** His hands will generally stay open although he may not be able to grasp anything for long. • **Head control when on his back** If you pull your baby up from a lying position by his hands he will keep his head up in line with the rest of his body without additional help from you. • **Head control when on his stomach** He will now lie quite flat and be able to raise his head and hold it in this position for quite a long time. He'll begin to take the weight of his shoulders and head on slightly outstretched forearms. • **Standing** Once your baby can support his head, he'll enjoy being held facing you with his feet touching your knees. Lift him up and down so he feels his feet in contact with your legs and learns the sensation of taking his weight.  AT THREE MONTHS

Month	Milestone
4	• **Mobility** Your baby should be able to roll from side to side and on to his back. He'll support himself on his forearms. • **Manipulation** Your baby will have discovered his own hands, which he'll suck and play with. • **Head control when on his stomach** Your baby will be able to raise both legs off the mattress. He'll be able to support his chest and head by propping himself up on his forearms. This way he'll be able to see what's going on around him. • **Sitting** If you hold your baby in the sitting position he will be able to sit with his head held up; the lower part of his back will still be rounded, but the upper part will be almost straight. • **Crawling** Your baby will probably raise both chest and legs off the floor while making swimming movements with his arms.
5	• **Mobility** When placed on his stomach your baby will push his head well clear of the mattress. He'll roll from back to side. • **Manipulation** He'll be able to grasp objects between both hands and will love sucking his own feet this way.
6	• **Mobility** Your baby will be able to twist in all directions and may sit unsupported briefly. • **Manipulation** Your baby will be able to hold an object between finger and thumb and may be able to rotate his wrist. • **Head control when on his back** Your baby's head and neck will be so strong and well controlled that he'll be able to raise his head from the mattress and look at his toes. • **Head control when on his stomach** Your baby will be able to take the weight of his head, shoulders and torso on his outstretched hands, and roll from his back to his side. • **Sitting** Your baby will be able to sit up without support, but only for a few seconds. • **Crawling** Your baby will be able to support the top half of the body on outstretched arms and you may see the first signs of crawling when he bends his knees up below his body. Although he's moving into the crawling position he probably won't quite have got the hang of it, the result of which will be his rocking back and forth. • **Standing** By now he'll probably make jumping movements by bending and straightening his knees and hips whenever he's held in a standing position.

AT FOUR MONTHS   AT SIX MONTHS

MILESTONES: 7 MONTHS TO 1 YEAR

Month	Milestone
7	• **Mobility** Your baby's ability to sit will improve, although he may have to bend forward to balance himself. • **Manipulation** The finger and thumb become completely opposable. Your baby will hold an object in each hand and can transfer small objects from one hand to the other. • **Sitting** He will be able to sit alone but will be very unsteady. His back will still be rounded and he will have to support himself with both arms, probably by placing them in front of his body as a kind of brace. However, in this position he won't be able to move his hands in any way because he'll be relying on them for balance. Any movement will result in his tumbling over. • **Crawling** Probably within a month of the previous stage your baby will have begun to take his body's weight on one outstretched arm when he wants to. • **Standing** He may start a sort of dancing movement instead of jumping and he'll also start to hop from one foot to another. Babies quite often place one foot on top of the other then pull out the underneath foot and repeat the whole movement over and over again.
8	• **Manipulation** Your baby's dexterity will improve and he'll use a pincer movement to grasp small objects. • **Sitting** Your baby will be able to sit up completely unsupported and will be able to turn round. He will still be a bit unsteady so always make sure that he is surrounded by soft cushions in case he topples over. • **Crawling** Your baby will have begun to pull himself forward on the floor with his head held erect, making kicking movements. • **Standing** If he hadn't started his dancing movement instead of jumping, this will begin about now and he'll start hopping from one foot to another. He may also start standing on one of his feet, pulling out the lower foot and repeat it endlessly.

AT SEVEN MONTHS   AT EIGHT MONTHS

Month	Milestone
9	• **Mobility** Your baby will make determined efforts to crawl and may be able to support himself on hands and knees. • **Manipulation** Dexterity continues to improve. He begins to use his index finger to poke into holes. • **Sitting** Your baby's balance will be so well developed that he'll be able to swing his torso to look around and will be able to reach forward without losing his balance. • **Standing** He can take his full weight on his feet, but can't balance yet. If you support your baby firmly underneath the arms he will be able to take his weight on his legs and will try to move one foot in front of the other. Supported on your lap, he will try to take a step or two forward. At this stage you must support your baby very securely to take most of the weight because his balance is still primitive.
10	• **Mobility** Your baby will be able to crawl with both his arms and legs straight. He'll pull himself to a standing position. • **Manipulation** Your baby will be able to hold two objects in one hand. He'll be a bit clumsy in releasing them. • **Standing** The muscle control of his knees and feet will have improved and he will begin to pull himself up to a standing position on furniture despite the fact that his balance is still far from good.
11–12	• **Mobility** Your baby will probably be able to totter when supported but will "cruise" along furniture by himself (*see p.188*). • **Manipulation** Your baby can hold crayons, feed himself, give and take objects. Co-ordination will improve daily.

AT TEN MONTHS

AT ONE YEAR

Physical milestones

There are key developmental milestones that each child goes through.

- All milestones are reached in the same order and your baby will not usually go on to another milestone before the previous one has been mastered.
- The rate of development is rarely constant. It goes through periods where it is very fast (growth spurts) and it may then slow right down. So, while development is continuous, many children can take huge steps forward in a developmental spurt, and then slow down for a while.
- A primitive reflex or movement has to be lost before a baby can acquire a particular skill. For example, your baby has to lose the primitive grasp reflex (see p.27) before he can acquire the skill to grasp an object purposefully.
- Development always proceeds from head to toe. The first milestone to be reached is control of the head; control of the body then progresses downwards to the arms, then to the trunk and finally to the legs.
- When your baby is very young his movements are usually jerky. As he gets older the movements become smoother and more precise.
- A generalized activity very often makes way for a specific activity, so your baby at six months old may be making apparently purposeless leg movements that resemble walking, although they are quite different from the movements that your one-year-old child will actually make when he does start to walk.
- Development is measured not only in terms of what is done but how it is done.

In other words, as your baby develops so do his skills.

- The brain and the nervous system control movement and co-ordination so your baby can only reach the milestones when the brain is ready. For instance, your baby will only learn to pick up a small object between his fingers and thumb when the nerve connections to the finger and thumb are fully developed.
- When a new skill is being mastered your baby may appear to lose a previously learned skill. This is simply because he is concentrating on the new one. As soon as it is mastered the old ones will reappear again.
- Milestones can be affected by your child's personality. Independent, determined children nearly always try out and practise new movements more than others so it's not surprising that they master them earlier. A friendly, outgoing child often has a strong desire to communicate with others and may develop speech earlier than other children. You can encourage both of these characteristics in your child by the way you behave towards him (see p.225).

Sitting

Bear in mind that before your baby is able to sit up he has to develop sufficient strength in his neck, shoulders and trunk so that he can control his head and keep his torso steadily upright. He also has to learn how to balance himself so that he doesn't topple over every time he tries to pick something up or twist around to see what's behind him; most babies don't achieve this skill before the age of about eight or nine months.

New view of the world
Propped up in a bouncing chair, your young baby will enjoy seeing what's going on around him and watching what you're doing.

- From the age of about two months you can help your baby to learn to sit up by supporting his tummy and shoulders and by talking to him so that he momentarily tries to raise his head to look at you.
- By the time your baby is three months old he'll be able to control head, neck and shoulders but his back needs support because it's still rounded.
- At four months he'll be able to hold his head, neck and most of his back straight and all you'll have to do is hold on to his arms to keep his bottom steady and stop him bending too much at the hips.

Helping your baby to sit up

Now that you know how a baby learns to control his head and to sit up, you can help your baby by playing similar sorts of physical games to those played in the first months of life. These games will introduce your baby to the use of the muscles he needs for grasping, pulling and pushing.

Propping your baby up

From as early as six weeks you should include your baby in what's going on by propping him up with cushions in his pram or in a bouncing chair. With all of my children I found the bouncing chair the best way of propping them up. The chair is

SAFETY TIPS WHEN PROPPING YOUR BABY UP

- At about five to six months old most babies learn to roll over from their back to their sides and then from their front on to their back. Once your baby acquires this skill he must never be left lying anywhere except on the floor, in a space that you've cleared of all hard or sharp objects. You should never leave your baby alone anywhere.
- When your baby is propped up, surround him with cushions. By the age of six months, when only his lower back needs support, he should still be padded round the bottom with cushions.

- Never leave him propped up on a chair or bed – he should always be on the floor.
- At about seven months old, when your baby starts to sit up, but topples over many times while attempting to do so, you must surround him with cushions or pillows so that he comes to no harm.
- Beware of leaving lightweight cots, chairs or prams within his reach. Your baby could easily pull the whole lot over by grabbing on to a side of something unstable when he attempts to pull himself upright.

soft and so it moulds to the baby's rounded shape; it can be safely padded with soft pillows and cushions. But the baby must be strapped into it to prevent him slipping and his head must be supported with a cushion or pillow. Because the chair is so springy it responds to any arm movements and kicking and so your baby is encouraged to try to make things happen for himself. Never put a bouncing chair on a table or other raised surface in case your baby's movements "bounce" it off.

SAFETY TIPS

- Never leave your baby alone.
- Remove furniture with sharp edges and corners.
- Remove anything breakable from a surface that is less than 1m (3ft) from the floor.
- Don't leave wires trailing across the floor.
- Cover electric points with safety plugs.
- Make sure that there are no electric switches less than 1m (3ft) from the floor.
- Put safety gates across doorways and at the bottom of the stairs.
- Try to keep the floor clear of small, sharp toys.
- Make sure all fires are guarded.
- Don't leave any cloths hanging from tables that a baby could reach up and pull.
- Make sure that all furniture and fixtures are sturdy and safely attached to the wall.
- Never leave anything hot on the table in the same room as your baby.
- Make sure that stair banisters are too narrow for a small child to squeeze through.
- Make sure that all cupboard doors are closed firmly and that the handles are out of a crawling baby's reach; if they aren't, lock them or seal them with masking tape.
- Make sure that all containers of poisonous substances are locked away or out of reach.

Crawling

Before your baby can crawl he has to be able to get into the right position. He has to be able to straighten his body so that his legs are outstretched. He has to learn adequate control of his head and neck. He has to have the strength to push up on both of his arms so that his chest and head are clear of the floor.

It's difficult to specify at exactly what age a baby will start to crawl, so you should see the times on pages 181–183 as stages more than ages. What's more, you shouldn't worry if your baby shows no interest in crawling. Some babies hate lying on their tummies and they are usually the ones who love seeing what's going on around them. They will probably leave crawling to a later stage; indeed, some babies never learn to crawl at all, but still go on to walk perfectly.

Helping your baby to crawl

While I am very much against teaching your baby to make orthodox crawling movements, you can encourage him to start moving forward from a lying or sitting position:

- The best possible way is for you to sit a few feet from your baby and to encourage him to come towards you, possibly using one of his favourite toys as an enticement.
- Help your baby whenever you think he needs it, particularly if he's getting tired and frustrated because his efforts are unsuccessful, and make sure that you always praise any efforts that he makes.
- As he becomes more adventurous you can help by placing a toy just out of reach so that he has to use all his own

resources, including his determination, to get hold of it.

- Babies learn by mimicry from a very early age so once he starts trying to crawl it's not a bad idea for you to get down on the floor yourself and crawl as well.
- Slippery floors, although usually dangerous, can be encouraging for crawling babies because even the slightest movement is rewarded with forward motion.

Shuffling

To move forwards your baby has to co-ordinate hand movements and knee movements, but initially he may find this difficult and may devise a unique shuffling movement to propel himself forwards and backwards. This can be anything from a sideways crab-like movement to a kind of shuffling on his bottom with one leg tucked underneath for leverage. It doesn't matter what kind of manoeuvre your baby works out – all are acceptable. The important thing is that he's mastered the art of moving; it's a great achievement and he should receive a lot of praise for doing so. Don't discourage your baby from any odd movements he makes, but rather let him discover how to control and move his body in his own particular way.

The crawling baby

Once a baby has learned the knack of crawling (or shuffling) he can pick up speed very quickly so he needs to be watched constantly. He'll also need a lot of room so that he can move about to the full extent of his capabilities. For this reason, and to encourage your child to be as curious and adventurous as possible, try to give him plenty of clear floor space. Your crawling baby is getting stronger every day so beware of anything that's rickety or fragile because he'll break it very quickly.

Your baby will also get much dirtier now, and will put any object he finds on the floor straight into his mouth so make sure that he doesn't go near pets' feeding bowls or rubbish bins. Your baby's knees will take quite a bashing so put him into overalls or trousers and try to ensure that the floor is very smooth or covered with something soft to prevent grazing; your baby doesn't need shoes and should go shoeless until he's walking.

Standing

Because a baby's development progresses from head to toe, control over the muscles of the knees, lower legs and feet is rarely achieved before the age of ten or 11 months. It's only at this time when he's strong enough and has sufficient balance to be able to take the whole weight on his feet and stand up.

Sitting down

Standing up is easy compared to sitting down, and it usually takes a baby three or four weeks to master getting back down to the floor again from a standing position. He usually does this by sitting down backwards with a thump, or by carefully sliding his hands down the support until his bottom's on the floor.

Until he's mastered this he'll probably just stand still and scream for your help. There may be a period of frustration for both of you before he learns to drop down into a sitting position. You can help your baby by lowering him down gently so that he gains confidence in the movement. You can also help by not getting annoyed when you have to do it over and over again.

"Cruising"

After your baby has gained sufficient confidence from pulling himself up into a standing position and getting back down on to the floor again it will probably be about four weeks before he starts "cruising". He does this by facing what he's holding on to and then gradually inching his hands along the support; he then brings the rest of his body into line with his hands by taking small sideways steps, one foot after the other. As he gets confident using this method he'll hold on to the support at arm's length and will only use it for balance.

Once your baby has reached this stage it's then only a very few weeks before he will let go of the support and move forwards to the next piece of furniture. These first few steps are very unsteady. To increase the width of the base, he will keep his feet quite wide apart and balance

Cruising around the furniture
If you have low, sturdy furniture, your baby will be able to pull himself up against it and "walk" around it supporting himself with his hands.

by holding his arms up and forwards, slightly bent at the elbows. It is not until your baby is quite proficient at walking that he will bring his feet closer together and let his hands drop to his sides.

HELPING YOUR BABY TO STAND

- Don't put socks or shoes on your baby's feet. He has much better grip and balance when his feet are bare. If your house is cold, put booties with suede soles on your baby's feet. Make sure that all your baby's clothing is loose so that movements aren't restricted.
- All the furniture in the room should be heavy, firm and stable so that there's no risk of it toppling on the baby as he holds on to it.
- Resist the temptation to hurry your baby with standing or walking. He'll do it in his own good time and nothing you do can hurry the process.

- Don't play tricks on your baby by suddenly removing your support. This will give your baby a bad fright and could damage his trust in you because until that moment you were the one thing that he could rely on.
- Don't start to use sleeping bags for the first time now – your baby will try to stand and will fall. If he's used to one it's all right to continue with it.
- Make sure that all wires and flexes are tucked away or firmly tacked down. He may start by cruising around furniture but a light flex may seem an ideal "hold" once he's on the move.

General development 1 to 2 years

During the second year your baby's body grows in length, loses its rather plump, podgy appearance, becomes firmer, stronger and more muscular, and starts to take on adult proportions. His balance and co-ordination will have improved and fine movements are mastered.

Size and weight vary a lot from one child to another, just as they do from adult to adult. Your child's weight gain will be proportional to your child's size, therefore small children gain less weight, less quickly, than large children.

Physical milestones

At 13 to 15 months Your baby should be able to stand by himself and take one or two steps to reach a support. However, he won't be able to get up from the sitting to the standing position without support (from you or by holding on to furniture).

At 15 to 18 months Your baby will be able to raise himself to the standing position unaided. He will probably begin to walk without any support in the early position of feet wide apart and elbows high. Practise more leg movements with your baby, using a large soft ball that he can try to kick to you. This also helps his balance

At 18 to 20 months Walking will become steadier and his arms will drop down by his side. Your toddler will almost certainly want to walk upstairs.

At 21 to 24 months Your toddler will be able to maintain his balance while he bends over to pick something up and will not fall over. Dance with him to help him practise a wide range of movements.

Manipulation milestones

At 12 months Your baby will have mastered the adult grip, which is a fine movement achieved by bringing the finger and thumb together. If you ask your baby for something he will give it to you, and will be able to roll a ball across the floor.

At 13 to 15 months Your baby will be able to hold two small objects in one hand; he will be able to put one block on top of another and may try to make marks with a pencil. When it is time to be undressed he may start taking off his shoes.

At 18 months Your baby can build a tower of blocks, possibly three or four high. He will be quite skilled at manipulating food with a spoon. If you show him how, he will open a zip.

At two years Your baby will have learned turning and screwing movements with his hands so he'll be able to open a door with the doorknob and may be able to unscrew a loose lid. He'll enjoy washing his hands.

Turning pages
By the time he is about 18 months your baby will be able to turn over the pages of a book.

Walking 1 to 2 years

There's no right age for your baby to start to walk. Your baby's first unsupported steps will probably occur some time between nine and fifteen months, but there's a wide variation either side of these figures. The reason for this is not known although very often there's a family history of early or late walking. Despite the very wide variation in the age at which babies learn to walk, they all have to pass through the same well defined stages of development before they can walk with confidence and good balance.

Babies can stay for a variable length of time in each phase and you should never make the mistake of trying to push your baby too hard to move from one to the other. You will give the greatest help if you are there with encouraging words so that your baby doesn't lose heart. Learning to walk is one of the most difficult things he'll ever have to do so make your baby proud of his achievements.

Stages of walking

1 Your baby will probably have started cruising around the furniture before he reached the age of one. He'll slide both hands along the support and bring up his feet to align with the rest of his body. Balance will be a problem.

2 He'll still cruise but he'll stand further away from the furniture and take more of his body's weight on his feet. He'll start to move one hand over the other instead of sliding them together and, as he becomes more confident, will start to move both hands and feet together. This is important because, for a second, your baby has the confidence and the balance to take all his weight on one foot.

3 Your baby will really enjoy the independence of moving around rooms using any support he can, and the next stage will be the negotiation of gaps between two supports. He will only do this if he can hold on to both supports at

HELPING YOUR CHILD TO WALK

- Arrange the furniture around the room so that he can go down one side, across and up the other.
- Initially, gaps between furniture should be no bigger than the width of your baby's arms so that he can hang on to something with one hand and stretch out the other to reach the next support easily. If the gaps are too big your baby won't be able to reach the support that will enable him to cross the gap.
- While your baby is learning to walk make sure that the floors aren't slippery – one bad bang may put him off walking for several weeks.

- Make sure the room is baby-proofed, with no flexes or objects that can be pulled over.
- He doesn't need shoes or socks; bare feet are safer not only because there'll be no risk of malformed feet but also because he'll be able to grip well and get used to the sensation of weight.
- A useful aid to complement cruising and your baby's first steps is a pushing trolley or cart. Make sure it has a stable wide base so it won't topple over. Don't use a baby walker.
- Always stay close at hand when your baby is taking his first steps.

Walking trolley
Your toddler's mobility and independence will be greatly enhanced by sturdy, wheeled walking toys such as this one.

once. At this stage he still has to feel securely supported, and will only let go of one support when he's holding firmly on to the other.

4 Your baby will start to cross gaps that are wider than an arm's span. While still holding on to the support with one hand, he will move into the centre of the gap and, having got his balance, will release the support and take a step towards the next one, making a grab for it with both hands.

5 Your baby will begin to "toddle". He will manage to stagger a couple of paces to reach the second support.

6 Your baby will launch himself into an open space and take several unsupported steps with confidence. He may only take half a dozen steps before losing his balance and sitting down with a thud.

SAFETY TIPS

- Remember, that once your toddler can walk, he'll also be able to climb, so fit bars to all the windows, or fit special fasteners that allow the window to be opened only a few centimetres.
- Keep possible hiding places like cupboards or chests securely locked so that your baby can't disappear and get locked in.
- Be sure that any locks on room doors are out of reach.
- Do not allow your unsupervised child into a garden with open access to the road. Teach the road training drill as soon as possible.
- Teach your toddler how to negotiate stairs properly, by sitting on the top stair, putting his legs down to the one below and then following with his hands.
- Keep all the handles of pans turned away from the front of the stove.
- Never leave anything hot lying where your toddler can reach it: keep it out of his reach until it is absolutely cold.
- Glass doors should never be so clean that your toddler bumps into them. Fix coloured paper or transfers on the glass to make them obvious.
- Keep all medicines in an approved medicine chest, high up and always locked. Never carry medicines around in your handbag.
- Move cleaning products out of reach or store them in a locked cupboard.
- Don't put rugs on polished floors unless they've been backed with double-sided tape or carpet grip to stop them slipping.
- Don't let your child near anything that is small enough to be swallowed or pushed up his nose or into his ear.
- Keep all sharp instruments, including kitchen equipment, out of your child's reach.
- Never leave sewing or DIY materials around.
- Never leave your child alone near water.

Your toddling child

When your baby first starts to toddle he will have very little control over his movements. However, by about 19 months he'll be able to walk backwards as well as forwards and may even have mastered running. Once he can run he'll be able to jump.

By two years old he'll be able to veer and swerve while he's running and will be able to glance over his shoulder without losing balance. He will be able to stop quite suddenly without toppling over and will have sufficient balance to be able to bend down to pick something up without having to sit down first. If you encourage him he'll be able to kick a ball, although it will be rather a dragging kind of kick because he can't maintain his balance on one leg for very long.

Your toddler will want, quite naturally, to race about as much as possible, but out of doors you'll have to be careful. He'll have no traffic sense as yet so you'll either have to hold his hand or use reins. I believe that reins are the most satisfactory solution

Starting to toddle
When your baby first starts to toddle she'll only be able to travel in one direction and will be incapable of swerving or stopping once she's got up speed.

for both of you: they hurt neither your arm nor your toddler's (like a wrist strap might) and they give him far greater freedom than he would have holding your hand

Although your toddler's strength will increase during this year, don't expect him to walk much further than a couple of hundred yards at a time. If you're in a hurry, or can't bear the idea of constant stops and starts to look at things, take a pushchair of some sort and use that when you need to.

If your baby has a set-back in the development of walking, don't worry. He's learning so much at the moment that it's quite understandable that he may slow down in one aspect of his development to concentrate on another; he may also suffer lapses after an illness. Just relax and let your baby develop along his own lines.

General development 2 to 3 years

By your child's third year his rate of growth and development will have slowed down. He will have almost complete control over his body, and many movements will have become automatic – he'll no longer have to concentrate or make an effort to do things requiring fine physical manoeuvring or co-ordination. He will have the co-ordination to build a tower of blocks, he will try to get dressed and undressed and may even manage to undo buttons.

Physical milestones

At two years Your child will be able to go up and down stairs alone, but he'll put two feet on each step before moving on to the next. He'll kick a ball successfully without falling over.

At two and a half years He'll be able to walk on tiptoe, jump in the air and on and off objects. However, he won't be able to stand on one foot yet.

At three years He'll walk upstairs with a foot on each step but will have to put both feet on the same stair coming down; he'll jump off the bottom step. He'll be able to stand for a few seconds on one foot but he won't be able to skip yet.

Manipulation milestones

At two years He'll put on his own gloves, socks and shoes successfully. He'll manage to rotate his elbow accurately so that he

Learning pencil control
He will be able to hold a pencil and will enjoy scribbling on paper. Give him washable felt pens as he won't necessarily confine his work to the paper.

can turn a door handle or unscrew a lid. He'll begin to draw pictures with pencils and crayons.

At two and a half years He'll be able to take off his trousers and underpants by himself. He'll be able to thread big beads on to a string and will be able to fasten large, easily placed buttons.

At three years He'll be able to dress and undress himself completely as long as all the fastenings are within reach; he'll manage a Velcro fastening on his shoes and even the buckle on his sandals. He'll be able to hold a pencil well enough to draw and colour quite accurately now and he may also master the difficult skill of using scissors.

Co-ordination birth to 1 year

During the first six weeks your baby's hands will be held in fists, although they'll probably open and close when he cries. By about eight weeks, your baby's hands will be open more often, and the grasp reflex (*see p.27*) will be replaced by a voluntary movement on your baby's part. Some parents worry at this stage because their baby doesn't hold on to objects as tightly as before. Don't worry – your baby is simply learning a new skill, which he will perfect within a couple of months.

Up to this age, he won't have tried to co-ordinate the movements of fingers and hands. Instead, he'll spend a great deal of time discovering how they look, feel and move; he'll hold them open most of the time and will move his fingers and watch them closely. It's as though he's assessing his powers before starting to use them.

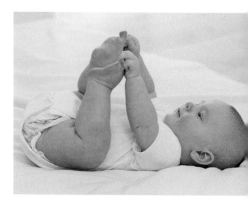

Playing with his feet
As your baby develops co-ordination he will try to grab everything. He will play with his feet as well as toys put within his grasp, and everything goes into his mouth.

Developing control

Between four and five months old he'll have voluntary control over reaching – he'll probably move both arms towards an object and grasp it between his two hands. At about six months old your baby will try to hold an object, either between two hands, or in one hand by squeezing it between the palm and fingers; there's no fine control.

However, he'll be able to differentiate between large and small objects and will open his hand accordingly. He'll love the feel of things, so provide lots of different textures to clutch and handle, as well as different shapes. When he's lying down he'll probably reach out, grab a foot and put it in his mouth. He won't know exactly what to do with all objects, so if you offer a cube he may hold on to it, but if you offer a second one, he'll drop the first without thinking. At around this time he'll start to explore how he can use his hands in feeding. Hand–eye co-ordination will be sufficient for your baby to pick up finger foods and start feeding himself, although it is anything but accurate.

Learning how to let go

At about eight months old your baby will hold something out to you but will not yet have learnt how to let it go and give it to you. He will not reach this milestone until he's about a year old, when dropping things deliberately from his highchair or buggy becomes a very entertaining game. From now on your baby's ability to grasp becomes more and more refined. By the

HAND–EYE CO-ORDINATION

Month	Skill	How to help
Up to 2	Until he is about eight weeks old your baby won't have learnt to use his hands. He'll be learning to focus; the maximum distance at which he'll be able to focus will be about 20–25cm (8–10in).	Your baby will try to focus on anything which is moving, for instance a highly coloured mobile. However, your face will be the most interesting object in his whole life, so make sure that he sees that often and close. Hang interesting objects within his eyeline, no further away from him than 25cm (10in).
2–2½	Your baby will have opened his hands and will watch them with fascination. Focusing distance is not much more than 30cm (12in) so he'll bring hands and fingers close up to his face so that he can watch them moving.	As soon as your baby's hands are open they are ready to have things put into them. The most interesting toys are the ones that make a noise, like a rattle. They are also useful because your baby starts to make a connection between what his hands are doing, what his eyes are seeing and what he can hear.
2½–3	Your baby will watch his hands very carefully and with a lot of concentration. Once he does this you'll know that he has made the connection between seeing and doing. At about this age your baby may make a clumsy movement with either hand to get near an object.	Your baby is learning to judge distances and to move his hands to where his eyes think something interesting is happening. Put a string above his cot or pram with lots of interesting objects hanging from it. Let them swing freely so that your baby can reach up to touch them to make them move and see them move as a result of his action.
3–4	Your baby will touch everything in sight, and will be learning how to measure distances using his hands and eyes. He'll look at an object and then confirm the distance by trying to reach it. Instead of using an open hand, he tries to make a fist before he connects with it.	Your baby will now be too old for swinging things. If something goes out of reach it will only frustrate him because he is longing to grasp it. Instead of having objects dangling from a string, secure them to the sides of the cot. Alternatively, hold out an object so that he can try to get hold of it. Always wait until he's touched it before handing it over.
4–6	Your baby's hand–eye co-ordination will be developing rapidly so he judges distance well and his eyes will be mature enough to focus on objects at any distance. He will also be learning to grasp, so when he reaches out and touches an object he'll open his fingers and curl them around whatever he wants to hold.	Your baby really needs lots of practice at reaching out and getting hold of things; he'll also have a great deal of fun doing it. You can encourage him to do this by holding out the most interesting objects you can find, for example anything that makes a noise or is an interesting shape. It could be a plastic bottle, a ball of wool, or car keys.

time he is nine months old he'll have stopped holding an object in the palm of his hand and will hold it between his thumb and the side of his index finger, and once he's a year old he'll be able to pick up quite a small object between the tips of his finger and thumb, and will usually point at it with his index finger before picking it up. He'll be able to pass an object from one hand to another, and hold two objects at once, one in each hand.

Manipulation

Between eight and ten months your baby really learns to manipulate. He squeezes things, slaps, slides, pokes, rubs, scrapes and bangs them. He explores every new substance with his hands, including food, and will mix, smear and splash anything that is liquid or runny. Most objects find their way straight to his mouth, whether they're feet, fingers, plastic lids or toys. As he gets more skilled at manipulation the fascination of putting things in his mouth begins to wane, and he begins to play games like pat-a-cake. He'll also have developed the social skill of being able to wave goodbye.

Right- and left-handedness

If both you and your partner are left-handed there's a one in three chance that your children will be left-handed; the chances of this happening with two right-handed parents is one in ten. There is no natural law that states that one hand is superior to the other so it should never bother you if your child is left-handed.

Your child has no control over which of his hands is dominant; it is decided by the developing brain. Think of the brain as two linked halves, each of which controls different activities. One of these sides becomes dominant as your baby's brain develops. If the left side dominates, the baby is right-handed and vice versa.

In the first months your baby may seem to have no preferences, but in fact most newborns turn their heads more to the right than to the left. As your baby's co-ordination improves, you may find that he starts to use one hand more than the other. Don't be worried if he doesn't do this; a baby will develop at his own speed.

Never, ever, try to dissuade your baby from being left-handed. You could risk causing psychological side-effects like stuttering as well as reading and writing difficulties by altering what your baby's brain naturally wants to do.

Children love to copy
Sit and draw with your baby; he may not have enough co-ordination to draw for himself, but he'll soon get the idea from watching you.

Co-ordination 1 to 3 years

By the time he's a year old he'll be able to pick up something quite small, such as a button, between thumb and forefinger. If you take a pencil or crayon and make marks on a piece of paper he will take the pencil when offered it, and will try to imitate the marks that you have made.

By about 13 months your baby will have learnt to hold more than one object in his hand. Co-ordination will also be improving so if you show him how to build a tower of blocks he'll follow your example, putting one block on top of another. He'll start to remove items of clothing (*see p.46*), and will love pulling around a toy on a string, hammering pegs through holes and fitting different shapes into the appropriate openings. He'll be able to feed himself without any help and without making too much mess by the time he's 15 months old. He will attempt to brush his hair if shown and will be keen to help you around the house.

New accomplishments

By the time he is 18 months old your baby will be able to build a tower of blocks, four or five high, and turn over the pages of a book, probably two or three pages at a time. By the time your child is two years old his hands will be very well co-ordinated and he'll manage the complex movement of twisting something round in his hands so he can open a door by turning the doorknob and unscrew a loose cap from a jar. Washing and drying the hands will be a favourite pastime and two-year-olds usually start making their first attempts to dress and undress themselves. They can usually manage things like putting on their shoes but probably need help with their socks.

Always remember that your child will proceed at his own pace and that he cannot develop muscular co-ordination faster than the brain and nervous system are developing; no two children develop at the same rate. Don't make the mistake of expecting more from your child than he is capable of. He has a tremendous desire to please and if you constantly set your goals higher than he's naturally capable of reaching he will then feel demoralized because he has let you down. Worse still, he may become resentful and frustrated if he aspires to do things that are more complicated than his body allows. Your role is to help and encourage your child, not to set unachievable goals.

Skills to master

By the time your child is three years old he'll probably be able to do the following:

- Build a tower of blocks, up to eight or nine blocks high.
- He'll continue to dress and undress himself with increasing skill.
- He'll undo buttons within easy reach but may not be able to do them up.
- He'll help with any household task or chore that you suggest and will love playing games that imitate the kind of jobs that you do whether it's mending something or doing the washing up.
- He'll be capable of carrying plates and dishes to the table, and will be a much more co-operative member of the family.

How to improve co-ordination

Between the ages of two and three your child is a great experimenter so feed this curiosity by opening up his world and planning new discoveries. This is the age when children find out about (and also understand): the force of gravity – something always falls down; anything that is round will roll; something that is square will not; liquids flow and have no shape; they take up the shape of their container. Clay and dough can be squeezed and made into different shapes.

These discoveries can only be made if your child's co-ordination, not just of the hand and the eye, but also of the body and the limbs, develops and matures. Toys that demand good co-ordination will help your child to develop it. You can help him improve balance by simply encouraging him to walk along narrow steps. Always stay close by otherwise your child could lose his confidence and fall. You can improve his ball sense by throwing and catching with him, initially using something large and soft like a beach ball.

Encouraging adventurousness

Once your child becomes mobile, it is better to encourage a spirit of adventure than to be over-protective. Of course your child will fall a few times, that is inevitable, but it's better than having a child who has no sense of physical freedom or confidence. If you don't you are also doing your child quite a disservice because for the next seven or eight years most of your child's pleasures will be derived from physical activities. If he can't move with the same pace and accuracy as other children he may be left out of many enjoyable activities. An over-protective parent is one who insists on holding the child's hand if he wants to climb along the edge of a low wall. Conversely a parent who encourages physical activity will be the one who introduces a child to balancing on a fairly narrow surface, practising at home on a plank supported by piles of magazines.

One of the best ways of encouraging activity in your child is to join in and do it yourself. You are the best person to introduce your child to new physical activities. Just by imitating your physical movements, he will be learning new skills, without either of you knowing it.

Adventurous spirit
Exercise is vital for your child so encourage him in active play whenever you can. He'll have lots of fun with a wheeled toy such as a tricycle.

Vision birth to 1 year

People used to think that newborn babies could not see. It was thought that because they could not focus to any great extent their visual world need not be stimulating and could even be neglected. We now know that this is far from the truth. A newborn baby can see. The only difference between a newborn baby and an older one with mature eyesight is that the newborn baby cannot see as much, as easily, or as well. In other words, your newborn sees in a limited way, and you have to fit the visual world into a range that he can perceive.

Your baby's visual powers will not be fully developed until he's between three and six months old. He won't be able to focus on anything more than 25cm (10in) from his face. As his eye muscles become stronger and he develops binocular vision, his acuity will improve greatly.

Even though your newborn baby's eyesight is limited, his eyes are very sensitive to two things: the human face, and anything that moves. If you bring your face to within 20cm (8in) of your baby's you'll notice his eyes move and his expression change. Even a baby only a few hours old can bring both eyes together on to an object (convergence) and follow it if it moves. As he gets older his whole body may react with excited jerking movements when your face comes into focus.

Colour vision

When your baby is born the cells in the retina of the eye that see colours are not fully developed, so your newborn baby only sees the world in terms of muted shades. The first colours that your baby detects are red and blue, and then green and yellow. For the first few months of life your baby can only see the brightest kinds of colours so make sure that you have brightly coloured objects around him. Babies are also very attracted to black on white pictures or objects.

Three-dimensional vision

Because your baby can only focus on objects that are closer than 25cm (10in) from his face, the world appears rather flat and many details are not seen. However, even at two weeks a baby will automatically raise a hand to protect himself from something that is moving quickly towards him. It is necessary for your baby to have three-dimensional vision before he becomes mobile, and he probably won't crawl until he sees and understands the third dimension. A complete, three-dimensional picture of the world is not usually built up until your baby is about four months old and may not be perfect until six months old.

Checking eyesight

During the first few months of your baby's life you are the best person to check his sight although you shouldn't become obsessive about it. By the age of four months even an inattentive or lazy baby should focus on a brightly coloured object held 20–25cm (8–10in) from his face, especially if it makes a noise, like a rattle, and especially if it is moved. One of the most joyful sights in your child's life is your

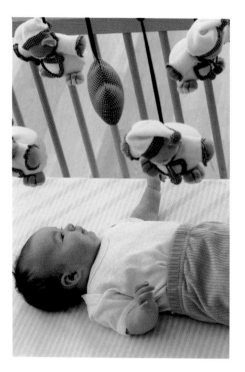

Something to watch
Your young baby is attracted to moving objects. String some brightly coloured shapes or a special mobile over her cot and she will love to watch them.

- Put very simple brightly coloured pictures around the rest of the cot within the baby's range of vision (no more than 25cm (10in) away for the first month).
- Put a mobile over the cot. This doesn't have to be an expensive item. It can be a couple of balloons or a few household objects hung on a coat hanger or on a wooden pole attached to the cot.
- String some interesting objects on elastic across the hinges of the pram hood so that your baby can watch them.
- If your baby's cot is near the wall, you can use toys with rubber suction pads to stick out from the wall between the bars of the cot for your child to watch and focus on.
- As your child gets older it is important that toys move and make a noise so dangle soft, light objects on strings so that they swing when your baby swipes them. Anything that jingles, such as a rattle or a toy with bells attached, is fun.
- In the car stick toys on to the back of the seat. You can also hang them from the side windows or the roof, as long as it doesn't cut down visibility dangerously.
- Your baby's never too young to go to museums or art galleries with you. If he's in a back-pack he'll be able to look at exactly the same things as you.
- When you put your baby outside in the garden either suspend some toys or mobiles from a tree bough or from a washing line. The washing itself is fun to watch as it blows in the wind.

face, and he should also react to your smile and bobbing head movements as you talk by around four months or so. If he isn't, don't be too concerned but mention it to your health visitor or doctor when you next go to see either one of them.

Stimulating your baby's eyesight

You can stimulate your baby's eyesight in many different ways.

- Put a fairly large photograph of your own face (or any face cut out of a magazine), at the side of your baby's cot so that he can practise focusing on one of his favourite objects – the human face. On the other side of the cot firmly attach a mirror so that he can look at his own face and also see it moving when he wriggles near it.

Vision 1 to 3 years

Around the age of one year your child begins to see, and can rapidly follow, moving objects with his eyes. His vision now is about as good as it ever will be in adult life. The main changes that occur during your child's formative years are to do with the ability to interpret what he sees so that he can use it to express ideas in words, pictures and movements. In other words, it is the connections in the brain between the eyes, the tongue, the pen, the brush, the intellectual thought, the hand and the rest of the body that mature, not the ability to see per se. As with other aspects of your child's growing up you should try to encourage the development of his eye/brain and eye/body connections so that he can reach his full potential.

You can do this by providing stimulating ideas, plenty of books, interesting toys and a varied range of activities.

Look out for changes

While I don't think regular eye checkups are necessary in a child who is developing normally you should be on the look-out for any changes in the appearance of your child's eye – that is a lazy eye, a drooping eyelid or a squint. Be responsive to signs that your child can't see clearly, for example, bumping into furniture or not being able to follow the trajectory of a ball that's thrown to him. Seek medical advice at once; don't wait to see if an abnormality clears up. Like a disused limb, a disused eye deteriorates rapidly.

Teeth birth to 1 year

There is no correct time for your baby to cut his first tooth. Some babies are born with a tooth, although this is rare, and yet it is still within the normal range to have none at 12 months old. It would therefore be misleading to give dates when you should expect your child to cut certain teeth, although it is possible to make a generalization about the order in which teeth erupt.

As a general rule, teething starts around six months old, after which many teeth appear up to the end of your baby's first year; the order in which they come rarely differs between children.

Teething

If you are on the look-out you will probably notice your baby's first tooth as it starts to push its way through the gum and form a small, pale bump. The only normal symptoms of teething are fretfulness and dribbling. You should never blame any other symptoms on cutting a tooth; it is a myth that teething can cause fever, diarrhoea, vomiting, convulsions, rashes or loss of appetite. Don't make the mistake of attributing any illness to cutting a tooth, so if you're at all worried get medical advice immediately. No parent likes to see their child in discomfort so I would suggest you do the following to help relieve pain:

- Offer your baby something firm to chew on like a raw carrot, a rusk or a cool teething ring. Your baby may find sucking rather painful, so give drinks from a cup instead.
- Try just gently rubbing your child's gums with your own little finger – this can help as much as anything. Certainly your attention and concern about his pain will bring him comfort.
- Avoid taking your child out in a cold wind, as this always seems to make the pain of teething worse. When you go outside in the winter try to cover most of your child's face and head with a warm hat or a hood and put a scarf around his neck and chin.
- Don't put teething gels containing local anaesthetics on his gums. They only have a transient effect, and local anaesthetics can cause allergies.
- Don't use teething powders and teething medicines. Your baby has many teeth to cut, and if you use any kind regularly you will be exposing your baby to a large amount of medication, much of which may be unnecessary and all of which may be accompanied by side effects.
- Take care if you use the water-filled teething rings that can be frozen to form ice if placed in the freezer. Careless use of these teething rings has been known to cause frostbite in babies. These rings can be used quite safely to cool down the mouth if they are just kept in the fridge as opposed to the freezer.
- Avoid the frequent use of paracetamol syrup. It is useful, but should not be given with any regularity except under doctor's orders. If you need recourse to it to soothe your fretful baby for more than two doses then you should consult your doctor or health visitor.

HOW THE TEETH COME IN

The first to erupt are usually the lower front incisors, then the upper two incisors. The two upper lateral incisors come next, followed by the lower ones. After this, the first upper molars erupt and then the first lower molars. The upper canines come in next, one each side, followed by the lower canines. The second molars erupt first in the lower jaw, and then appear in the upper jaw.

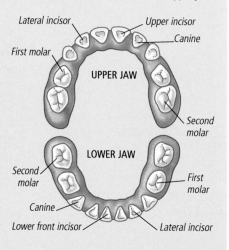

Lateral incisor
Upper incisor
Canine
First molar
UPPER JAW
Second molar
LOWER JAW
Second molar
First molar
Canine
Lower front incisor
Lateral incisor

Looking after teeth

When your baby has several teeth, you can start good habits early by encouraging him with a game of tooth brushing. First of all let your child watch you so that he can see how brushing should be done. Then just make an offer of a soft toothbrush as something to play with. He will almost certainly want to do what he has just seen you doing and will try to make the same kind of movements by putting the brush into his mouth and moving it to and fro.

Cleaning the teeth shouldn't be a serious business; it really should be playful. You are teaching your child to like and want to look after his teeth so you should avoid being censorious and make it a big laugh instead of a chore.

To actually get the teeth clean, take a piece of gauze with some toothpaste on it and gently rub it across the gums and any teeth that your baby has. It's important to clean the baby's gums even if there are no teeth because this keeps the mouth free of the bacteria that cause plaque. This also provides a good environment for milk teeth and later permanent teeth to grow into. The easiest position to clean his teeth/gums

First attempts at cleaning teeth
Encourage your baby to want to clean his teeth from an early age. At first give him a toothbrush to play with whenever you are cleaning your teeth.

will probably be with him on your lap, feet pointing away from you, mouth tilted up towards you.

Use a low-fluoride toothpaste at first, and avoid varieties made for children as they often contain a sweetener. Your baby may want to eat the toothpaste but you should stop him. Clean the teeth once if not twice a day and always after he's been given any medicine as they are often sweet and sticky to make them "more palatable".

Fighting tooth decay

The three most important factors in the care of your baby's teeth are diet and the absence of sugar, good dental hygiene and regular check-ups.

One of the best ways of taking care of your baby's teeth as soon as he has them is to see that his diet does not contain sugary foods such as sweets, chocolates, cakes, biscuits and very sweet drinks. Sugar, be it white or brown, is the arch villain in tooth decay. No child needs sugar. It is not necessary for health and you will be doing your child a favour if you don't encourage a sweet tooth, not only for his teeth but also for his weight.

Never leave a bottle containing milk or a sweetened drink lying around for your baby to suck on. His teeth will be constantly bathed in a sugary fluid, which will encourage decay. Give him a dummy if he wants to suck something.

Make sure that your baby's diet contains plenty of calcium and vitamin D, as they are essential for the healthy formation of the permanent teeth, which are already growing in your baby's jawbones. Foods that are rich in both of these nutrients are dairy products and fish; oily fish such as salmon, herring and sardines are particularly good.

Many people think that dental hygiene isn't important until your child has his permanent teeth. This is not true, so do follow a sensible cleaning programme for your child's teeth and, as soon as he's about two, start taking him for regular dental check-ups.

Teeth 1 to 3 years

At one time it was thought that milk teeth were not very important, but we now know that they are well worth looking after. First of all they guide in the adult teeth so that they grow in the correct position and secondly, if the primary teeth are lost through decay, the bone behind the teeth can be affected, eroding the support the adult teeth need. Your baby will be teething for most of the second year so be prepared for the molars to be a bit upsetting. The first molars are usually cut between 12 and 15 months when the upper molars appear first and are followed by the lower ones. The second molars appear between 20 and 24 months, in the lower jaw first and then in the upper jaw.

In general the later teeth are cut the less trouble they cause.

Once your child has all his teeth, give him plenty of chewy foods, and particularly fresh fruit and raw vegetables, to encourage the development of strong jaw muscles. As it happens this kind of food also has a cleansing effect as the fibres within them are shredded by the teeth. Take your child for regular check-ups.

Dental hygiene and care

The mineral fluoride has been proven to improve dental health and to reduce tooth decay. All water contains some fluoride but in some areas fluoride is added to drinking water. Dentists also recommend using

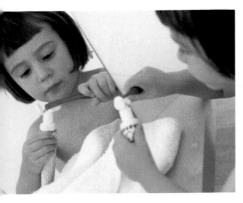

Gaining independence
Get your child into a tooth-brushing routine, which
should include always cleaning her teeth in the
morning and before going to sleep at night.

fluoride toothpastes, but in areas where water has added fluoride children under seven may be advised to use toothpaste containing lower levels of fluoride to avoid taking in too much (excess may cause fluorosis, which damages the teeth). Check with your dentist. He or she may even recommend supplements but these should only be given under dental supervision.

Help toddlers with tooth brushing

Until your child has reached the age of about six or seven he won't be capable of cleaning his own teeth thoroughly so you'll need to help him. He may object to this at first, and just clamp his jaws firmly shut. The best way around this is to make it into a game using a disclosing tablet. When chewed this exposes plaque as a dense area of colour, which can be brushed off.

Dentists generally agree that it doesn't matter how a toothbrush is used, as long as it removes plaque. At one time we were encouraged to brush the teeth upwards and downwards so that the gum margins were protected. However, it has now been shown that the best method, especially for children who don't have a great deal of co-ordination, is small circular movements on all surfaces of the teeth. However, make sure that the bristles have rounded tips and that they aren't too hard. If it is too hard it may cause the gums to bleed, then recede and the teeth to eventually become loose.

Always encourage your child to have a regular tooth-brushing routine, morning and evening. Don't feel they need to brush their teeth every time they have a sweet drink or a biscuit, but you can help by giving them a piece of cheese at the end of every meal. This makes the saliva alkaline and counteracts the sugary acid that erodes the protective enamel of the teeth and causes cavities.

VISITING THE DENTIST

Take your child for his first dental check-up before his third birthday, and make sure that this visit is as relaxed and pleasant as possible. It's important to take your child when his teeth are healthy, not to wait for any signs of problems.

Get your child used to the sight of the instruments and the smell of the surroundings by taking him with you when you go for your own check-up. If he can be trusted, and if your dentist has no objections, sit the child on your lap and let him watch while the dentist examines you. He'll no doubt be fascinated and will be delighted to copy your example. Just before your child's visit play a game of going to the dentist and look into each other's mouths. Then, when you actually get to the surgery, prearrange for the dentist to look at your mouth just before he looks at your child's.

12 Intellectual development

Your baby is the most responsive and most rewarding pupil you could ever meet. She wants to do more things, explore more areas and widen her horizons more than anyone else you know. She also wants to please you, and the combination of these qualities gives her an appetite for learning that should thrill you. One of the most important things to remember is that she's never too young to learn, although you'll have to tailor the way you introduce her to new experiences or the ways you try to teach her. Don't set her tasks that are beyond her capabilities as this will only lead to frustration. Guide her in all things, but never try to force her.

Learning birth to 1 year

Whatever you do don't waste the first crucial six weeks of your baby's life. Many people still think that because a baby isn't making sounds and moving very much she can't respond to what is happening around her and she can't learn. We know this to be entirely incorrect. Your baby's emotional and intellectual development during the first weeks of life is growing at exactly the same rate as every other form of her development, from her size and weight to her ability to co-ordinate.

I believe that, initially, the most important person in a baby's life is the one who most consistently looks after her. In the majority of cases this is the mother. You are her most important teacher. As adults we learn the most important and the most memorable lessons of our lives from people whom we like and with whom

we have a good rapport. If there is a special feeling of closeness, common ground, empathy and understanding with the teacher, then the lessons can be even more salutary and lasting. Exactly the same applies to your baby. All her learning will be made easier if she establishes strong bonds with you, her teacher, very early in life. A close runner-up to you is your partner. Your partner is your baby's next best friend; he (or she) should form a strong relationship with your baby as early as possible and be involved in as much of the "teaching" as you are.

The teaching you give your child is not teaching in a formal sense; there are no specific rules and no particular targets that your child has to reach. You can and should "teach" your baby by making the world interesting for her. Introduce her to

The five senses
Your baby has five senses and she wants to learn through all of them. She is eager and keen to meet new sights, sounds, smells, tastes and touches.

WHAT YOUR BABY UNDERSTANDS

Newborn baby Your baby will concentrate on your face if you bring it close to her, and she can distinguish your voice from anybody else's. When she hears your voice her eyes will move in the direction of it and she'll try to follow your face if you move it close to her. She can recognize your face if you place it about 20–25cm (8–10in) away from the time she's 36 hours old.

Four weeks If your face is close enough for her to focus on, she'll watch you while you are talking and she'll mimic your talking by opening and closing her mouth. She may stop crying when you pick her up because she knows you are a source of comfort. She imitates the movements of your face: she can use the right muscles to smile and grimace.

Six weeks She'll smile back at you and her eyes will follow a moving toy.

Eight weeks If you hold something brightly coloured above her head, she'll take a few seconds to focus on it and will then follow it as you move it from side to side.

Three months She'll immediately see a toy held above her. She'll smile when you speak and will

Stimulating games
Hold a mirror up so your baby can see herself. Point at her reflection and say her name as you do so.

make squeals and gurgles of pleasure. There will be obvious signs of curiosity and interest in what is going on around her.

Four months At feeding times she'll show signs of excitement. She'll laugh and chuckle when played with. She'll love being propped up because she'll be able to see what is going on around her; she'll turn her head in the direction of any sound.

Five months She'll be aware of strange situations and can express fear, disgust and anger.

Six months Your baby will become very interested in mirrors and in seeing herself in one.

Eight months She'll know her name and will understand the word "No". She'll probably have developed little sound signals like a cough to attract your attention when she reaches out for something that she wants. She'll probably want to feed herself at around this time.

Nine months She'll show a will of her own and may stop you when you try to wash her face. She concentrates very hard on toys and games and will even turn a toy over in her hand so that she can examine it carefully. When an object is hidden under a cloth she'll lift the cloth up to see the object.

Ten months She'll probably be able to clap her hands and wave bye-bye. She'll show that she understands a small number of words, and very short, simple statements.

11 months She'll know, and will enjoy, simple games like "Peek-a-boo". Her other favourite game will be dropping things and having you pick them up. She'll become very noisy and will want to shake and bang anything that makes a noise.

12 months She'll do anything to make you laugh and will repeat it over and over again. She'll enjoy "reading" simple books with you and will help you to undress her by lifting up her arms when you take off her clothes. She may know a few simple words like bottle, bath, ball, drink.

new experiences, explain everything that you see and, above all, join in with every activity so that you and your baby learn together. You have to give encouragement at all times, give praise when even the smallest thing is achieved, and provide constant support, especially if your child fails to do something that she really wants to do. Without your support your child won't gain the confidence she needs.

Look at your baby

In the early days it is a prerequisite to face your baby; facial contact is extremely important. One of the few things that a baby responds to visually in the first days of life is a human face (*see p.28*). Your newborn baby has to see that face as close as 20–25cm (8–10in) from her own, so bring your face up close to your baby's and make it "interesting". Move your head as you talk; raise your eyebrows and, most important of all, smile. Look deep into your baby's eyes all the time, and make constant eye contact. It has been shown that parents who face their children while they are feeding or playing with them, and look into their eyes, are much less likely to use corporal punishment to discipline their children as they grow up. It's hardly surprising that the children of such parents are much better able to form relationships with people as they get older.

Have conversations

Your baby holds her first conversation with smiles. The conversation goes something like this: you are chatting away to your baby about any subject you like with your face about 20–25cm (8–10in) away. You are animated and you smile a lot. Your

baby sees this as a friendly approach. Every baby has the natural human desire to respond in a friendly way, and so she smiles back. You are delighted with her recognition, her response and her friendly smile. You smile some more, you may laugh, you may cuddle her, you may kiss her. She loves that, so she smiles more to please you. You do more things to please her, and so the conversation goes on.

What is interesting about this kind of interaction between parent and baby is that your baby has learned two very important lessons. A smile from her gets a smile back. It may even get more substantial rewards like hugs and cuddles, as well as praise and approbation. The second lesson is that she has found a way of pleasing you and interacting with you. She will learn that she can initiate this interaction and she'll go on to use this method with other people. It is well known that the amount of smiling a baby does is related to her intelligence because it shows that she has learned that if she smiles the world will like her and life will be more pleasant. So you have given her a very good start in coming to terms with and managing the world around her.

Read to your baby

Children love books and your child will respond from a surprisingly early age if you look at them with her and read to her from them. Reading books together will teach your child about colours, the alphabet, numbers and names for simple objects. Your baby's never too young to be read to – your voice will be soothing to her, and you'll soon find that books at bedtime are a useful and pacifying part of your evening

Reading together every day
Settle into a comfortable chair and read a story to your baby. She will enjoy turning the pages of the book and looking at the pictures with you.

routine. The bonus you may never expect is that once you have introduced your child to books she may want to read them by herself too. You'll have done her a great service because you'll not only have introduced her to the idea of entertaining herself, but also to a pleasure that will last her for the rest of her life – reading and learning from books.

I suggest you start off with board books as they are brightly coloured and robustly made. For variety, buy some pop-up books as well but resign yourself to your baby's rough treatment of them.

Learning spurts

Your baby doesn't grow, develop and learn at a constant rate. Learning spurts are well known and every child has them. During a learning spurt, your baby will gobble up new ideas, acquire new skills and put them into practice immediately. However, while she's going through these learning spurts some activities, and possibly certain skills that she's already learned, may appear to slip. Don't worry. They won't have gone for good. It is just that your baby is using all her concentration to learn something new, but once it is learned she'll regain all the other skills.

During a learning spurt you should try to make your child's life as interesting as possible. Of course if your child shows that certain things are enjoyable then you should do them as often as you can, but don't hesitate to introduce your baby to new things too; she is ready to learn and absorb information at a very fast rate. And don't be too discriminating about the kind of entertainment you give either. Babies simply sieve out what they prefer and understand, and let the rest go by. In the first year learning is an entirely piecemeal process, so you'll help your baby most if you provide as wide and interesting a range of things as possible.

Learning spurts are invariably followed by periods when development appears to slow down. Treat them as recovery periods during which your baby consolidates newly learned skills and prepares herself for the next spurt. Don't get anxious about this – just let her practise the skills that she has already learned. You can help during these slower learning times by practising with her, saying something like "Let's sing that song again", or "Why don't we try to push the peg through that hole again?".

Let your child guide you

All the way through life, teachers who succeed do so by helping us to develop and reach our full potential. They help us maximize our strengths and minimize our weaknesses. As your baby's teacher, it's important to try to make the best of her good points and play down her bad ones. You also have to give your child the kind of help she needs when she needs it. Giving help is worthless if the person who

is being helped doesn't really require it or like it, so while you have to be an active helper, don't be an interfering one. Your baby should not be learning what you want her to learn, she should be learning what she wants to learn, and this should be your first priority.

You have to suppress any ideas of what you think a child of her age ought to be doing and respond to what she wants to do. This means that you have to be guided by your child. You have to respond to her needs. While it is your job as a good parent to introduce her to as wide a range of interesting things as possible, it is not your job to decide which of those things she should find interesting. In other words, having presented her with the menu, you must let her choose her own dishes.

Water play
All babies enjoy playing with water. Fill a plastic bowl with water and give your baby lots of unbreakable containers to pour and fill.

Learning 1 to 2 years

During the first year of your baby's life the accent was on learning physical things: she learned to crawl, to stand up and possibly even to take a few steps. The ability to do these things brought with it a sense of physical achievement and a sense of independence. She was able to go and explore the world without having to wait for you to bring it to her.

During this second year she'll not only consolidate all the physical skills she acquired in her first year, but she'll also master one of the most difficult intellectual ones – speech (see p.229). Your child will be struggling to express her thoughts and desires through speech and with her increasingly able brain she'll now see herself as a separate entity to you; she'll be aware of "self". She'll probably be quite frustrated this year and you may notice that more tantrums occur during this period. She'll need a lot of affection, encouragement and support.

Learning and speech

This is one of the most important intellectual lessons that your child will ever master. Without it, many of the other learning skills are delayed and may even be prohibited. Learning to speak is almost an act of survival; a child quickly learns that she has to communicate to survive.

Early communication, as we have seen, is not with words; initially it's with cries. The first conversation is usually with smiles; later it may just be with a head movement.

INTELLECTUAL DEVELOPMENT

12 months Your baby likes looking at simple books with you and loves a joke – she will repeat anything that makes you laugh. She'll understand that she should hold up her arms when you dress her and knows the meaning of simple, frequently used words like shoe, bottle, bath. Your one-year-old may even say one or two intelligible words.

15 months She will show you that she wants to brush her own hair. She'll know what kissing means and will give you a kiss if asked. She'll be very thrilled by any new skill and will want to help you with any household chores like dusting. Even though she doesn't understand individual words she can understand quite complex sentences.

18 months When you are reading together she will point to things, like a dog, ball, cow. She will recognize a cow and say "Cow". She'll know the different parts of her body: if you ask her where her foot is she will point to it, and to her hand, her nose, her mouth or her eyes. She'll know the difference between her nose and Mummy's nose. If you ask her to fetch something she will.

21 months She will come to you, attract your attention, and take you to things that she is interested in or has a problem with. She'll love scribbling with a pencil. She'll begin to understand and obey simple requests and questions.

Two years She likes her own company and will play happily on her own. Instead of just scribbling with a pencil she will make up and down strokes in imitation of writing. She knows the names of many familiar objects and toys and will use the words with meaning. Once she learns the meaning of a word she may repeat it continuously.

You may notice that your child just bobs her head to say thank you, and then a little later she may stand close to something that she wants and just shout for your attention. Once she has got it she will point to the object. These early lessons tell her that life will be a lot easier if she can communicate with the world around her in the language that is commonly used, that is, with words rather than gestures.

In learning to use words a child learns about the world around her and how people behave in it. Very often she will try to guess at the meaning of a word from the general sense of what is being said and the tone of voice that is used to say it. In discovering language, your child makes connections between sounds and what she understands about the nature of things that surround her.

When she first uses words she'll use them generically, and they'll have a much wider meaning for her than they do for an adult. For example, "Nana" (banana) may be her word for all fruit because that's the name she remembers first learning for a single fruit. However, with your help your child will learn the difference between a car and a lorry even though they both move on four wheels, and between a cat and a dog even though they are of similar size and shape and have tails.

Talk to your child

Your child is learning the art of communication. For this to happen you must communicate with her. If she wants something, tell her that you understand what it is that she wants and give it to her, naming the object as you do so. Don't talk to her without looking at her. If she wants

your attention stop whatever you are doing, turn to face her and listen. When your child first starts to learn language she learns it in broad strokes, so while she may not understand individual words, she very often gets the gist of the sentence. Give her lots of clues to help with this. In the evening when it's time for bed, start tidying up the playroom, ask her to help you to put the toys away, stack everything neatly in its place, then go to the door and say "It's time for bed now" and put your hand out for her. Although she may not yet understand the words, she'll have got the sense of them.

During the early stages of learning to talk, you can give your child a great deal of help in learning to understand language.

Eye contact
Give your child your full attention whenever you're talking together and make your meaning clear by your expressions and gestures.

Children love the sound of speech and they love your attention. Combine the two and talk to your child as often as you can. Make sure that while you are talking you are looking directly at your child and make eye contact. Slightly exaggerate your facial expressions and your gestures. Exaggerate the emphasis you put on words, the inflection and the tone of your voice. If you can, try to match your words with actions. For instance, "I think it is time for your bath" – go into the bathroom and start running the taps. "Let's comb your hair" – pick up the comb and start combing her hair.

Learning and playing

To a child, play is learning; it's also very hard work. While she is playing, she is learning and growing up. Play helps learning in many ways:

- It can improve manual dexterity. Building a tower of blocks or, when she is older, doing a simple jigsaw, teaches a child that she can make her hands work for her as tools and it prepares her for using her hands in delicate and refined ways.

- Playing with other children can help to teach a child how important it is to get on with others. Having playmates to the house teaches her to overcome shyness and introduces her to sharing; it presents her with problems to sort out without help from adults, and teaches her to control outbursts of antisocial behaviour. Through a special friend your child may learn to love people and understand feelings that she can't easily put into words. At the same time she will be learning about the feelings of others.

- Through play a child learns to communicate. Playing with other children demands a more complicated use of language. Talking while playing may be one of the sternest tests for your child because the more imaginative the play, the more complex the ideas, and these have to be expressed in words that her friends can understand.

- Play undoubtedly helps physical co-ordination. In fact it helps both physical and intellectual development.

Play helps co-ordination
By playing with a shopping basket she's imitating you, communicating that she is interested in what you are doing, and improving her hand–eye co-ordination.

The freedom to swing, climb, skip, run and jump helps to perfect muscular co-ordination and physical skills. It also improves hearing and vision.

Provide the right games

As your child makes no distinction between learning and playing, you can help her to learn a great deal, simply by the material you provide for her to play with and the kind of toys you introduce her to.

From a very early age, all four of my children loved playing with water, whether it was outside in a small paddling pool, or just standing on a chair at the kitchen sink with a bowl of water and an assortment of plastic dishes, cups, jugs, containers and funnels nearby.

Other games you can play

Water games were always good for an hour's concentration and all the time my children were learning lessons: that water feels wet, that it will pour, that you can fill things with it, that you can empty them, that you can blow bubbles in it; that things will float on it, things will sink through it; that vegetable dyes will dissolve in it and colour it and that other liquids won't; that when the tap drips it forms drops, and that cupped hands aren't watertight. And this wasn't the only game:

• Materials like play dough, plasticine or pastry was interesting, too, because it could be moulded by their hands. They soon discovered that it would keep its shape if left to dry out, or, if they wanted to, they could roll it into a ball and start all over again.

• Sand, whether in the sand-pit or sand tray, was also interesting because it was midway between a liquid and a solid. It felt like a solid but it poured like a liquid. If the sand was wet it would keep the shape of the bucket, and the children could make sand pies; if it was dry then the sand pies crumbled.

Helping the learning process

One of the most important concepts that a child grasps during her second year is that of classification – of sameness and difference. Toys can help the formation of this idea. Farmyard toys, with a variety of horses, cows and chickens, allow your child to sort out the animals that look the same, especially if you help by showing her the differences and naming the animals repeatedly as you put them into little groups. The same procedure can be applied to many other objects – fruit, cars, shapes or tins.

Children like being part of the domestic routine and learn a lot about what goes on in the house and what people have to do if they are allowed to participate. A young child can be given a little bowl with some flour to mix each time you bake; she can help with carrying and, when it comes to cleaning up, give her dustpan and brush; if it's not too big, give her your real one.

For years, an essential part of our playroom was the dressing-up box, into which were put all sorts of old clothes, uniforms, hats and shoes. Most children get immense pleasure from imitating other people. This is a very important learning step for a child because she begins to recognize that she has to share the world with other people and get along with them. Dressing up to look like them is one of her ways of coming to terms with this.

Children of both sexes like dolls. Boys should have their dolls too: they are their imaginary friends, their imaginary families and they help create an imaginary world into which they can escape. While your child is playing with dolls, she is learning about, and possibly mimicking, human emotions. She will mother the doll, talk to it very firmly, tell it off, then put it to bed and kiss it goodnight. Through this your child is working out the things that happen to her, and is learning to understand them fully and relate them to other people.

Creative games

Long before she'll be able to formally write or draw your child will love scribbling and using colours. A box of coloured chalks, a blackboard and an easel will be attractive because she'll be able to "draw" then rub out the scribbles and start again. Attach a sheet of paper to the easel and give your child a set of fingerpaints and let her make her own design of splodges, hand prints and smears on the paper.

Most children are musical and like to be sung to from the day they are born. Many children have mastered the tune of their favourite song or nursery rhyme long before they can talk. As soon as your child is old enough, buy her a simple musical instrument like a xylophone or a keyboard. Join in with marching and clapping and singing. She'll enjoy it even more if you have your own instrument too.

Help if she is frustrated

The best way to help your child with learning is to join in with her learning activities, especially if you make suggestions about how to do something

new with a toy and then demonstrate how to do it. However, you must do it tactfully and without interfering, and allow her to decide whether she wants to follow your advice or not. Many of your child's games won't be able to be played without a partner. You should offer to be "It" whenever you can, but only join in for as long as she wants you to; don't overdo it. Leave the initiative to her; she may want you to fill the bucket of sand and ask for your help, but the last thing she'll want is for you to turn the bucket upside down to make the sand pie.

Your child's concentration span is increasing, but she may still have problems concentrating on something that is difficult. You can help her to concentrate by making the task easier or by giving her a helping hand. If you show her how the task or the job can be completed, you can give your child a goal to work towards. She needs your loving support and encouragement and if you give it readily she will probably find the determination to go on longer than she would without you. Doing this will give your child a great sense of achievement.

Let your child play alone

Some parents make the mistake of thinking that their child's every waking hour has to be filled with interesting diversions and stimulating activities. This is wrong and can even be harmful. One of the most important lessons that your child has to learn, and will learn quite willingly if left to her own devices, is that she can be the source of her own entertainment. Very often a child wishes to be left to play by herself, to make her own decisions about what to play with and for how long. Let your child follow through little tasks that she has set herself, alone. If she can't do them she will ask for your help; if she doesn't, don't interfere. Interfering, interrupting or introducing a new activity will do the opposite of making her life more entertaining. It will make it boring because she'll never have the opportunity of seeing the activity through to the end. She will miss out on the sense of achievement that every child needs.

Another common mistake is to believe that children need to play with toys. Many of the most popular play activities don't involve toys at all. They may involve physical activities like swimming, climbing or running, playing with a bat and ball, building a camp out of twigs and leaves, just carrying water to the sandpit and filling the moat, collecting pebbles or shells. Give your child the scope and the autonomy to do all of these things. If you don't encourage private activities, your child will have a very uncomfortable sense of withdrawal or even deprivation when she is forced to entertain herself if you are absent, and this may lead her into mischief, delinquent behaviour or, even worse, danger. So you should be pleased if your child shows signs of self-sufficiency and being able to do without you and to entertain herself while excluding you.

Coping with mess

Leaving your child alone, however, will mean that you'll have to either ignore a mess or anticipate one. If she's playing water games, cover the kitchen floor with newspaper or old towels that will soak up the water. If she's painting, cover the

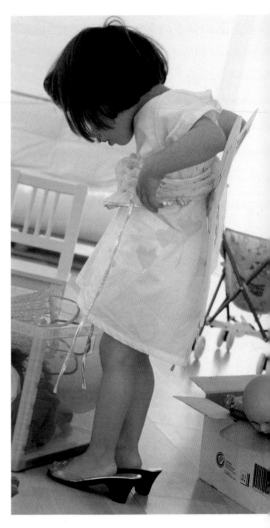

Costumes and dressing up
Children love dressing up, so keep a special box and fill it with old shoes, hats and clothes that you and your partner don't wear any more.

carpet with a sheet of polythene. If she's playing with mud or clay, cover your child's clothes with an apron and ignore the mess on her face and on her hair; it can all be washed off at the end anyway.

Learning 2 to 3 years

The way in which your child learns changes quite a lot in the third year, particularly in the second half. As a toddler, your child was learning about separate things, single events, one experience at a time. She may have satisfied her curiosity and explored that experience as far as she could, absorbing a great deal of new information in the process, but she rarely related it to anything else in her life.

Learning from experiences

What happens in the third year is that your child starts to think about her experiences and to learn from them. As your child develops the ability to think over new learning experiences her mind starts to work for the first time like a mini computer. Information is sieved and sifted, it is matched up to other experiences to see if they fit together or if they differ very greatly, and it is then put into similar or different pigeon holes. Your child starts to think and plan ahead, and becomes much more creative and imaginative. Gradually all the information that she has absorbed over the past years becomes available to apply to a given situation. Your child suddenly has an orchestra of thoughts that she can command at will.

This new ability to think, imagine and create changes your child's world considerably. Many familiar things close at hand in the house or garden no longer contain the same interest or excitement for her. She needs wider horizons; she needs to explore, to push the frontiers of her experience and knowledge further out.

Your child becomes very interested in how things work at this time and her conversation will constantly be punctuated with "Why?". She is avid for information and constantly asks questions. It's as if her brain wants more and more information to put

INTELLECTUAL DEVELOPMENT

Two years and three months She will try to build houses and castles with blocks and will repeat new words when you encourage her. She knows who she is and can say her name. She'll begin to pit her will against yours, and may become rather negative. She'll say the word "No" more and more often and won't always fit in with your wishes.

Two and a half years She loves helping you and will help with chores, putting things away, bringing things to the table. She'll know both her first name and surname. She can draw horizontal lines and vertical lines and can name several common objects. A boy will have noticed that his sex organs stick out from his body whereas those of his mother, and of his little girlfriends, do not.

Two years and nine months She'll begin to ask questions. She'll know the difference between boys and girls. She'll learn nursery rhymes and will be able to repeat them. She'll begin to understand numbers. She'll try to draw a circle but won't be able to complete it successfully without help.

Three years She'll like to play with other children. She'll know more nursery rhymes and will almost be able to draw a circle. She'll know the difference between such words as on, under and behind and will be able to form quite complicated sentences.

into the computer to start using immediately. One of the most important steps in your child's intellectual development is when she understands that time is not just in the present, but that there was a past and there will be a future; when she understands yesterday and tomorrow. Planning for the future is one of the most critical aspects of our intellect that makes us different from lower animals and it is during the third year that you will hear your child say for the first time, "I'll eat that later", or "We can go tomorrow".

Learning and speech

As your child grows older speech plays a more and more important role in communication and becomes more and more important in helping your child to learn. By now your child has got the hang of the basic rules of conversation. She knows, for instance, that people usually take turns at speaking; they know when it is their turn and they don't try to dominate the conversation. She also knows that instead of accompanying single words with gestures to explain what she means, she can vary the intonation of the words. She knows that an intonation that rises usually means a question and that a falling pitch indicates a statement. When your child was younger, speech was part of a simple pattern of communication telling you what she wanted or didn't want – it was used as a greeting or as a label. As your child's world widens she needs more sophisticated ways to express her thoughts.

One of the first expressions of this is her use of the possessive pronoun – "my doll, Mummy coat, Daddy nose". Another is the negative. Your younger child would

Learning colours
All children love to paint and draw and you can take the chance to name the colours of the paints and point out other things with the same colours.

just have said "No"; now she says "Can't" or "Won't". A little later she starts to express actions – "Dolly fall", "Dog bark", "Car bump". Another characteristic is the increasing use of questions combined with statements. "Daddy sleep, why Daddy sleep?" "Mummy must go shop, why Mummy go shop?" "Daddy gone out, where Daddy gone?" By the time your child is three she will be asking quite complicated questions in parallel with the way her thinking is developing. When you consider the following sentences, they contain quite sophisticated ideas: "I go get pencil and draw." "What that on table?" "See, this one better. But this not better."

Don't "talk down"

The kind of language you use with your child is very important. It's well known that adults change the way they speak to children as they get older. Sentences become more complex, they contain longer words, they describe abstract ideas. Don't fall into the trap of talking down to your child and don't use baby language when it is redundant. Throw into your conversation the odd word that you know is unfamiliar to your child but that she can guess at from the gist of the sentence. This way she'll learn new words and will learn how to use them and how to express herself in an articulate way. Research has proven that the children of articulate parents who don't "tailor" their speech to their children, use words more easily and freely at an earlier age than the children of parents who persist in simplifying their language.

Learning and playing

In keeping with your child's expanding way of thinking, she starts to get more out of playing. Playing still involves learning, but it's about learning different things.

- Play now starts to put the world around her into perspective. Before, a game like a farmyard with animals was simply a matter of sorting the animals into different types and putting them in the right place. Now she sees it with different eyes. It introduces her to an aspect of life that she knows is different from the one she leads. After all, she is probably not surrounded by animals most of the time, so it helps to reduce the world to a scale she can handle.
- Play increasingly becomes an outlet for emotions. Even an action-man type of doll can bring out feelings of protectiveness and gentleness. She can also use the same toy to get rid of aggressive instincts that, if directed against other children, would be labelled naughty and antisocial.

- Play creates an interest in other people. If the dressing-up box has a cowboy's outfit and a nurse's uniform your child can dress up and play a role. Even if she just puts a hat on at an angle and wears a pair of high-heeled shoes too big for her she can pretend to be her auntie and by acting out what she thinks she does, she is getting insight into her life and into other people's lives.

- Play develops a sense of territory and ownership. Safeguarding a new and cherished toy or her own private place to play, like a den, tent or a play house, teaches a child to respect the belongings and privacy of others. Play stimulates curiosity, independence, an adventurous spirit and intellectual growth. Mechanical toys and puzzles stimulate analytical thought. Painting, drawing, making shapes with clay and fitting together patterns encourage creativity. As your child gets a little older, toys like a microscope, telescope, a chemistry set or a magician's outfit allow experimentation. These kinds of toys teach her to meet challenges and master difficulties.

- As your child gets older, play helps to teach her how to cope with events beyond her control. She may break a treasured toy, she may fail to make a mechanical toy work or she may not have the competence to do what she wants to do. All these experiences help her to learn how to cope with problems

Make-believe games
Your child will love to create a little world of her own as part of her imitation of adults. Chairs can become a train or a car, and she can involve others in her game.

that arise in her world. There may be difficult choices to make but your child has to learn to make the decision. Play helps your child to get to know herself. As she gets older she has to interact with others, but before she can do that successfully she has to understand herself at least a little. Play allows her to discover her own physical and intellectual strengths and weaknesses.

- Play is an important aid in helping your child to mature. By the time your child is three she will be showing signs of having a sense of planning. She will keep her traffic jam of toy cars under the

surveillance of a police car, with a pick-up truck standing alongside. This shows that she is thinking ahead. She'll start to exercise her capacity to delay when she plays with toys that need the glue to set or the clay to dry. If she is prepared to share one of her toys with a friend who reciprocates by lending your child one of hers, then she is being taught the value of give and take.

Forming concepts

For your child to form concepts and put them to use in her world she has to have mastered two things. First of all she has to understand the basic concept of like and unlike. She learns to do this by recognizing similarities and differences in things and then fitting them together in her own mind. Once she can do this she has made an intellectual leap forward. From about 18 months to two years old you'll find that your child does this sorting automatically when faced with objects that have some things in common and some differences. All things that roll and are round are sorted into one group. All things that have edges and are rectangular, like blocks, are sorted into another. Things that have four legs and meow are cats. Things that have two legs and fly are birds.

We give our concepts verbal labels (names) and in her third year your toddler develops her understanding of concepts by using language. It would be very difficult for your child to progress with concept formation if she couldn't talk. Your toddler might use the word cat for every cat she meets, including the family pet, the cat drawn in a book, the cat she sees in a neighbour's garden and a toy cat. In her mind she uses a single label for all these different things. But by the time she approaches three she'll have made several rather sophisticated distinctions. She'll know that they are all cats so she'll have a concept of what makes "cattiness" but she'll also know that they are subtly different: "My cat", "Your cat", "Toy cat", "Cat in book", "Go see Granny's cat".

Abstract ideas

When your child is two years old it is impossible for her to describe things that are not real; things that she cannot see, which she cannot pick up and touch. She doesn't know what pretty means, she hasn't quite got the hang of emptiness and fullness and, while she knows that when she blows bubbles they will float, she can't yet distinguish lightness or heaviness. Your child may know the difference between one and several, but she has no idea of the magnitude of numbers, so anything more than one may be "lots". She has very little concept of time, she can't visualize what tomorrow means or last week; she has difficulty coping with tonight. Her understanding, however, improves throughout this year.

To have abstract ideas and to think in the abstract your child has to be able to picture things in her mind that are not actually there. If you ask her where a toy is, she has to remember when and where she was last playing with it. She has to see both things in her mind and then go and

Picture card games
During his third year your child will learn to think in a more abstract way. Memory games such as pairing pictures can help him develop this skill.

retrieve the toy. Once she is able to do this she can then make plans about things that are not actually there. So when you ask her where her boat is, she'll have a mental picture of the boat lying in the garden and will say: "Boat in garden, me get it in a minute". She'll carry on with her painting, finish it, wash her hands and then go out and get her boat without prompting. This means that she was able to carry the concept of fetching the boat in her head, have it interrupted by her painting, then complete several unrelated tasks and finally go back to the concept of bringing the boat in from the garden.

How to help your child

The most important way in which you can help your child develop is to listen to what she's saying. Because her world is now expanding at a colossal rate, not only in terms of her physical capability, but also her new intellectual development, it is very important that you communicate openly and freely with her. Listen carefully to everything she says, try to understand her thinking and answer her questions in terms that she understands. She is constantly asking you questions but ask her questions, too, so that you are aware of what she is thinking and what interests her.

Every time your child asks you a question or you have a conversation with her, you have a golden opportunity to help her to learn, even though the circumstances may be very casual and ordinary. If you are in the kitchen preparing lunch and your child asks you why you take the hairy bits off carrots you could start a discussion on how all plants have roots because they need food in order to

make them grow, and next time you are out in the garden you could pull up a tuft of grass and show her that root system. Or if you are really ambitious you could try putting a bean down the side of a jam jar lined with wet blotting paper and watching the root actually appear and grow down. When you are out in the street, keep up a running commentary on what is going on around you: traffic lights changing, cars stopping at pedestrian crossings, roadside drill, a policeman who is stopping and waving on traffic, and so on.

Around the age of three your child naturally becomes rather sensitive to what other people are feeling. She may show the first signs of empathy by wanting to

EARLY READING

Some children have a natural bent towards reading early and writing before their peers. If yours is one of them, encourage and help but never push. Your child can only master these advanced skills when the brain and intellect are sufficiently developed. You are not to know whether your child's brain is capable of reading (and later writing) so take your lead from her. Until this happens, simply continue reading to her, point out and name objects in books and encourage her to repeat them.

I'm against using "flash cards" when your child finds it onerous and a bore. In this instance you're only doing it for your own satisfaction and pride. This should never be the reason for making your child do anything. But if your child is avid for new words and gets pleasure from remembering flash cards, do by all means encourage her as much as you can. Don't try to make her read. When she's ready she'll start pointing out words; only then should you start to help her.

comfort you if you seem sad. Take advantage of this and start to teach her about the need to think of other people; that it is right to be kind and polite, helpful and thoughtful, co-operative and willing. Make sure she is introduced to people coming to your house like the window cleaner and the postman. Tell her about their jobs and some of the problems they may have to cope with, and suggest ways she might help, for instance taking the letters from the postman at the door and bringing them to you.

Nursery school

As your child reaches three years old start thinking about whether she would benefit from going to nursery school. The advantages are that she will meet lots of new friends, as well as interested and sympathetic adults who are good at knowing how to widen a child's horizons.

Learning to play together
When a child starts nursery it can be hard to learn to play together. Help your child to learn with games that involve sharing toys with others.

She'll have the opportunity to try new and interesting activities and she'll learn to socialize and be a member of a group. Lastly, and most importantly, she will have to be able to manage without you.

The decision as to whether she's capable of doing without you for long periods of time will be one of the factors that you'll have to weigh up when you are deciding the pros and cons of nursery school. If your child is very shy and clinging and doesn't talk easily to other adults and children, frets when you leave the room and follows you wherever you go then you are going to have problems with nursery school. You can, however, fall back on the knowledge that most children manage to get used to nursery school and indeed thrive on it so well that they miss school when they're on holiday. Bear in mind that with a little careful planning you can help your child get over the frightening first stages and she need not feel deserted.

Assessing a nursery or playgroup

There are several different types of group for pre-school children – play groups, nursery schools and day nurseries. Ring up your local council and get a list of all approved pre-school groups in your area. Choose two or three schools from this list that you can visit.

Go about your assessment in a thorough way. First of all, talk to the teacher in charge. Make an appointment to go and visit the group and sit in on some of the classes. If possible, spend a whole morning or a whole afternoon there so that you can get a feel of the routines, the amount of discipline, whether the teachers are strict, whether you approve of the way the children are treated, whether the environment is happy, informal and cosy and if the children seem happy. If you can, have a look at the facilities and talk to another mother whose child goes to that particular group.

Once you have chosen a nursery or playgroup, ask if you can take her along to sit in on a session a few weeks before she is due to start so that she can get used to everything. This will help her settle more easily when she starts going regularly.

Speech birth to 1 year

The moment when your child begins to speak is very exciting. Now you have some precise information about what your child knows and thinks; it's as if language provides you with a window to look in on your child's mental ability. It's also the tool with which she can learn. She no longer has to rely on crying to communicate.

Despite a great deal of research we still don't know exactly how a child acquires language. What we do know, however, is the general sequence that all children follow. We also know that your baby learns a lot about language before she even starts to talk: long before she knows what the words mean she'll listen to any changes in sound, to the rhythm and the intonation of your speech. She'll also learn about verbal rituals before she begins to speak and will soon know that first one person and then another speaks.

Early speech

For each month that your baby develops she will master new words and new grammatical rules. But learning to speak is infinitely more important than learning about vocabulary and grammar. Your child's main concern is communicating and interacting with people around her.

Children develop at their own speed and this applies to speech as well as other aspects of development. Don't worry if she doesn't seem to be as quick at picking up language as others – encourage her and let her take the time she needs.

How speech develops

Studies have shown that even a few days after birth babies will respond more to speech than to any other noise.

Up to six weeks As soon as your baby's born she'll start to make sounds. Initially they will be cries – cries for food, for affection, or because she's uncomfortable. Along with these she'll start to make little burbling noises as a mark of her pleasure and contentment.

Around six weeks She'll begin to respond to your smiling face as well as your voice with a more exaggerated gurgling. Although she's not literally talking to you she's communicating, and what's more she's learning to communicate in the way that adults do. For example, on seeing you vocalizing at her, your baby will respond with mouth and tongue movements and wait for your reply before reacting again.

Three to four months Your baby will make soft, cooing noises. At this stage the

sound will be of single syllables with an open vowel sound. The first consonants she'll use will be p, b and m so it's hardly surprising that she'll say "Maa" or "Paa", but she won't understand the significance of what she's saying at this time.

Seven months She'll be increasingly responsive to sounds, whether of the human voice or music. She'll expand her cooing into two-syllabled words by repeating the initial syllable: "Maama", "Beebe", "Daada". This stage will be followed by explosive sounds of exclamation: "Ai", "Imi".

Eight months Your baby will continue to babble, but she'll also learn how to shout to deliberately attract your attention. If she's near you when you're having a conversation with someone she'll pay close attention to whatever you're saying and will then turn to watch any reply that's made to you. Her babbling may become quite musical and she could try to imitate you when you sing a nursery rhyme to her or put on her musical box.

Nine months Your baby's speech will become noticeably more elaborate as she starts to join up the syllables she knows and pronounce them with sentence-like phrasing. So, with the rising and falling intonation of adult speech she'll say: "Ca-mama-dah-ba". Once she starts to make up sounds like this, technically called jargoning, you'll know that she's just about to start talking.

11 to 12 months Your baby will probably say her first "real" words some time during

Learning by imitation
Babies see their parents talking on the telephone and love to imitate. She'll enjoying "talking" to daddy or granny on the telephone too.

this month. The emergence of these first words is as much controlled by your baby's physical ability to articulate and make speech sounds as it is by her intellectual ability to make connections between objects and labels. The words she chooses will almost certainly be the names of things that are important to her: people (like mama, dada); animals (dog, cat); objects (cup, ball).

Simplifying words

The change from babbling to saying precise words means that your child has to change from making a stream of ill-controlled sounds to planned, thoughtful, controlled speech. Furthermore, the sounds have to be in a certain sequence so that the words are understandable to another person. This is a lot for a young child to cope with so the pronunciation of early words will very often be simplified.

Nearly all children reduce the number of consonants that they say at the beginning (or the end) of words so that spoon becomes "poon" and smack becomes "mack"; she might say "du" for duck, "be" for bed, "ca" for cat. This aspect of speech is one of the last to be mastered in English and children quite often have difficulty with consonants until they are four or five years old. This is quite normal.

Another way that children simplify the pronunciation of words is to put the consonants in the same place in the mouth where the basic sound of the word is made. This accounts for doggy being pronounced "doddy" or "goggy".

The other preference that children show is to substitute an explosive sound with a much less explosive one. So that

instead of saying pie your child may say "bie" and "doe" for toe and instead of pop, she'll say "bop".

Helping your baby to talk

- One of the first kinds of words that your baby learns are label words identifying the names of things. So in conversations with your baby stress the names of objects and repeat them frequently. When you are feeding your baby talk repeatedly about the spoon and the food. Make a special effort not to use pronouns. Say "I'll get your coat" instead of saying "I'll get it". Your child is learning the difference between herself and other people so use her name constantly rather than "you". "Where are Harriet's shoes?" "Harriet and Mummy will go into the car".
- Don't expect too much of your baby's pronunciation – if she can't say a word properly but you understand what she means don't make her try to say it perfectly. She'll only get frustrated.

BI-LINGUALISM

Children thrive on having two languages to learn. When young babies are learning to talk they can make all linguistic sounds. They find a new language much easier than we do. It also seems to be quite easy for them not just to pick them up, but also to think and speak in two languages. I remember watching my young godchild looking from her French mother who was speaking French to her English father who was speaking English. She was just two and a half years old; but she replied to her mother in French and her father in English. I would encourage exposing children to more than one language.

- Go to some effort to understand her own private, invented words or ones that are mispronounced. If she is trying to explain something to you, go through all the alternatives until you find the word that she actually wants. Her pleasure in having communicated with you when you find it will be enormous and will encourage her to try again.

- Help your baby to learn about how to apply words by describing and talking about things that are actually in front of her. Your baby can then make the connection between an object and what you're talking about if you repeat the word, especially if she can see, hold, touch and play with it. So, while you are playing with a ball, repeat the word ball as often as you can, and also discuss the innate properties of a ball – that it's round, and it will roll and bounce.

- In teaching your baby to talk you really have to be something of an actor. You must bring drama and interest to what you are saying. This means exaggerating your pronunciation and your intonation. Make it clear that you're asking a

Reading can help speech
Point to pictures in her book when you read to her, and repeat the names of the objects. She will eventually start to copy you.

question. Show when you're pleased and when you're serious.

- Your baby learns language from you more easily than from any other person but don't expect her to pick it up from the general babble of adult conversation. She won't be able to distinguish single sounds and sentences. Always stop what you are doing and look at your baby when she "talks" to you. Pay her the compliment of listening to her efforts when she tries to talk back.

- Ask your baby questions like "Where's your teddy?" and "Was that nice?" She may not be able to answer you initially but she'll understand what you're saying and may well point or nod.

SPOTTING IF SOMETHING IS WRONG

Don't worry if your baby doesn't speak in her first year. As in everything else, children develop speech at different rates. But if your child is still not speaking by the time she's two and a half you need expert help. If deficient hearing is responsible it's crucial to have the faults sorted out before she starts nursery or primary school. If it's a speech defect go to the best paediatric department, where there are therapists for children with speech disorders. Many problems can be sorted out if identified early enough.

- Don't oversimplify what you say to your baby – she needs the stimulation of adult speech, not a kind of pulpy baby talk.
- Take advantage of your baby's interests by talking about things on which she is already concentrating. She may not be interested in a story about a fictional character, but she will be riveted by a story in which she is the central character. She may not be particularly interested in animals but she will be fascinated by all animals if they are discussed in terms of mothers and babies because she can relate to that.

- Encourage her to use the few words that she has learned by using them in your conversations. She will be delighted to hear her own primitive conversation coming back at her, and this will encourage her to be adventurous with speech and to try out new words.
- Never, ever scold or correct early errors of pronunciation or understanding. With my own children I found some of these so charming that I left them uncorrected until quite a late age. In our house we all said "aterator" for radiator, "gamilla" for vanilla, and "binoclickers" for binoculars.

Speech 1 to 2 years

This year your child will make great strides forward in terms of both physical and intellectual development. She'll increase her vocabulary, and her grasp of grammatical construction will greatly improve. In order to speak properly she'll have to unlearn some of the habits she got into when her speech consisted of babbling. For example, in babbling, consonants are frequently dropped, and duplicated words are common. Once your child gains control of her speech she'll constrain the errors and substitutions that she used to make.

The beginnings of classification

As your child learns to recognize and identify objects she'll begin to classify and group them. However, at the beginning this process won't be completely accurate. She'll look at several objects and use the same word to identify all of them if they

have one or more features in common. This is referred to as overextension. The reason she uses words generically like this is because she hasn't the ability to articulate all words, but her desire to communicate with you is so strong that she has to use the nearest word that she can. Your child will link words together on the following bases:

Shape Balls, apples or stones may all be called "ball".

Size A handbag, a polythene bag and a shopping basket may all be "bag".

Sound A whistle, a siren and a car horn may all be "beep".

Movement A bicycle, a car, a bus and a train may all be "choo-choo". Although your child over-extends in this way she does know the difference between two things she calls by the same name. For example, she may use the word "guck" for truck and duck, and yet when faced with

THE FIRST SENTENCES

Some time before your child's second birthday she'll start to string words together. This is an important milestone because it shows that she's now aware of the relationship between objects. Your baby's first sentences will be limited in their meanings. They'll probably explain something that has just happened or describe what someone is doing. Her sentences will be concerned with:

What's happening:	Me run
	Cow go moo
	Truck bump
Who possesses what:	My dolly
	Mummy dress
	Granny bag
Where things are:	Doll in box
	Daddy in garden
	Ball in bath
Repetition:	Me more milk
	Play again
Where something's gone:	Drink all gone
	No more toy

Her sentences won't follow adult grammatical rules, that will develop later, but they will have a logical construction of their own. She'll learn fairly early that certain words are used together. She'll repeatedly hear "Pick up", "Put on ", "Go out", and will continue to use them as one word even when joining them on to others. So she'll have "Car pick up", "Door go out". She'll make the past tense by adding "d" to anything – "I wented", "You goed", "I gaved". To make words plural she'll add an "s" to the end –"Look, fishes", "Mouses", "Gameses".

pictures of them both and asked to point out a truck and a duck she'll make the distinction between the two.

In the same way, children can under-extend words. For most children the word animal usually just applies to mammals and the animals that they meet in their everyday life; they very often have difficulty in understanding that fish, insects and birds can be categorized as animals too. Whatever early words your child learns she'll soon begin to use them to mean a variety of things. A single word can be a label for a greeting, a demand or a question. At the beginning your child may often add gestures to single words to give them meaning. Later on she'll learn to change her intonation as a signal for different meanings.

Expanding vocabulary

Your baby's vocabulary will continue to expand and the words she'll learn most readily will be those whose use affects her daily life – people and animals, foods and most things from her daily routine. Early words nearly always include the names of animals like duck, dog, cat, horse, cow, plus the kind of noises that they make. Your child will also know the names of her favourite toys and, very importantly, the words that she can use to change or regulate the world around her by her interaction with you. So there may be words like no, up, more, out and open.

Some children learn a whole load of words as soon as they begin to speak, but it's more usual for them to acquire between one and three a month. By the time she's two she should be able to say about 200 words.

Helping your child to understand

Understanding always goes before usage and your 18-month-old child will understand a lot more of what she hears than her own language suggests. To help her you should make available far more information than your words alone provide.

- Talk to your child as often as you can and always look at her when you do so. In this way your child will be given the maximum number of opportunities for learning and understanding language.
- Help your baby's comprehension by acting out what you are saying with facial expressions and gestures, and make your words accompany some actions that can involve her: "Mummy will take off Mummy's shoes", or "Mummy will put on Jennifer's coat".
- For your child to learn that communication is always two-way, you shouldn't babble on with long sentences and stories without giving her the opportunity to participate and contribute. Punctuate your conversations with questions that demand a response of some kind.
- Your child finds it very difficult to understand language if there is a great deal of background noise that obscures speech sound. So if the television is on keep the sound low and don't play your radio loudly.
- Give her the confidence to try some conversation with strangers by acting as her interpreter. In this way she won't feel embarrassed and will have a go.
- Give her as many cues and clues to your meaning as you can, even though you know that she cannot understand exactly what you are saying. For example, at bathtime take her into the bathroom, run the tap, feel the temperature of the water and undress her, giving her information about what you are doing all the time and then say, "Now you are ready for your bath". Having had all the visual action and speech clues presented to her, she will certainly understand the meaning of your last comment.

Looking at books together

As with other aspects of her development, you are your child's first introduction to books. If she regularly sees you sitting reading a book or magazine, she soon will start copying your behaviour. You will find her sitting, studiously "reading" her book – which may well be upside down – and turning over the pages at intervals!

Gradually her attention will turn to the content of the pages as she starts to recognize objects. Popular books with this age group are those with clear, recognizable pictures of familiar, everyday objects that you can look at with your child, pointing and referring to the object by name. As your child's vocabulary expands during this year, she will be able to point to objects herself when asked. She will soon start to appreciate simple, illustrated stories, especially those with a repeated "chorus", which she will start to anticipate and join in with such as The Gingerbread Man or The Three Billy-Goats Gruff. As well as having a regular refrain, the most popular stories for this age group have simple, recurring themes – often involving the downfall of the big, fierce "baddie" (the wolf, the troll, the wicked witch) or the victory of the small or weak hero over her bigger and stronger opponent (the little pig in Three Little Pigs). Toddlers often want the same story read over and over again; for some reason, they find something in the story that they need. If that is what your child wants, let her have it – even if you are bored with it.

The value of nursery rhymes

Children love nursery rhymes – from the first game of "This little piggy" to all the old favourites – and will join in enthusiastically with whatever actions are involved. As with storybooks, the attraction of nursery rhymes lies in their simplicity, drama and recurring motifs and, above all, in the rhythm that babies and toddlers respond to from a very early age. Don't worry if you think you don't have a great singing voice: your child won't mind.

In fact, you'll never have had such an appreciative and adoring audience! Nursery rhymes play an important part in the development of your child's language skills, as well as providing an enjoyable and entertaining form of communication. Many can be sung as the accompaniment to activities – e.g. "See-saw Marjorie Daw" or "Incy Wincy Spider" – thus teaching and reinforcing the concepts in an enjoyable and memorable form. All will expand your child's vocabulary, extend her powers of imagination, and encourage a love of music and rhythm.

Clapping games
Teach your child lots of nursery rhymes. Many have actions to help with understanding. Show her to clap her hands as you sing them together.

Speech 2 to 3 years

During the third year, the structure of sentences will become more complicated and your child will start to fit whole phrases together. She'll begin to understand and use negatives, not just a simple "no" and "not". She will also start to phrase words so that they make a question and not just put "why" in front and, for the first time, she will begin to fully appreciate the relationship between one object and another. She'll start to use adjectives – big, small, fat, thin – and then comparative adjectives – bigger, smaller, fatter, thinner. She'll understand and start to use words that imply spatial relationships – this, here, that, there, and will learn the relationship between "I" and "my", "you" and "yours". She'll also learn how to use phrases with conjunctions such as "and", "then" and "but".

Having conversations

In her third year your child becomes a natural chatterer so take advantage of this tendency to show her how conversations are carried on; the to and fro pattern of verbal exchanges, how to make subjects interesting with questions and how to move on through various points of interest in any subject.

One of the best ways of involving your child in a conversation is to ask her what she likes or what she is doing or how things work. Having asked her the question you have to show real and sincere interest in her response for her to learn that conversation is worthwhile. Similarly, when she approaches you with a question or an appeal for help or just a request that you come and see something that is exciting, you have to show a genuine interest in what she is doing and saying. In this way you can contribute to what she is thinking, understanding and learning. If you respond to her running commentary of things that she is doing with a series of absent-minded "mms" she'll not only get little in return that she can learn from, but she will quickly learn that you are not interested so she'll stop referring to you.

Helping language to expand

You can help her by giving descriptions or instructions that are more detailed than you would normally give. For instance, if she is having difficulty getting her sweater over her head, you can say something like "Oh dear, the opening in your jumper is too small for your head." In this rather elaborate way of saying "I'll help you" you're introducing her to at least three new ideas and three new words. If she can't lift something and you can, you can point out that you can lift it because you are stronger than she is and the object is heavy.

Talk about colours, shapes and textures whenever possible. "You are going to have the red apple. I'll have the green one." "Look at the pretty blue flower with the long stem. Let's smell the flower." "Our car has four wheels. This truck has lots of wheels, let's try to count them. One, two, three, four, five, six, seven, eight."

You can also help her out with conversation. If you ask her what she has been doing in the garden and she can't quite get the words together, you could point her in the right direction by saying: "What did you make in the sand-pit? ... How did you get down from the top of the climbing frame? ... Where did you go on your tricycle?" You can prompt her responses by "What happened next?"

One of the favourite things that all my children enjoyed in a conversation was for me to leave a blank that they could fill in with the word that they knew. So in reference to getting down from the top of the climbing frame I could prompt them with "Oh, you mean you slid down the___ ", and my children would gleefully contribute "slide". Or in discussing what they had done in the sand-pit that afternoon I would say "Oh, you made sand pies with your___" and my children would shout "bucket".

HELPING WITH GRAMMAR

As your child begins to understand the more complicated aspects of grammar you can help, as before, by simply repeating what she has said in the correct form. So, as she starts to apply the constructions more and more widely, help her to use them in the correct way with new words and expressions.

Negatives

With your help your child can learn to put the negative where it belongs. By listening to what you say she learns to use won't, can't, wouldn't, hadn't, wasn't.

Your child says "I not eat biccit". You say "You haven't eaten your biscuit".

Your child says "No sweeties left". You say "Oh dear – there aren't any more sweeties".

Questions

In the same way you can teach her how to ask questions correctly and use the appropriate words that precede questions.

Your child says "Go out?". You say "Where shall we go?" .

Your child says "More?". You say "Would you like some more ice cream?".

Your child says "Coat on?". You say "Why do you put your coat on?".

In this way your child learns to use the "wh" words, such as what, who, which, where and why.

Adjectives

One of the best ways to teach your child about adjectives and the relationship of one object to another is to do it by opposites. So if your child says big ball, you can look around for a smaller ball, and then introduce her to the concept of opposites such as big and small.

You will be able to show her that compared to each other one is bigger than the other or that one is smaller than the other. Similarly, you can introduce other concepts to your child, such as wide and narrow, thick and thin, deep and shallow, heavy and light, hard and soft. Always demonstrate with the appropriate objects and if possible making it into a kind of game.

Possessive pronouns

Your child says "I bring book here", you can say "Oh you were over there and you brought your book to me here."

Your child says "I hate this biccit". You say "Oh then I'll have your biscuit and you can have my biscuit".

Your child says "This Jennifer coat, that Mummy coat". You say, "Yes, that is your coat, Jennifer, this is my coat".

This way your child learns how to use the words "my" and "yours".

Asking and answering questions

When your child approaches her third birthday she'll ask constant questions. While you may get tired of answering the constant whys you should be happy your child is showing so much curiosity in what is going on around her and making so many attempts to try to understand the world and to express her ideas in words.

Your child's questions should always be treated seriously so try to give the most accurate, truthful answer you can. Don't fob your child off with an answer like "Because that is the way it is" or "Things are just made that way" because that can't advance her understanding at all. You have got to give her information that adds to her knowledge in a form that she can cope with. So when your child says "Why is it raining?" don't respond with "Because it is." Try, instead, a simple explanation like clouds are full of water and the water is falling back to the earth in raindrops.

Your child's questions are usually very simple because she hasn't learned to use words to express her questions fully enough. So always examine the question to see what the point of it is. If your child says "What's that?" and you say "A ruler", she may want more than a name. So you could say "It's a ruler and you use it to measure things; look, this book is 23 centimetres long. It's also used to draw straight lines; let's draw one together". She may often ask questions that seem unanswerable at first like "Why birds fly?". But what she may really mean is "Why do birds fly? How do birds fly? Or why do birds flap their wings?", so test out bits of information and then say to your child "Is that what you mean?"

Always answer truthfully

If you don't know the answer to a question, be truthful, say that you don't know but also add "Let's go and look at it in the book"; or "Let's go and ask Daddy".

Sometimes parents shy away from giving truthful and accurate answers to children because they think a child won't be able to cope with the truth. This is often the case with questions about death and sex. It's always best to answer these questions truthfully and you should never avoid a difficult answer. However, don't make the mistake of thinking that when you tell the truth you have to tell the whole truth. You don't. It would be a mistake to try to do that because your child doesn't understand enough to cope with a complex full reply. What you can do is to supply that part of the truth that she can cope with and understand (see p.259).

LISPING

This is another common speech defect in children who are just learning to talk. It occurs, to start with, because the child simply has not mastered all the sounds needed and so she substitutes a similar sound that she can make. This can become a habit, however, or the child may be copying another child with a lisp. Neither of these is anything to worry about and usually stops without treatment.

Lisping may, however, indicate a more serious underlying problem: it may be due to a degree of deafness, to a cleft palate, or to a faulty action of the tongue. Although these possibilities should have been excluded at your child's regular developmental check-ups, if you are at all worried about persistent lisping, consult your doctor so that speech therapy can be started if necessary.

13 Social behaviour

The foundations of your child's social behaviour are laid in babyhood. The way you treat your child and the way in which he responds to you, and to the outside world, will be part of his make-up. Social development in early childhood goes through fairly well defined stages. From being a very non-gregarious newborn your baby will join in the surrounding social group by imitating others. One of the most important guides in this early period is the mother, or primary caregiver. Babies who establish warm, loving, outgoing relationships with their mothers are motivated to make friendly relationships with other people by the pleasure they feel in this early relationship.

Personal development birth to 1 year

Your baby is different from all others. He is unique, and no matter how many books you read, none can tell you about him. You are going to have to discover your baby for yourself and little by little, with careful observation, paying close attention to all the signals, you will come to know and prize his individuality. It is one of the most precious possessions a child has, and one of the most important jobs you do is to nourish that individuality. Help it to grow and flower and maintain it intact.

Getting to know your baby as a person is like reading an exciting story very slowly. You'll find out if he likes very gentle treatment or slightly rougher handling; you'll discover if he has a ready sense of humour, enjoys a joke and is eager to join in with things, or whether he prefers to be quiet. It may take you several weeks to know how he behaves when he's really well and happy, and until you do you may worry about whether he's ill or not. It may even take you a couple of months to know his crying patterns – an early signal of whether he's going to be a fretful baby or a placid one (*see p.158*). But don't worry. You'll gradually come to know all of your baby's idiosyncrasies: if he's a fast or slow feeder; if he needs a lot of sleep or is wakeful; if he likes to be cuddled or not.

While you are learning about your baby you will have to make many reassessments and adjustments as you fit your daily routine to his needs.

Early socializing
You are your baby's favourite person and she will love to explore your face as way of saying "hello" and showing interest.

Social milestones

By the time that your baby is six months old he will have learned a lot about being a sociable human being. In ways that we do not quite understand, he will have become an expert at the flow of social exchange. He'll know how to start a conversation with you and how to get you to play. He will have learned how to hold your attention by smiling, by babbling and by being interested and curious; and how to end a conversation by looking away or appearing bored.

The stages at which he acquires this ability are outlined below:

By three months Your baby won't like to be deprived of social contact and will quite often cry as soon as he is left alone. However, he'll stop crying when an adult reappears and when he is talked to or is diverted by a toy or a rattle. He'll turn his

Learning to laugh
Use laughter to show approval and punctuate games with laughs and jokes to develop your baby's sense of humour in social exchanges.

head when he hears human voices and will smile when an adult smiles at him or makes a kind of clucking sound. He'll express pleasure when others are present by smiling, kicking and waving his arms. He'll recognize his mother and other familiar people by acting sociably, and will show fear of strangers by turning away and possibly even crying.

By the fourth month He may lift his arms in anticipation of being picked up. He will focus on faces and will nearly always follow the direction of the person who puts him down. He'll smile at the person who speaks to him and whenever anyone pays special attention to him he'll show delight. He'll laugh out loud when he is being played with.

Between the fifth and sixth month
He will show quite a different reaction to smiling and to a scolding tone of voice. Familiar people are greeted with a smile, and strange people with recognizable expressions of fear.

At six months Social behaviour becomes much more active so he may pull the hair of the person who is holding him or rub their nose or start to pat the person's face.

At seven to nine months He will socialize by imitating speech sounds and gestures.

By 12 months He will refrain from doing things if told "No", and will show fear and dislike of strangers by rushing to his mother, and possibly even crying when the stranger approaches. He may become slightly clingy at this age.

Respond to his behaviour

The generally accepted definition of a good baby is one who cries very little, settles down easily and sleeps for long periods; the definition of a bad baby is the opposite. On the basis of these definitions all of my friends had good babies and I had bad babies. However, I would not describe any of my babies as bad. My babies were demanding and occasionally difficult but I am sure this arose only because they wanted my attention and, to me, this seems perfectly normal.

In the first few weeks you and your baby have to get used to each other. Do not be put off by how your baby behaves initially. He has no control over how he responds to the outside world and may exhibit tendencies that will not remain

beyond the first couple of months.

He may be miserable, jumpy, excessively wakeful or excessively sleepy. What you must do is deal with your baby's needs as competently and calmly as possible, giving all the love that you have.

"Difficult" babies

A baby who is really difficult, who, for instance, cries and cannot be comforted by any of the usual methods (see p.162), is extremely hard to deal with calmly. The sound of a baby crying constantly is irritating and upsetting at the same time and, if your baby also rejects your efforts to comfort him, you may then feel spurned and inadequate. You may even become angry because you believe that your baby is crying on purpose. This is absolutely impossible: your baby cries because he is biologically programmed to do so until his needs are understood and fulfilled. When you fail to do this a vicious circle ensues. You become tense because the baby won't stop crying. When you're tense you cannot cope calmly with your baby and as a result he'll cry even more. That way ill temper increases on both sides. Try hard not to lose your temper or to get too worked up.

- Share the responsibility with your partner and take it in turns, wherever possible, to deal with your baby.
- Follow the advice on crying (see p.162–166), and don't forget, yours is not the only baby in the world who is going through this "difficult" spell. Whatever you think, this spell will be brief.
- Don't treat your baby's behaviour as a deliberate rejection of you – at the moment he can't help behaving like this as he's desperately trying to adapt to the

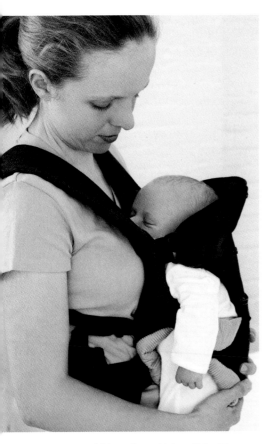

Keep him close
In the early weeks, carrying your baby with you in a sling as you go about your day gives him lots of close contact with you, and may even help him sleep.

cry, won't be very alert and won't take much notice of his surroundings. He may fall asleep mid-feed, he won't respond when talked to and shows little emotion.

A baby like this is marvellous initially because he leaves you to regain your strength after delivery. But he's missing an awful lot in life and needs to be coaxed into realizing that in fact being awake is much more fun.

- Don't try to keep your baby awake forcibly. He knows how much sleep he needs and you should respect this. However, you should make sure that he's not going for too long without food. If, for example, he can sleep through the night you must wake him up before you go to bed because it is otherwise too long for a new baby to go without liquid.
- Whenever he is awake provide as much stimulation and affection as possible. Surround the cot or crib with mobiles and photographs so that even if you're not there he has something to focus on and be occupied by.
- Try carrying your baby in a sling so that at least he gets to know your warmth and smell, even though he's asleep.

new world he's found himself in. You have to accept your baby as he is and deal with him accordingly; as he grows he'll change eventually.

- Accept any offer of help from friends and relations so you can take a break and recharge your batteries.
- Try talking to another parent or to your doctor or health visitor about ways of coping or contact a support group.

Sleepy babies

These babies are often called placid babies. Your baby may sleep 21 hours out of 24; he'll make few demands on you, will rarely

Wakeful babies

Instead of sleeping the usual 16 out of 24 hours for the first few weeks of life your baby may sleep as little as 12, and he'll take these in short bursts. He'll be full of life, interested in everything that's going on and will be very keen to learn. Wakeful babies are usually very sociable and affectionate. Although he may exhaust you, he'll be very rewarding.

Until your baby's old enough to entertain himself, you and your partner will be the sole form of entertainment, and he may demand your attention all hours of the day and night. If you don't work out some sort of shift system with your partner you may become so fatigued that you cannot carry on. Don't be resentful of your baby's wakefulness; try to accept it and take practical steps to make sure that you get enough sleep.

- Carry the baby around in a sling.
- When you're at home take the crib or basket wherever you go and place it safely on a table or work surface so that your baby can hear your voice.
- Have plenty of pictures and mobiles over the cot or crib so that he'll be occupied.
- Prop him up in a bouncing chair or in the pram or buggy (with straps on) from about six weeks.
- Keep the baby's room warm because this sometimes encourages sleepiness.

Discontented babies

You may have a discontented baby, one who is irritable when he's hungry yet doesn't enjoy feeding. He takes the feed slowly and with difficulty. Afterwards he isn't very sociable and doesn't like to be held. When you talk to him he doesn't seem to take much notice; he seems tired but fretful and not very relaxed. When laid down to sleep he starts to cry.

Don't feel that you'll never succeed in making your baby comfortable and happy or you'll begin to feel inadequate and eventually resentful. Try to keep all negative emotions out of your head. Your baby's behaviour is aimed at the outside world to which he's not yet acclimatized, and not at you.

Never interpret your baby's unhappiness as a personal criticism. Try very hard, no matter how much your baby rejects you, to get him to smile at you. Try to engage him in play; sit with him on your lap and play, or even give him a massage. Get your baby to respond. Once he does this then you know that you've turned the corner and you can get to know each other.

- When he cries, try all the crying remedies.
- Make sure his nappy is clean and dry and his room is warm and cosy before he's put down to sleep so he feels secure.
- Give as many feeds as he wants and never keep him waiting and crying.
- Put lots of mobiles above the cot to occupy his attention.
- Carry him around with you if that provides comfort.

Jumpy babies

All newborn babies are sensitive to loud noises and sudden, jerky movements, but jumpy babies over-react to quite normal stimuli. For example, when he gets hungry he doesn't show hunger with the usual persistent cry but within a few seconds of waking is screaming hysterically. When he's picked up his body stiffens and if he's put down again the body may jerk. He'll seem to be alarmed by any kind of noise or rapid movement around him.

- Understand, once again, that your baby's behaviour is not a rejection of you as a parent. It's just an inability to deal with the new world that he's in.

- Hold your baby securely most of the time in such a way that there's no risk of his arms or legs flopping back, which can make him feel insecure.
- Pick him up gently and slowly. When you bend down speak softly and gently; you could even try singing a song.
- If he seems to feel more secure when he's near you put him in a sling and carry him with you all of the time.
- Don't give your baby baths, just top and tail him every day (*see p.72*). Never take all of his clothes off at once, as this makes babies feel insecure; always leave the vest or the nappy on and try to keep his body covered, even by a towel, for as long as possible.
- Don't leave him in a noisy or very brightly-lit room. For example, avoid rooms that face noisy schools or roads with heavy traffic, and rooms that have chiming clocks or telephones.

Your baby as part of the family

During the first few weeks of your baby's life the household will revolve around him, but from then on he'll have to learn to fit in with the household and the rest of the family. It is important that your new baby learns to live with a group of people for whom there are routines, accepted customs and modes of behaviour, quite a number of guidelines and a few rules.

However, your baby can't be expected to fit into family routines if he isn't introduced to them, so include your baby in family activities like mealtimes, games,

outings, shopping, household chores, looking after pets and visiting friends as soon as possible. All of these encounters are important to your child because through the working of the family group he will learn about the working of people in general. In this way he'll relate how he behaves with his own family to how he should behave with strangers.

Through the family your baby will eventually learn the social customs and attitudes of your society. One of the most important ways your baby learns is by imitation – so by watching and copying how you behave, your child develops his own behaviour patterns.

Involve your baby in family life
Include your baby in as many activities as possible. Give her a ringside seat at mealtimes for example, and let her get to know friends and family.

Boundaries birth to 1 year

Very few children under the age of a year need true disciplining. Up to this age a child is not open to reasonable argument and your main form of discipline will simply be to set boundaries and say "No" and, if your baby doesn't obey, to resort to the physical removal of either the baby or the object. I don't believe that young babies should ever be smacked or punished.

As they grow up all young children need to be shown the boundaries of socially acceptable behaviour by their parents. Many of these limits are implicitly set by the way members of the family behave to one another. Setting a good example by your own behaviour is the best way to teach your child what good behaviour is. It is part of your responsibility as the parent to give your child guidelines on behaviour so start to do this during your child's first year. If you don't, your child will soon find that other children and adults won't tolerate someone ill-mannered and selfish. You're going to have to keep to some guidelines in your home, as in any other organized group of people, for the sake of efficiency, justice and safety.

Understanding bad behaviour

No baby behaves badly deliberately, although many a tired and exhausted parent feels convinced that they do. Your baby may cry constantly and be very irritable and grumpy, but this is usually due to being over-tired, hungry, ill, anxious or scared of your leaving or of meeting strangers. This is not your baby's fault and he should never be blamed for what really is beyond his control. Nor should you blame yourself if you've done everything within your power to prevent or correct what is causing your baby's unhappiness.

Towards the end of this year one of the major causes of "bad behaviour" will be frustration. Your baby may be a fairly strong-willed character to begin with and as he gets older and more independent he's going to want to express this. A battle of wills will soon emerge and he'll no longer accept that you have total control over his life. He'll challenge your preferences and begin to assert himself strongly. Objections to your choice of food are common, so let your baby choose what he wants to eat, and the order that he eats it (see p.120). Equally, if he wants to wear certain items of clothing let him go ahead and wear them. If you don't allow your baby some freedom at this time he will become very frustrated and angry.

Help your child

Doing things alone may bring their own frustrations because your child's ambitions will often exceed his capabilities. He won't be able to make his body do what he wants it to, and he'll find that he cannot manage the world in the way that he wants to. This will inevitably result in tears and possibly temper tantrums (see p.166). Try not to get annoyed at this – every child goes through similar behaviour – but do give him your assistance. If you don't offer to help at this point he may waste a lot of energy trying to do something that is completely beyond him and repeated failure will be very demoralizing. When your baby is in this kind of mood, bullying and pressurizing will simply cause more stubbornness. Be tactful, humorous even, and a little devious. If you let your baby feel that he is taking control you'll find that he very often fits in with what you want. So, instead of saying "Don't" to your baby who is throwing plastic mugs everywhere, make the clearing up into a game. Sit down and suggest that he tries to pick them all up before you count to ten.

When to say "No"

During your baby's first year there are very few reasons for saying "No". I had only one unbreakable rule in my children's first year. That was when they were doing something that was unsafe for themselves and others. In these instances I would say "No" firmly and at the same time remove the object from my child, or stop my child from performing the dangerous activity. I did not wait for my child to stop. As I was trying to teach my child what was unsafe, I always offered an explanation as to why I was stopping him from behaving in a certain way. I simply stated what was dangerous about it and repeated it every time the same thing occurred in the hope that my child would remember, learn and not do it again. I did not chastise and I tried not to become angry. Only as they got older and learned the rule did I give them the opportunity to resist without my intervention first.

I believe the best way to teach a child how to behave is by praise and reward for good behaviour, or by example with an explanation from other members of the family. However, this will only be successful when your child has the intellectual ability to recognize what's wrong and can decide what the correct way to behave actually is.

Possible concerns birth to 1 year

Your feelings for your baby

Many women believe that mother love will be turned on like a tap as soon as their baby is born. It can come as rather a shock when after even two or three days they don't feel anything for their baby that resembles love. They may feel tenderness and protectiveness towards this tiny new being who is dependent on them, but they don't feel a strong, binding love.

This is very common and not at all abnormal. Love usually does develop after one or two weeks and until it does, concentrate on enjoying your baby physically: the feel of your baby against your skin; his smell as you put your nose into the crease of his neck; his grip as you put your finger into his tiny palm and feel it grasped tightly.

Postnatal depression

Most women have feelings known as the baby blues after childbirth, caused by the dramatic drop in hormone levels, but these usually soon pass. About 10 per cent of mothers, however, develop postnatal depression (PND), which is more serious and can affect your relationship with your baby. Rapid medical attention is needed – the longer PND is untreated, the longer it can take to resolve. PND has many symptoms, and women experience these in varying combinations. As well as feelings such as hopelessness and despondency, sufferers can experience lethargy, anxiety, tension, sleep difficulties, loss of interest in sex, obsessional thoughts, feelings of guilt, and lack of self-esteem. If you have any of these symptoms don't bottle up your feelings – seek help. The sooner treatment starts, the better and your depression should improve in a few weeks.

Independent babies

Just as there are adults who keep themselves to themselves, so there are some babies like this too. These babies don't smile very much, they respond little to being talked to, they seem not to enjoy playing games, and they don't always like being cuddled. On the other hand, they can become grizzly if placed in a pram or cot and left alone. They can be rather irritable and get upset easily. They tend to cry and are slow, fussy feeders.

When such a baby is tired he is fretful but doesn't go to sleep. All your best efforts fail to make this kind of baby sunny, and you may feel you are lavishing love to little effect. But don't blame yourself – some babies are just like this and you are not alone.

A baby who smiles a lot and exudes joy gets friendship, love, companionship and help in return. The baby who is miserable or who just stays in neutral gets less in return. Life is not so pleasant for him and so he may grow up to be a rather troubled individual. As a parent you may have to work hard to get your child to be more positive. Although you may find it difficult,

you have to try your best to get your baby to focus on you, to listen to you, to smile at you. If you can get to this stage, where your baby is responding to your overtures, most of his unhappiness and yours will be a thing of the past.

Babies with disabilities

Babies develop at all speeds from very fast to very slow and it can be difficult to judge what's normal and what's not. If you feel that your baby is not really keeping up with the general social milestones (see p.260), check with your doctor. However, minor problems may not show up for several months, so follow your instincts if you think your baby is not developing quite normally and seek early help. The earlier you get help the greater the chance you have of dealing with any abnormality.

If your baby has a physical disability it's often comforting and helpful to talk to people in similar situations so contact any relevant national agencies.

HEAD BANGING

Towards the end of the first year some babies take to banging their head against the end of the cot. This is rarely a sign of abnormality, and there's little risk of brain damage; most babies grow out of it quite quickly. However, do minimize the risk by padding the ends of the cot with a quilted fabric, and by buffering the cot and the wall if this causes an irritating banging noise. Try giving your baby a relaxing bath at bedtime and an extra long cuddle (some psychologists think that such children may need more physical attention and stimulation). Music may also be soothing. If your baby continues to bang his head for several months talk to your doctor.

Personal development 1 to 2 years

During the second year much of your toddler's behaviour is attention-getting. He will try to do this by speaking, by crying, by hitting or by doing other things that he knows are forbidden. When he's successful at getting your attention he'll show how satisfied he is by smiling or laughing.

Two year olds often seem to be very negative and their favourite word appears to be "No". This is a transitional stage between babyhood and childhood, and during it your toddler will be trying to assert his independence. He'll want to do everything immediately, and will frequently want a specific routine adhered to. Your toddler's mood may change frequently and his emotions may veer between extremes of lovingness and temper tantrums. One of the things that you must do is follow your child's mood when he shows this kind of negative assertiveness. Unless your child is given the opportunity of being independent at this stage such early resistance can lead to strongly negative behaviour now and later.

On a much more positive level, two-year-old toddlers become much more co-operative in play. Early play with an adult teaches toddlers how to be socially co-operative, as long as the adults are patient in showing children how to share. Your toddler will learn to share by being shared with. Gradually he will begin to co-operate with other children in play, although in the beginning other children may be unwilling to share. Encourage your child to persevere and don't give up showing your child by your example.

Likes and dislikes

A child begins to show all kinds of assertiveness during this year and it is quite natural that he should demonstrate preferences dramatically. He is very keen to grow up and to show that he is growing up. He no longer sees himself as a mirror image of you; he now sees the two of you as separate people, and therefore finds no reason for doing exactly what you want. He will be determined to exercise his independence and will refuse offers of help and shrug off your assistance, even when he really needs it.

Your child is developing likes and dislikes, and has a very strong urge to fulfil his own desires, even though they may not be the same as yours, and yet the conflict that this may bring can make him feel very unhappy. Your child is torn between the very strong drive to exert independence and the drive to be loved by you.

Even when he is trying to win a battle with you he needs your help and emotional support because he is too immature to manage without them.

Balancing his needs

Your job is to take the middle road and to try to balance your child's need for independence with the need for love and protection. It isn't always easy. Your toddler's thinking is immature; his memory is short, and judgement is unreliable. He cannot think ahead and may be impatient when things don't get done immediately.

At the same time your child is eager to control and dominate the world around

Co-operation in play
Help your child to learn about playing happily with other children by encouraging him to take turns when he plays with you.

him. His strength of will is ahead of his intellectual capacity so you'll have to decide when it is time to baby your toddler and when it is time to encourage and push him on, allowing independence and adventurousness, while still guarding against any dangers. Do be flexible in allowing your toddler to exercise these

likes and dislikes, and don't enforce your will simply to win or to show your authority. You can always win a battle by pulling rank, but you shouldn't be unreasonable for the sake of it.

Judge the situation carefully. You'll find that there are very few instances where it is important for you to get your own way (one would be if your toddler's safety or well-being was threatened, for example). Where it doesn't matter and no harm will come of it, it's best to let your child do what he wants to.

Personality

Your child is born with his own personality, which shows itself within the first few weeks of life. However, there are certain social situations that will develop a child's personality during early childhood. They can bring out both the good and bad aspects of your child's personality so try to make sure that the good traits are accentuated and bad ones played down.

THE TIMID CHILD

Some children are naturally shy, keep themselves to themselves and speak very little. Don't immediately think that your child has problems and become over-anxious and over-protective. A child who is quite talkative on home ground may be completely silent and withdrawn in a strange place or when confronted with strangers. This happens in many children around the age of one. In a new situation don't increase your child's difficulties by insisting that he join in immediately. Allow him to sit quietly on your knee or to stand by your side while he takes in what everyone is doing and becomes familiar with it. After half an hour or so, when you can sense that he is feeling more comfortable, gradually encourage him to join in your conversation. Even a shy child, if encouraged in this gentle, slow way, will join in with new friends and new games after an hour or so. But do remember to introduce new experiences slowly and allow your child to get used to them before moving on to other ones.

If your child's very timid and shy he may become very upset if you try to leave him with a babysitter. You must try to understand your child in this and still give him your love no matter how irritating the situation is. He'll grow out of this clinginess with your help, but he'll need to gain a sense of security first.

- If your child has a strong desire for approval, he will be motivated to fulfil the expectations of those around him. The desire for your approval and the approval of other adults usually comes before the desire for the approval of friends. Whenever you can, get your child to do the "right" things for your approval, then praise him for doing it.
- Young children express their sympathy by trying to help or comfort a person who is sad or in distress, but they are unable to sympathize until they have been in a situation similar to that of a person who is distressed.
- When children understand the facial expressions and speech of others they develop the ability to empathize with them and to experience what the other person is feeling.
- Children who tend to be rather dependent, who like to be helped and given attention and affection, are often motivated to behave in a socially approved way. The more independent children are motivated less by the desire for approbation.
- Children who are friendly express their friendliness by wanting to do things for and with others. These children express their affection for others in all kinds of words and gestures.
- Children who are not allowed to be constantly in the limelight of family attention, and who are given opportunities and encouragement to share what they have, want to think of others and do things for them rather than simply concentrating on their own possessions, their own interests and getting their own way.

Playing and sharing

Your toddler should mix with others as soon as possible. In the first year your child becomes used to interacting, not only with members of the immediate family, but also with the extended family such as grandparents, aunts, uncles, nieces, nephews, cousins and friends who come to the house. Your toddler will be a great deal more comfortable with strangers and adults if he starts off feeling that every friend of yours is a friend of his. He needs to know too that there are other members of the family who will help and care for him and whom he can rely on and trust.

If you help your child to accept others readily then he won't have too much difficulty mixing with other children when expanding experience and the desire to strike out make him want the company of others of the same age. At about the age of 18 months children will usually tolerate

Encouraging toddlers to share
Between the ages of one and two years, children play alongside rather than with each other. Giving them something to share can help them interact more.

other children although they won't necessarily play together; they may play side by side doing the same thing, but rarely interact. A little later, when they start to play with toys, grabbing and hitting between children is not unusual. However, if your child repeatedly does this then you must explain that it's not a good way to behave, and point out that he wouldn't like the same doing to him.

While your child has to learn to share, it is hardly realistic to expect him to automatically give a toy to another toddler if he wants it. This is not because your child is selfish or a bully; it is because he hasn't appreciated the concept of sharing. If your child makes a grab for a toy that another child is playing with, you can teach him about sharing by saying that if he has his friend's toy, he must give one of his to the friend. A child of two is usually able to understand the justice of this reciprocity. You have to deal with sharing in very simple terms because intellectually he is

ONLY CHILDREN

Although only children undoubtedly benefit from the constant love that they receive, and grow up feeling very close to both parents and friends, there are few who don't confess to having wanted brothers and sisters at some stage in their lives. This is rarely a serious problem but one of the things you can do to mitigate any possible problems is to introduce your baby to other babies of the same age. As your baby reaches the sociable age, around 18 months to two years, you should make a real effort to find friends for him and invite them to your home.

Try not to over-indulge

It's easy for parents to over-indulge an only child and to make them feel too important. You're going to have to curb your desire to give him all that he wants and, just as important, all your attention. It's important that he learns to accept that he can't have everything that he wants and be the permanent centre of your world, just as a child in a larger family has to (see p.242).

It may be tempting to be possessive and over-protective. This can be bad for you and your child. You'll feel bereft when he becomes independent and needs you less, but your child will lose out on a sense of curiosity, adventure and independence and may become clingy. You mustn't shy away from disciplining your child either. Like any other child he has to be shown the right way to behave if he's to grow up able to mix with others.

not grown up enough to have more adult behaviour forced upon him. It is not until he is about two and a half to three that you can use reason and expect your child to be more altruistic.

Encouraging generosity

You can encourage your child to be generous from a very early age. As you are the most important person in his life it is easiest to be generous with you. You can take advantage of his desire to please you by teaching little generous acts (like giving Daddy a toy) and to then go on to encourage more and more unselfishness in his behaviour towards you and other members of the family. It is only natural for your child to want to please and be friendly with people who obviously care for him and love him and for whom he feels great affection.

Having accepted generous behaviour as the norm towards people whom he loves, it is a fairly logical extension to show unselfish, generous behaviour to people who are just friends. So, ask your young child to give you a toy or to give Daddy a toy, or to give you one each. If he finds a particular activity exciting and pleasurable, you can ask if you can join in and share the pleasure and excitement. Then encourage your toddler to do the same with other members of the family and friends who come to your home.

By the time your child is about 18 months old he should be able to share activities and treats with anyone who enters your home and is seen as a friend. If he can manage to do this he is well on the way to being generous and unselfish with his peers.

Boundaries 1 to 2 years

Children like to know what the boundaries of behaviour are and need these to be happy and well adjusted. Boundaries are essential to a child's development because they fulfil certain needs.

- By knowing the boundaries, children learn how to behave in ways that mean they are praised. They interpret this praise as acceptance and love. Both are essential if your child is to adjust well to growing up and being happy.
- When discipline appropriate for the age of your child is applied it serves as motivation. This encourages your child to strive to accomplish what is required and this brings comfort and satisfaction.
- Boundaries help a child develop a sense of self-control and of conscience. This inner voice will later guide him in making his own decisions and controlling his own behaviour. Without them he may be indecisive and act in an antisocial way.
- Undisciplined children are often scolded. This gives them a feeling of guilt and shame. These feelings will inevitably lead to unhappiness and poor adjustment.

When to use discipline

Discipline, overdone or underdone, can be equally bad for children because both of them lead to insecurity. There is no place for ruling your child by fear, force, corporal punishment or humiliation. While you can tell your child the reasons why you want some things to be a certain way, you cannot use reason until he's about two and a half or three, so disciplining has to be simple and easy to understand and it has to be in direct relationship to what he is being punished for. There must be no delay between what your child does and the discipline he is given, and the action has to fit whatever it is your child has done.

If you're often extremely angry over minor misdemeanours your child will simply be left bewildered. Keep disciplining for really serious matters like destructiveness, being physically violent or telling lies. In this way your child gets very clear messages of what is tolerated and what is not. Your child's memory is short and if you brood over what he's done he will simply not understand. He will think that you are purposely withdrawing love from him and be very perplexed, so make all discipline clear and swift, then forget it.

Understanding boundaries
Once you establish boundaries of behaviour for your child, stick to them. Children thrive on consistency as they know where they stand.

Avoiding problems

Children are very receptive to fairness and justice, and if you adhere to these two principles you will probably avoid most difficulties in disciplining.

Avoid corporal punishment at all costs. Research has shown that children don't know what they are being smacked for. They cannot remember, so they don't associate the punishment with the crime, and smacking doesn't act as a deterrent. Never punish a child as a calculated act.

The child is much less damaged by a sharp word in the heat of the moment that is quickly forgotten when the air is cleared, than by a long argument with a threatened punishment as soon as you get home or, worse, when your partner gets home.

You will not go far wrong if you are very clear about your motives for disciplining. Make sure that they are for the happiness and safety of the child, and not simply as a means of impressing on your child your authority and superiority.

BEHAVIOUR GUIDELINES

Learning the rules of social behaviour and learning self-control takes time; it doesn't take months, it takes years. Don't expect him to remember what you said last time. He isn't necessarily defying your previous instruction, he may have simply forgotten it. A child of two has a very short memory, so be forgiving and repeat your instructions. Words never mean as much as actions and you really do have to show your child how to behave. Here are some of the things that you can do.

- Have as few "rules" – those instructions that can be broken under no circumstances – as possible. "Don't" is a very negative word and if you are not careful, by the time your child is two, you could be prefacing everything you say by "Don't". "Do" is a very positive word so reinforce with positive "dos" and cut down the "don'ts".
- Don't give vague instructions; try to be very clear. Instead of saying "Don't be naughty", tell him exactly what you don't want him to do.
- If you give your child instructions, always give a reason why. If you tell your child that his tricycle has to be put under cover when he's finished using it at night, explain that it may otherwise get rusty in the rain and not work. Try to refrain from saying "Because I say so" when he asks you why.

- Always reward good behaviour with praise and affection, possibly even with a treat if your child has accomplished something difficult. You can help him distinguish between good and bad behaviour just by withholding praise and rewards from acts that you don't approve of.
- There is no better way of getting your child to do something than to show that you do it too. If you want your child to take off his dirty shoes at the door, show him you do the same with your shoes.
- Be consistent. Don't let your standards slide and give one instruction on one occasion and the opposite on another (although you can show that under certain circumstances you are prepared to be flexible). There is no reason why your child shouldn't have several ice creams on his birthday, because he knows that that day is special, but he should learn not to expect the same on the following day.
- Always admit your mistakes, no matter how young your child is, and always be generous when you do something wrong. It makes your child feel that the world is fair and just, therefore don't be afraid to say, "naughty Mummy", or "Mummy shouldn't have done that" or "You are quite right, I won't do it again".

Possible concerns 1 to 2 years

The aggressive child

Aggression is a basic act of hostility and the ways in which we use it usually mean that it is unprovoked by anyone else. Most children have feelings of aggressiveness to some extent and usually express them in verbal or physical attacks on another child, very often choosing a child who is smaller than they are.

Aggressiveness, bullying and destructiveness are modes of behaviour that usually represent cries for help. They frequently result from parental neglect, absence, over-discipline, under-discipline or too much smacking. A child who behaves in this way is really not at fault, although he may be very hard to help. It is worth remembering that a nasty child is usually nasty because someone has been nasty to him. You shouldn't be too ready to blame the child but should look beyond the behaviour, to his home and his general environment. Weaning a child off his normal pattern of behaviour, and the distrust of adults, may take years because he has to re-learn the attitudes that he has been learning from the day he was born.

If your child starts to show signs of being very aggressive, try to nip it in the bud. Don't punish and don't smack your child for being aggressive; this will only make the behaviour worse. Instead, show him very firmly that you are not prepared to put up with it and that he will gain nothing but your disapproval if he continues with his current behaviour. Show him that if he can change he will be highly rewarded, and will gain lots of praise for all good efforts. If your child seems to be highly disturbed, or if you're at all worried by an aspect of his behaviour, you must seek expert help immediately.

Jealousy

Rivalry is a perfectly normal emotion for a child to feel. Sometimes it can have a positive effect and can act as a spur to make the child do his best. In this instance it adds to his friendliness and his desire to socialize. However, if it leads to quarrelling and boasting, your child will have a hard time of it.

A child feels one of the strongest forms of jealousy when a new baby arrives. This is because your child feels that he's been "dethroned" and that he has lost the special place he had in your life. He may try all sorts of attention-seeking devices and may even revert to such babyish behaviour as losing bowel control, refusing to feed himself or refusing to dress alone. Or he may direct his jealousy directly at the baby and try to hurt it. Alternatively he may feel unable to cope with these jealous emotions and may internalize them so that he becomes quiet and stays away from you; he may even reject you altogether.

It is very easy to understand all of these emotions. You must try to help your child by preparing him for the arrival of a new baby and by showing that his place in your affections is quite secure. Make a special time when he has all of your attention. Involve him in looking after the baby by asking for assistance in certain easy tasks, and praise and reward all helpful behaviour on his part, and whenever he shows love and affection for the new arrival.

Over-indulgence

It is very easy for any parent to over-indulge or spoil their child. After all, you have a natural desire to please your child and to make his life happy. It's all too easy to err on the side of giving a child too much, of making life too easy for him and allowing him to become the centre of your universe. You will have to control these desires in yourself for your child's sake.

One of the ways in which you can help your child not to be egocentric is to make sure from early on that he is not always the centre of your attention. He must learn that the world does not revolve around him; that the household and the family do not see him as the pivot for their constant attention. If you let your child know quite clearly that there are times when he's expected to do without you and to do things alone, you will be doing him a favour. None of these should involve cruelty or force. You should show your child as much love as you can, but he should be made to see that everyone has certain boundaries within which they live. As he gets older, teach him that you have a need for privacy just as he does, although you're always there if needed.

Don't make the mistake of thinking that over-indulgence has anything to do with the number of possessions your child has or how much affection he gets. It is to do with allowing your child to grow up so that he impresses his will on you and on others by using power games such as wheedling or bullying. It is a parent's duty to prevent this occurring.

Temper tantrums

Between one and two years old temper tantrums are normal, attention-seeking devices (*see p.168*). Children of this age have not yet acquired the judgement to match their strength of will, and clashes with parents are therefore frequent. If anger or frustration are excessive they may culminate in a tantrum. Children usually throw themselves on the floor kicking and screaming because they do not have the control to do anything else. It is their way of showing their helplessness to overcome their problem in a controlled way.

Far and away the best thing to do is to stay calm. If you don't your child will catch your mood and it will make his behaviour worse. Ignore your child and, if possible, leave him alone. A tantrum loses much of its point if there is no audience.

As your child gets older he will become better able to tolerate delays and accept compromises. At the same time you will become more expert at anticipating problems and forestalling head-on clashes and will become more skilled at finding distractions for him.

STUTTERING

Nearly all children of this age have jerky speech which, on occasion, may turn into a real stutter. This may be because your child has so many ideas in his head that he thinks more quickly than he can speak. It may also be that he is very excited and simply can't articulate properly. Stutters can also appear for a short time and then disappear again. Stay calm and don't draw your child's attention to the stuttering. Don't jump in with the word that you think your child is looking for but simply accept his speech. Making your child feel nervous and self-conscious about the way he talks will only increase his tendency to stammer.

Conflicting desires
*As your baby grows she can sometimes get confused
and unhappy at the conflict between her urge to be
independent and her desire to please you.*

"Naughty" or disobedient?

There are some children who are habitually
naughty and some who are habitually
disobedient. These two things have to be
handled differently.

To me, a naughty child is one who is
immature and not able to exert sufficient
self-control to do what he knows is right.
A disobedient child is quite mature and
knowingly flouts your wishes and rules.

A naughty child is often forgetful and
simply forgets your remonstrances. You can
tell him off for doing something wrong
and find him doing it again an hour later.
He'll be genuinely surprised to find himself
in the wrong again so quickly. Naughty
children frequently get so wrapped up in
an activity that rules go by the board. This
kind of child needs more repeated tellings
than the average, and careful, sympathetic
correction. Usually a naughty child is
apologetic and contrite, which should be
warmly received. However, there does
come a point when a naughty child needs
punishing. I favour withdrawal of treats
and pleasures that can be reinstated when
a given goal has been achieved.

Your child may go on being naughty
for a long time. Be prepared for this and
don't become too angry; sheer naughtiness
is more of an irritation than a serious
annoyance. You may feel you can
sympathize to a certain extent with the
naughtiness; even if you don't feel like
this try not to be too hard on him.

Disobedience is another matter. Most
of us feel little sympathy for a constantly
disobedient child who rarely apologizes or
expresses any kind of repentance. If you
have a disobedient child you may have a
constant stream of negatives, rows and
recriminations. Guard against this if you
can. A child has a limited repertoire with
which to respond to your anger. Brutality in
your behaviour leads to brutality in his.
Physical punishment from you encourages
violence, truculence and aggression in him.
It's hard, but try a programme of positive
actions and words. Try to explain to him
why he shouldn't be so disobedient;
explain when his actions are dangerous
or antisocial and suggest how he should
behave. Outlaw punishments, reward all
good acts. It often works. Whatever you
do don't alienate your child. You are all he
has. Always show your love, always let him
know he can come to you.

Personal development 2 to 3 years

Your young baby's dependence on you stemmed from the fact that you were the centre of his universe, you were the caretaker and the affection-giver. He couldn't get through life without your help and support and he sought your approval and affection.

However, as he gets older and sees himself as an independent person, not just a reflection of you, he also begins to see you as a separate personality and as a whole person. He is experiencing many different feelings and new emotions with which he has to become familiar. He begins to know real love for many of the things around him: his favourite toy, a pet, a favourite grandparent. All of these feelings bring your child closer to the adult idea of love.

Children respond to your moods

If he sees that you are tired he is genuinely concerned, and if you are unhappy he is sincerely sympathetic. When he is enjoying something he will want to share the experience with you and will offer to share it. If you need help, he will offer it to you spontaneously because he really wants to give it. If you are upset or frightened, he feels profoundly sorry for you, and tells you so with words and expressions. He has a strong desire to make you feel better and happier, and does so in the only way that he knows, by telling you that he loves you and by hugging you.

This is quite a step forward in your child's personal development, because all these feelings and actions are truly unselfish. He is now putting someone else before himself; he is becoming genuinely caring and loving; he wants to understand someone else and do what is best for them; he wants to bring them pleasure and comfort. These are very grown-up things to want to do. Always encourage these tendencies and make sure you praise him when he exhibits them.

Imitation and identification

Your child has always learned by imitation and as he gets older he begins to learn by "identification", too. He begins to put himself in your position and into the position of others and starts to behave as he would have others behave towards him. This means that he is starting to control himself and take command of himself. You may even overhear your child scolding himself when he has done something that he thinks you will disapprove of. The big difference is that he now disapproves of it in himself as well.

You will find your child observing and identifying with most of the adults who are close to him and any interesting ones who are not. He may exercise his imagination by dressing up and acting out roles and by being all kinds of different people. But most of all what he is doing is practising being you. He will play Mummy or Daddy with dolls and toys and you may even hear the imitation of exact phrases that you use with exactly the same intonation you have in your voice. These are all his ways of exploring and experimenting with the way he thinks the world works.

Making friends

Your child's galloping desire to learn brings with it the desire for the company of children of a similar age. He will probably be showing signs of gregariousness and of wanting to join in games with others during this year and he'll need the stimulation of other children's ideas and their company.

You cannot make friends for your child, but you can help him to find friends. Your child has to learn how to make friends slowly, just as he has learned all the other lessons in his life, so introduce your child to making friends with only one at a time.

Start off on home ground first and invite a child who lives nearby so that your child is in familiar surroundings and has a sense of confidence about what he is doing and where he's doing it. Make sure that you are near at hand to give him help and support should he need it, and

Playing together
Children need to learn how to make friends. Invite first one, then several friends to your home for a tea party maybe, or a picnic in the garden.

encourage him to settle down to playing by playing along yourself. Once he has got over the first hurdle of making friends, try inviting two or three children to the house at the same time. Once your child becomes a member of a group of friends make it clear to him that they are welcome at your home and that he can bring them into the house once he has asked your permission. As your child makes his first steps into the outside world, it is important that he has a comfortable feeling about it and has confidence about his own place within it, so helping gather around a small group of friends whom he knows and with whom he gets on, is an important way of laying down the right patterns for later life.

Encouraging security

All children have fears. Anxiety and fear are normal emotions, but they make a child feel very unhappy and uneasy, and it will be some time before your toddler has the ability to cope with fears or avoid the things that make him afraid (*see p.170*).

One of the most common early fears is of your absence or of being abandoned. The easiest way to cure this is to show your child that you will always come back as you promised and when you said you would. Fear will not be cured by staying with your child; that will only make him more fearful because he never learns to cope without you.

Your small child also begins to feel anxiety if he finds that his own feelings are getting out of control, like frustration, anger and jealousy. The way to help here is to listen and observe your toddler as closely as possible, so that you can pick up all the clues as to what is causing the anxiety and then reassure him. Talking about some of the fears and explaining what's happening will give the reassurance that he needs.

Remember that whether you think your child's fear is reasonable or unreasonable, as far as your child himself is concerned the fear is still the same. All fears have to be handled sympathetically and gently. Never suddenly present your child with whatever makes him most frightened. You wouldn't dream of asking your child to stay outside in a thunderstorm if he was afraid of thunder, so why should you expect him to pat the dog he's scared of? Whenever your child shows fear, accept that fear as real and don't brush it aside as nothing. Always tell your child when there is nothing to fear, but don't just tell him not to be afraid, because he won't understand that. Explain why there is no reason to be frightened, always tell him that you understand why he is, and sympathize with his fear. Never ridicule the fear; that will simply make your child secretive, and it is much harder for him to cope with a fear alone, than to cope with your help.

Nudity and sexuality

A child's sex education begins with the first cuddle. All children take pleasure in physical contact and joy in their parents' reciprocity. They grow up realizing that people touch one another as an act of friendship as well as an act of love.

As your child gets older he will become pleasantly aware of his body, without being at all self-conscious about it. You can encourage this by having an open attitude to nudity within the family. Like everything else, a child learns patterns of behaviour and attitudes from you. The child who sees his parents unclothed and unembarrassed will take nudity as a matter of course and is unlikely to grow up concerned about nakedness. On the other hand, if you are worried about it he will almost certainly worry about it too.

It is natural for a child to be curious about the differences between male and female bodies. Your child will probably have been aware of the difference in genders since the age of 15 months or so, and once he sees his parents naked he'll be aware of sexual differences. Curiosity about his mother's breasts and his father's penis is best satisfied by a frank chat and a good look. Neither of these things is likely to stimulate sexual feelings in your child and he'll only be embarrassed if you are.

Answering children's questions

Children who are encouraged to ask questions, and who are given explanations, take for granted that their parents will listen to them. These children grow up to be happier and less authoritarian than children whose questions are ignored and who are rarely supplied with explanations. Parents who take note of what their child says are showing that they consider him an individual with something useful to say. If your family believes and operates in this free and easy manner, it's going to be a much happier unit.

In the early years your child regards you as omniscient and will naturally turn to you for advice on most subjects. If you remain approachable and welcome questions your child will grow up feeling that he can talk to you about anything. Discouraging your child from asking questions when he is young and uninhibited will only make any inhibitions worse as he grows older. If you want to be the confidant of your children you should try to keep the channels of communication open at any cost.

You should not avoid answering questions, even if they embarrass you. If you are concerned about when to tell your child about sex, the answer is that you explain the first time that he asks you. A child's curiosity should always be met by your willingness to answer truthfully. It is much better if he learns about sex in an accurate, matter-of-fact way from you than in a secretive melodramatic way from friends who may well have some of the information wrong.

From about three years onwards, a child can handle at least part of the truth on sexual questions, although it is not until he is about six or seven that he can understand the mechanics of sex. I told my own children about conception, the growth of a child in the womb and childbirth whenever they asked about it. I left talking about sexual intercourse until the age of six or so depending on the child. All discussions on sex should include aspects of caring, loving and the responsibilities involved in intimate relationships.

HANDLING GENITALS

Babies usually become aware of their genital organs toward the end of the first year but handle them without any obvious pleasure. Handling eventually does bring a pleasurable sensation, and then fondling becomes more like real masturbation. Most children of both sexes masturbate, and it's simply unreasonable to expect them not to. Despite the myths, it will not lead to blindness or insanity.

It is perfectly normal for a boy to handle his penis. After all, he handles every other part of his body that sticks out. In young children, this is rarely done for any length of time or for any purpose. The pleasure it brings is more general than sexual. It is not until children are much older that they feel sexual excitement.

Don't scold your child

There is no reason to discourage a child from handling genitals, nor should you stop him from masturbating. That will only cause furtiveness, and worse, it may stop your child discussing anything about genital organs in later life. Unless masturbation is an obsessional means of escaping from reality, the best way to treat it is by paying no attention to it at all. If by accident it happens in public, distraction is the best course of action, but never, ever, scold your child for it.

Boundaries 2 to 3 years

As your child becomes old enough to reason with you, you can explain what discipline is. This way he will grow up knowing that discipline is based on mutual responsibility and participation in decisions. Don't expect blind obedience from a child. It is far better to reason and persuade. If, however, you take the trouble to discuss why it is wrong to behave in a certain way and right to behave in another, you'll find that your child is interested in motives and is much more likely to do what you want because he understands why you want it.

On the other hand, don't make the mistake of talking over every decision, and never just telling your child what to do. When you think the situation warrants it, give a simple order unless you feel that your child is going to be recalcitrant and a softer approach may be better.

Good disciplining should give your child the opportunity to make a choice. Part of growing up is about exercising choices and options and he has to learn this skill like any other. Choose very carefully when you are going to give him a choice: let it be one he will find fairly simple, one you don't really think is important which way the decision goes. Don't try to fool your child by giving a choice when your decision is already made; you won't fool him.

When to insist

To my mind there are just a few instances when you have to insist on discipline.

- When your child's safety or the safety of another person is threatened. There have to be rules, for instance, whenever fireworks are used or whenever you make a camp fire or have a barbecue.
- Children have to grow up learning that the wishes and comforts of other people must be honoured. I have been very strict on matters where thoughtfulness, helpfulness, unselfishness and courtesy with anyone are concerned.
- I feel that there can be few concessions about honesty. With my own children I was always severe with lying and stealing. I didn't do this through punishment but by proving to the child that it was better and easier on them to tell the truth, no matter how bad it was, and no matter how dreadful the crime seemed, than to tell a lie. I wanted my children to know that I appreciated the courage it takes to own up to something.

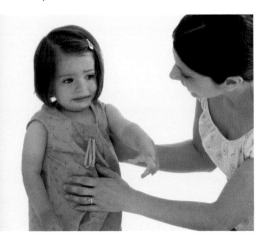

Understanding right and wrong
Your child will only be able to learn the differences between right and wrong if they are clearly pointed out by you and explained every time.

Possible concerns 2 to 3 years

An aggressive antisocial child

We've all experienced feelings of aggressiveness towards other people, especially when we feel that our security is being threatened. It is only by great self-control that we conquer such feelings, and that is something that takes many years of learning and maturity to achieve. It is not surprising, therefore, that many children give full rein to their aggressive instincts.

When aggressive behaviour in a child becomes a regular feature, however, it is usually a response to two things: a lack of effective restraint and discipline from the time he was born, and a feeling of insecurity in the child, who may be experiencing a lack of parental attention, love and affection. In both ways the parents are almost entirely responsible for the child's difficult behaviour.

If you have an aggressive child look closely at the way that you and your partner behave, and if you're honest with yourselves you'll almost certainly find that you are falling short in your position as teachers and role models for your child. It is fairly easy to prevent a child ever becoming aggressive but it is very difficult to retrain an aggressive child to be less so. One of the first and most important ways to teach gentleness and flexibility in your child is to be flexible, tolerant and gentle in all your dealings with him. Don't forget your child will imitate everything you do, including being aggressive.

If your child suddenly becomes aggressive or starts bullying, this is a sure sign of some tension or unhappiness in the child's life, and you should look carefully for the cause of it. In a young child it will nearly always be found in his relationship with you, your partner or the rest of the family, or to tension in the home. Don't think that you can pull the wool over a young child's eyes by sweeping things under the carpet; children will always pick up on the atmosphere, and this can cause great insecurity.

Shyness

Some children are shy by nature, and studies show that up to ten per cent of infants are born with a nervous system that predisposes them to shy behaviour. Such children show their shyness by giving evidence of disliking new experiences; even when taken to a family gathering or party, they will spend most of the time clinging to their mothers' legs or hiding their faces.

STEALING

Most young children are used to taking things that belong to others – their mother's make-up, a sibling's toy, or their father's keys – just because they want to play with them, and at home this isn't usually a problem. However, young children are incapable of understanding the "property rights" of others, and you may discover that your child has taken something while you were out shopping or visiting a friend's home. If this is the case, explain to the child that this is stealing, and that stealing is not allowed. Eventually, your child will get the idea. It isn't necessary to have the child accompany you when you return the object, unless the habit has become persistent and you feel that extra enforcement is necessary. Most children feel penitent enough on being found out.

"HABITS"

Nail biting, thumb sucking and carrying a comforter are not abnormal in a young child. Don't try to stop them, and certainly never by force, ridicule or deprivation. They are nearly always caused by tension of some kind and they happen in more than half of otherwise quite normal schoolchildren. For the most part they are unconscious, nervous habits and are best cured by encouraging a pride in appearance. The majority of children stop nail biting when they become concerned about their appearance and interested in the opposite sex. At this age social considerations begin to outweigh their personal habits. I don't believe in discouraging these habits. As they get older children sense what is acceptable, impose self-control and only indulge in their habit in private. No one can persuade me there's much that needs correcting about this mature behaviour.

Comfort habits
Thumb-sucking and carrying a comforter can continue right into the teens, but eventually a child will give up the habit of his own accord.

They also show reluctance in conversing with strange children or adults, and typically prefer to play alone rather than in a group. When such a child grows older and attends school, he may be diffident about making new friends.

If your child is shy, my advice is not to criticize him or to try to change his nature – not only is this unrealistic but it also may add to the problem. Instead, when you know that a new experience is in the offing, try to prepare him ahead of time so any strangeness is diminished. And, when he is meeting new people, allow him plenty of time in which to get used to them before you expect him to feel comfortable in their presence.

A cheeky child

It is not always easy to draw the line between cheek and impertinence. Occasional cheekiness is, to my mind, a perfectly acceptable trait. I like it in a child because it suggests spirit, mischievousness and a healthy attitude towards authority.

There is also the mistaken belief that questioning decisions is being cheeky. This is because some parents feel that cheekiness undermines their authority. However, if you encourage your child to talk things over with you, you will encourage the sense of responsibility for disciplining himself rather than blindly obeying your decisions. In this way he will grow up aware of the value of persuasive argument. On the other hand, if you always encourage your child not to say what he thinks because you always interpret arguing as being naughty he will rarely get the chance to understand the reasoning behind your decisions.

The other good aspect of being cheeky is that it provides a verbal mechanism for getting rid of anger and frustration. Anger is a perfectly acceptable emotion in a child, but isn't acceptable if he is venting his anger in a physical way. It is much better for your child to shout about anger than to hit someone. So when your child is cheeky weigh up why you think he is being so and if the reasons are healthy ones, just keep it in check. Insolence goes beyond cheekiness because it flouts good manners. It ignores thinking about how the other person feels and it may be hurtful. If your child goes over the boundary into insolence you'll need to teach him this is not acceptable.

Selfishness in children

All children are naturally selfish, but as your child comes out of toddlerhood the most important lesson to learn is "Do as you would be done by". This means learning that he can't always have the treats he wants because they have to be shared with others; he may not have the biggest, rosiest red apple because there is only one and another child may want it; he has got to learn to lose because only one child will win and he won't always be the one.

The most important way of convincing your child that he should not be selfish is to try to get him to feel how other children will respond to selfishness. If he can understand that generally speaking all other children are feeling the same way as he is, then it is obvious that people have to take turns at getting what they want, whether it is being the top dog or having more turns on the swing than anyone else. It's up to you, by your actions, to show your child the benefits of unselfishness.

An over-indulged child

A child who is over-indulged is a self-centred child. Here are some of the things that you may have been doing that will make your child egotistical:

- If you are over-protective you can make your child feel that he is extra-special. Children who are waited on hand and foot by others and protected from experiences grow up to expect that others will continue to do things for them instead of making the effort to do them themselves. This stifles independence and co-operativeness.
- If you show favouritism towards a child you encourage a sense of self-importance. Children who are not favoured have feelings of inferiority or martyrdom. Either way it encourages the child to become self-centred rather than outgoing and thoughtful about others.
- Some parents set too high a goal for their children, and encourage them to become egocentric when they strive for these goals.

One of the best cures and possibly the only cure if you won't change your ways for an over-indulged child is to let him go to school early. He really needs the levelling process of a play group or a nursery school, and getting used to mixing with a group and being considered as no different from anybody else. Later in life he may respond well to boarding school. If neither of these things is possible, an over-indulged child can still be pulled down a peg or two by choosing bright, outgoing, intelligent friends for him. Contact with another sensible adult can help your child through the painful process of losing this sense of self-importance.

14 Playing

Play has a vital role in your child's development and provides a platform for learning, especially about becoming sociable. To learn to become sociable a child has to have contact with children of the same age, and these contacts will mainly be made through play. Parents now know that for their children to be healthy and happy and to grow up well adjusted, they need to be given liberty to play for as long as possible. To this end parents provide their children with all sorts of play equipment and toys, with an emphasis on their educational value.

Play birth to 1 year

During the first year your baby will go through what is called the exploratory stage. Until she is about three months old play will mainly consist of observing people and objects and of making rather random attempts to grab hold of anything that is held in front of her. After three months your baby will gain enough control over her hands and arms to enable her to grasp hold of, and examine, small objects. As soon as she can creep, crawl or walk her world will explode. She'll forage for herself and will examine everything within her reach.

TOYS AND GAMES FOR BABIES

Never in a baby's development is play more synonymous with learning than in the first few years of life. She is learning to see properly and discovering how to use her hands and how to master hand–eye co-ordination (*see p.195*). She may learn quite a lot by simply watching and moving her own hands, but she'll practise and perfect her new skills with any toys you give her.

What toys to give

From about five weeks Her visual field will be increasing and she'll enjoy watching anything that moves, so hang mobiles above her cot and changing mat. They're easy to make from household items if you don't want to buy them (*see p.267*).

Suitable toys

- Mobiles • Rattles • Mirror • Music box • Large/small balls • Soft toys • Squeaky toys • Bendy toys • Activity centre • Books • Cooking utensils

Developing skills
You can help your baby improve her skills by giving her a variety of toys that encourage the development of hand–eye co-ordination.

By three months She'll love objects that make noise so provide her with a rattle or a toy that she can shake or strike out at. Choose a brightly coloured lightweight, unbreakable, washable rattle that has a slight enough handle for her to grasp easily (at this stage she won't have the muscle strength or co-ordination to grip on to anything for more than a few seconds).

By four months Plastic beakers filled with beans, or water-filled canisters will also make interesting noises and she'll be able to hold them between both hands.

SAFETY TIPS

- Make sure the toys you buy are for the appropriate age group and have a CE label.
- Never give your child anything to play with that is so small that she might swallow it by accident or gag on it, push it up her nose or into her ear.
- If you buy an second-hand painted toy make sure that the paint is lead-free. Young children put everything into their mouths and children have been known to get lead poisoning from toys covered with paint containing lead. (This applies to second-hand furniture too.)
- Never leave your baby alone while she is playing, not even in a playpen.
- Always provide non-toxic crayons and pencils. For your own sake, make sure that the crayons, pencils and felt tips you provide will wash off surfaces and fabrics.
- Don't buy toys made from thin rigid plastic. They break easily and leave sharp edges.
- When you buy soft toys check for a safety label. If there's no label make sure that there are no sharp pieces of wire used to hold any additional pieces on, and check that eyes and noses are firmly secured to the fabric.

By six to ten months Any object that is fairly small and has crevices, holes or handles that your baby can poke her fingers into or wrap them around will be ideal. They should be brightly coloured and, if possible, make a noise, like rings with bells on them.

Put a fairly large specially designed baby mirror in her cot – she'll love staring at her own face. Never be tempted to put one of your own mirrors in the cot – it could easily break.

Musical boxes seem to provide endless fascination for small babies and can play a part in your bedtime routine (*see p.146*). The best ones have a string that the baby can pull herself.

Activity centres that have a series of knobs and buttons that your baby can push or turn to make noises can be attached to a piece of furniture or the bath. As your baby's manipulative abilities improve she'll love playing with this.

Ten to 12 months Once your baby can pick up something small she'll be able to hold chalks, pencils, crayons and, eventually, paint brushes. She'll be more mobile now and will enjoy being able to pull or push toys like trains, cars or walking dogs. Provide her with some toys on strings so that as she sits on the floor she can draw them in towards her.

Games to play together

Play peek-a-boo with your baby, either when she's in her cot or if she's sitting on your lap. You can vary the game by hiding your face behind a headscarf or towel instead of your hands.

Buy a large inflatable beach ball and gently roll it towards your baby. Once she can sit

unsupported she'll be able to bat a ball back to you with her hand. You could even throw a small soft ball (such as a beanbag or foam ball) gently into your baby's lap for her to "throw" back to you. Show your baby how to fill up a container with a selection of toy animals, plastic spoons – anything really that isn't breakable. Then encourage your baby to have a go and you'll soon find that she'll sit for hours filling up and emptying her container.

Babies seem to have endless patience with and fascination for stacking beakers or rings, both of which help your baby with co-ordination. They come in a variety of styles although the basic principle is the same. The ones with large pieces are better for younger babies because they're easier for less co-ordinated hands to grab hold of and manipulate.

All fall down
Play games with bricks: your child will try to make a tower and you can demonstrate cause and effect by knocking them down and saying "All fall down".

Making use of household objects

A baby under one year old really doesn't need formal toys, although she'll inevitably be given some. Everything she comes across is fascinating. Any object that smells, looks or sounds interesting will appeal to your baby. Many household items, which we take for granted, will hold a world of excitement for your baby. Here are a few everyday things that you might like to try as "toys" for your child:

- Wooden spoons and spatulas, small saucepans and their lids, plastic or metal colanders and sieves, funnels, a set of plastic measuring spoons, plastic cups with lids, plastic bottles of different sizes with their caps taped or glued on securely, small plastic boxes that you might use in the fridge, plastic ice-cube trays, a whisk, an old egg carton, old loaf and bun tins. Just hand them to your baby and she'll work out what she wants to do with them herself.

- Anything that rolls: the cardboard tube inside rolls of kitchen paper, film or foil, and cotton reels.
- Round objects like balls – balls of every type, balls of wool, balls of string, grapefruit, oranges, apples.
- Things that are very light: sponges, foam rubber, polystyrene.
- Anything that rattles: transparent plastic jars with pulses, coloured beads or paper clips inside. But do make sure that the lid is firmly on.

- Things that are flat and hard: a wooden plate, a table mat, a ruler.
- Things that are stretchy: stretchy cloth, elastic itself, a piece of cloth that's been cut on the bias.
- Anything that has a hole that a baby can poke her fingers through: a roll of sticky tape, an old roll of sticking plaster, a napkin ring, a set of shaped plastic biscuit cutters.
- Things that are quite large and heavy but perfectly safe, like a cushion, a football, a soft-backed book, rice or dried fruit in a tough polythene bag, a loaf of bread (not bread with seeds though).
- Objects that have different textures that will be interesting for your baby to feel. Good examples are pieces of felt, strips of fine sandpaper, thick strands of wool, a fabric-filled bean bag.

FUN WITH EVERYDAY THINGS

Noisy toys
Wooden spoons and metal pots and pans or a toy drum make noise and help your baby understand how to exert control over things and over himself.

Trying to reach
When your baby is starting to be able to lean forwards, put something just out of his reach to encourage him to stretch forwards and try to pick it up.

BABY MASSAGE

Massage is a wonderful way to express your love for your baby; in the early days it helps the bonding process between you and your child; it helps to calm an unsettled baby and can help an anxious mother to come to terms with handling her precious new baby. Older babies and toddlers also benefit from massage; it is an effective way of soothing a fretful baby and can help an over-excited toddler to relax. Work from the head down, with light strokes, ensuring that both sides of the body are massaged symmetrically. Use sweeping strokes and do each part two or three times. On small areas, use just your fingertips. On some parts of her body you will need two hands and on others one.

1 Lightly massage the head with a circular motion, then stroke down the sides of the face. Massage the forehead, working from the centre out.

2 Gently stroke the neck from ears to shoulders and from chin to chest. Then stroke the shoulders working from the neck outwards, towards her arms.

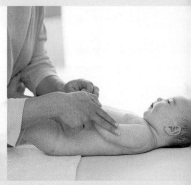

3 Stroke down the arms to the fingertips. With your fingers and thumb gently squeeze the arm from top to bottom. Massage the wrist and hand; stroke each finger.

4 Continue down her chest, following the ribs. Massage the abdomen in a circular motion working outwards from the navel, using fingertips or fingers and palm.

5 Massage all down her legs, as with the arms. Massage ankles and feet and stroke each toe. Finish with long, light strokes the whole length of her body.

6 Once you have massaged your baby from head to toe on the front, turn her over and massage her back, again working from the head down.

Play 1 to 2 years

Like almost everything else your child is doing and experiencing, play develops. Your child is now entering what I call the proper "toy" stage. This usually begins towards the end of the first year and goes onto reach its peak when your child is between five and six years old.

When children first play with toys they just examine them and explore them. As they get older they use their imagination to breathe life into the toys. They like toys that imitate the adult world. Dolls, toy houses and cars, for example, allow children to act out the scenes they see in real life. At this age, they endow toys with human qualities, they set up houses, homes and camps and imagine that their toys are capable of talking and feeling just like themselves.

TOYS AND GAMES FOR TODDLERS

Your toddler's co-ordination will improve greatly this year, as will her manipulative skills. Toys that make use of both of these will provide the most enjoyment, but be prepared for your child to be a bit ham-fisted at first and give her quite large, straightforward items. Household objects will continue to be popular, but other toys may stretch both co-ordination and mental processes further.

Suitable toys
• Posting box • Stacking blocks • Building blocks
• Hammering table • Push/pull toys • Dolls
• Cars • Crayons and felt tips • Paints and brushes • Blackboard • Books • Modelling clay
• Sand-pit • Paddling pool • Slide • Swing
• Frame • Walking trolley

Toys to help manipulation

"Fitting" toys, where your toddler has to fit a shaped block into the correct hole, are ideal. A variation of this is sometimes called a "post box" and consists of a plastic box or cylinder with shaped holes cut into the surface. Your toddler can "post" the appropriately shaped blocks through the correct holes with the extra pleasure of them disappearing with a clunk. Stacking blocks provide hours of fun because they can be used in the bath, in the garden and on the beach, as well as on the floor. If you haven't already got them, building blocks are perennial favourites with children because they can be used as part of imaginary play to make so many shapes or objects – towers, forts, corrals, houses. Buy the ones sold with a trolley and you'll combine manipulation and walking.

Playing with paint

All children love to paint and draw, but during this year you may find it difficult to interpret exactly what's been drawn. Make sure that you prepare both the painting area and the child by covering the table and floor with a waterproof covering or newspaper and your child with an overall.

Two paint techniques that your child might enjoy trying out are block painting and butterfly painting. In block painting you have to provide the equivalent of a rubber stamp. This can be a small sponge, a ball of cotton wool, a cork, half an apple or a potato – anything, really, which your child can hold easily and use in a stamping movement. Make up the stamp pad by sprinkling two tablespoons of powder paint on some moistened squares of kitchen paper that you've put in a flat dish. Gently use the back of a spoon to mix the paint into the paper.

In the second technique blobs of coloured paint are dropped on to a piece of thick paper. This is then folded so that the two sides mirror each other. If your child has learnt how to blow through a straw she can blow the paint into shapes before you fold the paper.

Only keep paintings that you and your child both agree are worth keeping. Display them with magnets on refrigerator doors or, if you find a place where your child's fingerprints always seem to mark the walls, such as down the side of the staircase, cover these with your child's drawings. Your toddler's pictures can make ideal cards to send to relatives or to say "thank you" for presents; they're also easy to make into calendars, which make lovely little presents for grandparents.

FUN WITH PAINT

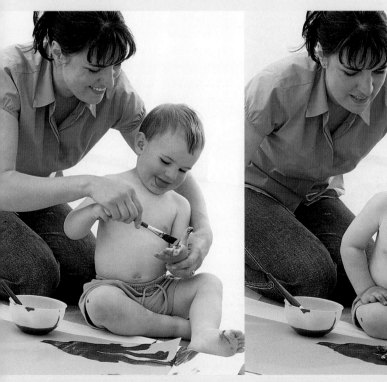

Fingerpainting
To make some fingerpaint, mix 60ml (2floz) liquid starch with either four drops of food colouring or a tablespoon of powder paint.

Using his hands
Once the paint is made, let your child daub some on his hands and make handprints and shapes on huge pieces of paper.

PAINT TIPS

- Buy powder paints and mix the quantity that you need; only buy blue, red, yellow and white.
- Keep paint in small plastic jars, preferably in the non-spill variety that have a hole in the top for the paint brush.
- Plastic egg cartons make a difficult-to-spill artist's palette for your child.
- To thicken up powder paint without using extra powder add some liquid starch.
- Children love making their own paint so make up a little liquid starch in a small container and provide some bottles of food colouring. They can add this until they have the colour that they require.
- Cleaning up is easier if you add a little bit of detergent to fingerpaints.
- You can make a paint that will stick to a shiny surface such as glass or aluminium foil by mixing a few drops of food colouring, and an egg yolk with powdered detergent.
- If you buy your child felt tip pens or crayons, make sure they're the fat, chunky ones because they're easier to hold.
- Take a fairly large block of synthetic foam rubber or polythene foam and cut different-sized holes in it. Stand up all your child's bottles, brushes and jars in it. That way they won't fall over.
- A cutlery tray makes a very good store for bottles, jars and paint brushes.
- Put drawing paper on a kitchen paper dispenser and attach it to the wall in your creative corner.
- Keep your old newspapers for floor covering, or use a large plastic table cloth.

What paper to use

Inexpensive makes of paper, wallpaper, shelf paper, old envelopes or brown paper bags, even old newspaper, can be painted on. Alternatively, buy a roll of lining paper and cut off what your child needs. Make a reusable colouring board by covering a piece of cardboard with clear, stick-on paper. In this way paintings can be washed off with a damp cloth or kitchen paper (experiment with paints to see which one sticks on the surface best).

What brushes to use

When your child begins to paint, use thick brushes so that she sees immediate, bold results. Provide pastry brushes, cotton wool balls, orange sticks and pipe cleaners for variety. Let her use her fingers or her feet from time to time. Make an alternative brush from an old roll-on deodorant bottle: lever out the ball from the neck of the bottle with a spoon, fill with paint and replace the ball.

Preserving drawings

You can preserve a crayon drawing by ironing it on to a piece of cloth. Lay it face upwards on the ironing board, cover it with a piece of light coloured cloth and then iron it firmly at a low-to-medium temperature. The drawing will transfer to the cloth. Make sure you let it cool before you move it from the ironing board. Another tip is to spray drawings with fixative, or hair spray if you use it. This will keep the colours from being rubbed off. Alternatively, there is a "magic" solution that is estimated to keep a drawing for 200 years! Dissolve a tablet of milk of magnesia in 500ml (2 pints) of soda water

Water fun
Give your child lots of empty plastic bottles, beakers
and colanders to play with in a bowl in the garden or
in the bath.

and let it sit overnight. The following day
soak a paper drawing in the solution for an
hour; remove from solution and leave until
it is completely dry.

Playing with water

Most children love playing with water and
by the time they're in their second year will
have forgotten about any fears they may
have had. Try some of the following, but
never leave your child alone near water:

- Paddling pools are ideal summer
  playthings. The smaller, round variety that
  you blow up are just as much fun as a
  more elaborate, permanent one.
- In the summer lay a tarpaulin sheet on
  the ground and play a hose or plant
  spray over it. When it's completely wet
  it'll make a perfect slide for your child.
- Make a small hole in the bottom of a
  plastic container and fill it with coloured
  water. Attach it to the back of your
  child's tricycle (and later, bicycle). She'll
  be able to see the coloured trail the
  water has left as she cycles along.
- If you have a tap in the back garden put
  a container of soil near it so that she can
  mix water with the soil and make up her
  own mud. Messy but lots of fun.
- Make an "iceberg" that can be played
  with in the bath or in a paddling pool.
  Put some food colouring into a balloon
  then fill it with water. Put it into a pan
  and place it in the freezer. When it's solid,
  prick the balloon and peel it off – you'll
  be left with a perfect, round "iceberg".

CREATIVE MATERIALS

Glue
Mix 250g (8oz) flour with one teaspoon of salt in
a pan. Add 600ml (20floz) water slowly until it's
absorbed into a paste. Simmer for five minutes
then cool and refrigerate in an airtight container
until required.

Modelling dough
Mix three parts of flour to one part of salt, then
stir in one part of water. Colour with food
colouring and store in an airtight container.

Mock-clay dough
Mix together equal parts of salt and flour. Add
a little oil and then add enough water to mix to
a stiff dough. Knead until soft and stretchy.

Playing with sand

Sand-pits are marvellous play areas for children. Whether you buy a ready-made one or make your own by filling an old plastic paddling pool, an old rubber tyre or a cement-lined hole, you should always use washed river sand. Although more expensive than builders' sand it doesn't stain like the latter. Always cover the sand-pit over when not in use or every cat in your area could use it as a litter tray.

Slides, frames and swings

As your toddler becomes more co-ordinated throughout the year you may want to invest in a large piece of play equipment. If you decide to buy a swing, buy the kind that your toddler has to be bodily lifted into and out of. If you buy a slide make sure it has safety sides and no parts that will splinter.

Sand-pit play
A sand-pit can give young children hours of fun pouring it, digging or making castles. Make sure it is shallow, however, so your child can't get buried.

Rough and gentle games

Not all children like the same sort of game, nor does the same child like the same kind of game all the time. Some children have an obvious preference for more athletic, boisterous games, while others prefer quiet, contemplative activities.

Two of my sons were of the former type, and two of them the latter. From an early age I indulged the two who preferred rough and tumble games by providing large, soft cushions and foam-filled soft furniture for them to jump and leap about on and do their acrobatics. Outdoors there was a rope to climb, a tree with a favourite way up and down, a climbing frame with rope ladders and netting for them to cling on to and a tyre swing. I think they each had their first tricycles around the age of about 13 or 14 months. Ball games like football or bat and ball were always favourites with my children and had the advantage that they tired them out.

For the other two children, we had to provide lots of books and countless sets of paints, easels and drawing boards. At a very early age the children made toy ships or toy steam engines from household junk like empty egg boxes and kitchen paper tubes, yogurt cartons and plastic margarine containers, and as they got older they went on to making paper aeroplanes. One of our sons became quite an expert on origami at the age of three. Both of these children loved musical instruments and had recorders, toy flutes, toy xylophones and toy guitars before graduating on to proper instruments at a later age.

Are the toys creative enough?

There is hardly any toy or game that isn't creative for your child. Whatever she plays with or sees when she's awake will help her create imaginary worlds. She'll create patterns with colours and shapes and will create miniature models of her own home all the time that she's playing.

By far the most enjoyable and beneficial are games that don't need much supervision from you. They allow your child to follow any interesting development if the fancy takes her, and concentrate on doing something of her own choosing. She can use her own judgement so that her interest is completely fulfilled. If you constantly interrupt her and tell her to be clean and tidy, or careful, or if you try to help her too much, her interest in the game will wane. She will lose sight of the point of her game and will become disheartened. This sort of adult interference can also result in a child being unable to concentrate when she gets to school.

Is my child stimulated enough?

If you provide the right environment and the right equipment, you needn't worry about whether your child is being stimulated enough. At this stage she is developing her thinking about playing, and what she needs is freedom to allow her thought processes to expand so that she can follow new ideas as they occur to her, and see play through to its conclusions.

Your child is attacking play very much like an explorer. She must be given privacy and time to herself with no interruptions (unless she asks for them). It is your job to be an assistant and make sure that she has all the facilities that she needs. Once you have provided all these facilities, it is up to your child to decide what to do, not you. It's best to let her be to use her own imagination and not to interfere.

SAFETY TIPS

- Keep her well away from any kind of pool containing water. No matter how small or shallow it is, even if she can swim, she should never be left unattended.
- Any game that involves metal implements is potentially dangerous, e.g. metal buckets and spades or toy pistols. So is any game with sharp or pointed instruments, e.g. bows and arrows or toy knives.
- Never let your toddler go anywhere near or handle fireworks or matches.

How you can help

You can't teach your child to use her imagination, but you can encourage her natural gift for fantasy by trying some of the following:

- Play a variety of make-believe games with your toddler.
- When you tell a story act out the characters' parts and make up all the different voices. If your child has a favourite, suggest that she takes that part for herself.
- Play games of "What's this". Get your child to shut her eyes then gently stroke some object across her skin. She's got to guess what the object is.
- Help your child in her imaginary world by giving her some glove puppets – either bought ones or brown paper bags with faces drawn on them.
- Provide good fantasy toys like dolls; children of both sexes love dolls because they're so easy to incorporate into their imaginary worlds. Stuffed animals, house cleaning sets, tea sets and gardening or carpentry sets are also ideal
- Start to stock a dressing-up box. Put in some of your old shoes, shirts, skirts, dresses, hats and scarves. Have some special cheap jewellery as well. If you can find some authentic uniforms from second-hand shops so much the better. Make a cloak from a length of fabric and attach a clasp at one end.
- Play at being an animal. Get down on all fours and move about the floor making all the animal noises that you know. This will show your toddler how to do it.
- Play telephone conversations. If you've given your child a toy telephone, pick up the real phone and pretend to have a telephone conversation with her.

STORAGE TIPS

- Always keep any plastic containers with lids for storing blocks, marbles or small toys. Those made for ice cream or margarine are ideal.
- Use brightly coloured labels for easy identification of what's inside your containers.
- Large glass jars are good for storage because you can immediately see what's inside them.
- Never throw out any shoe boxes – they make good beds for dolls as well as houses or barns.
- Loop a plastic mesh basket over the taps in the bath to store all bath toys.
- Use a flat-topped chest for storing larger toys. This can double up as a table.
- Your child's toys are bound to get strewn around your home. Try to keep a basket in each room to make for quick and easy tidying up.
- Keep a special bag or box of toys in the car.

CLEANING AND PREPARING TOYS

- Always buy machine-washable stuffed toys.
- Alternatively use a carpet shampoo and brush to clean stuffed toys.
- Try to buy plastic toys that can be put into the dishwasher when they are dirty.
- If plastic toys have got out of shape, you can soak them in hot water and then re-mould them with your fingers.
- Clean and deodorize smelly toys by sponging them with a cloth that has been wrung out in a solution of baking soda.
- You can dry-clean your child's soft toys by shaking them in a bag containing a generous amount of baking powder.

Play 2 to 3 years

Your child will probably still play with some of her existing toys although the ways in which she plays with them may differ. She may continue to play with building blocks, but instead of just piling them on top of each other will use them as part of a larger concept: she may use them to make the wall surrounding an imaginary house.

During this third year your child will want to imitate the way you behave and the way you look. Manipulation skills will be greatly improved so larger jigsaws and more fiddly puzzles will be popular.

Imitative games

As part of her imitation of the adults around her, your child will create a little world of her own. You don't need to buy a proper play house for her to do this. A couple of chairs, or a small table draped with a large blanket will make an instant tent or playhouse, as will an old playpen covered with a sheet. Children love playing in the dark, so draw the curtains if that's what they want. All of my children loved playing with cardboard boxes of any size, as long as they were big enough to climb into. Small ones became boats and cars, piles of them were made into castles, forts and houses. Boxes laid on their sides became tunnels and when laid end to end became trains. More elaborate "houses" can be made by taking a large box or a series of tea chests with all the nails and strips of metal taken off and cutting out doors and windows. Your child can draw in curtains and put pictures on the wall inside, and outside she can draw shutters,

TOYS FOR 2 TO 3 YEAR OLDS

Children of this age are gaining steadily in independence, control of language and new skills. They like to build things up and knock them down, and they love "let's pretend" games.

Suitable toys
• Large-piece jigsaw • Plasticine • Plastic building bricks • Scissors (blunt-ended) • Glue • Prams and pushchairs • Tea sets • Toy washing machines, cooking utensils • Play house • Tricycle • Cars and trucks • Climbing frame

Imaginative play
Toys such as tea sets, play groceries, dolls' house furniture and dressing-up clothes all encourage imaginative play.

a door and a knocker. If you put several stools or small chairs in a line across the room your child will make them into a train, a boat or an aeroplane.

Games to help manipulation

Your child will use her hands to explore objects and discover what they do – it'll be an important part of the learning process for her. All of the games and ideas listed below require good co-ordination.

- During this year your child will have enough co-ordination to help with tasks in the house, and she'll see this as a form of play because she's so keen to copy what you do. She'll enjoy helping you wash fruit and vegetables, and she'll be able to snap the tops off beans and tear lettuce leaves.

Encourage hand skills
Construction toys such as building blocks or train sets with lots of pieces help stimulate your child's manipulative skills as well as his imagination.

- Many children love taking anything mechanical to pieces so don't throw away old clocks, old motors, cameras or CD players when they break; let your child have fun taking them to pieces. And if there is anything around the house that needs to be dismantled, such as an old wall or fence, or cardboard boxes that need breaking down, let your child join in.
- Your child might enjoy trying out spatter painting. To do this she places leaves, grasses, coins, whatever shape she wants, flat on to a piece of white paper.

She then takes a toothbrush, well soaked with paint, and gently draws her thumb or a plastic knife across it so that the paint is spattered randomly across the paper. To make it look even more exciting she can try different colours. When the paint is dry she can remove the objects.

• Give your child a small plot in the garden that is entirely hers. Provide her with her own trowel and a watering can and help her plant some quick-growing flowers such as marigolds or vegetables such as radishes, runner beans or peas.

Jigsaw puzzles

Your child will probably be able to deal with jigsaws of up to six pieces. Wherever possible you should try to buy ones with easily identified bits when the puzzle's apart. Your toddler will find it much easier if she can see what's a leg or an arm or a tree rather than just a shape. Buy wooden jigsaws where possible: they're easier to handle and don't bend like the cardboard variety. If you find your child still can't hold them make it easier by gluing on small plastic hooks from the hardware store. Start off with the inset puzzles where the pieces fit into pre-cut areas on a tray. Your toddler will soon pick up how it works.

With some jigsaws you may have to show your child exactly how to assemble the pieces. When you do this explain to her why certain pieces go together and interlock. "Look, this bit has two bumps that look like eyebrows ... this piece is for the head that always goes on top of the body". Once you've done this and helped your child through it herself a couple of times she'll happily sit and do it over and over again. If you have a number of puzzles, make them easier to sort by marking the back of each piece with a different colour pen.

Make your own puzzles out of your child's favourite picture by pasting it on to heavy card and covering it with clear contact film. With a craft knife, cut the puzzle into about six pieces made up of triangles, diamonds and squares.

Learning through play

There's no time in your young child's life when play does not contribute to her development. Quite often your child's needs and desires can be fulfilled in play when they cannot satisfactorily be met in any other way. For instance, a child who's unable to be a leader in real life may gain great satisfaction from being the leader of her collection of play people or bossing her stuffed animals around.

For most children, play involves experimentation. Through trial and error, your children can discover that creating something new, something that they haven't met or done before, can be very satisfying. Once they have fulfilled their creative interests in play, they can then transfer them to the real world as they grow and mature.

At home and in school children learn what the generally accepted roles of the different sexes are. Knowing what they are, accepting them and taking up the relevant role are different things. Soon after joining a playgroup your child learns that she must play that role if she wants to become an accepted member of the group. It may be in this group that your child meets the most rigid enforcement of moral standards that she'll ever experience. There is nothing like a group of children at play for encouraging the development of desirable personality traits. By contact with friends, your child will be given lessons every day in how to be generous, truthful and co-operative, how to be a good sport and pleasant to be with. These lessons are especially forceful, because your child is constantly seeking the approval of friends and peers, and the playgroup in general.

Learning about colours

Always mention the colour of something that you are using or looking for. For instance, "I'm looking for the green packet", "Where's that red tin gone?", "Oh, I've found the jar with the blue label" or "I'm going to use this yellow pencil". Always describe the colour of your child's clothes: "That's a pretty pink dress". "What a nice red jumper". Always point

TELEVISION

Some babies are introduced to television while they are still in their cots. Their parents see television as a built-in babysitter to keep children amused. For quite a lot of children television is more popular and consumes more of their playtime than all other play activities added together. Here are some of the reported facts about television:

- Television is at its least useful when a child is left to watch it alone. Even if she's watching a highly educational programme she'll get less out of it if she watches it in an entirely passive way. But if she watches with other children who comment on it, or with an adult who asks questions and makes observations, the programme can act as a springboard for ideas and discussion.
- Some parents let television interfere with the usual eating and sleeping routines, leading to upset digestion and tired children.
- Watching television can curtail other activities, especially outdoor play and playing with other children; it may leave little time for creative play.
- Television often presents information in a more exciting and dramatic way than school books and school teachers. Children therefore often find books and school work boring.
- Television cuts down on conversation and other social interactions in the family.

- Characters on television are often presented as exaggerated stereotypes and children come to think that people in a given group have the same qualities as the people portrayed on the screen and this influences their attitude towards them.
- If a child watches too many programmes portraying crime, torture and cruelty, this may blunt her sensitivity to violence so that she accepts violent behaviour as normal.
- Two groups of children were studied for the effects of violence on television. One saw violent programmes, the other did not. The studies showed that the young children who watched the violent programmes were noticeably more aggressive, both with other children and with their toys, than those children who had not been exposed to the same programmes.
- Children are great imitators and as the law breakers often seem more glamorous than the heroes, children tend to identify with the villains.
- Television can present models for the behaviour of the different sexes and for life roles and careers. This in turn gives rise to similar expectations in children that are not always the best.
- If children are really interested in programmes they have seen they may want to find out more by reading or asking grown-ups about the subject.

out the colour of flowers, in your garden, your windowbox or in the park, and show your child the different colours that animals, and birds especially, can have. Show your child how colours are made, "Look, if we mix a little bit of red with white we get pink; yellow mixed with blue makes green". Teach her the colours of the rainbow; rainbows are magical to children.

Learning about numbers

Always take the chance to count while you are doing routine things. For instance, count one, two and three as you do up the buttons on your child's dungarees or jacket, or when you're washing her hands or feet. Help with number learning by counting things as you shop. Ask your child to fetch you two oranges or three carrots.

Count bottles and jars and arrange them into groups such as two bottles, three cans and four packets. Draw numbers on small sheets of paper and help your child to number little groups of her toys, for instance, three balls, five blocks, seven farmyard animals. When you go for walks count the number of houses or gates, trees in a garden or ducks in a pond.

Learning about letters

Take every opportunity to help your toddler become familiar with letters. Teach your child the alphabet song so that remembering it is all the easier. Serve alphabet soup or alphabet spaghetti and

help your child to spell out her name with the letters. Alternatively, buy your child some magnetic letters that she can play with on the refrigerator door. Children love moving the words around.

My children liked us to spell out words by drawing the letters in the palms of their hands while their eyes were closed, and they tried to recognize the letters and build up the word. Play word games when you read a story. As you read a sentence, leave out a word and get your child to say what it is. "The cat was sitting warming itself by the ... ". As you point to the fire in the picture your child can shout out "fire".

Have fun learning
Bring learning into your child's games in a relaxed way. Ask her to count her toy figures or dolls as she plays with them and maybe give them simple names she can spell out with you.

15 Outings and travel

No baby is too young to take on an outing. Indeed, with a young baby you can go just about anywhere and, provided he can look about him, he'll enjoy the change of scene, even if he doesn't understand quite what's going on. Planning ahead is the secret and the younger your baby the more carefully you need to plan. If you are well organized, outings with your baby can be a great joy, and the sooner that you start after bringing your baby home the better. Looking after a baby needn't preclude parents from resuming the active life that they had before. One word of warning, though. Don't be too ambitious or undertake very long trips at first.

Local outings birth to 1 year

Planning your outings

It's always worth spending a little time planning how you're going to get to your destination, what you need for the journey, where you're going to feed your baby when you get there and how you're going to change him. Until you feel confident, take your partner or a friend along with you. An extra pair of hands to share the load, and an ally to share the novelty and possibly any problems, will make any trip with your baby more enjoyable.

When you're out and about, you'll need to make sure that there's somewhere that you can feed your baby in peace, especially in the first months when your baby won't have settled into a predictable feeding routine. You'll have to change your baby as well, so try to find out if there's a nearby department store or public convenience with a mother and baby room you can use. There should be a work-top at waist height for easy changing, which will save you having to change your baby on the floor, or even worse, on your lap. In the summer, it's fun to sit in a nearby park to feed your baby.

WHAT TO TAKE FOR A YOUNG BABY

- A changing surface (that can be a fold-up plastic mat or a fabric nappy)
- Disposable nappies
- Baby wipes
- Breast pads if breast-feeding
- Bottle and milk powder if bottle-feeding
- Hat (sunhat for summer, warm one for winter)
- Sweater
- Toys for distraction
- Plastic bag for dirty nappies

Get out and about
Simply taking your baby out for a walk in the park in his pushchair is good exercise for you while being fun and stimulating for him.

Using a baby sling

Slings are one of the most convenient methods of carrying a baby as well as one of the oldest. They hold your baby securely against your chest so that you and your baby have the security of being close to each other; they also leave your hands free. Buy a washable sling because your baby is bound to posset over it, and do try it on before you make your final choice. It's got to be easy to put on and to wear. The shoulder straps must be wide enough to support your growing baby's weight comfortably and both you and your partner must feel relaxed wearing it. It has been said that a baby shouldn't be carried in a sling until he can support his own head. This is not true. You can carry your baby in

a sling as soon as you and he are happy about it – your baby will find close contact with you so soothing and reassuring that he'll probably curl up and doze.

Using a pushchair

A pushchair is absolutely essential if you don't want to carry your baby in a sling or once he's too heavy. Pushchairs with seats

WHAT TO TAKE FOR AN OLDER BABY

- A changing surface
- Disposable nappies
- Baby wipes
- Baby food and spoon
- Non-messy snacks
- Feeding beaker with fruit juice
- Bib
- Hat
- Sweater
- Toys for distraction
- Plastic bag for dirty nappies

Know your pushchair
You'll often have to collapse the pushchair when you're out and about, so make sure that you can kick it shut and open it up while holding your baby.

that lay completely flat are essential for very young babies. Although babies fit quite snugly into the curved shape of the pushchair, it is important to make sure they are well supported. Even a tiny baby, if awake, can be propped up to take in the interesting sights around him. Always make sure that your baby is safely strapped in.

Using a back-pack

A back-pack is a useful means of carrying an older baby who can sit up well and who has become rather heavy to carry in a sling. Once again, it leaves your hands free, but it also allows your baby to see much more of what's going on around him. Before you buy a back-pack, do the following:

- Try on the back-pack in the shop, with your baby in it.
- Check that the baby's seat comes halfway down your back. This is very important because it places the strain on your back and not on your shoulders; it also keeps the baby stable.
- Make sure that the pack has a safety strap to keep the baby in place and a waist belt for you to keep it secure. Check that the shoulder straps are well padded.

TIPS FOR PUSHCHAIRS

- Never leave your baby unattended.
- Always make sure that the pushchair is fully extended and that the frame is locked in position.
- Never let go of the pushchair for a moment without putting the brakes on first.
- Always put the safety harness on your baby.
- Never, ever put shopping on the handles of the pushchair, it could tip over backwards.
- From an early age teach your child to keep his fingers away from the wheels.

- One disadvantage of pushchairs over prams is that in cold weather your child is more exposed. If you don't have a padded chair cover, lay a blanket over the pushchair before you put the baby in and wrap the blanket over and around him.
- If your baby falls asleep before you get home either put the pushchair down into the lie-back position or tuck him up comfortably with pillows.
- If you have a toddler, fix a buggy-board to the back of the baby's pushchair in case he won't walk.

- Check that your baby can sit comfortably and that the leg openings don't restrict him in any way.
- Try to buy a pack with a built-in loading stand so that you can put it on without any help; such back-packs often convert to free-standing seats.

Going shopping

Try to shop early in the morning when the shops are least busy. When you go to a supermarket, always strap your baby into your shopping trolley. Most supermarkets have lie-back seats for young babies as well as seats for older ones. Wheel the trolley down the centre of the aisle. Your baby will want to grasp everything in sight, which can easily cause chaos with a supermarket's carefully stacked packets or tins. If you're still breast-feeding, plan to shop between feeds; or if you're going to be out for a while aim to have most of your shopping done before you have to find a quiet spot to give the next feed.

Having a car is one of the greatest freedoms a new parent can have. There's no worry about how to cope with public transport, and it provides an ideal feeding and changing area.

Eating out

In the first months your baby will doze off almost anywhere, so eating out will be quite easy. However, by the time he's nine months old he'll be capable of keeping himself awake; he'll be keen for any new experience and a restaurant, with strange people doing even stranger things, will fascinate him. Choose your restaurant carefully and try to find a child-friendly place that provides highchairs. Always take your own snacks with you, and as soon as you've settled your baby in his seat, give him these to occupy him. Have plenty of toys for distraction (rearranging paper napkins is a good quietener). You may find it works better if you feed your child before you and your partner start.

Using public transport

If you're shopping on your own, with a pushchair, a changing bag and a grumpy baby, getting on public transport can seem like the last straw. However, there are some tips to get over the worst problems.
- Avoid travelling in the rush hour.
- Where possible, carry your baby in a sling or back-pack. This leaves your hands free and makes getting on and off easier.
- Carry plenty of distracting toys.
- If you're asked to, leave your pushchair in the special luggage section. If this is the case make sure you get up in plenty of time before your stop to retrieve it.
- Never be embarrassed to ask for help.

TIPS FOR SHOPPING WITH BABIES

- When you're carrying your child in your back-pack remember your child's grasping fingers can reach jars and tins in a shop.
- When you take your child to the supermarket always find a trolley with a babyseat and strap him safely.
- For emergencies keep a few disposable nappies, wipes and plastic bags in the glove compartment of the car for quick changes.
- Shopping seems to make children hungry and therefore fretful. Avoid this by taking a snack.
- You can use the opened boot of the car, with a blanket laid over it, as a surface on which to change your child.

Local outings 1 to 3 years

By the time your child is walking you may find that your greatest problem is keeping him safely restrained and happily occupied when you go out. You'll also have to be prepared for very slow journeys with endless stops to look at the many objects that take your child's fancy. Most parents continue to use their pushchair, although reins, back-packs and bicycle seats are useful alternatives and can sometimes be more fun for your child.

Using the pushchair

As your child gets older he won't be happy just sitting in the pushchair, but will often want to walk along with you. This may be inconvenient, especially if you are shopping, and you will have to do your utmost to persuade your toddler to stay in the chair. In my experience the best way of doing this is to take along one of your child's favourite toys as well as a snack.

If your child is so restless that he makes shopping impossible, you could take along a pair of reins and put your child in them. He will feel a sense of freedom and independence, but you know that he can't wander away from you and get lost. A wrist link that's securely attached to the reins will prevent your child becoming separated from you.

Using a bicycle seat

If you have a bicycle you may find it fun to take your toddler on the back. There are two kinds of bicycle seat – front-mounted and rear-mounted. These lightweight plastic structures fit neatly and securely on to the bicycle frame and can accommodate a child of up to 22kg (48lb). Make sure that your child's feet are well away from the wheels and that there's a strong safety belt for your child. If you decide you do want to use this method of transport, both you and your child must wear protective cycle helmets.

SHOPPING WITH TODDLERS

- Encourage your child to become familiar with shopping. Give him the wrappers or boxes of things on your shopping list and suggest he finds them for you by matching them up with products on the shelves.
- Toddlers can get lost in shops. Dress yours in an easily spotted coat or hat in a bright colour.
- As soon as possible, teach your child his name, address and telephone number. In the meantime, insert a label with this information inside his coat in case he does get lost.
- I used to use a referee's whistle on a string round my neck to summon my children. We had a code: one whistle – come briskly; two whistles – run; three whistles – emergency.
- Any outing can be a lesson in disguise. In the supermarket you can teach your child about healthy eating (that beans are better than tinned spaghetti hoops) or best buys (that large tins work out cheaper than small ones).
- It's a scary prospect but you can make sure your child could find his way when he's near home by giving the same running commentary as you approach your house. "And here's that big tree on the corner, now we turn right, past the post box, and here's our road, and our house, the fourth on the left".

Shopping with an older child

As soon as your child can toddle you'll be faced with a new problem: how to keep an eye on, and occupy, a lively young child and concentrate on what you have to do. The only efficient way of getting about, especially when shopping, is to take your partner or a friend along with you. In this way, one adult can get on with the shopping while the other occupies the child. (There is also the added bonus of another pair of hands to help carry shopping home.)

The most important tip is to keep your toddler on reins so that you can concentrate on what you're doing without having to worry about what he's doing. It also helps to sit your child in the supermarket trolley so that he can't run away. As you go around the shop ask your child questions like "Can you see the baked beans?" "Which is the largest tin?" "Which apples do you want – the red or the green ones?". Most children love being involved in this way and you can even let them choose a few of their favourite foods and put them in the trolley.

My supermarket solution for keeping them quiet was to let my children put anything into the trolley as we were going around and then take it all out at the end (unbeknown to them): it was time-consuming, but more peaceful.

If you aren't going food shopping but, say, clothes shopping instead, still keep your toddler on reins but take along his favourite books. When you go into the changing rooms sit your child on the floor beside you and encourage him to look at the pictures, maybe telling you what's in them or what the story is about.

Special excursions

Going out to the shops or to the park will probably be part of your toddler's daily routine but there will be occasions when you want to plan a special excursion like the zoo or a boat trip. In your plans, take your child's personality into account. What's his attention span? Is he very active? If he is, don't plan to go anywhere where he's going to be confined to his pushchair for long or you'll ruin everybody's day. If, when the day arrives, your toddler's in a bad mood, postpone the outing; similarly, if you no longer feel like it. Take enough snacks for the whole day and include quite a variety of them.

Family outings
Your toddler will love going out with his mum and dad. Be prepared to make endless stops to look at anything that catches your child's attention.

Car journeys birth to 1 year

Travelling in cars is a normal part of everyday life, and the sooner your baby learns about it the better.

Car safety
The most important aspect of travelling by car is the safety of your baby. Never sit in the front or back of the car with your baby on your lap. Always use a car seat suitable for your baby's age, weight and size and make sure that the seat complies with current standard and safety regulations. Before choosing a restraint, seek independent consumer and safety advice.

Feeding your baby
Obviously feeding is much easier if you're breast-feeding. If you're bottle-feeding, however, you must never try to keep a made-up feed warm because any germs will quickly multiply. If you can't get hold of disposable bottles and feeds, mix the formula, when you need it, in a sterilized bottle with some boiled water that you've kept in a thermos.

Once your baby's weaned you'll need to take baby food, a feeding dish, a plastic spoon and a drinking cup with a spout. You can feed your baby from the jar, but remember to throw away anything he doesn't finish because the food will be contaminated with saliva, and germs will grow in it very quickly.

Changing your baby
Disposables are by far the easiest to use when you're travelling. There's no need to do more than top and tail your baby when travelling so all you need are some baby wipes and a plastic bag for dirty nappies.

Travel with your baby
Car journeys can be easier than public transport with a young baby as you can keep changing kit in the car – and you'll have somewhere you can feed in peace.

CAR TIPS
- Never leave your child alone in the car.
- When the temperature is very hot, avoid heat exhaustion and heatstroke by only taking your baby on essential short journeys early in the morning and at night when it is cooler.
- Secure a sun blind or piece of thick cloth on the car window to protect a baby from the sun.
- Remove all loose objects from the back ledge in case of accidents.
- Always keep a bag with spare nappies and changing equipment in the car.
- Have a rug or cot quilt to put over the baby when he falls asleep.

Car journeys 1 to 3 years

It's between the ages of one and two and a half that car journeys become most difficult. Your child will hate being made to sit still in one place and he'll want to assert himself. A new sense of independence emerges at this time and he'll be keen to express what he wants to do, especially when you don't want him to do it. Here are some tips that may help.

- Make an early start or travel at night. Pack soft clothing that will do double duty. For example, anoraks in a pillow case make good car pillows.
- Buy or make seat backs with pockets for the front seats of the car and put games, snacks, drinks and books in them.
- Curb restlessness by stopping for five minutes every hour or so, so that the children can stretch their legs.
- Always tape knives, forks and spoons to the inside of the food containers.
- To minimize mess in the car have a store of carrier bags to put rubbish in and a supply of paper tissues and baby wipes to clean sticky hands and faces.
- Have nutritious snacks, for example, raisins, fruit, pieces of cheese, in plastic bags so that you never have to say no if your child wants to nibble.
- Always take more drinks, such as small, sealed containers of milk or juice, than you think you'll need.
- Most children love grapes (the seedless kind) and they quench thirst as well as satisfying hunger.
- Music and stories to listen to will keep most children happy in the car.
- Get your child to take some responsibility for his own entertainment by letting him select a few of his toys and put them in his own case or bag.
- Magnetized games prevent bits getting lost, alternatively sew or stick Velcro on to toys or games so that they will stay steady or in one place.
- Keep a few treats hidden away for the moment when your child gets grumpy.
- Don't stand for any misbehaviour like screaming or kicking. Pull in to the side of the road and say that you're not going any further until he behaves.

PREVENTING CAR SICKNESS

Some children are more prone to car sickness than others. Most grow out of it as they get older, but there are ways to minimize the risks:

- If your child gets car sick, ask your doctor or health visitor to suggest a suitable medicine.
- Keep your child occupied.
- Don't give your child rich or greasy food within a few hours of leaving.
- If your child wants a snack during the journey give him dry biscuits or a glucose sweet.
- Don't become over-anxious. Children quickly pick up on their parents' moods and this can make them apprehensive and more prone to car sickness. Excitement and apprehension do play a part and children tend to suffer more on outward journeys than on return ones.
- If your child goes very pale or very quiet, stop the car. Provide a plastic bag or bowl to be sick in, if necessary.
- Keep a supply of plastic bags in the car, baby wipes to clean your child up (and a change of clothes) and something to take away the taste.

Air travel birth to 3 years

When you make your reservations say that you're going to be travelling with an infant. Ask to be put on a flight that's not crowded and ask for a bulkhead seat, because there's more leg room there. Ask if they provide cots; if they do, order one so that your baby will be comfortable during the flight. Bulkhead seats are advisable if you have a toddler, too, because you can lay a towel on the floor in front of you for him to play on. Carry a small baby in a sling so that you have both hands free. Alternatively use a pushchair. Find out from the travel company if the airport provides pushchairs – you'll probably have to walk a long way to reach the boarding area and if you're trying to manage hand-baggage and a baby you could find it exhausting. If they don't provide pushchairs take your own – it can be carried as hand-baggage.

Arrive at the airport with plenty of time to spare. This means that you'll be able to check-in before the queues start and get yourself organized. Carry everything you need in a lightweight shoulder bag or rucksack – toys as well as nappies and changes of clothing – so that your hands are free. Families with young children are often allowed to board first, or you can arrange for priority boarding. Check with your travel agent or on the internet.

WHAT TO TAKE WITH YOU

- Child's passport and immunization documents, if necessary.
- Lightweight bag for baby's equipment.
- Travel cot if cot unavailable at destination.
- Pushchair, carrycot, back-pack or sling.
- Plastic mat for nappy changing.
- Bouncing chair if used.
- Pack of disposables; buy supplies at destination.
- Nappy changing equipment.
- Potty if needed.
- Plastic bags for dirty nappies.
- Vacuum flask for days on beach.
- Bottle-feeding equipment if required.
- Non-spill mug and plastic dish if weaned.
- Toys and games.
- Comforters if used.
- Quick-drying, non-crease clothes.
- Sunhat, if necessary.
- Long-sleeved and long-legged clothes.

Making the best of plane journeys

There are several ways you can make the journey easier for you and your child.
- Ask the airline if they carry baby food.
- Change your baby's nappy just before you board the plane.
- Keep some food or drink at the ready to give your baby at take-off or landing to help equalize the pressure in his ears and avoid discomfort.
- Shortly after boarding ask one of the flight attendants for help and find out when it will be convenient for him or her to warm your baby's food and drink.
- Make sure your inflight baby bag, with feeding equipment and changes of nappies and clothing, is clearly labelled in case it gets mislaid during the flight.
- Amuse your child with the same kinds of games as you play in the car (*see p.289*).

- Don't try to eat or drink hot food while you're holding the baby for fear of spillage and scalding him.
- Take along a few of your child's favourite toys but only bring them out one at a time and at intervals through the journey.
- Let your baby play with all the inflight equipment – spoons and forks from the food tray, plastic safety instructions from the seat flap, earphones for the films.

Towards carefree foreign holidays

Your baby's never too young to travel (although most airlines require a doctor's note if she is under two weeks old). The type of holiday you choose is up to you and your individual tastes – it may be camping, staying in a luxury hotel or swapping houses with another family. Wherever you go make sure that they have adequate facilities for young children. Without them you're not going to enjoy the holiday yourselves. If it is a hotel ask if they provide highchairs, play pools, laundry service and early meals for children or babysitting. If you're going to a beach it's advisable to choose one that's sandy. Ask your doctor's advice well ahead of your trip about health precautions, vaccinations (*see p.343*), or any medication that you should take with you. With a baby, consult your health visitor about food, facilities and hygiene in the country or area that you're going to.

If you're adventurous with the family diet at home, let your children eat what they want. If you or they are more conservative and you're not self-catering, make arrangements with the hotel for them to have simple meals. Don't try to introduce your young child to exotic food for the first time in a foreign country.

SAFE SUN TIPS

Keep babies in the shade at all times. Do not expose them to the sun. Babies have little skin pigment so they have much less protection from the sun than adults, and exposure to the sun's ultraviolet rays can lead to skin damage and skin cancer in later life.

- In very hot weather, avoid taking your baby out in the sun between 11am and 3pm when the sun is at its highest.
- Dress your baby in a wide-brimmed hat and loose light clothing that covers his shoulders and neck, such as a shirt with sleeves and a collar.
- Be aware that your baby is still at risk on cloudy days.
- Make sure the pram or buggy has an adjustable hood or umbrella to shade your baby.
- Be particularly careful near snow and water where reflected light is strong.
- Apply sunscreen of at least factor 30 to your child before he goes out and reapply often. Use waterproof sunscreen when swimming.

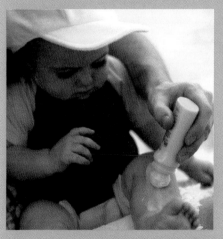

Keep your child protected
A young child's skin is easily damaged by the sun. Always protect your child by using sunscreen, cotton clothing and a hat.

16 Home safety

Accidents in the home cause a large percentage of deaths in children between the ages of one and four. Most of these incidents are avoidable so do take the time and care to minimize the chances of anything happening in your home. Most accidents are caused by a chain of events rather than a single occurrence, for example when someone is ill or tired, or when something unusual is happening.

Room-by-room safety

All children are naturally adventurous and inquisitive, and it is all too easy to underestimate the dangers your child may face in your home as soon as she becomes mobile. Many household items are dangerous to children. Every year children have accidents and many could have been avoided with a little forethought.

General tips
- Buy all medicines in child-proof bottles, and always keep them out of the reach of your child in a locked medicine cupboard. Ask your pharmacist if he can supply prescription medicines in child-proof bottles.
- Always keep medicines and chemicals in the clearly labelled containers that they originally came in. Never put a poison into a bottle that previously held a harmless liquid such as fruit juice.
- Store all drugs and chemicals as far away from food as possible.
- Don't leave aerosol cans lying around – the nozzle could easily be depressed by your child and could cause eye damage.

RISK FACTORS

The chances of an accident happening are increased by the following factors:
- If your child is tired, ill or hungry.
- If parents are tired or ill or if the mother is premenstrual or pregnant.
- When there's great excitement in the home, such as when you're going on holiday or expecting the arrival of a new baby.
- If your child is considered hyperactive.
- If you and your partner aren't getting on, or if you're actually rowing.
- If your child hasn't got anywhere safe to play.
- If correct safety precautions haven't been followed.
- If the equipment you use for your baby doesn't comply with safety standards.

- Fit socket safety covers to all power points that are not in use.
- Make sure that flexes and electrical appliances are kept out of the reach of your child.
- All electrical flexes should be in good condition and not frayed or otherwise damaged; replace them if necessary.
- Fit window locks or safety catches to prevent windows opening more than 10cm (4in). Bear in mind that windows can be an essential escape route in case of fire so make sure the window keys are easy to find in an emergency.
- Never leave anything near windows that your child could climb up on.
- Keep pins, needles, matches, lighters, sharp knives and scissors out of the reach of your child, in a child-proof drawer.
- Cover hot radiators and pipes with towels

Stair gates
Put a gate across the kitchen doorway so your child can still see you but won't be under your feet while you are cooking. Put one at the bottom of the stairs as well.

or seal them off with pieces of furniture that your child can't move. Teach your child from an early age that radiators are hot and shouldn't be touched.
- If you own a gun always store it, and its ammunition, in a locked safe.
- Always buy flame-resistant clothing for your child.
- Make sure furniture is too solid and heavy for your child to pull over.
- Fit smoke alarms to ceilings on each level of your home. Check them regularly to make sure that they are still working.
- Replace old foam furniture; it gives off toxic fumes if it catches fire.

The bathroom

- Make sure that it's possible to open your bathroom and lavatory door from the outside in case your child locks the door.
- Medicines, scissors and razor blades should be kept out of your child's reach in a locked cupboard.
- Don't leave any perfumes and cosmetics lying around.
- Keep the lavatory lid closed.
- When you run your child's bath always run the cold tap in first so there's no risk of her being scalded; test the water before putting your child in.
- Fit thermostatic taps to reduce risk of scalding.
- Fit handles to the sides of the bath.

- Use a non-slip bath mat in the bath.
- Have a non-slip floor surface.
- Teach your child how to swim as soon as possible.
- Make sure bathroom windows are fitted with locks or safety catches.
- The bathroom cabinet, which must have a child-proof lock, should be out of the reach of your child.
- Don't fit a bathroom cabinet above the lavatory – your child could climb up on the seat to open it.
- Never leave your child alone in the bath.
- Hot towel rails should be covered with towels and your child should be taught from an early age that they're hot and shouldn't be touched.
- Don't mix lavatory cleaners with bleach as they can give off dangerous fumes.
- Keep all cleaning agents, bleaches and disinfectants in a locked cupboard.

The kitchen

- The floors should be non-slip.
- All work surfaces should be well lit.
- The floor should be uncluttered.
- Windows and glazed doors should be fitted with toughened safety glass.
- Keep cupboard doors closed and preferably fitted with child locks.
- Keep drawers shut and put child locks on them if possible.
- Always wipe up spilled liquid at once.
- Keep work surfaces as clear as possible so that sharp implements such as knives can be spotted immediately.

Safety in the bath
Put a non-slip mat in the bottom of the bath so your baby does not fall. This is just as important when your child is older as he may try to climb in and out.

- Fit a cooker guard around the hob.
- Never leave a boiling pan or chip pan unattended on the stove.
- Use the back rings of the cooker, and always turn the pan handles towards the back of the stove.
- Never reach across a heated burner or ring; you could burn yourself, or knock a pan off the stove.
- Whenever using electrical equipment always follow the manufacturer's instructions exactly.
- Don't use tablecloths. Even a crawling baby can reach up and pull whatever's on the table on top of himself.
- Keep matches in a safe, cool place.
- Don't cook with your toddler around you. Arrange a safe play area in a special part of the kitchen so that you can still talk to each other.
- Keep the flex on any electrical equipment short and out of the way.
- Don't store things that you use frequently on a high shelf. When you do have to reach into a high place, stand on a secure kitchen ladder, and make sure that your balance is good before you reach up.
- Always keep cloths away from the stove in case of fire.
- Make sure your dishwasher, washing machine and dryer have safety locks.
- Keep a fire blanket next to the stove in case anything catches fire.
- Keep plastic bags well out of reach of your child.
- Your child's fingers could easily catch in a swing door. Either get rid of it or secure it in an open position.
- Any "glasses" that your child uses should be unbreakable.

- Never leave a room with the iron on; it's all too easy for your child to topple both board and iron on top of himself.
- Always keep your baby and her toys away from the immediate cooking area so that there's no risk of you tripping and spilling hot liquid over her. Put her in either a playpen, baby bouncer or highchair while you are cooking.
- If you put your child in a playpen in the kitchen make sure that it is well out of reach of the work tops.
- Store all cleaning materials – such as bleach or soap powders – out of reach.

In the highchair
A baby should be strapped into his highchair every time you put him in it – even if you think he can't climb!

Children's bedrooms

- Fit safety locks on all windows and don't leave furniture near them.
- Put special plastic safety covers on any furniture with sharp corners.
- Store toys and games at a low level so that your child doesn't have to stretch or be tempted to climb up to get at them.
- Don't leave toys lying around on the floor.
- Don't put an electric fire anywhere near your child's bed at night because she could throw off her blanket or quilt and cause a fire.
- Buy non-flammable nightclothes.
- Wall-mounted lights are safer because they have no flexes trailing on the floor.
- Never leave your baby in her cot with the side down.
- Never leave your baby alone on the changing table, even for a second.
- Keep a baby monitor by your child's bed so you can hear if she wakes up in the night
- Put a stair gate across your child's bedroom doorway once she is crawling. Don't put one at the top of the stairs as you might trip over it.

The living room

- If you have an open fire, always keep a spark guard in front of it as well as a safety guard that is fastened to the wall.
- Run flexes around the walls.
- Disconnect appliances when not in use.
- Keep flexes on electrical appliances short.
- Don't place a hot or heavy object on a low table where your child could reach it.
- All shelving should be securely fixed to the wall and should be well out of the reach of your child.
- Make sure your houseplants aren't poisonous.

Sturdy furniture
When your child is nearly ready to walk she will pull herself up on everything. Put unstable furniture out of her reach even if it's only until she is more stable.

- Keep the television out of reach.
- Anything breakable should be out of the reach of your child.
- Fit toughened safety glass to windows that are near the floor, especially patio windows, so that it won't shatter even if your child falls on to it. In addition put stickers on the glass so it can be seen.
- Never leave hot or alcoholic drinks lying around within reach of your child.
- Don't leave lighters or matches lying about; lock them away.

Halls, stairs and passageways

- Fit a safety gate across the bottom of the stairs; don't put one across the top as they are a trip hazard.
- Electric light switches should be in convenient places.
- Banisters should be secure; check them regularly and repair any loose ones.

- Never leave anything lying on or near the stairs. Make sure that doors, hallways and stairs are well lit.
- Don't have open-plan staircases – your child could easily fall between the stairs or off to one side.
- The gaps between the banisters should be no more than 6.5cm (2½in) apart so children can't climb through them.
- Stair carpets should be fitted well so that they don't slip. Any tears or holes should be patched immediately.
- Put safety locks and a chain on your front door; make sure the lock is well out of your child's reach.

The garden

- Put child-proof locks on all gates.
- Fence off a swimming pool or pond.
- Never leave a paddling pool with water in it; empty it and either deflate it or store it upside down.
- Fit any rainwater butts or similar water-collecting devices with a secure lid. Your child can drown in as little as 5cm (2in) of water.
- Bury any animal excreta before your child has the chance to poke it, play with it or even try to eat it.
- Store all your gardening tools and machinery in a locked shed and keep the key where a child can't reach it. Explain that there's dangerous equipment in the shed, which is why it is locked.
- When mowing the lawn or cutting a hedge, keep your toddler well away.

Garden plants

Let your child do some gardening, but remove all poisonous plants; ask your local nursery if in doubt. Tell your child not to eat any plants or berries she finds.

- Your clothesline should be high up out of a child's reach. If you have a rotary washing line cover it up when not in use.
- Pull up any mushrooms or toadstools as soon as they appear.
- Never work on your car when your child is playing outside.
- Lock away all pesticides, plant sprays and car cleaners.
- Never leave lengths of rope lying about.
- Fence off your rubbish bins so that your child can't rummage inside them.
- Make regular safety checks on any swings, slides or climbing frames in your garden and always watch your child.
- If your child is playing in a paddling pool in the garden never leave her alone.

Out and about

Your child will enjoy playing out of doors – she'll be able to run around freely, get dirty, and explore a different environment. The main danger associated with playing outside is that she may run out of the playground and into the road. You can prevent this by making sure that your child always plays in an enclosed environment and that any garden and playground gates are locked with child-resistant locks.

Your child must learn that roads are dangerous places and that she must never run out into a road.

Playground safety

Young children need challenging equipment to test their skills and use up energy, but make sure they're safe.

The play area should be surrounded by a fence so that animals can't get in.

- Young children should sit in box swings, not open ones.
- Swings should be enclosed by a fence.
- Climbing equipment should be situated on a rubber surface, grass or sand so children don't injure themselves.
- Tell your child not to put her feet under a roundabout or jump off one when it's still moving.
- Slides constructed on an earth mound will break a fall.
- The surface of a slide should have no joins in it.
- Playground equipment that is at ground level, like tubes and tyres, is safest for toddlers and younger children.

ROAD SAFETY

It's never too early to teach your child the safety code for crossing the road. Whenever you want to cross the street, always go to a pedestrian crossing if possible or find the safest place to cross – one where you can see clearly in all directions and drivers can see you. Stop by the kerb, hold your child's reins or her hand, look in both directions for traffic and listen. If traffic is coming, let it pass. Look in both directions again and when nothing is coming walk across; don't run. Continue to look and listen as you cross. Keep up a running commentary of what you're doing, looking out for and listening for.

Keep safe
Never let a young child on the road alone and make sure she understands that she must never run into the road. Use reins especially if you are carrying shopping.

Emergency first aid

Choking

If your child chokes on a piece of food, her airway can become blocked, she will be unable to get oxygen into her lungs and she may lose consciousness. If the blockage is mild, she will be able to cough, cry and breathe; if severe, she can't cough, breathe or make any sound. Normal breathing may return if she loses consciousness and the muscles relax. If she is not breathing, start resuscitation (*see pp.300–302*).

For a baby under one year

1 *Lay your baby face down along your forearm, keeping her head low and supporting her head and shoulders on your hand. Give her five sharp blows between the shoulder blades with the heel of your hand.*

2 *Turn your baby face up and look in her mouth. If you can see the obstruction, pick it out with your fingers, but don't put your finger down her throat.*

3 *If back blows don't work, put two fingers on the lower half of her breastbone (see right), and give five downward thrusts. Check the mouth again. If the blockage hasn't cleared, repeat steps 1 and 2 three times, then call an ambulance. Continue back blows and chest thrusts until help arrives, or the baby is unconscious.*

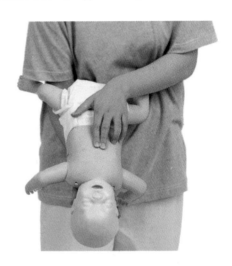

For a child

1 *If choking is severe and she can't cough or breathe, help her to bend forwards and give her five sharp blows between her shoulder blades with the heel of your hand. Check her mouth and pick out anything you can see.*

2 *If that fails, stand behind her and place one fist, thumb inwards against her abdomen, just below the rib cage. Cover it with your other hand and pull sharply inwards and upwards. Repeat up to five times. Check mouth again.*

3 *If this fails, repeat steps 1 and 2 three times, then call an ambulance. Continue back blows and abdominal thrusts until the ambulance arrives, or the child loses consciousness.*

Give five abdominal thrusts

Unconsciousness

If your child is unconscious and isn't breathing, she's at risk of brain damage and her heart may stop. If your child collapses, assess her condition quickly so you know what first aid treatment to give. If she is unconscious but still breathing, call for help and place her in the recovery position (see *opposite*). If she's unconscious and not breathing, you will need to give rescue breaths (see *opposite*) to get oxygen into her body, then give chest compressions with rescue breaths to get the oxygenated blood circulating (see *p.302*). This is called cardiopulmonary resuscitation (CPR).

Assessing a baby under one year

1 *Find out if your baby is conscious by calling her name and tapping the sole of her foot. If she doesn't respond, shout for help.*

2 *Open the airway by lifting the chin with one finger and tilting the head back.*

3 *Look, listen, and feel for signs of breathing. Look along your baby's chest and abdomen to see if there is any movement. Listen for sounds of breathing and feel for breaths on your cheek for up to 10 seconds.*

● If there are no signs of breathing, you should give five rescue breaths (see *opposite*). If you have help, get someone else to call an ambulance. If you are on your own do CPR for one minute, then call an ambulance.

● If she is breathing, hold her in your arms with her head lower than her chest and call an ambulance.

Assessing a child

1 *Find out whether your child is conscious by tapping his shoulder. Keep calling his name. If he doesn't respond, shout for help.*

2 *Open the airway. Tilt his head back by placing one hand on his forehead. Put two fingers under your child's chin and lift his jaw.*

3 *Look, listen and feel for signs of breathing. Look along your child's chest and abdomen for movements; listen for sounds of breathing; and feel for his breath on your cheek.*

● If he is not breathing, give five rescue breaths (see *opposite*). If you have help, get someone else to call an ambulance. If you are on your own, do CPR for one minute, then call an ambulance.
● If he is breathing, place him in the recovery position and call an ambulance.

Look and listen for signs of breathing

Rescue breathing for a baby under one year

1 If your baby has stopped breathing, keep her head tilted, and lift the chin with one finger. Check the baby's mouth for obvious obstructions. Pick out anything you can see.

2 Inhale, put your mouth over your baby's nostrils and mouth making a tight seal. Breathe gently into her mouth and nose so that her chest rises – about one second. Remove your lips and let the chest fall. Give five rescue breaths. If you can't get the breaths in, begin chest compressions (see p.302).

Breathe into baby's mouth and nose

Rescue breathing for a child

1 If your child has stopped breathing, keep his head tilted, and lift his chin with two fingers on the point of the chin. Check the child's mouth for obvious obstructions. Pick out anything you can see.

2 Support the chin with one hand, and using the finger and thumb of your other hand, pinch your child's nostrils closed. Inhale, put your mouth over his mouth, making a complete seal, and breathe out until his chest rises – about one second. Remove your lips and let the chest fall. Give five rescue breaths. Then begin chest compressions (see p.302).

Lift the chin with two fingers

RECOVERY POSITION

For a baby under one year

Cradle your baby in your arms with her body facing slightly towards you. Keep her head lower than her body to help keep the airway open.

For a child

An unconscious child who is breathing should be placed in the recovery position to keep her airway open and to allow liquids to drain from her mouth. Roll your child over onto her side with the uppermost leg

bent and the lower leg straight. Make sure her lower arm is clear of her body. Bend her upper arm at the elbow so that it supports her body, place her upper hand under her cheek to help keep the head back.

Chest compressions for a baby under one year

1 Lay your baby down on a firm surface and position two fingers only on the centre of the chest.

2 Press down sharply on the chest with the tips of your two fingers to a depth one-third of the depth of the chest; release the pressure, but don't remove your fingers. Give 30 compressions at a rate of about 100 compressions a minute.

3 Give two rescue breaths (see p.301). Continue alternating 30 chest compressions with two rescue breaths. After one minute, send for an ambulance, if it has not already been called. Take your baby to the phone with you if necessary. Continue resuscitation until the ambulance arrives, the baby starts breathing or you are too exhausted to keep going.

Chest compressions for a child

1 Lay your child on his back on a firm surface. Place the heel of one hand in the centre of the child's chest.

2 Press down sharply to a depth one-third of the depth of the chest. Release the pressure, but don't remove your hand. Give 30 compressions at a rate of 100 compressions per minute.

3 Give two rescue breaths (see p.301). Alternate 30 chest compressions with two rescue breaths for one minute. After one minute, call an ambulance if it has not already been done. Then continue resuscitation until the ambulance arrives, the child starts breathing or you are too exhausted to keep going.

Serious bleeding

Severe bleeding can lead to a serious condition called shock and eventually unconsciousness. Act quickly and calmly. If bleeding is severe treat for shock (opposite).

1 Expose the wound – cut away clothing if necessary – and press on the wound with your hand or over a clean dressing or cloth. If there is glass sticking out of the wound, don't remove it. Instead, apply pressure on either side of the object to compress the ends of the damaged blood vessels.

2 Raise the injured part, so that it is above her heart. This will slow down the blood flow to the injured area. If possible lay her down, keeping the injury high. Call an ambulance or take your child to hospital.

3 If blood appears through the bandage put another one on top. If it comes through the second bandage you may not be applying pressure in the right place. Take both dressings off and start again.

Shock

After a serious injury such as severe bleeding or burns, recurrent vomiting, severe diarrhoea or extreme pain or fear, a child may suffer from shock. Symptoms include: pale, cold, clammy skin; shallow and rapid breathing with yawning and sighing; sickness and vomiting; and, eventually unconsciousness. If you notice any of the symptoms, especially if there is no obvious bleeding, act immediately. Send someone for help while you attend to her. If she becomes unconscious, *see p.300.*

1 *Lay your child down, preferably on a blanket and keep her head low.*

2 *Raise her legs, unless you suspect a broken bone, to keep the circulating blood in the centre of the body. Loosen any tight clothing and, if it is cold, cover your child with a blanket. Call an ambulance.*

Warning
- Do not give your child anything to eat or drink. If she's thirsty simply moisten her lips with water.
- Do not warm her with a hot-water bottle or electric blanket; it takes blood away from the vital organs.

Electric shock

Your child may get an electric shock from frayed flexes or wires, light switches, defective electrical appliances or from touching an appliance with wet hands. In severe cases your child may lose consciousness. In mild cases she may have burns – often at the point of entry and exit of the electricity.

1 *Break the contact between your child and the source of electricity. Switch the current off at the mains or pull the plug out of the wall.*

2 *If you have to break the contact manually make sure you do it safely: push your child away using an object made of a non-conducting material, such as wood or plastic, and stand on an insulating material. Or drag your child away by his clothes; your hands must be dry and you mustn't touch his skin.*

3 *Examine your child for burns. If burns are severe or your child is unconscious call an ambulance. In the meantime, treat the burns (see p.304).*

Break the contact with a non-conducting object

Burns and scalds

These are usually described in terms of the amount of damage to the skin. Superficial burns are the least serious and can result from a minor spillage or touching a very hot surface. Partial-thickness burns are more serious and fluid-filled blisters form on the skin. Full-thickness burns are very serious since all layers of the skin, and possibly nerves, are damaged and fluid loss is high due to weeping of the skin. Seek medical help for any burn on a child. If the burn is large, or deep, take her to hospital.

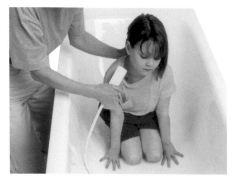

1 *Cool the area by running cold water over the affected part of the body for about ten minutes. If there is no water available you can use another cool liquid such as milk.*

2 *Remove or cut away any burned clothing, shoes, or jewellery before the damaged tissue begins to swell.*

3 *Cover the injury with a sterile dressing to protect it from infection. Clean kitchen film makes a good temporary dressing; don't wrap it around the limb.*

4 *Call for medical advice, or an ambulance. You may need to treat her for shock (see p.303). If she loses consciousness, see pp.300–302.*

Warning
- Do not touch the affected area or attempt to burst any blisters that form.
- Don't put lotion or fat on to the area.
- Don't stick a adhesive dressing to a burn.
- Don't cover the burn with a "fluffy" dressing or any cloth that sheds lint.
- Don't remove anything that is sticking to the burn: you may cause further damage to the skin or tissue and introduce infection.
- Don't overcool your child; it could cause hypothermia.

Clothing on fire

1 *If your child's clothing should catch fire, the first priority is to stop him moving. Any rapid movement will make the flames worse.*

2 *Stop him running around in a panic because this will fan the flames. Lie him on the floor with the burning side uppermost.*

3 *Wrap him in a heavy woollen coat or blanket to stifle the flames. Never use nylon – it's flammable.*

4 *Roll him on the ground to put out the flames. Douse him with water if you have some, or with another non-flammable liquid.*

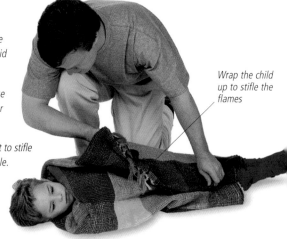

Wrap the child up to stifle the flames

Heat exhaustion and heatstroke

These can occur when the body becomes overheated. Heat exhaustion is caused by loss of body mineral salts. Heatstroke develops when the temperature control mechanism in the brain fails. Your child's temperature may rise above 40°C (104°F)

1 Take your child's outer clothes off and lay her down in a cool shady place.

2 Call a doctor if your child's temperature is as high as 40°C (104°F) and, while you are waiting, sponge her with tepid water or wrap her in a cool wet sheet. Place a covered ice pack on her forehead, give her water to sip and direct a fan on to her body.

and in extreme cases she may lose consciousness. Her skin may look and feel hot, but is dry. Your child will seem drowsy and lethargic, and may have a rapid pulse. In severe cases your child may be confused and may even lose consciousness.

3 Monitor her pulse rate and temperature closely. Check her temperature every minute until it lowers to 37.2°C (99°F), then stop cooling, but continue to monitor her temperature.

4 If she loses consciousness, treat as on pp.300– 302. Call an ambulance.

Hypothermia

This is a condition that develops when the body temperature falls below a certain level – usually because of exposure to extreme cold outdoors or inadequate heating in your home. A baby who has become dangerously chilled will appear quiet, drowsy and limp and will refuse food. Her hands, feet and face may be bright pink. If you suspect hypothermia in your baby, request urgent medical help. It is very important to warm your child gradually.

Cuddle your child to warm her

1 Replace any wet or damp clothes, dress your child in dry clothes and put a hat on her head. Wrap your baby in a blanket. Call for medical advice, or call an ambulance for a baby.

2 Use your body heat to warm your baby or child. Take her to bed with you, or get into a sleeping bag with her and cuddle her against your body.

Broken bones

Rough play not infrequently results in broken bones. Children are most prone to greenstick fractures, where the bone doesn't break completely and there is minimal damage to the skin. Suspect a fracture if your child cannot move the affected area normally or without pain; if there is bruising and/or swelling around the site of the injury; if the area appears deformed in any way.

1 *Support the joints above and below the affected area with your hands to prevent worsening of the injury.*

2 *For extra support, put an affected arm in a sling; immobilize a leg by tying knees and ankles together.*

Support the affected area

3 *Take your child to the nearest accident and emergency department if someone else can support her while you drive, or call an ambulance.*

Warning
- Don't try to straighten her limb if it is bent or curved.
- Don't touch an open wound. If there is an open wound or if bone is sticking through the skin, cover it with a sterile dressing.
- Don't give your child food or drink because she may need a general anaesthetic.

Poisoning

1 *If you suspect that your child has swallowed a poison call an ambulance immediately. Tell the ambulance control what you think she has taken and how much.*

2 *Your child may have severe stomach pains and will probably vomit. Hold her head lower than her body so there is no risk of her inhaling and choking on any vomit.*

Assess her condition

Warning
- Never attempt to induce vomiting – you could cause more harm if what she's swallowed is corrosive. Corrosive substances include caustic soda, weed killer, paraffin, disinfectant, bleach and other ammonia-based household cleaners. Look for signs of burning around her mouth. If there are any, she's probably swallowed one of these substances. Give water or milk to drink to cool the burning.
- If your child's unconscious assess her condition. If she is breathing place her in the recovery position (*see p.301*); if she's not breathing begin resuscitation (*see pp.300–302*). Use a plastic face shield for giving rescue breaths, or close her mouth and breathe into her nose.

Find out what your child has swallowed

Head injury

This is a potentially serious injury. A blow to the head can cause injury to the skull or brain, and there may be delayed reaction to the injury hours or even days later. It's important, therefore, that you watch your child after any head injury.

1 Help your child to sit or lie down, and place a cold pack against the injury.

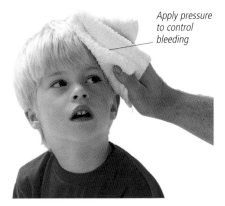

Apply pressure to control bleeding

2 If there is an wound, cover it with a dressing and apply direct pressure to stop the bleeding.

3 Watch your child and monitor especially for any changes in his level of consciousness. If he was slightly dazed but recovers quickly he may be concussed (his brain was "shaken" in his skull). If he appears fine initially but deteriorates later, he may have a serious condition called compression, caused by bleeding within the skull, or a fractured bone fragment pressing on the brain.

4 Seek medical advice for all head injuries.

Warning
- Never shake your child to check his level of consciousness.
- If your child is unconscious assess his condition. If he is breathing place him in the recovery position (see p.301); if he's stopped breathing begin resuscitation.

FIRST AID KIT

Always have a first aid kit in your home (and a separate one in the car). Keep it out of reach of your children in a cool dry place. Check the contents regularly and restock as necessary.

- Sterile gauze squares in various sizes for cleaning wounds
- A box of adhesive dressings in various sizes ·
- Sterile dressings with bandages attached in various sizes
- Small and large roller bandages such as conforming or crepe bandages
- A roll of 2.5cm (1in) hypoallergenic adhesive tape
- A sterile eye pad with bandage attached
- 2 triangular bandages
- Safety pins
- Blunt-ended tweezers

- Blunt-ended scissors
- Disposable gloves
- Face shield for rescue breathing
- Antiseptic cream
- Calamine lotion

Other useful items
- Junior paracetamol or ibuprofen syrup
- Insect repellent
- Antihistamine syrup
- Sunscreen with the highest protection factor
- Digital thermometer

17 Home medicine

All parents are worried when their child is ill. The difficulty can lie in not being able to identify what's wrong with the child, especially when he's too young to tell you how he feels, and in not knowing how serious the ailment really is. All children get ill sometimes, but modern medicine is so efficient that few illnesses now pose the threat that they once did. Healthcare professionals can identify and prescribe for the ailment; it's the parents' job to provide nursing and comfort. Sometimes it's hard to know when to ask for help, but if you're worried, follow your instincts and seek medical advice.

When to ask for medical help

Doctors, nurses and other healthcare professionals won't mind if you consult them for reassurance if you're worried about your child's health. For minor ailments you can try your local pharmacist before ringing your doctor's surgery. Or you can ring NHS Direct 24 hours a day, 365 days a year (0845 46 47). In some areas there are walk-in clinics open seven days a week. Like many doctors, I quickly learned that one person whose opinion can't be dismissed is the mother's. So when in doubt seek medical advice, especially if you notice any of the following:

Temperature
- If your child's temperature rises above 38°C (100.4°F) and he is obviously ill.
- If the temperature rises above 39.4°C (103°F) even if there are no apparent signs of illness.

- When a fever, having been high, drops and then rises again.
- When the temperature is accompanied by infantile seizures (see p.332).
- When your child has fever, stiff neck, a headache and sensitivity to light.
- When a baby has had a temperature of 37°C (98.6°F) for 24 hours.
- When a child has had a temperature of over 37°C (98.6°F) for three days.
- When your baby's skin feels cold and he is drowsy, unusually quiet and limp, though his face, hands and feet are pink (possibly hypothermia).
- If a fever is accompanied by a rash of red or purple blood spots that don't disappear when pressed. Check this by pressing a glass to the skin and looking through it to see if the rash is still visible. If it is, get medical help immediately: it could be meningitis.

Ask for advice
If you suspect your baby isn't well, don't hesitate to get medical advice. You know your baby and you're the best judge of when she is unwell.

Pain and discomfort

- When your child feels sick and dizzy and complains of headaches.
- When your child complains of blurred vision, especially after having had a blow on the head.
- When your child has severe griping pains at regular intervals.
- When your child has a pain in the right side of his stomach and feels sick.

Breathing

- If your child's breathing is laboured and you notice that his ribs are being drawn sharply inwards with each breath.

Loss of appetite

- If your child is normally a good eater.
- If your baby's under six months.

Wounds

- When your child has had any kind of serious accident or burn.
- When your child has lost consciousness, no matter how briefly.
- When acid gets into your child's eye.

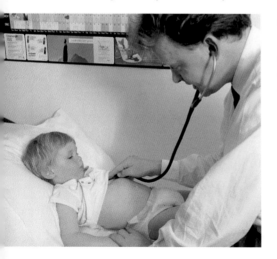

- When the wound is deep or has caused serious loss of blood.
- When your child has been bitten by an animal, a human or a snake.
- When the eye has actually been pierced by an object.

Vomiting

- If the vomiting is violent, prolonged or excessive.
- If your baby is very young – it may cause rapid dehydration.

Diarrhoea

- If your baby's very young – it could cause dehydration.
- If it is accompanied by abdominal pain, temperature or any obvious illness.

Questions you may be asked

When you seek medical advice you are likely to be asked a number of questions and it's important to answer these as accurately as you can.

Some specific questions may include the following: has your child vomited or had diarrhoea? Does he have any pain? Where is it? How long has it lasted? Have you given him anything for it? Is his temperature raised? How quickly did the fever come on and what was his highest temperature? Has he lost consciousness? Have you noticed swollen glands or a rash? Has he had any dizziness or blurred vision? You may also be asked about your child's appetite and sleeping patterns.

Examining your child
If you take your child to your doctor's surgery or a walk-in centre, expect him to be examined once you have answered the doctor's questions.

Using a thermometer birth to 3 years

Your child's temperature will probably fluctuate between 36°C and 37.5°C (97.5°F and 99.5°F). It will be at its lowest at night when your child is asleep and highest in the afternoon; it'll also be high if your child has been running around.

Although you'll probably be able to tell your child is feverish just by looking at him and laying your hand on his brow, there may be occasions when you need to take his temperature. Don't, however, rely on the temperature reading as an accurate reflection of your baby's health. Children can be very ill with no fever, or well with a high temperature, so always take account of any other symptoms.

TYPES OF THERMOMETER AVAILABLE

Never use a mercury thermometer in your child's mouth; he may bite it and swallow mercury, which is a poison. Digital thermometers are harder to break and are safe and easy to use with children of all ages. They can be used to take a child's temperature in the mouth or under the arm.

To take the mouth temperature, ask your child to open his mouth and raise his tongue. Place the thermometer under his tongue and ask him to place the tip of his tongue behind his lower front teeth to hold the thermometer in place. Ask him to close his lips, but not his teeth, over it. Leave until the thermometer bleeps and read the number in the window. Ear thermometers are also accurate and give a reading in seconds. Strip thermometers are less accurate than the others, but simple and safe to use. Always wash a thermometer after use in soap and cold water and store in its own case.

Using a digital thermometer
With a young child you may find it easier to take his temperature under his arm than in the mouth. Put the thermometer into his armpit and lower his arm over it. Hold his arm down until the thermometer bleeps, then remove and read it.

Using an ear thermometer
Digital ear thermometers are a quick, safe method of taking a child's temperature. Gently insert the tip into your child's ear and read the temperature from the display. The ear thermometer has a hygienic disposable tip.

Using a strip thermometer
Carefully position the heat-sensitive side on your child's forehead and hold it there for a minute or so, keeping your fingers clear of the panels. One of the panels lights up on the side of the strip facing you indicating the temperature.

Giving medicine birth to 1 year

When your baby is ill your doctor may prescribe a medicine, such as liquid paracetamol, ibuprofen or an antibiotic. Give the dosage recommended by the doctor or as instructed on the bottle. Follow any instructions exactly and if using a teaspoon, make sure it is the correct size.

Most medicines for children come in syrup form with a spoon, dropper or syringe to administer them. The syringe is the easiest method for giving medicine to babies and makes it very easy to measure the amount accurately. Ask your pharmacist to give you an adapter to put in the top of the bottle. Put the adapter in the bottle and the fit the syringe ito it.

If your baby refuses to take medicine, get your partner to help you, or wrap your baby up in a blanket so that you can hold him steady. Your baby may start to cry when he takes the medicine. Don't worry about this; it's far more important that your baby swallows it and keeps it down so that he can recover from his illness. Try to stay calm when giving the medicine, as your baby will sense your own anxiety.

When a child is ill I think special measures are called for. Getting your child to take his medicine outweighs every other consideration. Use the most powerful reward that you can think of as a means of getting your baby to accept the medicine.

GIVING MEDICINE TO A BABY OR CHILD

Whether you are using a syringe or a plastic measuring spoon to administer medicine to your child measure out the dose before you start. Make sure that you have understood your doctor's instructions if you're giving a prescription medicine and follow them precisely. When giving over-the-counter medication, read the directions on the packet very carefully. If you are at all unsure, check with your doctor or pharmacist.

You'll need to hold your child securely. It's best to hold his hands gently out of the way to prevent him knocking the medicine out of your hand.

Using a syringe
Hold your baby in the crook of your arm. Draw up the correct amount of medicine from the bottle into the syringe. Place the end of the syringe into the side of your baby's mouth and push the plunger down gently to release the medicine into your baby's mouth. Hold him still while he swallows it.

Using a spoon
Sterilize the spoon with boiling water or sterilizing solution. Pour the medicine into the spoon. Hold your child in a half-sitting position and, if necessary, pull his chin down with your finger, and place the spoon on his lower lip. Raise the angle of the spoon so that the medicine trickles into his mouth.

Giving medicine 1 to 3 years

Medicines for older children usually come in a liquid form, which is simply taken off a spoon. Ear or nose drops would be given in the same way as for a younger baby. If your child is making a great deal of difficulty about having drops it's important to stay as calm as possible so he doesn't panic. Get your partner to help you by holding the child firmly while you administer the drops.

As your child gets older, try not to make a fuss, or be very insistent that he takes the medicine as this will make your child respond negatively. It usually helps if you show your child that you are willing to take some yourself. If your child really

doesn't like the taste of medicine, then try diluting it with his favourite drink.

Tips for giving medicine

- Suggest your child holds his nose while taking the medicine, so lessening the effect of the taste. Don't forcibly hold his nose, however, as he may inhale some of the medicine.
- Show your child that you have his favourite drink ready to wash the taste of the medicine away.
- Help your child to clean his teeth thoroughly after taking any liquid medicine to prevent syrup sticking to his teeth.

ADMINISTERING DROPS TO BABY OR CHILD

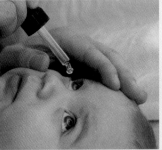  

Eye drops
Lay your baby on his back and tilt his head in the direction of the affected eye. Put the dropper into the medicine, and draw up the right amount. Gently pull his lower eyelid down with your finger and raise his upper lid. Let the drops fall into the corner of his eye. Get someone to help if necessary.

Nose drops
Lay your baby on his back with his head tilted backwards. Put the dropper into the medicine, and draw up the right amount. Hold the dropper just above your baby's nostrils and let the required number of drops fall into each nostril. Keep your baby still while the drops run into the nose.

Ear drops
Lay your baby on his side. Put the dropper into the medicine, and draw up the right amount. Hold the dropper over your baby's ear opening and let the required number of eardrops fall into the centre of his ear. Keep him still for a few moments while the drops spread into the ear canal.

Being a nurse to your child

Few mothers will escape being called upon to act as a nurse – all children fall ill at some time. Mothers, however, make excellent nurses because they put the health and comfort of their children before almost anything else. Many children become "babyish" when they are ill and want to be with their mothers all the time. Very often it's not just your company they require but also your physical contact. Ill babies need a lot more nursing, cuddling and affection than usual. If you're still breast-feeding you'll probably find that your baby wants more "comfort sucks". However, at the same time as being as loving as possible, guard against starting habits you don't want to continue.

Should he go to bed?

Unless your doctor advises otherwise, it's best to trust your own common sense and your child's natural inclinations. If he wants to stay up he should be allowed to do so. Even if he has a temperature he should be allowed to stay up if he wants to. But do make sure that he gets plenty to drink so that he doesn't become dehydrated, that he rests when he feels tired and that the room temperature is kept even and warm.

There is nothing sacrosanct about bedrooms either. One of the most potent medicines is the sight and sound of you and the reassurance you bring, so your sick child will be very much better off being near you. If possible rig up a couch, sofa or comfortable chair so that he can be in the same room as you. This way your child will have the opportunity of seeing, talking to

and being entertained by anyone who comes into the house rather than being cut off from the rest of the family in his bedroom. When your child is tired, however, it is time to put him to bed. But don't just leave him alone. Make sure that you visit him at regular intervals (every half an hour), and find the time to stay and play a game, read a book, or do a puzzle. If you have other children, encourage them to do the same thing. If he is asleep check him to make sure he is not too hot.

When he's on the road to recovery make sure that enough happens in his day to make the distinction between night and day. If he hasn't been watching television, let him watch it before he goes to sleep. Then read him a story to calm and quieten him, as you would usually do.

Feeding your sick child

There are no longer any hard and fast rules about the sort of food that you should give your child when he's sick and unless directed by your doctor you can feed your child whatever he wants to eat. It's time for you to relax most of the rules, dietary and otherwise. Let him eat and drink what he wants, and as much as he wants. You'll probably find that he prefers little but often. If your child is off his food never force him to eat.

Even though your child will seem to eat very sparsely while he's ill, he will quickly make up the deficit as his appetite increases. The return of his appetite is invariably the sign that your child is on the mend. When he is on the road to recovery,

Stay close
Give your child as much comfort and love as you can when he's ill. Stay with him as much as you can and give him his favourite foods and drinks.

spoil him with his favourite foods and perhaps those that have been previously restricted to treats. He'll be keen to make up for all the lost meals, and any weight-loss will be made up quickly.

Giving drinks

It is essential that your child drinks a lot when he's ill – when he has a fever, diarrhoea, or is vomiting – because he will need to replace lost fluids to avoid becoming dehydrated. The recommended fluid intake for a child with a fever is 100–150ml per kg (1½–2½floz per lb) of body weight per day, which is the equivalent of 1 litre (2 pints) per day for a child who weighs 9kg (20lb). Encourage your child to take fluids by leaving a drink at his bedside (preferably water or fruit juice), by putting drinks in glasses that are especially appealing and by giving him bendy straws to drink with.

Treating your child's temperature

The first sign of a raised temperature is often a hot forehead, but to check that your child is feverish take his temperature (*see p.311*). Call your doctor if a fever lasts more than 24 hours for baby (or three days for a child), or if there are other symptoms.

Temperatures over 37°C (98.6°F) should be taken very seriously in children under six months, so you must take action to reduce

Reassure your child
*Be there for your child and support her if she is being
sick. Allow her to play whenever she feels like it or
read her stories to comfort her.*

doses in 24 hours. Check his temperature
regularly. It is important for the child to
drink a lot as he will lose fluid through
sweating. Ibuprofen can be given to a child
instead of paracetamol, or they can be
alternated to help control the fever. Never
give aspirin to a child under the age of 16.

Keeping your sick child amused

Illness is an occasion when you can
completely indulge your child. When he is
not resting, spend time playing games and
talking to him. Relax all the rules and let him
play whatever games he wants to, even if
you've previously disallowed them in bed.

a high temperature as soon as possible.
Children are at risk of febrile seizures when
the temperature is high.

To reduce fever, lower the temperature
in your child's room and give him iced
drinks. Try to cool your child by removing
his clothes; if he is in bed, use light
bedclothes. Give the recommended dose
of paracetamol syrup to help control the
fever, but do not give more than four

If your child wants to do something
messy like painting, let him, just spread
an old sheet over the bed first. If you can,
move a television with a DVD into his room
temporarily – this will keep him entertained
and make him feel special as well. You can
sit and read aloud to him too. Alternatively

COMFORT AND RECUPERATION TIPS

- Give your child treats. If he has a sore throat give him ice cream.
- Cool cotton sheets are soothing for a feverish child. Change the bed regularly.
- When your child is being sick always be there, and always cover his forehead with the palm of your hand. Give him some water to rinse his mouth with, and perhaps a mint to suck to take away the bad taste.
- Put a table next to the bed for his toys, books, fruit juices or water.

- Make a work table by cutting a semi-circle out of an inverted cardboard box. This can be placed over your child's lap. Alternatively you can put a sanded wooden plank over two chairs, either side of the bed.
- Buy some new toys for your child. Don't give them to him all at once, but give them one at a time.
- If your child isn't feeling too ill you could try wrapping the toys up so that you can play a game together. Ask him to guess what's in the packages by feeling them, then let him tear off the paper.

get out some of his old toys and play with them together; buy him small presents and let him unwrap them; sing songs or make up a story together; ask him to draw a picture of what he is going to do when he feels better; and, unless he has an infectious illness, let some friends visit him for a brief period during the day. As your child begins to get better you can let him play outside, but if he still has a fever discourage him from running around.

If your child has to go to hospital

At some point in your child's life he may have to go into hospital. But given a little forethought, a stay in hospital does not have to be upsetting or frightening for your child. If you don't like hospitals and you convey this feeling to your child you may inadvertently make his stay in hospital much more difficult than it has to be.

Try to teach him that a hospital is a friendly place where people go to get better. Whenever the chance arises – if you have a friend or a relative in hospital, for instance – take your child along when you go to visit and be matter-of-fact, not gloomy, about their illness. If a child's first experience of being in hospital is when he becomes sick, it will seem even more alien than it would otherwise.

Preparing a child for hospital

If you know that your child is going to hospital, read him a story about a child who goes into hospital, and role play

Packing for hospital
Involve your child in the preparations for going into hospital if possible and make sure she takes some of her favourite toys and books.

doctors and nurses with toy stethoscopes. Be as honest as you can about why he's going to hospital, and emphasize that it's to make him better. Reassure him that you will be with him as much as you can while he's in hospital, and if he is old enough to understand, tell him when he'll be well enough to come home.

If your child needs to have an operation he's bound to be curious about what's going to happen to him and what the doctors are going to do. Answer his questions as honestly as you can – if he asks you if the operation will hurt, don't pretend that it won't, but tell him that doctors have medicines to make the pain go away quickly and he will soon be better.

Medical index

▨ Asthma

In a person suffering from asthma the allergic reaction shows itself in the lining of the air passages. This lining is very sensitive. It not only responds to the allergen with wheezing, but it also responds more than usual to exercise, infection and emotional disturbances. The lining of the airways goes into spasm and secretes mucus. Your child will have difficulty breathing out and you will hear a wheezing noise when he does this. His face may become pale and he could look anxious and perspire. If his lips turn blue, this is a late stage and an indication of a serious need for urgent medical help.

The allergen that causes your child's asthma may be dust, pollen, feathers, animal hair or fungal spores. Also many young babies wheeze if they have an attack of bronchitis or bronchiolitis (inflammation of the smaller tubes). This baby can legitimately be labelled a wheezy baby, but it is wrong to assume that all babies who wheeze are asthmatic. They are not. Once they grow a little bigger and the bronchial tubes become wider the wheezing will stop. This condition is not allergic in origin and the wheeze associated with respiratory viral infections is not necessarily asthma.

What to do If your child has an attack of wheeziness, seek medical help. This usually means making an appointment to see your doctor. If the doctor diagnoses asthma your child will be given medication, and if necessary you will be taught how to administer it. He will be monitored in an asthma clinic in the community or hospital depending on the severity of his asthma.

As your child gets older he may be tested with various allergens to see if he is sensitive to a specific substance. If this substance is isolated you can then do something about avoiding it. For instance, if your child is sensitive to feathers and house dust (both of these being very common causes of allergy), try to get rid of any bedding that contains feathers, down or hair, and make sure that the furnishings plus the carpets and curtains in your child's room do not hold a lot of dust. House dust allergy is commonly caused by a microscopic mite (the house-dust mite) that lives in house dust. There are nearly always more mites in damp houses than in dry ones, so there is a scientific rationale for a asthma being worse in a damp house than in a dry one.

Besides an allergic component of asthma, there may be an emotional one. If your doctor suggests that emotional factors are playing a part in your child's asthma it is up to you and your family to see what you can do to improve the atmosphere and minimize the stress in your child.

It's very important that you and the rest of the family don't get asthma out of perspective. Many parents of asthmatic children are over-anxious and over-stress the condition so that eventually the whole household revolves around the child. This is an unwise way of behaving because your child may soon learn how to manipulate the household around his asthma attacks.

The treatment of asthma is rather complicated so you will be given very clear instructions as to what you should do under certain circumstances, and certainly what you should do if an asthma attack comes on suddenly out of the blue.

▦ Balanitis

This is the inflammation of the tip of the penis in uncircumcised boys. It may be caused by nappy rash, which is often a reaction to detergent, or it can be due to an infection. It is not serious, but for the child's comfort, you should treat it promptly. The penis will be red and swollen, there may be a pussy discharge from the tip and the foreskin cannot be drawn back.

What to do If you notice any redness around the tip of the penis, draw back the foreskin very gently, wash and apply some antiseptic cream until you can get medical advice. If the foreskin won't draw back, leave it and see your doctor as soon as possible. Your child will probably be prescribed both topical and oral antibiotics.

▦ Bites

The chances of your child being bitten by an animal such as a dog, or another child are relatively high; the chances of your child being bitten by a snake depend on where you live.

What to do The treatment given for a cat, dog or other mammal bite depends on the depth of the wound and whether your child's tetanus immunization is up to date. If the bite is superficial, clean the wound and leave it open or put a loose-fitting

gauze dressing on it if necessary. If, however, the wound is serious, or on your child's face, then you must seek medical advice as soon as possible. Animal bites are usually deep and dirty so your child may be prescribed an antibiotic.

Bites from other children can be even more septic than animal bites. These should be cleaned and left open, and if you're at all worried by them you should seek medical advice.

If your child is bitten by a snake, dial 999 for an ambulance. Do not let him walk, but lay him down. While you are waiting for medical help, wash the surface of the skin and apply a pressure bandage from above the bite as far up the limb as possible. If possible, identify the snake.

▦ Blisters

These may be formed as a protection to the body where the skin has been chafed, burned or rubbed.

What to do A blister should be left intact. Never prick it; leave it intact as long as you can. If a blister is on an exposed area simply cover it with a small pad of gauze kept in place with tape. The blister will subside of its own accord and the skin will become dry and fairly hard. It will change its colour to a rather dark pink and it will gradually fall off. Don't do anything to disturb this natural process.

▦ Bruise

This is a purplish-red stain in the skin, usually resulting from a blow or a knock that ruptures the small blood vessels near the skin's surface. It usually takes 10–14 days for a bruise to disappear completely;

as it fades, it changes colour to maroon, then green or yellow as the blood pigments break down and are reabsorbed by the body. Resting, cooling and raising the affected part will soothe any pain. A bruise is rarely serious. If a bruise appears without any reason, this could relate to uncommon, but serious, conditions such as leukaemia and haemophilia.

What to do A minor bruise needs no treatment at all, just a cuddle and reassurance if your child is upset. If the bruise is large, apply a cold compress for half an hour or so. This will contain the bruising. Seek medical advice immediately if the pain and bruising aren't getting better within 4–6 hours; this might suggest an underlying fracture. Also seek medical advice if a bruise appears spontaneously with no apparent cause.

▧ Burns

It is almost inevitable that your child will burn himself on a radiator or hot tap at some stage, despite your efforts.

What to do Cool the burn by placing it under cold running water for ten minutes, or until pain subsides (see p.304). The best treatment is to protect the burn with a non-stick dressing. Otherwise use a piece of kitchen film, a sterile gauze dressing or non-fluffy material (a clean cotton handkerchief will do). Don't remove any clothing that is sticking to a burn.

Seek medical advice if you are worried. For any burn If your child has been severely burned he must be taken to the nearest hospital emergency department as soon as possible for proper medical treatment.

▧ Catarrh and runny nose

Neither persistent yellow catarrh (catarrh which continues for longer than five or six days), nor a runny nose is normal. Both of these signs indicate that your child may be suffering from an upper respiratory viral infection. If yellow secretions go on for more than six or seven days your child may need antibiotics. A clear watery nasal discharge over a long period is more likely to be caused by allergic rhinitis.

What to do As the ear, nose and throat and the lungs are connected by a small set of tubes, anatomically speaking, an infection in any one place can very quickly creep along the tubes to infect another. For example, a chronic infection of the middle ear can lead to a condition called glue ear which can affect hearing and the development of speech. See your doctor if you suspect your child may have an ear infection.

▧ Chicken pox

This is a very common infection that children invariably catch as it's one of the most contagious of all childhood diseases (see p.340). Your child will be contagious from one to two days before the rash starts to the time when the blisters scab over. The chicken pox virus is the same one that causes shingles (herpes zoster), so adults, particularly older ones, can get shingles from a child with chicken pox.

Chicken pox often starts with a temperature of 38–39°C (100.4–102°F). In very young children, however, there is hardly any rise in temperature; the rash may be the first sign. This will appear in crops over five to seven days and will be extremely itchy. At first the spots are like dark red pimples, but within a couple of hours they will have developed a small blister on top that resembles a drop of water. The spots will eventually scab over and drop off. The rash usually starts on the child's trunk and then spreads to his face, scalp, arms and legs. In the worst cases, the spots can also appear inside the child's mouth, nose, ears, vagina and anus.

What to do The most important thing to do is to stop your child from scratching the spots. If you don't do this the scab may come off and the resulting wound may become infected and can leave a scar. The best treatment for this is a moisturizer containing antiseptic applied at regular intervals. Keep your child's nails short to minimize the risk of infection should he pull the scabs off. Your child may find that the itchiness is so intense that he can't get to sleep so your doctor may prescribe antihistamine to relieve this. Give your child the recommended dose of paracetamol and/or ibuprofen syrup to control his temperature and make sure he drinks plenty of fluids. If your child is still wearing nappies leave them off as much as possible to prevent infection.

▥ Colds

A cold is caused by a virus that we cannot treat specifically. There is no antibiotic to which the virus is sensitive so it cannot be killed. This means that it has to be overcome by the body's own defence mechanisms and this usually takes 10–14 days, whatever we do. The common cold virus infects and inflames the membranes of the nasal passages and throat.

This produces the well known symptoms of sore throat and runny nose.

Sometimes the viral infection weakens the body and allows a secondary bacterial infection to develop. The tonsils and adenoids may become swollen and so may the glands in the neck. If the tonsils become infected (tonsillitis) antibiotic treatment may be required so ask for medical advice (see p.336).

Colds are common in young children, and to have five or six colds a year is quite usual. Babies under six months are less likely to catch colds because of the antibodies they receive from their mothers, especially if they're breast-fed.

What to do In a young baby a cold can cause quite a lot of distress because it may block the nose and prevent breathing during feeding. Don't let your child suffer in this way; seek medical advice. You will probably be given nose drops to use before each feed and these will keep the nasal passages clear long enough for the baby to feed. Never use nose drops for more than a few days at a time unless they are prescribed by your doctor.

Because all the upper air passages, the nose and the sinuses in an infant are connected by short tubes, an infection of one part can quickly spread to another. For this reason a cold may rapidly become bronchitis (an infection of the respiratory tract), tonsillitis (see p.336) and sometimes otitis media (infection of the middle ear). If your child complains of a sore throat or earache (see p.325), seek medical advice because he may need to take antibiotics.

Older children seem to feel the symptoms of a cold less than adults. They seem to suffer it quite cheerfully so there is no reason to use proprietary cold cures for a child in the way one might for an adult.

▓ Cold sore/Herpes simplex

Despite their name, cold sores have nothing to do with a cold other than the fact that the cold affects the immune system and reduces the resistance to infection, allowing the herpes simplex virus to activate. Primary herpes simplex infection may occur in young children. This is an acute illness with a very high fever, lots of painful mouth ulcers and great difficulty swallowing.

What to do If you notice a herpes blister coming up, get some acyclovir (Zovirax) cream, available as an over-the-counter medicine, as soon as possible. If painted on to the affected area early enough, this can contain or minimize the attack of herpes.

The herpes virus is passed on by direct contact. Most children who get cold sores, usually around the lips, nose and possibly on the cheeks and chin, get them from adults who kiss them. It is quite common if one parent in the family has a cold sore for other members of the family to catch the virus from that one parent; it is equally possible for your child to infect others.

▓ Colic

In a baby under four months of age, colic describes a crying spell, during which the baby's face becomes very red and both legs are drawn up to his stomach as if he is in great pain. This crying spell usually comes in the early evening; during the rest of the day the baby is generally contented. The crying can reach screaming pitch and last

from one to three hours. It doesn't usually respond to soothing techniques that work at other times. Colic is so common that it is regarded by paediatricians as normal, but for parents it can be difficult to endure. The cause is not known. It is often at its worst at six weeks but disappears by three to four months without treatment.

What to do Try all the ways of soothing your baby that work at other times of the day. This may mean you are constantly offering the breast or bottle; changing nappies; winding; nursing and rocking; walking with the baby held over your shoulder; putting the baby in a sling against your body; playing music to give a constant background noise; or walking him in a pram. Try offering your baby a dummy if he seems to want to suck all the time. Having a warm bath relaxes most babies and helps when the crying is at its worst.

If you find it hard to cope, seek medical advice to reassure you that your baby is healthy and will grow out of the colic eventually. Health visitors can provide valuable advice and counselling while your baby is still having attacks.

▓ Conjunctivitis

This is an inflammation of the conjunctiva, the outer covering of the eye. It makes the eye look red, and it can feel itchy or sore.

What to do If your child develops a "red eye", examine it first to see if there is a foreign object trapped underneath the lid. If there is, try to rinse the eye with tepid boiled water to see if you can wash the foreign body out. If not, go to your doctor. If there is not foreign object or trauma the cause of the "red eye" could be viral or bacterial infection or an allergic reaction. In case your child's conjunctivitis needs antibiotic treatment, seek medical advice.

Coughing

A cough is the body's natural reflex to irritation of the throat, the very back of the nose and the membranous lining of the air passages. It often accompanies an infection of the upper airways, the throat or the lower airways and the purpose of the cough is to remove excess mucus or phlegm. By coughing the phlegm is loosened, brought up into the mouth and then swallowed. Any germs existing in it are then killed by the acid in the stomach. (A common cause of coughing at night is mucus dripping from the nose and sinuses into the back of the throat.) However, coughing can also be due to allergy or asthma and not infection.

What to do A cough that is merely a response to irritation and not to the presence of excess mucus is called an unproductive cough because it doesn't cough out any phlegm. A cough that does get rid of the mucus is called a productive cough. An unproductive cough serves no useful purpose and can be extremely irritating to a young child; it can even prevent sleep. It is important to differentiate between a dry, unproductive cough and a wet, productive one that produces phlegm, because the treatments are entirely different.

Cough medicines in general are not effective, but a cough suppressant can be useful if a child has a very severe, dry, unproductive cough that's disturbing his

sleep. Expectorant cough medicines are not generally recommended for children.

You can ease the irritation of a night-time cough by turning your child on to his side or his front, or by propping him on pillows (if he's over a year old). Never let the coughing become so severe that a prolonged bout causes your child to vomit. Seek medical advice if your child has a persistent chronic dry cough, as it could be asthma or an allergic reaction.

A productive cough, however, should never be suppressed because it is serving a useful purpose. It is helping to overcome infection by clearing mucus from the air passages. A productive cough that lasts for more than 24 hours may need treatment, so seek medical advice.

Cradle cap

A thick yellow encrustation on the scalp, cradle cap occurs mainly in babies, although children up to the age of three can have it. The yellow scales appear in small patches or can cover the entire scalp. Cradle cap is not due to poor hygiene. Babies who suffer from it probably just have greasier scalps. Cradle cap may look unsightly, but it is quite harmless unless it is accompanied by red, scaly areas elsewhere on your baby's body, in which case your baby may have eczema.

What to do Don't try to remove the scales with your fingers. If they won't brush out, they must be loosened first. Smear a little baby oil or aqueous cream on your baby's scalp and leave overnight. This makes the scales soft and loose and they'll wash away when you shampoo the next day. If the cradle cap becomes hard and thick, you may need to continue the treatment over a ten-day period. Seek medical advice if you're worried or if your baby has red scaly areas elsewhere.

▥ Croup

In children between the ages of one and five, croup quite often accompanies a cold. The name is given to the sound of air being inhaled through a constricted windpipe, past inflamed vocal cords. Your child may go to bed feeling quite well, but wake with a tight chest and have great difficulty breathing in; exhaling is easier.

What to do If you notice this kind of breathing you should seek medical advice. On occasion the breathing can be so laboured that there's a risk of suffocation. If this is the case try to keep your child calm and in an upright position in a moist humid atmosphere and call an ambulance. Stay with your child until help arrives. If necessary, take him to the hospital yourself.

To make breathing easier, prop up your child in an upright position with pillows, and make sure that he is comfortable. If he's very alarmed take him on your lap, hold him firmly and try to get him copy your breathing. Listening to you breathing in and out will take his mind off his fear – if he's relaxed breathing will be easier.

Make sure that the air in your child's bedroom isn't too warm as this can dry and irritate the already inflamed air passages. Open the window and let some cool air blow in. Moistened air is soothing to the passages so try taking him to the bathroom, running the hot tap of the shower with the door and the windows shut. This will make the atmosphere steamy and if you sit in there with your child on your lap (maybe telling him a story at the same time), it will help.

If you can do nothing else, boil a kettle in your child's room, but keep your child away from the kettle; never leave without removing the kettle.

After the first episode of croup seek advice about treating croup so that you can deal with it should it happen again.

▥ Cuts and grazes

Examine any wound to see how deep it is and whether it is bleeding profusely. If it is serious get medical help (*see p.302*).

What to do If it is a small graze, clean the area with clean water and apply a clean, dry, non-stick dressing that's larger than the injury. If the cut is bleeding apply pressure directly over the wound and raise it above the level of the heart (see p.302). Cover the wound with a a sterile dressing.

▥ Diarrhoea

The main symptom of diarrhoea is the frequent passage of loose, watery stools and the condition is a sign of irritation of the intestines. Bear in mind, however, that it is quite normal for breastfed babies to pass frequent watery stools.

Diarrhoea in a baby is always serious because of the danger that the baby may become dehydrated. If accompanied by vomiting in a young child is also serious for the same reason, especially if it is accompanied by fever and sweating.

What to do Seek medical advice immediately if your baby is under one year old and has had diarrhoea for six hours, or if a child has diarrhoea with fever and vomiting, if he still has diarrhoea after 12 hours, or if the stools are greasy or contain mucus or blood. Give your child frequent small sips of an oral rehydration solution. This contains sugar and electrolytes that help reduce the amount of fluid lost as well as replacing fluid in the body.

Pay close attention to hygiene. The infection could spread throughout the family if your child doesn't wash his hands after going to the toilet or if you don't wash yours after changing his nappies.

▣ Drowsiness

In a normally alert child drowsiness can be a symptom of a fever, hypothermia (when the body temperature falls below normal), or dehydration. It can also occur before or after a seizure, following a blow to the head, or as a result of medication, such as antihistamines.

If your child is drowsy but contented, is feeding well and has a normal body temperature, there is no cause for alarm; he's probably just feeling a little sleepy. If, however, your child becomes drowsy while recovering from an infectious disease such as measles or chicken pox, and he complains of headache and neck pain, this could indicate encephalitis or meningitis, both of which are serious conditions and require immediate medical attention.

What to do Check your child's body temperature. If it's over 38°C (100.4°F), he has a fever, and if it is under 35°C (95°F), he will be suffering from hypothermia. In either case, seek medical advice.

If drowsiness is accompanied by diarrhoea and vomiting, keep up your child's fluid intake to prevent the risk of dehydration. If his condition does not improve, seek medical advice.

Check to see if your child has recently received a blow to the head; find out if your child has a headache or neckache; smell your child's breath and check the drinks cabinet – he may have drunk alcohol. Check the medicine cabinet for sleep-inducing drugs. In any of these cases, seek medical advice imediately.

If your child has had a seizure, leave him to rest after the seizure has passed and seek medical advice (see p.332).

▣ Earache

The main reason for earache being a common ailment in babies and young children is the anatomy of the ear. Think of the ear as two sections separated by a membrane, the ear drum. The first section is a passage leading from the opening of the ear to the ear drum. This is the auditory canal. The second section, behind the ear drum, is the middle ear. Inflammation of the outer ear is called otitis externa; inflammation of the middle ear is called otitis media. The Eustachian tubes, which are rather short and wide in young children, link the middle ear to the back of the throat. The purpose of the tubes is to equalize pressure in the ears, but they are often the source of ear problems in young children.

Otitis media is the most common ear ailment both because of the construction of the Eustachian tubes and because babies spend most of their time lying down. The combination of these two factors makes it much easier for bacteria to travel from the nose and throat straight to the middle ear. Inflammation of the mucus membrane of the Eustachian tubes causes them to become blocked. This traps the bacteria in the middle ear, where they multiply. Obviously, no young child can tell you he has earache, but if he has inexplicable fever, vomiting, diarrhoea and loss of appetite, and if he pulls at his ear, you'd be right to suspect earache.

What to do Seek medical advice if you suspect your child has earache. He will need to be examined to confirm the diagnosis and, if the cause is otitis media, your doctor may recommend oral decongestants, such as antihistamine, paracetamol for the pain, and possibly nasal drops to clear the upper airways. If the pain has gone on for more than 24 hours you child may need antibiotics.

Never, ever put anything into your baby's ears, and don't apply hot compresses to the outside of the ear. Similarly, if the cause of the earache is a boil, or something else in the outer ear, don't treat it yourself. Seek medical advice.

■ Eczema

Infantile eczema often goes hand in hand with asthma and the two are quite commonly seen together. Eczema produces a fairly generalized rash on the face, behind the knees and on the inner side of the arms and wrists. The rash is usually itchy, dry, red and scaly; in its worst state it can weep quite profusely. You will notice that the eczema waxes and wanes. It may be brought on by a cold or if the baby has had a sleepless night or a tummy upset.

Often asthma or other allergic conditions may run throughout the family,

so you may find that a relative has penicillin sensitivity, another has asthma, another has eczema, another has hay fever.

What to do You'll need to seek medical advice for your child and you may be referred to a skin specialist if the eczema is difficult to treat.

The story on infantile eczema is rather good: many children improve by the age of two, and many more do so by the age of seven. Usually it will have disappeared by the teens although the person always retains the possibility of eczema flaring up in later life if he should ever have a severe mental or physical trauma.

For the everyday care of a baby with eczema of the skin I would suggest the following: avoid over-bathing – soap and water are dehydrating. Use baby lotion on cotton wool which will do the same job just as well. Pay attention to cleanliness, particularly round the nappy area and face. Dress your child with cotton next to the skin at all times and avoid wool as it can be irritating and make the eczema worse. Rub in the soft, bland creams and ointments exactly as prescribed.

■ Epilepsy

After febrile seizures (*see p.332*) the next most common cause of seizures in children is epilepsy. Epilepsy can take two forms: general or tonic-clonic (grand mal) seizures and absence (petit mal) seizures.

With an absence seizure your child suddenly "blanks out" for a couple of seconds and looks very pale and vacant. He won't fall down or become incontinent, but he'll be completely unaware of his surroundings. When he snaps out of it, he'll carry on as normal, as if nothing had happened. A child suffering from a general seizure will have similar symptoms to febrile seizures (see p.332).

What to do You should deal with all seizures with them in exactly the same way (*see p.332*), then seek medical advice. Your child may have tests to assess the likelihood of the seizures recurring and will then receive medical treatment.

It is psychologically inadvisable to treat children suffering from epilepsy as "epileptic". Treat him as normal, but take precautions; leave the bathroom door open in case he has a a seizure in the bath and keep a close eye when he's swimming.

▧ Fever
The range of normal body temperature is 36–37°C (96.8–98.6°F). Anything over 37°C (98.6°F) is a fever, although the height body temperature reaches is not necessarily an accurate reflection of the seriousness of the illness. A fever is not in itself an illness, but rather a symptom of one. Apart from any illness, your child's temperature will reflect the time of day and activity level: after a very strenuous game of football, for example, the temperature could temporarily be over 38°C (100.4°F). A temperature of over 37°C (98.6) could be serious in a baby under six months old. If the temperature remains high, there is also a slight risk of a febrile seizure occurring (*see p.332*).

What to do If you suspect that your child has a fever, take his temperature, then check it again in 20 minutes to see if it has varied. Make a note of each reading.

Put your child to bed and remove most of his clothing, even if the room is cool. A child with a fever need only be covered by a light cotton sheet. Give children's paracetamol in the recommended dose to help bring down the temperature. If the temeperature is high, give him paracetamol and ibuprofen; alternate the two in order to reduce in fever and then a steady control of the temperature. Never give aspirin to a child under 16 years of age as this has been linked to Reye's syndrome.

Encourage your child to drink as much liquid as possible by offering small amounts of fluid often. Seek medical advice if: your child is under six months old; he has a febrile seizure; he has had a seizure before or if seizures run in the family; if your baby has a fever that lasts more than 24 hours (or three days in a child), or if you are worried about any of the other symptoms.

▧ Fingers caught in door
Until your baby learns how doors work there's always the risk that his fingers may become trapped. Injury may result in wounds or even broken bones.

What to do If the skin is broken and there is serious bleeding take your child straight to the nearest hospital emergency department. If it is bleeding profusely, press on the wound and hold your child's hand up in the air. When the bleeding stops, cover it with a clean, non-fluffy dressing and put your child's arm in a sling for the journey to hospital.

▧ Gluten sensitivity
This is a problem that occurs when gluten, a protein contained in most cereals, except

for rice and corn, damages the lining of the intestines, which causes a gluten sensitivity. Unwittingly, therefore, you may feed your baby with an allergen as some baby cereals contain gluten.

A child with gluten sensitivity initially shows a "failure to thrive". This means that the child will perhaps not have as much energy as you'd expect, may be a little sleepy and won't gain weight quite as quickly. You will also notice that the stools alternate between a fatty consistency so when you to try to flush them away they won't go – they stay and float – and quite loose stools. This is because the allergic reaction in the lining of the bowel prevents the correct digestion and absorption of fatty substances. Your child may have frequent bouts of diarrhoea and be pale and irritable a lot of the time. He will also have abdominal distension and vomiting. If this condition goes undiagnosed in young girls it can lead to a delay in the onset of menstruation.

In its very advanced stage gluten sensitivity, or coeliac disease, produces quite abnormal body configuration. The abdomen becomes distended, there is hardly any fat on the limbs or body, the muscles of the legs and arms become wasted, the tongue becomes smooth and there may be swelling of the ankles. The hair will be thin. However, gluten sensitivity is not very common and even though it's caused by a common food-stuff don't be over-anxious about your child's diet.

What to do Once a diagnosis has been made your child has to be given a gluten-free diet, which means that wheat, rye, barley and oats will have to be excluded.

Your child will have to remain on a gluten-free diet for life. The first thing that you will notice is an improvement in the mood of your child. This usually appears within a few days, and is followed by a greatly improved appetite and consequent weight gain. You will then notice a change in the appearance of the stools and the frequency of bowel movements, although this may take weeks. After being on a gluten-free diet for six months to a year, your child should be within the normal weight range; height takes about two years to recover.

▦ Hayfever

Hayfever, or allergic rhinitis, is similar to asthma except that the allergic reaction occurs in the mucous membranes of the nose and eyelids, not the chest. The condition causes sneezing, a runny nose with clear discharge and itchy, watery, red-rimmed eyes. It mostly occurs in spring and summer and is usually due to a reaction to plant pollen. Hayfever is troublesome, but does not usually have serious consequences.

What to do If your child is sneezing a lot, check his temperature to make sure that he isn't ill with an infection such as influenza or a common cold. Discourage your child from rubbing his eyes; this will make them worse. Bathe his eyes with cool water to ease the irritation. Seek medical advice as soon as possible if you think your child may be suffering from a more serious infection, or if the hayfever is making your child miserable.

If your child's condition is severe, he may need to see an allergist and have a series of tests to track down the allergen that is causing the symptoms of hayfever.

There are various measures you can take to try to minimize the severity of attacks. Watch the pollen count each day and, if it is high, discourage your child from playing near freshly mown grass, for example. Use synthetic fillings for your child's bedding, rather than feathers. Keep your house as dust-free as possible. Even if your child isn't allergic to dust, a dusty atmosphere makes hayfever worse.

Prepare an emergency pack for outings. It should contain paper handkerchiefs, eye drops to reduce the eye irritation, a moist towel to soothe your child's eyes, and whatever medication has been prescribed. Your doctor may be prescribe a steroid nasal spray to help relieve the condition.

◼ Hives (see Urticaria)

◼ Infectious fevers (*see p.340*)

◼ Measles

This is a highly infectious disease. In addition there can also be quite serious complications, in particular, pneumonia (*see p.331*) and meningitis (*see right*). Your child is most likely to catch the disease between the ages of one and six years. Measles takes its most serious form under the age of three.

It generally takes 10–14 days for the symptoms to appear after your child has been infected. The first symptoms are similar to a normal cold – runny nose, a hoarse cough and a fever. For the first two days the temperature will be 38–39°C (100.4–102°F). It may fall briefly before becoming as high as 40°C (104°F). It's at this stage that the rash generally starts as brownish-red spots behind the ears and then spreads to the face and the rest of the body. There may be small red spots, each with a white centre in the mouth (Koplik's spots) before the rash starts. Your baby's eyes may become red and sore.

At around the age of 13 months your child can be immunized against measles, when he has his MMR (measles, mumps and rubella) immunization (*see p.339*).

What to do Look in the child's mouth for signs of Koplik's spots. Ask for medical advice to confirm measles. While your child has the fever, follow the general instructions for coping with high temperatures (*see p.315*). Bathe his sore eyes with lukewarm water and dim the lights if that makes him more comfortable. He probably won't be very hungry when he's feverish, but make sure that he drinks adequate amounts of liquid by providing small but frequent drinks. Seek medical advice immediately if your child has any of the following: a high temperature four days after the rash has appeared; earache or laboured breathing; a phlegmy cough; or if he becomes semi-conscious.

◼ Meningitis

An inflammation of the meninges, the membrane that surrounds the brain and spinal cord, meningitis is caused by viral or, much more seriously, bacterial infection. The illness starts with flu-like symptoms, high temperature, mottled skin, limb pain and cold hands and feet. As the infection develops the child will have a headache, stiff neck, sensitivity to bright light, increasing drowsiness and vomiting. Bacterial meningitis may also lead to a rash that does not fade when pressed. Check this by pressing a glass onto the rash. If it is caused by meningococcus the small purplish-red spots will not disappear.

What to do Meningitis is life-threatening and the disease can develop very quickly, so it needs urgent action. If you suspect meningitis, be prepared to insist on urgent medical attention. Take your child to the emergency department of the nearest hospital or dial 999 for an ambulance.

Meningitis is confirmed by taking a sample of cerebro-spinal fluid through a lumbar puncture. Your child will be treated in hospital and if it is bacterial meningitis all close contacts will be treated with a preventative medication to prevent further spread of the disease.

■ Mumps

This disease is uncommon in children under five (see p.340). It usually takes 16–21 days for the symptoms to appear after infection. When the infection does occur, you may first notice that your child seems under the weather. The positive symptom will be if the glands swell up in front of and under the ear on one or both sides of your child's face. This swelling will be accompanied by fever and the glands will be tender.

At around the age of 13 months your child can be immunized against mumps, when he has his MMR (measles, mumps and rubella) immunization (see p.339).

What to do Ask for medical advice to confirm the diagnosis. Although there's no specific treatment, you can do a lot to make your child more comfortable. Reduce his fever using the recommended dose of children's paracetamol (see p.327). Give

your child liquid foods if he finds it difficult to chew; give your child plenty to drink.

■ Nettle rash (see Urticaria)

■ Nose bleeds

Haemorrhaging from the nose, or nose bleeds, are most often caused by damage to a patch of small blood vessels lying very near the surface of the skin, just inside the nose. Nose bleeds are usually caused by a blow or injury to the nose during rough games, or simply because your child persistently picks his nose.

What to do This small patch of blood vessels can bleed rather a lot, but try not to panic. Never tip your child's head back because blood that is swallowed can irritate the stomach and cause vomiting. This will only increase the blood pressure in the head and create a tendency for the nose to bleed again.

Apply gentle pressure with your thumb and first finger on either side of the soft part if the nose up to ten minutes or until the bleeding has stopped. If bleeding does not stop, pinch the nose for another ten minutes. If it still does not stop, get medical advice.

If your child has nose bleeds quite frequently ask for medical advice. Your child may be referred to an ear, nose and throat specialist for cauterization of the delicate areas inside the nose.

■ Pneumococcal infection

This is caused by a strain of the streptococcus bacterium. In most people the bacterium is carried in the nose and throat without causing any harm, but infection can lead to meningitis, ear infections and pneumonia (see below) so it is potentially serious in young children.

What to do Pneumococcal infections can be treated with antibiotics. Babies are now routinely offered a vaccination against pneumoccal infection (see p.339).

▦ Pneumonia

Common childhood viral infections and the rarer infectious childhood diseases such as measles and whooping cough may be accompanied by pneumonia. What happens in this situation is that the infecting organism enters the lungs and weakens their defences. The bronchial tubes become inflamed and produce a lot of mucus, the lung function begins to deteriorate so they can't expel the mucus. It then forms into little pools in the lungs, which become infected.

The initial signs of pneumonia are an increased breathing rate; difficulty with breathing and possibly a rather bluish colour around the mouth. When pooling of mucus occurs in a small air passage, the deeper part of the lung beyond this blockage becomes sealed off and the fluid may collect to the extent that it renders a little section of the lung completely solid; this is a small area of pneumonia. If a larger air passage becomes blocked off, the area of pneumonia can be quite extensive.

What to do If you notice any of the above signs seek medical advice immediately. Meanwhile, stay calm and try the following measures to help your child: try to keep the air moist by boiling a kettle in the room, but never leave your child

alone in a room in which a kettle is boiling. Stay with your child; make him feel comfortable and secure. Try to support your child in an upright position because this will make breathing easier.

▦ Rashes

Most rashes have an internal cause and in young children they are a classic symptom of some of the more common infectious fevers (see p.340). They may also be the result of an allergy.

What to do Rashes usually involve damage to the small blood vessels in the skin and there is very little that one can do to correct this by applying anything on the skin surface. However, try to relieve the symptoms of itching and burning by applying a cooling lotion, like calamine, since prolonged scratching may break the skin and introduce infection. It is better not to use anti-sting or anti-burn sprays on a rash because they often contain local anaesthetics that may trigger allergic reactions in the skin. If you are concerned about your child's rash, or if the rash becomes infected, seek medical advice.

▦ Roseola infantum

This disease is often confused with rubellla (see p.340). Your child will suddenly get a high fever of about 39°C (102°F), without any other symptoms. As the child's temperature returns to normal he'll develop a rash of pale red spots. Roseola infantum is most common in children under the age of two years.

What to do Seek medical advice to get an accurate diagnosis. No specific treatment is needed, other than keeping the fever down (see p.315).

▦ Rubella (German measles)

This is a viral disease, like measles, but it isn't as serious or as contagious (see p.340). The initial symptoms resemble a mild cold with a runny nose, a sore throat, and a temperature of 38°C (l00.4°F). The rash usually appears a couple of days after your child starts to feel unwell. The spots, which start behind the ears and on the forehead before moving down on to the body, are pale and flat and are not as close together as those in measles. They only last for two to three days. The glands on the back of your child's neck will almost definitely be swollen and they may stay like this after the rash has gone. The symptoms usually last about ten days.

At around the age of 13 months your child can be immunized against rubella, when he has his MMR (measles, mumps and rubella) immunization (see p.339).

What to do Get an accurate diagnosis so you can notify any pregnant woman with whom your child has been in contact; it's also important in relation to possible immunization at puberty. The infection is so mild that there is nothing you can do, other than keep your child comfortable and give him plenty to drink. Keep him at home until the rash has been gone for a few days.

▦ Scarlet fever

Also known as scarlatina, this is a throat infection that is caused by a strain of streptococcus bacillus that is no longer very common. It starts with a sore throat and a fever, the tonsils become swollen and inflamed and your child may have headaches and vomit. About three days after this a rash of tiny spots may appear around the neck and in the armpits; this will then spread over the whole body. The tongue's surface may become red and swollen and look like a strawberry.

What to do Get medical advice so you have an accurate diagnosis. Penicillin is the antibiotic of choice for this condition provided your child is not allergic to it. Other than this, there is nothing specific that you can do. Treat the fever and make sure your child has plenty of fluids.

▦ Seizures

In some children we never discover the cause for seizures, but in the majority of children between the ages of six months and five years seizures (also known as febrile seizures) are caused by a rise in body temperature. Young children's brains are more easily affected by this than adults; the irritation stimulates the nerves that control the muscles, which in turn react by contracting violently.

When having a seizure your child will become unconscious and will twitch uncontrollably. His eyes will roll up and he may froth at the mouth slightly. His breathing will be heavy and his teeth will be firmly clamped; he may become incontinent during the seizure. When the seizure is over your child will fall asleep – he may drift straight off or he may briefly come to and then sleep deeply.

What to do Never leave your child alone. Although you may desperately want to call for help you must stay by your child until the seizure is over to make sure he doesn't hurt himself. Loosen his clothing and remove any nearby furniture in case he kicks or rolls against it, but don't try to restrain him. Don't try to place anything in his mouth. Contrary to popular belief, people rarely bite or swallow their tongues during a seizure and you could do more damage by trying to prize open his jaws. Once the seizure is over, place him in the recovery position and call for medical help.

If your child has a seizure of this sort, try to prevent high fevers from occurring in the future. Remove extra clothing and blankets when he gets hot and give him regular doses of children's paracetamol and ibuprofen. Alternate the two in order to bring a reduction in fever and then a steady control of the temperature.

Sleep-walking

A sort of "mobile dreaming", sleep-walking occurs when a child wanders about the house while asleep. A sleep-walking child does not walk about with his eyes closed and his arms held straight out in front. His eyes will be open but he will be asleep; he won't see you and won't understand anything you say to him. Many children go through a short phase of sleep-walking, but this soon passes.

What to do If you find your child sleep-walking, don't try to waken him. Lead him slowly and gently back to bed. There is no need to get medical advice unless the sleep-walking is very frequent and you need reassurance that nothing is seriously wrong. Protect your child, for instance, by putting a barrier at the top of the stairway

at night so he can't fall down the stairs, and by making sure that no windows are left open. Try to reassure your child if you think you know the underlying cause of the sleepwalking.

Splinters

All splinters carry a risk of infection because they are rarely clean so should always be dealt with promptly.

What to do Usually a splinter can be removed with clean tweezers. Gently wash around the splinter with soap and warm water. Grasp the splinter and draw it out at the same angle as it went in. Clean the area and confirm that your child has been immunized against tetanus.

If the splinter is deeply embedded, lies over a joint or is difficult to remove, take your child to the emergency department of your nearest hospital.

Sprains

Because children are so active and may not have very good co-ordination when young, they can sprain their wrists and ankles quite easily. In a sprain a ligament is quite often stretched or torn, and this causes swelling. Your child won't want to put pressure on the joint, and will find it painful to move.

What to do The best treatment for a sprain is rest; any kind of strain on the sprained part should be avoided. You can also help by putting an ice pack on the sprained joint and elevating the limb to reduce swelling and bruising. Then surround the joint with padding and secure this with a bandage. Check the circulation beyond the bandage every ten minutes to make sure that the bandage isn't too tight. Loosen if necessary.

Sticky eye

A sticky eye is fairly common in the first week or so after your baby is born and it is nearly always due to blood or amniotic fluid getting into the eye during birth.

What to do There is always the possibility that the sticky eye is due to a bacterial infection so seek medical advice just in case. However, usually all that is needed is careful cleansing with a clean cotton wool swab soaked in sterile water. When you wash your baby's eye you should always draw the swab from the inside corner, near the nose to the outer corner and then throw it away. It's important to use a separate swab for each eye.

Stings

It's almost inevitable that your child will be stung by a bee or wasp at some stage, and that he'll be very upset when it happens. A sting is rarely serious, but if it causes an allergic reaction, or if your child is stung by a number of insects, get help immediately.

What to do If your child has been stung do not try to squeeze the sting as this may spread the irritating chemical in the sting into deeper parts of the skin. Instead, scrape it off with your thumbnail or the side of a credit card. Don't use proprietary preparations that contain antihistamines; they may cause an allergy of the skin.

If your child is stung in his mouth dial 999 or 112 for an ambulance. Cool his mouth with sips of water while you wait.

Styes

A stye is an infection in the hair follicles of the lower eyelashes. It looks like a small boil on the eyelid – a red swelling with a central area of pus.

What to do Eyes are very precious. Never take chances; get medical advice if you are at all worried. Don't use any of the patent treatments from chemists as they may make specific antibiotics less effective should they be prescribed by your doctor. You may notice that the eyelash is loose and if your child is co-operative you can release the pent-up pus inside the stye by just pulling the hair out. It won't be painful as the infection will already have dislodged it from its hair follicle. Alternatively, you can bathe the stye with a cotton wool bud dipped in cooled, boiled water.

Squints

Your newborn baby may squint until the age of eight or ten weeks, by which time he'll have learned to use his two eyes together (stereoscopically).

What to do There's nothing wrong with this early squinting, but if it persists after three months seek medical advice. Early treatment is important or the imbalance of the muscles of the eye, which usually causes a squint, may remain uncorrected.

Sunburn

Sunburn is inflammation of the skin caused by excessive exposure to sunlight. The best cure is prevention and you'll need to be strict with children who may not appreciate the dangers and the potential for long-term damage. Most children's skin is very sensitive to sunlight – more sensitive than adults' – so be careful about exposing their skin to the sun at any time.

What to do Preventing sunburn is a lot better than treating it. Protect the exposed parts of the skin with a generous application of sunscreen cream of at least factor 30 about 20 minutes before going out. Repeat at least every two or three hours and every time your child has been in the water.

Always cover your baby's head with a wide-brimmed hat and dress him in loose light clothing that covers the shoulders and neck, such as a shirt with sleeves and a collar. Make sure the pram or buggy has an adjustable hood or sunshade with which to shade your baby. If the sun is extremely strong it is better to keep your child indoors, especially between 11am and 3pm when the sun is at its highest. Remember that your baby is still at risk of ultraviolet rays even on cloudy days in summer.

If by chance your baby does get sunburned, calamine lotion is a good cooling application, and children's paracetamol will do a lot to relieve the soreness in the skin and bring his temperature down. If your baby is restless and ill, take his temperature; if it is raised this may herald heatstroke and you should seek medical advice immediately.

▥ Teething

This is the term used to describe the eruption of a baby's first teeth. Teething usually begins at about the age of six or seven months, with most of the teeth breaking through before your baby is 18 months old. Your baby will produce more saliva than usual and will dribble; he will try to cram his fingers into his mouth and chew on his fingers or any object that he can get hold of. He may be clingy and irritable, have difficulty sleeping and he may cry and fret more than usual. Most of these symptoms occur just before the teeth erupt. It is important to realize that the symptoms of teething do not include bronchitis, nappy rash, vomiting, diarrhoea or loss of appetite. These are symptoms of an illness and should be treated as such.

What to do If you can't work out why your child is so irritable, and he has no other symptoms of illness, feel his gums. If a tooth is coming through you will feel a hard or sharp lump and the gum area will be swollen and red. You should not need to get medical advice unless your baby has other symptoms that cannot be attributed to teething, or you are unduly worried. Nurse your baby often. A teething baby needs your comfort and closeness. Don't think that the arrival of teeth means you have to speed up the weaning process. Babies with teeth can be breast-fed with no discomfort to the mother.

Distract your child with a chilled teething ring (never freeze the ring or your baby may get frostbite) or a piece of carrot or apple – something firm. Stay with your baby in case he chokes on the food.

If your child seems to be in a lot of pain, give children's paracetamol or ibuprofen, but take care with the number of doses given. Never exceed the recommended dose. If your child refuses food, encourage him to eat by giving him cold, smooth foods such as yogurt, ice cream or jelly.

▥ Thread worms

This is the most common type of infecting worm. These thin, 6mm (¼in) long white worms live in the rectum and the females crawl through the anus to lay their eggs on the surrounding skin. This produces the classic symptoms of itching, especially at night. When your child scratches his bottom he may pick up some of the eggs under his fingernails. If he then puts his hand in his mouth the eggs will be ingested again.

What to do If you notice your child scratching his bottom, especially at night, save your child's stools and examine them for the thread-like worms. If you find them, get medical advice. Medicine to eradicate the worms is available from your pharmacist over the counter, and because worm infection spreads easily to other members of the family everyone should be given the treatment. Keep your child's nails short, and make sure he washes his hands after going to the lavatory.

▥ Tonsillitis

The job of the tonsils is to trap infections as they enter the body through the mouth, and localize them in the throat. For this reason tonsillitis is usually part of a throat infection. The tonsils also send warning signals to the rest of the body when an infection is beginning so the body can alert all its defences. The adenoids serve exactly the same function but are at the back of the nose instead of in the throat. It is fairly logical, therefore, for the tonsils and adenoids to be thought of together. Tonsils are most important to a child up to the age of ten years and this coincides with the

time they are most likely to meet infection and their defences have to be very strong. If your child has tonsillitis he will complain of a very sore throat and his tonsils will look red and swollen; they'll probably have white patches on them.

What to do You'll need to ask for medical advice – usually your child will be prescribed an antibiotic to combat the infection. To make your child's throat feel better give him as much ice cream and cold liquid as he wants.

Despite their useful function it used to be fashionable to remove tonsils and adenoids. Nowadays, ear, nose and throat surgeons feel that certain criteria must be fulfilled before tonsillectomy can be considered. These would probably include recurrent, severe attacks of tonsillitis, possibly associated with ear infections and deafness. Despite these criteria tonsils are rarely removed in a child under the age of four. The most serious side effect of tonsillitis is infection of the middle ear, which can lead to chronic deafness. Always be on the look-out for signs of deafness if your child has recurrent attacks of tonsillitis.

▥ Toxocara

This roundworm is found in cats and dogs. Its eggs are passed on in their faeces so your child is at risk when he plays on ground where animals have defecated. Your child can ingest the eggs if he puts his dirty hands into his mouth. The eggs burrow through the intestinal wall and are carried in the bloodstream to the lungs. They are then coughed up, swallowed and continue to develop in the intestines. There are generally no symptoms, although if your child has more than one worm he may have abdominal pain and suffer from a loss of appetite.

What to do Prevention is better than cure. Don't allow pets into your child's play area at home and take care when you go to public parks. If your child is diagnosed as having toxocara he will be prescribed a medicine to get rid of it. Follow the instructions carefully. The most serious effects of this illness involve the eyes so your child may need to see a specialist.

Urticaria

A general term used for an allergic skin reaction, urticaria is also known as nettle rash or hives. Most children have a tendency to develop hives, but this is gradually lost as they grow older. It is very easy to diagnose because it is the only skin rash which will disappear completely within a few minutes.

The rash, which is very itchy, often looks like a fairly bad nettle sting; it can also form large red patches with uneven edges. It may result in swelling of the eyes, the lips and possibly the tongue. If the latter occurs you must dial 999 or 112 for an ambulance immediately.

What to do You can do quite a lot to relieve the itchiness by cooling it with calamine lotion. There is no need for any specific treatment unless the attacks are persistent. In this case you should ask for medical advice.

There is a particular form of urticaria called papular urticaria that is caused by flea bites, usually from the fleas on the family cat. I well remember a case of a child who used to appear in our clinic once a month and it turned out that it was always the day after she had been to visit her granny and it was granny's cat who had the fleas. The cure is to get rid of the fleas on the pet, not to get rid of the pet.

Vomiting

This is the expulsion of the contents of the stomach through the mouth. A baby may posset up small quantities of curdled milk after a feed, but this should not be confused with vomiting. Vomiting has many causes but in the majority of cases there is little warning and after a single bout your child should be comfortable and back to normal.

Vomiting can be a symptom of a specific disorder of the stomach such as pyloric stenosis, or a symptom of an infection such as an ear infection. It frequently accompanies a fever, and even the common cold can cause vomiting if your child swallows enough nasal discharge to irritate his stomach. If your child has a bad cough this can also cause him to vomit up food that he has recently eaten. Other causes of vomiting include appendicitis, meningitis, migraine headaches, food poisoning and travel sickness. Some children vomit because of excitement and anticipation, but this is usually limited to toddlers. Vomiting should always be taken seriously because it can rapidly cause dehydration, particularly in a baby or young child.

What to do Put your child to bed and place a bowl for him to vomit into within easy reach. Give your child frequent, small amounts of liquid, preferably cool water.

Check your child's temperature to see if he has a fever too. If he has a fever, treat it and make sure he does not become too hot (see p.327). Get him to brush his teeth to take away the taste. Ask for medical advice if your child continues to vomit over a six-hour period; if he also has diarrhoea and/or a fever over 38°C (100.4°F); or if the vomiting is accompanied by any other worrying symptoms such as earache. Feed your child bland foods when the nausea and vomiting have passed. Reintroduce solid foods slowly.

■ Warts

These are small benign lumps caused by the wart virus. They are made up of an excess of dead cells that protrude above the surface of the skin. They can appear singly or in alarming numbers over all parts of the body, including the face and genitals. If they occur on the soles of the feet, they are known as verrucae. It takes about two years for the body to build up resistance to the wart virus, and after that time the warts usually disappear spontaneously. Warts are spread by direct contact with an infected person.

What to do If your child wants the warts removed, or they appear on a part of the body where they would easily infect other people, try the patent wart cures from your pharmacist. These work by the application of a weak acid solution to the wart and the daily removal of the resulting burnt skin. Follow the manufacturer's instructions carefully and avoid applying the solution to healthy skin. Don't use patent wart cures on warts that appear on the face or genitals: you may cause scarring.

Ask for medical advice as soon as possible if you are unsure whether the lumps are really warts. Any growth or lump on your child's skin that you are uncertain about should be checked. Get medical advice as soon as possible if the warts continue to multiply or they appear on the face or genitals and you want to have them removed.

■ Whooping cough (Pertussis)

Like most childhood illnesses, whooping cough starts off with a runny nose, a cough and a slight temperature. This period can last for up to two weeks. This will be followed by severe, paroxysmal coughing when your child will have difficulty drawing breath. This is when the characteristic "whoop" occurs. Breathing difficulties are even greater for babies, who may not develop the technique of whooping to get air into the lungs.

A vaccination against whooping cough can be given at the same time as the diphtheria and tetanus vaccination (see Immunization chart, opposite).

What to do Ask for medical advice. Antibiotics are effective in the runny nose stage. People who've been in close contact with the infected child may be protected from whooping cough if given antibiotics during the incubation period. When your child starts on a coughing bout, hold him firmly and try to calm him down. If he's tense he'll find it even more difficult to catch his breath. Support him in a sitting position to make breathing easier. Eating may provoke vomiting. Try giving small amounts of easily eaten food (mashed if necessary) immediately after a coughing fit.

Immunization

Immunization is one of the most successful forms of preventive medicine and has helped to eradicate many formerly lethal diseases throughout the world. However, its continued success depends on strict maintenance of an immunization programme in the community, and it is the responsibility of all parents to ensure

AGE	VACCINATION	HOW GIVEN	REACTION
2 months	• Pneumococcus	One injection	Possible redness and swelling at injection site, mild fever; irritability.
	• Diphtheria, tetanus, pertussis (whooping cough), polio and Hib	One injection	A slightly raised temperature; sickness and/or diarrhoea, a small lump at injection site that will disappear in a few weeks.
3 months	• Meningitis C	One injection	As for pneumococcus
	• Diphtheria, tetanus, pertussis (whooping cough), polio and Hib	One injection	As for diphtheria etc
4 months	• Meningitis C	One injection	As above
	• Pneumococcus	One injection	As above
	• Diphtheria, tetanus, pertussis (whooping cough), polio and Hib	One injection	As above
Around 12 months	• Hib,Meningitis C	One injection	As above
At 13 months	• Pneumococcus	One injection	As above
Around 13 months	• Mumps, measles and rubella (MMR)	One injection	As above and fever; rash; generally unwell/malaise.
3 years and 4 months or soon after	• Diphtheria, tetanus, pertussis (whooping cough), polio	One injection	As above
	• Mumps, measles and rubella (MMR)	One injection	As above

that their children are fully protected. Some parents are anxious about the possible side effects that may occur as a result of a vaccination. If you have concerns, it's important to talk them through with your doctor and health visitor. The risk of complications is very small whereas the risk of harmful effects from the diseases themselves is much more serious. However, if your baby develops side effects at any stage of the programme your doctor may delay or stop immunizations.

COMMON CHILDHOOD INFECTIOUS DISEASES

Disease	Incubation period	Symptoms
Measles (see p.329)	10–14 days	Runny nose, cough, inflamed eyes, fever, vomiting, diarrhoea, Koplik's spots on the inside of the cheeks, at first then after four days a rash behind the ears, then on the face, then on the body.
Rubella (German measles) (see p.332)	14–21 days	Slight temperature, enlarged glands at the back of the neck, rash behind the ears then on the forehead, then the rest of the body. Rash lasts three days.
Roseola (see p.331)	4–7 days	A high temperature with slight cold symptoms; a pink rash after three days when temperature goes down.
Chicken pox (see p.320)	10–21 days	Dark red, irritating groups of spots that emerge every three or four days. Initially look like blisters then scab over.
Whooping cough (pertussis) (see p.338)	Around 7 days	Slight temperature, runny nose, slight cough then a convulsive cough followed by whooping breath, vomiting, cyanosis (blue colouring to skin) during coughing spasms, then exhaustion.
Mumps (see p.330)	17–21 days	Swelling and soreness of the glands at the sides of the face, in front of the ears, painful swallowing and dry mouth. Fever and generally unwell.
Scarlet fever or Scarlatina (see p.332)	2–5 days	Sore throat, lack of appetite, fever, vomiting, swollen glands, tiny red spots, scarlet facial flushing and strawberry-coloured tongue.

The immunization schedule shown on (see p.339) started in September 2006. Any child who began his immunizations before that date would not have been given the pneumoccocal injection at two months, but would have started with a meningococcus C immunization. This schedule is for healthy children. If a child is unwell the day he's due for an injection it will be deferred until he has recovered. If he has a chronic illness that affects his immune system he will have an individualized schedule.

Treatment	Complications	Immunity	Prevention
No specific treatment other than junior paracetamol and/or ibuprofen to reduce the fever. If secondary infection of the ears or lungs occurs antibiotics will be necessary.	Ear infection, pneumonia encephalitis, gastroenteritis	Lifelong	MMR immunization at around 13 months and at three years and four months or soon after.
No specific treatment.	None to your child but fetal damage could occur in a pregnant woman	Lifelong	MMR immunization at around 13 months and at three years and four months or soon after.
No specific treatment.	Rarely causes infantile convulsions	Usually lifelong	None
Relieve itching with moisturizer that contains an antiseptic.	Encephalitis, pneumonia	Lifelong	None
Antibiotics must be given early to be effective; fresh air. Possibly raise your child's head in bed to make breathing easier.	Possibility of seizures, bronchitis or pneumonia	Lifelong	Immunization at two, three and four months and at three years and four months or soon after.
Plenty to drink, soft food if chewing is painful.	Meningitis, inflammation of the testicles	Lifelong	MMR immunization at around 13 months and at three years and four months or soon after.
Penicillin, plenty to drink, and rest in bed as long as fever lasts.	Rheumatic fever	Lifelong	None

Immunization and travelling abroad

If you are planning to take your baby or toddler abroad, it is vital that you find out beforehand about the health risks in the country you're going to be visiting and the precautions, including vaccinations, you may need to take. Ask your travel agent, the embassy (in London) of the country you are going to visit, or the Department of Health, who issue a useful leaflet (SA 40) *Before You Go: The Traveller's Guide to Health* that gives comprehensive advice on the subject. They also publish a companion leaflet, (SA 41) *While You're Away*, which is worth taking with you. You could also check the website of the National Travel Health Network (www.nathnac.org).

If vaccinations are needed, see your doctor at least two months before you go as some take time to be effective and some cannot be given at the same time as other vaccinations. If your child is very young and several injections are required, you may want to reconsider your plans.

Holiday health precautions

First aid kit Take a first aid kit with you containing: a packet of adhesive dressings, sterile needles, insect repellent, antiseptic cream, water sterilization tablets and any prescription medicines.

Water Babies' feeds should, of course, be mixed with boiled water as usual. Otherwise, unless you know that the local water is safe, use bottled water or sterilize it by boiling or using sterilization tablets. This applies not just to drinking water but also to the water you use for cleaning teeth or rinsing the mouth out.

Food Beware of raw vegetables, salads, unpeeled fruit, cream, ice cream, ice cubes, under-done meat or fish and uncooked or reheated food. Freshly cooked foods are safer.

Travelling in Europe

If you are travelling in Europe, free or reduced-cost emergency medical treatment is available in the European Community countries. To get medical care you need an EHIC card (available from the Department of Health), which should be applied for at least one month before your trip starts. You can apply for this card if you live in the UK and are a national of the UK. Children each need their own separate cards. You can get a forms from a post office or contact the Department of Health website, www.dh.gov.uk/travellers.

Travelling outside Europe

The UK has made arrangements with some countries outside the European Community for urgently needed medical care to be provided free or at reduced cost to UK nationals or residents. You may have to produce evidence of UK nationality and residence in order to qualify for such treatment. Check what is available in the country you are to visiting before you go.

Taking medicines abroad

If you need to take any prescribed medicines for your baby or toddler with you, your doctor may be able to supply a limited quantity under the NHS. Check if there are any restrictions on taking drugs, prescribed or over-the-counter, into the country you are visiting. To avoid any problems at security or customs, take a letter from your doctor with details of any medicines prescribed.

Travel insurance

Whatever countries you intend to visit, it is very important that you take out adequate private medical insurance. The arrangements provided for emergency medical treatment in EEC countries, or in countries covered by reciprocal arrangements, do not cover every eventuality; the cover is not always as comprehensive as in the UK and it never covers the cost of bringing a person back to the UK in the event of illness.

DISEASE AND PRECAUTIONS

Disease	Risk area	Vaccination
Cholera	Africa, Asia, Middle East, especially in conditions of poor hygiene and sanitation.	Two injections. Cholera is contracted from eating or drinking contaminated food or water.
Malaria	Africa, Asia, Central and South America; possibly southern Europe and United States (check before travelling).	None, but anti-malarial tablets must be taken before, during and for a month after your trip.
Polio	Everywhere except Europe, North America, Australia and New Zealand.	Given as a routine to babies in the UK.
Rabies	Many parts of the world, including Europe.	Not routine, but ask for advice as it is recommended for travel to remote areas.
Tetanus	Occurs worldwide, but greatest risk in areas where children are not immunized.	Given as a routine to babies in the UK.
TB	Africa, Asia, Central and South America, some poorer inner city areas elsewhere.	Skin test and injection, preferably three months before travel. Not necessary for short visits and when staying in modern hotels, but advisable for longer visits if you will be living or working closely with the local population.
Typhoid	Everywhere except Europe, North America, Australia and New Zealand, in conditions of poor hygiene and sanitation.	Two injections, 4–6 weeks apart. Typhoid is contracted from drinking contaminated water.
Yellow fever	Africa and South America.	One injection at least ten days before travelling. Infants under nine months should not be vaccinated, and should not therefore be exposed to the disease.

Index

Acknowledgments

Medical consultants for new edition:
Dr W John Fysh MBBS FRCP FRCPCH.

Cooling Brown would like to thank:
Constance Novis for proofreading; Hilary Bird for the index.

Picture library: Romaine Werblow

The publisher would like to thank the following for their kind permission to reproduce their photographs:
Alamy Images: Picture Partners 208; Chris Rout 57; **Corbis:** Cameron 29;

Getty Images: Photodisc Green; 9;
Mother & Baby Picture Library: 71, 97bl, 143, EMAP: 287 291.
Photograph of breast pump on page 35 provided courtesy of Avent Ltd.

Jacket images: Front and spine: Photolibr‹ Marina Raith. Back: Author portrait: Carc Djanogly for DK; Punchstock: Brand X Pictures.

All other images © Dorling Kindersley
For further information see:
www.dkimages.com